Heath Social Studies

The United States Past to Present

HEATH

Program Authors
Gloria P. Hagans   Social Studies Coordinator, K-12, Norfolk Public Schools, Virginia.

Barbara Radner Reque   Director, DePaul University Center for Economic Education.

Richard Hall Wilson   Social Studies, Coordinator, Montgomery County Public Schools, Maryland.

Senior Texas Edition Consultants
Peggy Dildy-Holland   Coordinator of Elementary Social Studies, Midland ISD, Midland, Texas.

Glenn M. Linden   Associate Professor of History and Education, Southern Methodist University.

Texas Edition Consultants
Cherylyn Manning   Teacher, Raymond Elementary School, Aldine ISD, Houston, Texas.

Nancy Gregory Streeter   Social Studies Coordinator, Carrollton-Farmers Branch ISD, Carrollton, Texas.

Learning System Consultant
Kathleen McDonnold   Teacher, Doss Elementary School, Austin ISD, Austin, Texas.

Bilingual Consultants
Vicky Lozano   Principal, Neil Armstrong Elementary School, South San Antonio ISD, San Antonio, Texas.

Blanca I. Solitaire   Teacher, Clearwater Elementary School, Brownsville ISD Brownsville, Texas.

Contributing Writers
Nancy Hughes, Birdie Lamkin, Jan Miller, Caroline Sowell, and *Kay Thomas*   Teachers, Midland ISD, Midland, Texas.

Karen McAuley   Former teacher and author of educational materials, New York, New York.

Area Specialists
Bert Bower   Curriculum Developer on the Latin American Project, Stanford Program for International and Cross-Cultural Education (SPICE).

Carol M. Hansen   Former Coordinator of the South Asia Area Center Outreach for the University of Wisconsin-Madison.

Lawrence A. Kletter, Esq.   Author of numerous articles on the Middle East.

Jo Sullivan   Outreach Coordinator, African Studies Center, Boston University.

Leslie M. Swartz   Chinese specialist and Outreach Coordinator in the Harvard University East Asian Program.

Janet Vaillant   Associate Director of Soviet and East European Language and Area Center at Harvard University.

Reading Specialists
Nan Jackson   Reading/Language Arts Specialist, Montgomery County Public Schools, Maryland.

Ted Schuder   Reading/Language Arts Coordinator, Montgomery County Public Schools, Maryland

Executive Editor   Allen Wheatcroft
Editorial Services   Marianna Frew Palmer
Editors   Marian Cain, Susan Belt Cogley, Martha Green
Freelance Editors   Kathryn Riley, Susan Marx
Series Designer   Robert H. Botsford
Production Coordinator   Carol S. Lanza

The United States Past to Present

Karen McAuley
Richard Hall Wilson

D.C. Heath and Company
Lexington, Massachusetts   Toronto, Ontario

ACKNOWLEDGMENTS

Design Credits *Photo/Art Coordination*: Connie Komack   *Art Editing*: Pat Mahtani   *Photo Research*: Martha Davidson; Pembroke Herbert/Picture Research Consultants   *Map Coordination*: Toni Jurras

Cover: Michael Philip Manheim (Photo Researchers, Inc.)
Maps: R. R. Donnelley Cartographic Services, Dick and John Sanderson
Graphs and Timelines: Omnigraphics, Inc.

Tax Credits: **325** From *Pioneer Women* by Joanna L. Stratton. © 1981

Illustration Credits: **20-21:** James Teason. **38:** James Hamilton (drawings); Dick Sanderson (map). **39, 40:** Sally Schaedler (Mulvey Associates, Inc.). **41, 47:** Pam Ford Johnson (Publishers' Graphics, Inc.). **56, 66, 84, 92, 105:** Katy Linnett. **116:** James Teason. **121:** Katy Linnett. **127:** Andrew Z. Shiff. **138:** Katy Linnett. **186:** Ron Toelke. **204, 212:** James Hamilton. **222:** Andrew Z. Shiff. **244:** Nancy Evers. **246:** Katy Linnett. **258:** Andrew Z. Shiff. **300:** Nancy Evers. **445:** James Hamilton. **534, 536:** Tom Leamon (PC&F Inc.)

Photo Credits: Unit One: 22-23: "Mayflower in Plymouth Harbor" by William Halsall (detail). The Pilgrim Society, Plymouth, MA. **24:** The Granger Collection. **27:** *l* The Bettmann Archive; *r* Scala/Art Resource, Inc. **28:** Musée Condé, Chantilly (Photographie Giraudon). **29:** Ted Spiegel (Black Star). **31:** Archivio IGDA. **33:** Arnold J. Saxe (Coverage). **35:** Library of Congress. **44:** The Hispanic Society of America. **48:** Cortez and Montezuma, #1412. Library Services Department, American Museum of Natural History. **50:** Museum of the American Indian, Heye Foundation. **51:** *l* Library of Congress; *r* The Bettmann Archive. **52:** State Historical Society of Wisconsin. **55:** "Mission San Francisco de Solano" by Oriana Day. M.H. De Young Memorial Museum; gift of Mrs. Eleanor Martin. Permission of the Fine Arts Museum of San Francisco. **57:** The Bettmann Archive. **60:** NYPL. **62:** "Village of Pomeiock" by John White. Trustees of the British Museum. Photo by Bradley Smith, from *The U.S.A.: A History in Art*. **63:** Rare Books and Manuscripts Division, New York Public Library. Astor, Lenox and Tilden Foundations. **65:** "Pocahontas" by unidentified artist after Simon van de Passe. National Portrait Gallery, Smithsonian Institution. Transfer from the National Gallery of Art; gift of Andrew W. Mellon. **70:** "Signing of the Contract" by Percy Moran. The Pilgrim Society, Plymouth, MA. **72:** Courtesy, John Hancock Mutual Life Insurance Company. **74:** "Pilgrims Going to Church" by George H. Boughton. The Bettmann Archive. **75:** The Maryland Historical Society, Baltimore. **78:** The Architect of the U.S. Capitol. **81:** Detail from *Vallard Atlas*, chart #9 (HM 29). Reproduced by permission of the Huntington Library, San Marino, CA. **85:** The Granger Collection. **89:** "The Half-Moon Passing the Palisades" from the painting by H.A. Ogden (detail). New York Historical Society. **91:** Museum of the City of New York.

Unit Two: 96-97: "South East View of the Great Town of Boston" (detail). Library of Congress. **98:** "A Morning View of Blue Hill Village" by Jonathan Fisher (detail). © 1973 by the William A. Farnsworth Library and Art Museum. **100:** Society for the Preservation of New England Antiquities. **101, 102:** The Bettmann Archive. **103:** "Hooker and Company Journeying through the Wilderness from Plymouth to Hartford in 1636" by F.E. Church. Wadsworth Atheneum, Hartford, CT. **106:** "Isaac Royall and Family" by Robert Feke. Harvard Law School. **107, 109:** The Granger Collection. **110:** Peabody Museum of Salem/Mark Sexton. **112:** Massachusetts Historical Society. **114:** "The Plantation" by unknown American artist (detail). The Metropolitan Museum of Art; gift of Edgar and Bernice Chrysler Garbisch, 1963. Photo © 1971 by the Metropolitan Museum of Art. **118:** Colonial Williamsburg Photograph; detail used by permission. **123:** Historical Pictures Service, Chicago. **124:** Virginia State Travel Service. **126:** Harvard College Library. **129:** The Granger Collection, New York. **130:** Detail from "The Residence of David Twining" by Edward Hicks. The Abby Aldrich Folk Arts Center, Williamsburg, Va. **132:** I.N. Phelps Stokes Collection, New York Public Library. Astor, Lenox and Tilden Foundations. **135:** Historical Pictures Service, Chicago. **136:** The Granger Collection. **139:** The Hagley Museum and Library. **142:** The Granger Collection. **143:** "Bowles' Moral Pictures, or Poor Richard Illustrated" by Bowles and Carver. Yale University Art Gallery, Mabel Brady Garvan Collection. **144:** The Granger Collection. **145:** "Benjamin Franklin, the Fireman". Collection, CIGNA Corporation, Philadelphia, PA.

Unit Three: 148-149: "Pulling Down the Statue of George III" by William Walcutt. Private Collection. **150:** Courtesy of the New-York Historical Society. **152:** *l* Private Collection; *r* The Granger Collection. **153:** "He That by the Plough Would Thrive...". Addison Gallery of American Art, Phillips Academy, Andover, MA. **155:** American Antiquarian Society. **157:** Massachusetts Historical Society. **158:** American Antiquarian Society. **159:** "The Trial of John Peter Zenger". The Metropolitan Museum of Art; A Bicentennial Gift to America from a Grateful Armenian People, 1978. **160:** Virginia State Library. **161:** The Bettmann Archive. **162:** 31.212 Mrs. James Warren (Mercy Otis) c. 1763, John Singleton Copley, Amer. 1738–1815, oil on canvas 51¼" × 41." Bequest of Winslow Warren, 1931: Courtesy Museum of Fine Arts, Boston. **164:** Concord Antiquarian Museum. **166:** "George Washington" by Charles Willson Peale. Washington/Custis/Lee Collection, Washington and Lee University, Va. **170:** The Bettmann Archive. **171:** *bl* The Bettmann Archive; *tr* Shelburne Museum, Shelburne, VT. **172:** New York Historical Society. **173:** American Antiquarian Society. **174:** The Harry T. Peters Collection, Museum of the City of New York.

(continued page 559)

Contents

Maps

Graphs, Charts, and Diagrams

1

Reviewing Map and Globe Skills

Using a Legend

Geography is the study of places on Earth and life in those places. **Maps** are important in understanding geography. A map is a drawing of all or part of Earth. Maps use symbols to tell about a place. A symbol can be a line, a dot, a color, or a picture. To find out what a symbol stands for, study the map's **legend,** or key.

The map on page 3 shows how two parts of Earth—North and South America—looked over 500 years ago. The map shows that the Americas had many forests. It shows too that in some places the land was covered with tall grasses. There were also sun-baked desert lands dotted with hardy cacti and other plants that need little water. The Americas also had tundra. In these very cold lands, the ground is always frozen. Still, during the short summers, mosses and tiny flowering plants quickly blossom.

Forests, grasslands, deserts, and tundra are **natural vegetation.** Natural vegetation is the kind of plant life that grows wild in a place. Use the map's legend to answer questions about natural vegetation in the Americas.

1. What do the colors on the map stand for?
2. Where is the tundra in North America?
3. Name the two kinds of grasslands shown on the map.
4. Early visitors to North America wrote of a land almost completely covered with trees. Which parts of North America did these visitors probably travel through?

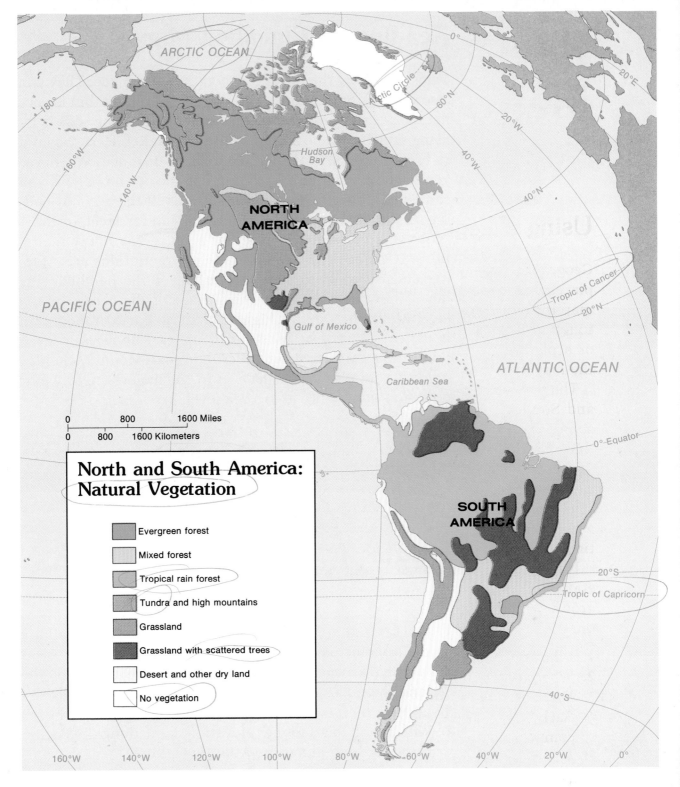

North and South America: Natural Vegetation

- Evergreen forest
- Mixed forest
- Tropical rain forest
- Tundra and high mountains
- Grassland
- Grassland with scattered trees
- Desert and other dry land
- No vegetation

ARCTIC OCEAN

Arctic Circle

Hudson Bay

NORTH AMERICA

PACIFIC OCEAN

Gulf of Mexico

Caribbean Sea

ATLANTIC OCEAN

Tropic of Cancer

SOUTH AMERICA

Equator

Tropic of Capricorn

0   800   1600 Miles
0   800   1600 Kilometers

160°W 140°W 120°W 100°W 80°W 60°W 40°W 20°W 0°

Where are the forests of North America? Of South America?

Reading an Elevation Map

Maps can show the natural vegetation of a place. They can also show tall mountains, rolling hills, and land that is very flat. How can maps show these differences? One way is by using shading to show places with high **relief.** Here the land rises and falls sharply within a short distance. Whenever you see heavy shading on a map like the one on page 5, you can be sure there are many mountains. If there is no shading, the land has low relief. Here the land is level, or flat.

Shading can tell you whether a place has many mountains. It cannot tell you how high the mountains are. Mapmakers use color to show **elevation,** or the height of the land. They measure from the surface of the ocean, or **sea level.** Mountains are the highest lands on Earth. A mountain is at least 2000 feet (about 610 meters) above sea level. Some mountains are even taller than that. Mount McKinley in Alaska stands over 20,000 feet (6,100 meters), nearly four miles (6 kilometers), above sea level.

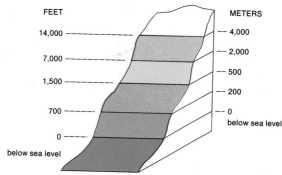

FEET   METERS

14,000   4,000

7,000   2,000

     500

1,500

     200

700   0

     below sea level

0

below sea level

1. (a) How tall are the Rocky Mountains? (b) How tall are the Appalachians?
2. (a) What is the elevation of the Great Basin? (b) Is the land there flat or very hilly? (c) How can you tell?
3. (a) How high is the Coastal Plain? (b) Is it flat or hilly?
4. Which land has a higher elevation, land along the Pacific Ocean or land along the Atlantic Ocean?

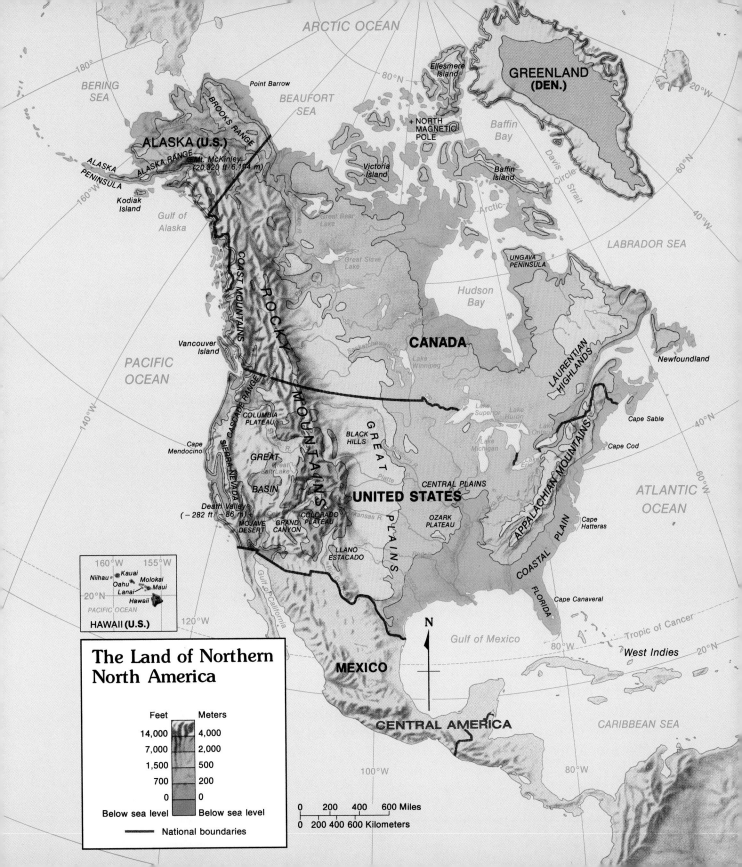

ARCTIC OCEAN

180°

BERING
SEA

Point Barrow

BEAUFORT
SEA

80°N

Ellesmere
Island

+ NORTH
MAGNETIC
POLE

GREENLAND
(DEN.)

20°W

BROOKS RANGE

ALASKA (U.S.)

Baffin
Bay

60°N

ALASKA RANGE

Mt. McKinley
(20,920 ft/6,194 m)

Victoria
Island

Baffin
Island

160°W

ALASKA
PENINSULA

Kodiak
Island

Gulf of
Alaska

Great Bear
Lake

Arctic

Davis Strait

40°W

LABRADOR SEA

Great Slave
Lake

COAST MOUNTAINS

ROCKY MOUNTAINS

Hudson
Bay

CANADA

UNGAVA
PENINSULA

Vancouver
Island

PACIFIC
OCEAN

Saskatchewan R.

Lake
Winnipeg

LAURENTIAN
HIGHLANDS

Newfoundland

140°W

Cape
Mendocino

CASCADE RANGE

COLUMBIA
PLATEAU

SIERRA NEVADA

GREAT
BASIN

Great
Salt Lake

BLACK
HILLS

Lake
Superior

Lake
Huron

Cape Sable

40°N

GREAT PLAINS

Platte R.

CENTRAL PLAINS

Lake
Michigan

Lake
Ontario

Lake
Erie

APPALACHIAN MOUNTAINS

Cape Cod

60°W

ATLANTIC
OCEAN

Death Valley
(−282 ft/−86 m)

MOJAVE
DESERT

GRAND
CANYON

COLORADO
PLATEAU

UNITED STATES

Arkansas R.

OZARK
PLATEAU

COASTAL PLAIN

Cape
Hatteras

160°W   155°W

Niihau • Kauai
Oahu • Molokai
Lanai • Maui
Hawaii

20°N

PACIFIC OCEAN

HAWAII (U.S.)

120°W

LLANO
ESTACADO

Rio Grande

FLORIDA

Cape Canaveral

Tropic of Cancer

20°N

Gulf of California

N

MEXICO

Gulf of Mexico

80°W

West Indies

The Land of Northern
North America

CENTRAL AMERICA

CARIBBEAN SEA

100°W

80°W

Feet	Meters
14,000	4,000
7,000	2,000
1,500	500
700	200
0	0
Below sea level	Below sea level

National boundaries

0   200   400   600 Miles

0 200 400 600 Kilometers

Using a Scale

The United States covers over 3,600,000 square miles (9,360,000 square kilometers) of land. Maps of the United States are, of course, much smaller than that. Maps are always smaller than the places they show. This is because a map is drawn to **scale.** Scale is a way of showing distances on a map. Every inch on the map stands for a certain number of miles or kilometers.

To find out to what scale a map is drawn, look for a numbered line. It tells how many miles or kilometers each inch on the map stands for. You can use that line to figure our how far apart places on the map really are. You can do this by copying the numbered line on the edge of a sheet of paper. Make sure you mark the beginning and the end of the scale.

On the next page, you will find two maps on the United States. Each was drawn to a different scale. Use the maps to answer the following questions.

1. (a) About how many miles does each inch stand for on the top map on page 7?   (b) About how many miles or kilometers does each inch stand for on the second map on page 7?
2. (a) About how many miles is it from San Francisco to New York City on the top map?   (b) How many miles apart are the two cities on the second map on page 7?
3. Use either map and its scale to find the distances between the following pairs of cities:
   (a) Denver and San Francisco;
   (b) Houston and Birmingham;
   (c) Jackson and Louisville;
   (d) Atlanta and Miami.
4. Would the distances between cities listed in the activity above change if you used a map drawn to a different scale? Why or why not?

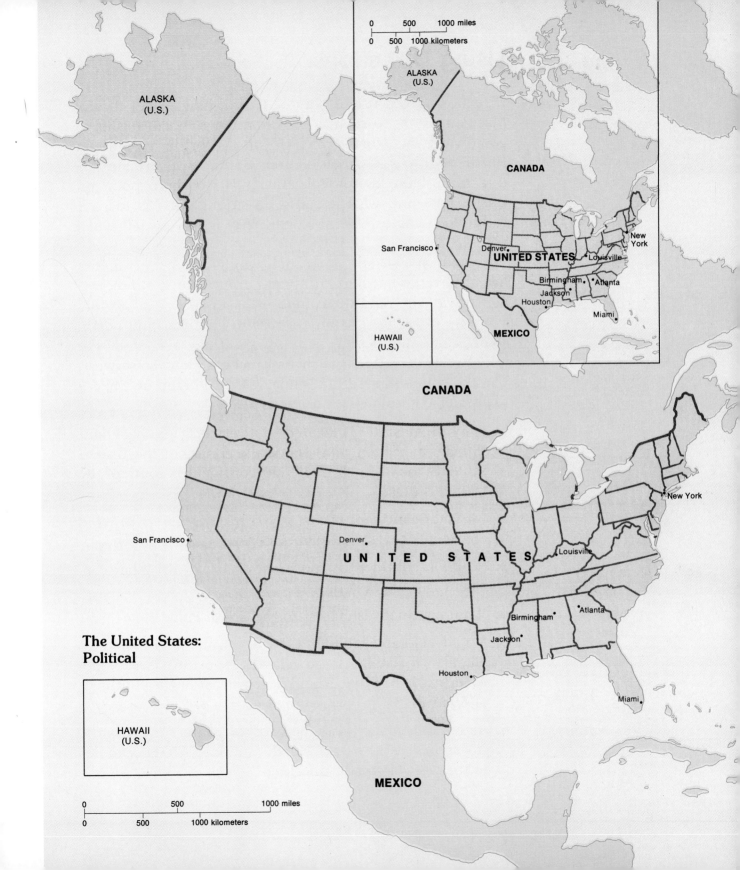

ALASKA
(U.S.)

ALASKA
(U.S.)

CANADA

UNITED STATES

San Francisco

Denver

New York

Louisville

Birmingham

Atlanta

Jackson

Houston

Miami

MEXICO

HAWAII
(U.S.)

0   500   1000 miles
0   500   1000 kilometers

CANADA

San Francisco

Denver

New York

UNITED STATES

Louisville

Birmingham

Atlanta

Jackson

Houston

Miami

The United States:
Political

HAWAII
(U.S.)

MEXICO

0   500   1000 miles
0   500   1000 kilometers

Using Directions

Directions are a useful way of telling how to get to any place on Earth. North is a direction. To go north means to go toward the North Pole, the most northern point on Earth. South is a direction too. South is always in the direction of the South Pole, the most southern point on Earth. East and west are also directions. East is to your right when you are facing north. West is to your left when you face north.

A **compass** can tell you which way is north. A compass has a movable needle that always points north, no matter which way you hold the compass.

A map often has a **compass rose** to help you find north, south, east, and west. A compass rose may also show the in-between directions, such as northeast and southwest. Use the compass rose that appears on the map on page 9 to answer the following questions.

1. The United States is located on a very large body of land called a **continent.**   (a) Name the continent the United States is located on.   (b) What continent is south of the United States?

2. (a) What continent is east of North America?   (b) What continent is west of North America?

3. (a) What continent is southeast of Asia?   (b) What continent is southwest of Asia?

4. What continent is closest to the South Pole?

5. A body of land smaller than a continent is called an **island.**   (a) What large island is northeast of North America?   (b) What island is southeast of the continent of Australia?

6. An **ocean** is a very large body of salt water. The Atlantic Ocean lies to the east of North America. What ocean lies to the west of North America?

7. Name the ocean that lies to the east of Africa, to the south of Asia, and to the west of Australia.

8. What ocean lies to the north of both Asia and North America?

9. Describe the Pacific Ocean's location in relation to the continents it touches.

10. Describe the Atlantic Ocean's location in relation to the continents it touches.

11. (a) You can travel no farther north than the North Pole. After passing the North Pole, in what direction are you going?   (b) What is the farthest south you can travel?

12. (a) If a map has no compass rose, north is always toward the top of the page. Where then is east? (b) Where is south on such a map?

The World: Land and Water

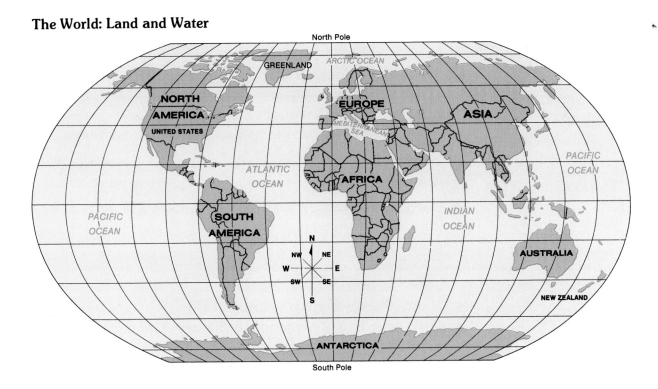

Using a Grid

Washington, D.C., is the **capital** of the United States. The capital is the place where the government of a country meets. Every year millions of Americans visit Washington, D.C. They come to see the White House, the home of the president. They also come to see the Capitol, the place where our country's laws are made.

Many visitors to Washington, D.C., use street maps like the one shown here. Maps like these show hundreds of different places. People need a quick way to find the exact place they are looking for. To help them, many mapmakers place a **grid** on their maps. A grid is a series of lines that cross one another. The lines of the grid are labeled with letters and numbers. These letters and numbers give every place shown on the map an exact location. To help you find that location, mapmakers provide an index. The index is a list of the places shown on the map.

To find a place on a grid map, you must look it up by name in the map's index. The index gives the letter and number of the grid section where that place is located. For example, according to the index, the White House is located at C3. Look at the map and find section C3. Is the White House in that grid section?

Use the index and the map to answer the questions.

1. (a) Where is the National Visitor's Center? (b) What building is nearby?
2. (a) What building is at D2? (b) What building is at C3? (c) Is it east or west of the one at D2? (d) Is it north or south of the one at D2?
3. (a) Where is the Capitol located? (b) What monument lies west of it?
4. Name the art gallery located at C5.
5. (a) Where is the Museum of African Art? (b) What famous building lies southwest of it in D7? (c) What memorial lies in E3?

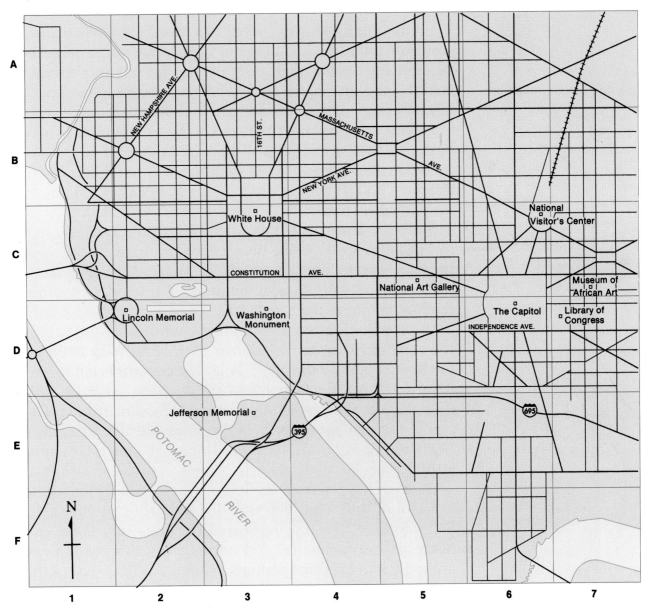

Washington, D.C.

Using Latitude and Longitude

Latitude Lines (Parallels)

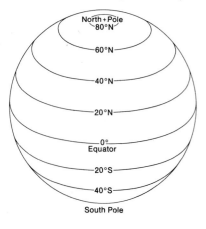

Longitude Lines (Meridians)

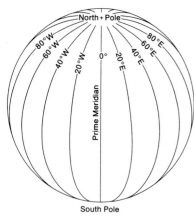

Everyday many ships cross the oceans. They make their way over hundreds of miles of open sea with no sign or landmark to guide their way. Every day many airplanes also fly long distances. They too have no sign or landmark to mark their path. How do they keep from getting lost?

Sailors and airplane pilots use grids to figure out where on Earth they are. The grid they use is much like the one used on street maps. However, this grid is not labeled with numbers and letters. Instead it uses two sets of imaginary lines labeled in degrees (°).

One set of lines, called **parallels of latitude,** circles Earth from east to west. These lines are called parallels because they are always the same distance apart. The other set of lines is called **meridians of longitude.** These lines run from the North Pole to the South Pole. They do not circle Earth.

The starting point for measuring parallels of latitude is the **equator.** It is the line that is exactly halfway between the North Pole and the South Pole. The equator is numbered 0° latitude. All places north of the equator are north latitude. All places south of the equator are south latitude. The places farthest away from the equator are the poles. The North Pole is 90° north latitude. The South Pole is 90° south latitude.

The starting point for measuring meridians of longitude is also a 0° line. That line is called the **prime meridian,** or first meridian. The line numbered 180° longitude is the end point for measuring lines of longitude. It is exactly halfway around Earth from the prime meridian. All lines east of the prime meridian to the 180° longitude line are east longitude. All lines west of the prime meridian to the 180° longitude line are west longitude.

Using latitude and longitude lines, you can locate any place on Earth. Answer the questions using the world map.

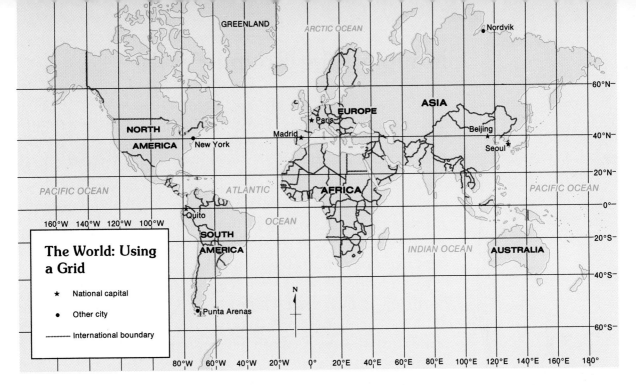

The World: Using a Grid

* National capital
● Other city
------- International boundary

1. (a) Which city on the map is farthest north? (b) Which city is farthest south? (c) Which city is closest to the equator? (d) Which city on the map is closest to the prime meridian?
2. If you were at 10°N, 60°E, would you be on land or sea?
3. If you were at 40°N, 120°W, would you be on land or sea?
4. (a) Which of the following cities have the same latitude: New York, Madrid, Beijing, Seoul? (b) What is the longitude of each of those cities?
5. The equator divides Earth into two equal parts called **hemispheres.** Places north of the equator are in the Northern Hemisphere. Places south of the equator are in the Southern hemisphere. Is New York City in the Northern or Southern Hemisphere?
6. The prime meridian and the 180° longitude line also divide Earth into hemispheres. Places east of the prime meridian to the 180° line are in the Eastern Hemisphere. Places west of the prime meridian to the 180° are in the Western Hemisphere. Is Beijing, China in the Eastern or Western Hemisphere?

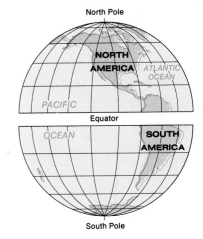

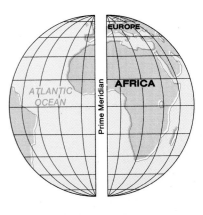

Mapping the Round Earth

Earth is round like an orange. A **globe** is round too. A globe is a model of Earth. It looks much the way Earth would look if you could see it from space. Therefore, a globe is a very accurate map of Earth. Maps drawn on flat sheets of paper do not show Earth as accurately. On some of these maps, the oceans seem very small. On others, land near the North and South Poles looks much larger than it really is. Why? Whenever you show a round object on a flat sheet of paper you have a problem.

To see why mapmakers have trouble showing the round Earth on a flat sheet of paper, try flattening an orange without tearing the peel. To do so, you must make a number of cuts in the peel. Mapmakers often do the same thing when they make a map of Earth. They cut into a globe and then flatten it out. The more cuts they make, the more accurate the land looks near the equator. What happens to the land near the poles?

Mapmakers also use mathematics to show the round earth on a flat sheet of paper. On such a map, the shape of the land is correct. Distance and direction, however, may be distorted, or changed. For example, which seems to be farther west, Los Angeles or Seattle? To find out, check the longitude of both cities. Be sure to check longitude before answering. Do not let appearances fool you.

1. Which lies farther west: North or South America?
2. Which lies farther east: Greenland or South America?
3. Which stretches farther east: Asia or Australia?
4. Which stretches farther west: Europe or Africa?
5. Which is farther east: Lima or Havana?
6. Which is farther east: Lima or New York City?
7. Which is farther west: Havana or New York City?
8. Which is farther west: Greenland or South America?
9. Which is farther east: Leningrad or Alexandria?
10. Which is farther west: New Orleans or Mexico City?

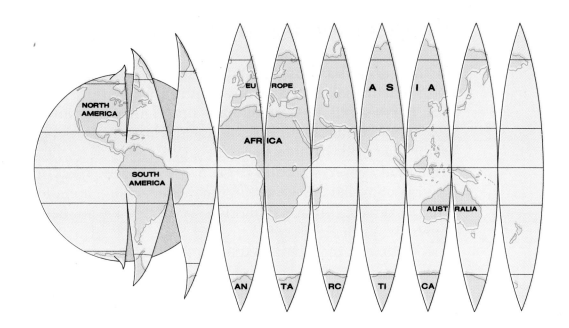

The World: Locating Cities

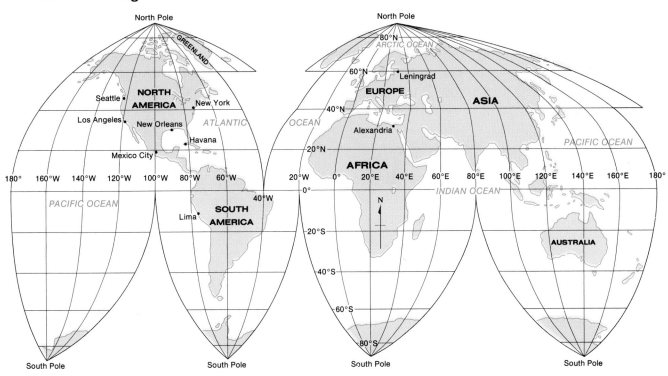

Understanding Earth's Movements

Earth is always moving. It moves in two ways. Every 24 hours Earth makes one complete turn, or rotation, on its **axis.** Earth's axis is an imaginary line that runs from the North Pole to the South Pole. As Earth turns, it is daylight on the side of Earth that faces the sun.

Earth also moves around the sun. This journey takes 365 days to complete. Every year Earth makes one complete journey, or revolution, around the sun. The diagram below shows the path Earth takes around the sun. It also shows where Earth is in regard to the sun at four different points in its journey.

Notice that as Earth turns, it leans or tilts on its axis. That tilt never changes. So for one part of the year, the Northern Hemisphere points toward the sun. For the rest of the year, it points away from the sun. When the Northern Hemisphere points away from the sun, the Southern Hemisphere points toward it.

Earth's tilt as it makes its yearly journey around the sun is the reason there are differences in the weather from one season to the next. When the Northern Hemisphere points toward the sun, it is summer there. The temperatures are

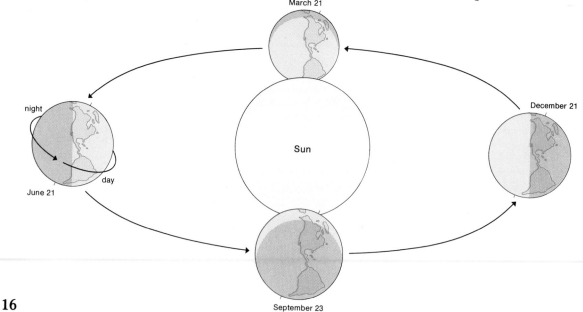

warm, and there are more hours of daylight than of darkness. In the Southern Hemisphere it is winter. Temperatures are cold and there are many more hours of darkness than of daylight.

Study the diagrams showing Earth's rotation around the sun carefully. Then answer the following questions.

1. North America is in the Northern Hemisphere. (a) When does winter begin in North America?
(b) When does summer begin?

2. Much of South America is in the Southern Hemisphere. (a) When does winter begin in the Southern Hemisphere? (b) When does summer begin?

3. When it is spring in the Southern Hemisphere, what season is it in North America?

4. (a) What is the first day of autumn in the Southern Hemisphere?
(b) What is the first day of autumn in the Northern Hemisphere?

5. What part of Earth changes least from one season to the next? Why?

6. The North Pole never gets the direct rays of the sun. Therefore, it is always cold at the North Pole. However, when the Northern Hemisphere faces the sun, days at the North Pole are so long that the sun never sets. What is it like at the South Pole at this time of year?

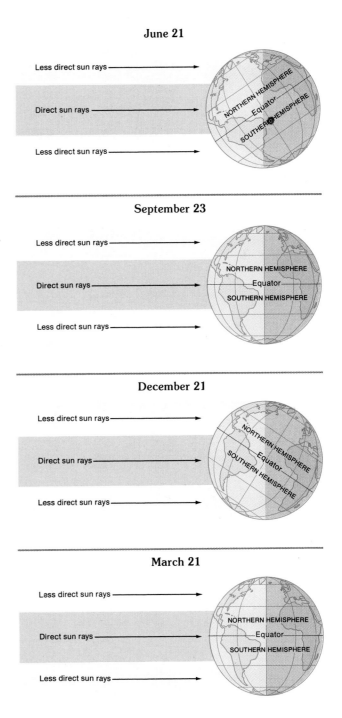

June 21

Less direct sun rays

Direct sun rays

Less direct sun rays

September 23

Less direct sun rays

Direct sun rays

Less direct sun rays

December 21

Less direct sun rays

Direct sun rays

Less direct sun rays

March 21

Less direct sun rays

Direct sun rays

Less direct sun rays

Reading a Climate Map

North and South America stretch almost from the North Pole to the South Pole. On the two continents, you can find nearly every kind of **climate.** Climate is the usual weather of a place. It is the weather you can count on.

In some parts of North and South America, the climate is hot and dry all year long. This does not mean there cannot be several rainy days and a number of cool ones in the course of the year. It does mean that most of the time the weather will be hot and dry.

The map on the next page shows the climate in different parts of North and South America. Study the map and answer the questions.

1. Which continent has the coldest climates?
2. If you were going to visit Phoenix, would you take an umbrella? Why or why not?
3. What city in South America has a climate most like that of Atlanta?
4. Find Manaus, Brazil, on the map. (a) What kind of clothing would you need if you were going to visit Manaus in the summer? (b) What kind of clothing would you need in the winter?
5. Find Boston on the map. (a) What kind of clothing would you need if you were going to visit Boston in the summer? (b) What kind of clothing would you need if you were going to visit there in the winter?
6. Find Thule, Greenland, on the map. If you were going to visit there, would you take a bathing suit or a warm winter coat?
7. Which has colder winters, Seattle or New York City?
8 Which has rainier summers, San Francisco or Atlanta?
9. Which city on the map has a climate that is usually cooler and wetter than the lands around it?
10. What city in North America has a climate most like that of Santiago, Chile?

North and South America: Climates

Tropical climates

- Hot and very rainy all year
- Hot all year with one rainy season and one dry season

Temperate climates

- Hot, dry summers and mild, rainy winters
- Hot, humid summers and mild winters
- Mild and rainy all year
- Warm summers and cold, snowy winters
- Short summers and long, cold, snowy winters

Polar climates

- Always cold and dry, with a short, chilly summer
- Icecap—frozen all year

Dry climates

- Desert climate with almost no rain
- Semi-desert climate with some rain

Highlands

- Usually cooler and wetter than the lands around them

0   500   1000   1500 Miles

0   500 1000 1500 Kilometers

Words for Land and Water

basin   the land drained by a river and the streams that flow into it; land surrounded by higher land

bay   part of a larger body of water that extends into land

canyon   a narrow valley with high, steep sides

cape   a point of land that extends into water

coast   land along the ocean

delta   land built up by deposits of soil which collect at the mouth of a river

divide   the highest ridge of land that separates two regions drained by different river systems

gulf   part of a body of water that extends into land, often larger than a bay

harbor   an area of deep water that is protected from winds and ocean currents, forming a place of shelter for ships

hill   a raised part of Earth's surface, smaller than a mountain

inlet   a narrow body of water, smaller than a bay, that extends into land

island   a body of land surrounded by water, smaller than a continent

The Grand canyon

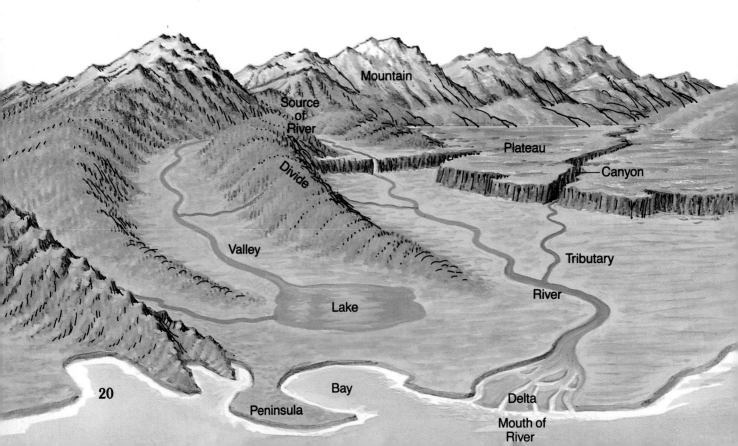

20

lake   a body of water smaller than an ocean surrounded by land

mountain   high rocky land, higher than a hill

mountain range   a row of connected mountains

mouth (of a river)   the part of a river where its waters empty into a larger body of water

peninsula   a body of land almost totally surrounded by water

piedmont   the hilly land lying at the foot of a mountain or mountain range

plain   a stretch of level or gently rolling land, often called a lowland

[plǽtou] **plateau**   flat or gently rolling land that stands high above sea level

river   a large stream of water that flows through land

sea   a large body of water, partly or wholly closed in by land

sound   a long narrow body of water, larger than a strait, that connects two larger bodies of water or separates an island from the mainland

source (of a river)   the place where a river begins, usually in highlands

strait   a narrow body of water, smaller than a sound, that connects two larger bodies of water

tributary   a river or stream that flows into a larger river or stream

valley   lowland that lies between hills or mountains

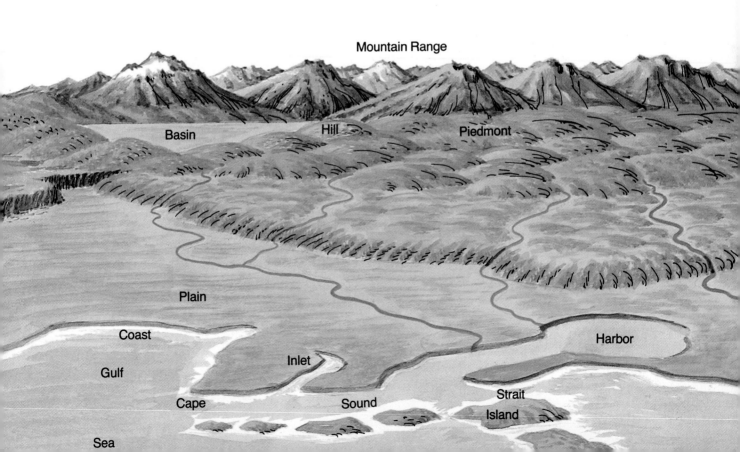

Mountain Range

Basin   Hill   Piedmont

Plain

Coast

Gulf   Inlet

Harbor

Cape   Sound   Strait

Island

Sea

A painting of the *Mayflower* arriving in North America

Unit One

Newcomers to the Americas

Until about 500 years ago, people in other parts of the world did not know there was a North and South America. Then, beginning in 1492, people from Europe began to explore and then settle the Americas. In doing so, they brought many changes to the land and the people of the Americas.

1

A Voyage That Changed History

Have you ever read a book over and over again? About 500 years ago Christopher Columbus did. The book told of countries where people dressed in clothes made of silk. It described rich palaces and streets paved with gold.

The book had been written by an Italian named Marco Polo in 1298, over 150 years before Columbus was born. It described the 17 years Marco Polo spent in India, China, and Japan. Columbus dreamed of seeing those Asian countries for himself. In 1492, he set out on a voyage to make that dream come true. Columbus, however, never reached Asia. Instead, he stumbled upon two continents that were on none of the maps he had studied. That accidental discovery changed the **history** of countries everywhere. History is the story of the past.

As You Read

This chapter tells of how the search for new routes to Asia led to the European discovery of the Americas. As you read, think about how different our history would have been had Columbus not tried a new route to Asia. The chapter is divided into four parts.

- Seeing New Routes to Asia
- Crossing the Atlantic
- A Continuing Search for Asia
- What the Explorers Found

◀ *A painting made in the 1500's of Marco Polo in China*

Seeking New Routes to Asia

Marco Polo was from Venice, an Italian city in Europe. He went to Asia as a **merchant.** A merchant buys and sells goods. Marco Polo bought ivory, jade, silks, and many other treasures in Asia. He then sold these treasures to Europeans at high prices.

Other people in Europe also wanted a share of the trade with Asia. However, the only known routes were dangerous. They crossed huge deserts and tall mountains. They were also controlled by Italian merchants like Marco Polo.

Long ago, merchants could not move freely from one country to another. They had to buy or win trading rights from the ruler of every country they traveled through. In the 1300's, Italians had those rights for every country along Marco Polo's route to Asia. In the 1400's, people in other parts of Europe began to seek other ways of reaching Asia.

Portugal's Plan to Reach Asia

Portugal was the first country to seek a new route to Asia. The search began in 1416. Prince Henry, a son of the

Trace each route from west to east. Why was a new route to Asia important to the Portuguese? Who first reached Asia by an all-water route?

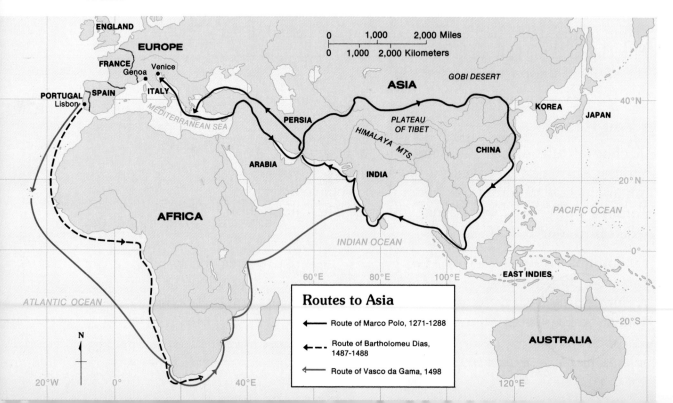

Routes to Asia

← Route of Marco Polo, 1271-1288

←- - Route of Bartholomeu Dias, 1487-1488

← Route of Vasco da Gama, 1498

king of Portugal, led the search. He hoped to reach Asia by sailing around Africa. Because such a route would be entirely over water, it would be faster than the one Marco Polo took.

As a young man, Prince Henry had sailed along the northern coast of Africa. However, neither he nor anyone else in Europe knew much about the rest of Africa. Nobody even knew how large it was. As Prince Henry's sailors traveled south along the west coast of Africa, each voyage took them a little farther into the unknown.

Prince Henry died in 1460, but his work was carried on. In 1488, Bartholomeu Dias (bär′tủ lü me′ủ dē′äs) reached the most southern part of Africa. Ten years later, in

Columbus wanted to sail west across the Atlantic to find a new route to Asia.

1498, Vasco da Gama (vä′skō də gä′mə) sailed around Africa and finally reached India. Nearly 40 years after his death, Prince Henry's dream had come true. Portuguese sailors had found an all-water route to Asia.

Columbus' Idea for Reaching Asia

While the Portuguese were searching for a route to Asia around Africa, Christopher Columbus was thinking about another route. He believed he could reach Asia by sailing west across the Atlantic Ocean.

Columbus' idea grew out of his experiences. As a boy, he had lived in Genoa, a city in Italy. There Columbus spent much of his time wandering around the harbor. He talked

Prince Henry began the search for a water route around Africa to Asia.

with sailors and studied their maps. He learned how to sail a ship. He hoped to be a sailor too some day.

Years later, on one of his early voyages, Columbus was shipwrecked near the coast of Portugal. He swam to shore and made his way to the city of Lisbon. In Lisbon, he learned even more about sailing routes. He listened to the stories Portuguese sailors told about their voyages along the coast of Africa. He even took part in a few of those trips.

A Plan Takes Shape. The more Columbus learned, the more certain he became that the fastest way to reach Asia was to sail west. Columbus believed that because Earth was round, a western route would be more direct than one around Africa. Columbus

Columbus asked Queen Isabella and King Ferdinand to sponsor his voyage west.

did not have the money to prove he was right. He needed several ships, sailors, and supplies to make such a long trip.

Columbus asked the kings of Portugal, England, and France to help him. All three refused. They said Earth was much larger than Columbus thought. They were certain that Columbus' western route to Asia would be much longer than the one around Africa.

After several years of trying, Columbus convinced Queen Isabella of Spain to trust him. No one knows for certain why she gave Columbus her support. Perhaps it was his strong feelings that convinced her. Perhaps she agreed because she wanted to spread Christianity to the people of Asia.

Isabella may have reasoned that a route to Asia promised great riches for Spain. Whatever her reasons, she and her husband, King Ferdinand, gave Columbus the backing he needed for his voyage.

Earlier Voyages. As Columbus made plans for his voyage, he was unaware that a westward route had already been tried. Earlier westward voyages had been made by Vikings, the most daring sailors in all of Europe.

The Vikings lived in what is now Norway and Sweden. In the 800's, they built settlements in Iceland, an

Long before Columbus was even born, the Vikings sailed west on the Atlantic Ocean. From where did they first set sail? Trace their routes. Where did they settle?

island west of Europe. According to the stories the Vikings told, they reached a larger island even farther west in the late 900's. Eric the Red, the leader of the voyage, called the island Greenland. Soon there were Viking settlements along the coast of Greenland.

Then, in the year 1000, the Vikings came to a land west of Greenland. The stories say that Eric's son Leif journeyed through part of that land. He found it was covered with great forests. Grapes and other fruit grew wild on twisted vines near the shore.

Today we know that Leif Ericson had reached the mainland of North America. The Vikings called the land Vinland. They built a settlement but abandoned it. Memories of Vinland lived on only in stories.

To Help You Remember

1. Why did Europeans look for new ways of reaching Asia?
2. (a) Who was Prince Henry?
   (b) What role did he play in Portugal's search for a route to Asia?
3. What route to Asia did Vasco da Gama find?
4. How did Columbus plan to reach Asia?
5. Why did Queen Isabella help him?
6. (a) Who were the Vikings?
   (b) Where did they settle?

29

This book is divided into 26 chapters. Each chapter begins with a *title*. The title tells you the main idea of the whole chapter. Every chapter is divided up too. Each major part begins with a *heading*. The heading tells the main idea of that part of the chapter. Each major part of a chapter is divided into smaller subparts. Subparts begin with *subheadings*. A subheading tells you what that subpart is about. To remind you of the difference between titles, headings, and subheadings, they are printed in different-sized letters.

The chart below shows the major headings and subheadings in the part of the chapter you just read. It also shows the headings and subheadings in the part of the chapter you will be reading next. Use the chart to answer the following questions.

The Voyage That Changed History

Part One	**Part Two**
Major Heading	*Major Heading*
Seeking New Routes to Asia	Crossing the Atlantic
Subheadings	*Subheadings*
Portugal's Plan to Reach Asia	Over the Wide Atlantic
Columbus' Idea for Reaching Asia	Land at Last!

1. What is this chapter about?
2. What is the main idea of the first part of the chapter?
3. What are the first two subheadings about?

The chart also shows the headings in the part of the chapter you will be reading next. Use those headings to answer the questions below. Check your answers as you continue reading.

1. What is the main idea of the second part of the chapter?
2. What does each subheading in Part Two describe?

Crossing the Atlantic

On August 3, 1492, just before dawn, Columbus and ninety men set out in three small ships to find the lands Marco Polo had described. They did not know it, but their voyage would change the history of the world.

Over the Wide Atlantic

Westward, always westward, the ships sailed across the wide Atlantic Ocean. August turned into September, and September into October, but there was still no sign of land.

Columbus feared that his sailors would be frightened if they knew how far from Spain they were. So he lied to them. Each day, they traveled farther than he told them.

Still the men wanted Columbus to turn back, but he refused. Then, before dawn on October 12, a sailor looked to the west. *"Tierra! tierra!"* he cried. *Tierra* is the Spanish word for land. A thin strip of sand glowed in the moonlight. Columbus ordered the sails lowered. The sailors waited for dawn to come before going ashore in a strange new land.

Land at Last!

When morning came, Columbus and his men rowed to shore in small boats. Columbus placed the Spanish flag in the sand. Then he **claimed** the island for Spain. That is, he said that Spain now owned the island. The islanders all watched Columbus in amazement. They did not understand what it meant to claim land.

Columbus called the island San Salvador (san sal′və dôr), meaning "Holy Savior," for he was grateful to God that he had reached land safely. Although Columbus did not know it, the island already had a name. The people who lived there called it Guanahani.

Columbus thought that he had landed in the Indies, a group of islands south and east of Asia. Because

Columbus set sail with three small ships—Pinta, Niña, and Santa María. He crossed the vast Atlantic in two months.

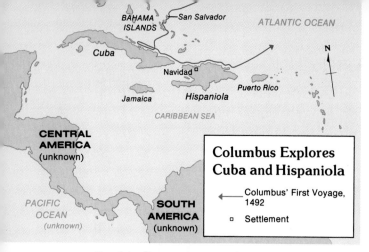

On his first voyage, what islands did Columbus and his crew explore?

of this mistake, he called the island people Indians. In fact, Columbus stood on an island in what is now the Bahamas, near Cuba (kyü′bə). The people of the island called themselves Arawaks (ä ′rä wäks).

The Arawaks were one of many groups who lived in North and South America. Each group had its own name and language. Yet Columbus and other Europeans thought of them as one people—the Indians. The name *Indian* has been used ever since.

The Arawaks were a peaceful people who had once lived on the mainland of South America. They were kind, generous people. They gave freely of all they had—bread, corn, cotton thread and cloth, and even dart guns for fishing. They did not, however, have any gold or other treasures. Therefore, Columbus decided to **explore** the islands farther west.

To explore means to search for new things or new places. Columbus asked the Arawaks to help him.

For the next three months, Columbus and his Arawak guides sailed around the Caribbean Sea. Columbus was sure the rich cities of Asia were very close. He explored the islands of Cuba and Hispaniola (his′pə nyō′lə), where Haiti and the Dominican Republic are today.

As Columbus was exploring the islands, one of his ships was wrecked on the northern coast of Hispaniola. Columbus' men used the wood from the ship to build a fort. They named it Navidad (nä vē däd′). It was the first Spanish settlement on the western side of the Atlantic Ocean. Columbus left some men at Navidad and returned to Spain.

To Help You Remember

1. Why did Columbus keep the distance he traveled a secret from his men?
2. (a) Where did Columbus think he had landed? (b) Where had he actually landed?
3. For whom did Columbus claim San Salvador?
4. (a) What did Columbus call the people living on the island? (b) What did they call themselves?
5. Why did Columbus sail around the Caribbean Sea?

A Continuing Search for Asia

When Columbus returned to Spain in April 1493, he received a hero's welcome. The king and queen of Spain named him "Admiral of the Ocean Sea, Viceroy and Governor of the Islands that he had discovered in the Indies." Still Columbus was not happy. He had not found the rich cities of Asia.

Columbus Sails Again and Again

On September 25, 1493, Columbus set out on his second voyage across the Atlantic. He took 1,500 men and 17 ships with him. When they reached the island of Hispaniola, they found no sign of the men Columbus had left behind. Columbus started a new settlement about 100 miles east of Navidad. He named it Isabela (iz′ə bel′ə).

Columbus did not spend much time building the settlement. Most of his time was spent looking for gold and other riches. He searched one island after another, but he found little sign of treasure.

In 1496, Columbus returned to Spain. He was a disappointed man. Yet he still believed that China was near the islands he had explored. In 1498 he set out again. This time Columbus sailed farther south, along the northern coast of South America.

Columbus explored several beautiful islands in the Caribbean. Yet he found no sign of cities rich in gold.

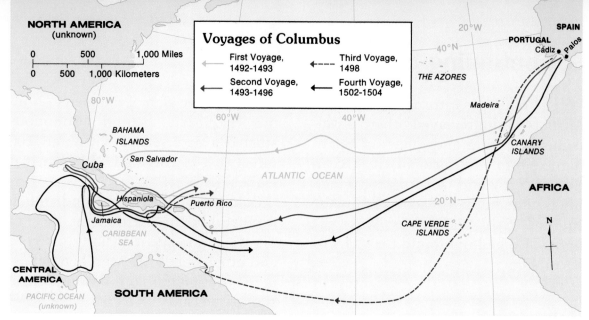

How many voyages did Columbus make? On which voyage did Columbus reach the coast of South America?

As before, Columbus brought men who planned to settle in the Indies. Women came too. The settlers brought seeds, plants, animals, and tools—all the things they needed to start a new life. Still, many of the settlers spent most of their time looking for treasure. So did Columbus.

This time, Columbus did find pearls in the waters off the coast of South America. However, he still could not find the rich cities of Asia. He was back in Spain before the year was out. There he was greeted with the news that the Portuguese had finally reached Asia by sailing around Africa. The news crushed him. He was desperate now to find a route across the Atlantic to Asia.

In 1502, Columbus made his last voyage. With him were 135 men and boys. His 13-year-old son Ferdinand came too. They sailed into every inlet, stream, and bay they saw, but Columbus never found the treasures of Asia. Instead, he found a land unknown to Europeans.

Columbus never knew how valuable the lands he discovered really were. He died a poor and unhappy man. Yet a few years after his death in 1506, Spain would become rich because of Columbus' discovery.

Naming Columbus' Discovery

Columbus never knew why he failed to find Asia. The reason is easy to understand today. Columbus was thousands of miles from Asia. North and South America and the Pacific Ocean lay between him and Asia. He had reached the shores of two continents Europeans knew nothing about.

One of the first people to realize that Columbus had not reached Asia was Amerigo Vespucci (ä mâr'i gō ve spü'chē). Vespucci was an Italian trader who lived in Spain. He had sold Columbus many of the things Columbus needed for his trips across the ocean.

Vespucci talked several Spanish sailors into taking him along on their westward voyages. On these trips, he became more certain that the land they saw was not a part of Asia. Many of the plants and animals he saw were unknown in Asia, Europe, or Africa. For that reason, he decided this land must be a new continent.

Vespucci wrote much about the new continent. Then a German mapmaker made a new map of the world. In it he included the continent Vespucci had described. The mapmaker even named it America in honor of Amerigo Vespucci.

As Europeans learned more about America, they found that it was not one continent but two. They named them North and South America.

Why did people keep coming to the two Americas long after everyone knew they were not a part of Asia? Some, like Columbus, were seeking a

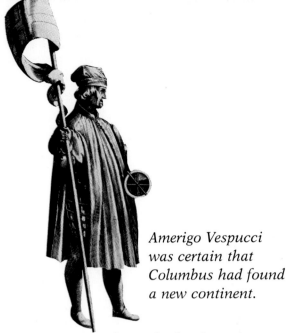

Amerigo Vespucci was certain that Columbus had found a new continent.

water route through the Americas to Asia. Others were eager to see if the Americas had treasures too.

To Help You Remember

1. Why was Columbus unhappy when he returned to Spain in 1496?
2. (a) What things did people bring on Columbus' third trip? (b) Why did they bring those things?
3. (a) Why had Columbus failed to find Asia? (b) What land had he found instead?
4. Why did Vespucci believe that the land Columbus reached was a new continent?
5. Give two reasons people continued to come to the Americas long after they knew the two continents were not part of Asia.

What the Explorers Found

European explorers found that the Americas were much larger than anyone had dreamed. They were, in fact, about four times larger than Europe. They contained many different **environments.** An environment is everything in a place. It includes land, climate, plants, and animals.

Environments in the Americas

The explorers who followed Columbus found that North and South America were alike in many ways. Both were shaped somewhat like triangles. They were wide to the north, and became narrow, curving points to the south. They were alike in other ways as well.

Both continents had low mountains in the east. These mountains had once been much higher, but they had been worn down over many, many years by wind and rain. In North America, the eastern mountains are called the Appalachians. They were named after a group of Indians who lived nearby. In South America, the eastern mountains are known as the Guiana Highlands and the Brazilian Highlands.

In the center of both North and South America, the explorers found plains. In North America, these lands of low relief were covered with grass.

Great herds of buffalo lived there. The explorers had never seen such strange animals before.

In South America, only part of the plains were covered by grass. The rest was covered by the largest rain forest in the world. Trees and other plants grow so tall and so close together in a rain forest that the sun's rays never reach the ground. Plants grow thickly because they get a lot of water. In a rain forest, it rains nearly every day.

The explorers also found high mountains along the western coasts of both continents. In North America, these mountains were later called the Rockies. In South America, the mountains were named the Andes.

Two of the longest rivers in the Americas flow from the Rockies and from the Andes. The Indians called the North American river the Mississippi. The explorers named the South American river the Amazon.

Columbus and other explorers also found that the Americas were rich in **resources.** A resource is any part of the environment that people use to meet their needs. Early explorers saw such valuable resources as wood, fish, and furs. They did not, however, see those resources that were buried deep in the earth. The Americas had much gold, iron ore, and other valuable metals.

In what direction does the Mississippi River flow? The Amazon River? Into what body of water does each empty? ▶

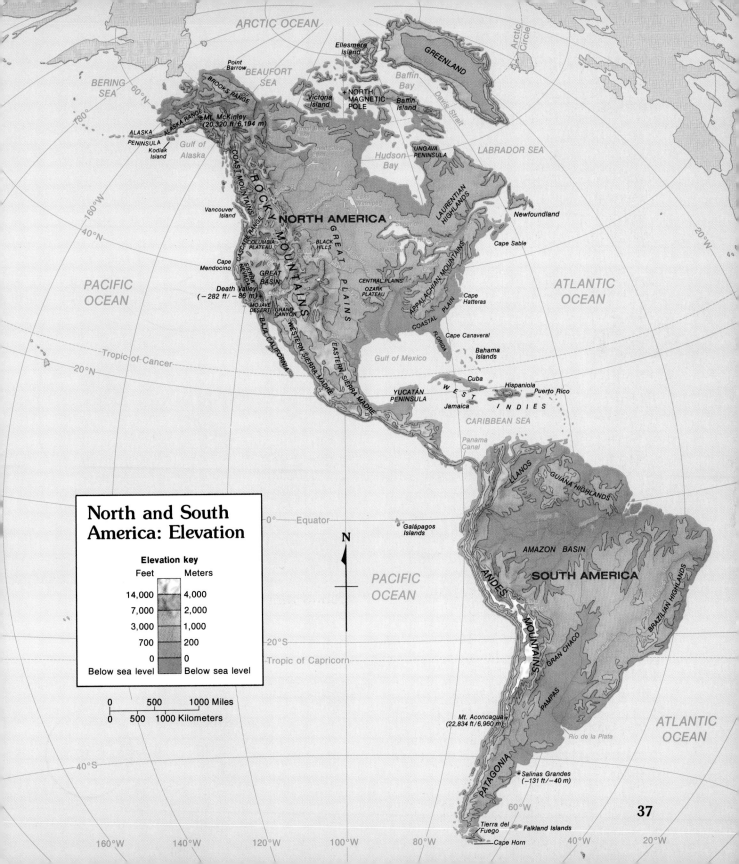

North and South America: Elevation

Elevation key

Feet	Meters
14,000	4,000
7,000	2,000
3,000	1,000
700	200
0	0
Below sea level	Below sea level

0   500   1000 Miles

0   500   1000 Kilometers

ARCTIC OCEAN

BERING SEA

BEAUFORT SEA

Point Barrow

Ellesmere Island

GREENLAND

Arctic Circle

Baffin Bay

+ NORTH MAGNETIC POLE

Victoria Island

Baffin Island

Davis Strait

BROOKS RANGE

ALASKA RANGE

+ Mt. McKinley (20,320 ft/6,194 m)

ALASKA PENINSULA

Kodiak Island

Gulf of Alaska

Great Bear Lake

Great Slave Lake

Hudson Bay

UNGAVA PENINSULA

LABRADOR SEA

COAST MOUNTAINS

Vancouver Island

Lake Winnipeg

LAURENTIAN HIGHLANDS

Newfoundland

NORTH AMERICA

Cape Sable

CASCADE RANGE

COLUMBIA PLATEAU

ROCKY MOUNTAINS

BLACK HILLS

GREAT PLAINS

Lake Superior

APPALACHIAN MOUNTAINS

Cape Mendocino

SIERRA NEVADA

GREAT BASIN

CENTRAL PLAINS

OZARK PLATEAU

Cape Hatteras

Death Valley (−282 ft/−86 m) +

MOJAVE DESERT

GRAND CANYON

COASTAL PLAIN

BAJA CALIFORNIA

WESTERN SIERRA MADRE

EASTERN SIERRA MADRE

Cape Canaveral

FLORIDA

Gulf of Mexico

Bahama Islands

YUCATÁN PENINSULA

Cuba

Hispaniola

Puerto Rico

W E S T   I N D I E S

Jamaica

Atlantic Ocean

PACIFIC OCEAN

Tropic of Cancer

20°N

CARIBBEAN SEA

Panama Canal

LLANOS

GUIANA HIGHLANDS

0° Equator

Galápagos Islands

AMAZON BASIN

SOUTH AMERICA

N

PACIFIC OCEAN

ANDES MOUNTAINS

BRAZILIAN HIGHLANDS

20°S

Tropic of Capricorn

GRAN CHACO

Mt. Aconcagua (22,834 ft/6,960 m)

PAMPAS

Rio de la Plata

ATLANTIC OCEAN

40°S

PATAGONIA

+ Salinas Grandes (−131 ft/−40 m)

60°W

37

Tierra del Fuego

Falkland Islands

Cape Horn

160°W   140°W   120°W   100°W   80°W   40°W   20°W

80°N

60°N

40°N

20°W

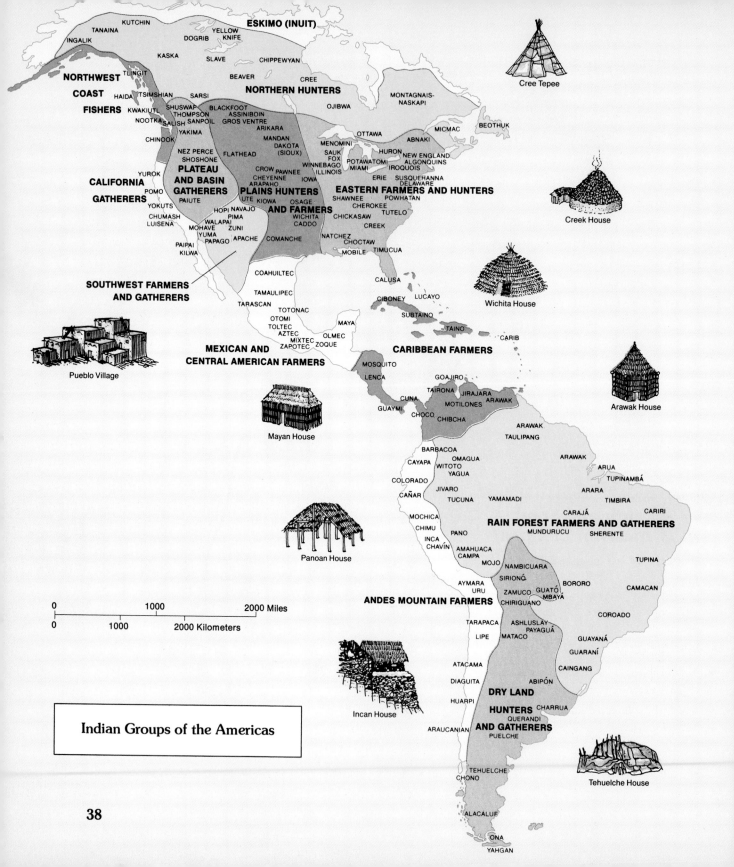

Indian Groups of the Americas

Cree Tepee

Creek House

Wichita House

Arawak House

Pueblo Village

Mayan House

Panoan House

Incan House

Tehuelche House

ESKIMO (INUIT)

KUTCHIN
TANAINA
INGALIK
TLINGIT
HAIDA
TSIMSHIAN
KWAKIUTL
NOOTKA
CHINOOK
SALISH
SHUSWAP
THOMPSON
SANPOIL
YAKIMA
NEZ PERCE
SHOSHONE
YUROK
POMO
YOKUTS
CHUMASH
LUISENA
PAIPAI
KILWA

DOGRIB
KASKA
SLAVE
CHIPPEWYAN
BEAVER
SARSI
BLACKFOOT
ASSINIBOIN
GROS VENTRE
ARIKARA
MANDAN
DAKOTA
(SIOUX)
FLATHEAD
CROW
CHEYENNE
ARAPAHO
PAIUTE
UTE KIOWA
HOPI NAVAJO
PIMA
WALAPAI
MOHAVE ZUNI
YUMA
PAPAGO APACHE

YELLOW
KNIFE
CREE
OJIBWA

PAWNEE
IOWA
WICHITA
CADDO
COMANCHE

NORTHWEST
COAST
FISHERS

NORTHERN HUNTERS

MONTAGNAIS-
NASKAPI

BEOTHUK

OTTAWA
MENOMINI
SAUK
FOX
WINNEBAGO
MIAMI
ILLINOIS
HURON
POTAWATOMI
NEW ENGLAND
ALGONQUINS
IROQUOIS
ERIE
SUSQUEHANNA
DELAWARE
POWHATAN
SHAWNEE
CHEROKEE
TUTELO
CHICKASAW
CREEK
NATCHEZ
CHOCTAW
MOBILE
TIMUCUA

ABNAKI
MICMAC

EASTERN FARMERS AND HUNTERS

PLATEAU
AND BASIN
GATHERERS

CALIFORNIA
GATHERERS

PLAINS HUNTERS
AND FARMERS

SOUTHWEST FARMERS
AND GATHERERS

COAHUILTEC
TAMAULIPEC
TARASCAN
TOTONAC
OTOMI
TOLTEC
AZTEC
MIXTEC
ZAPOTEC
OLMEC
ZOQUE
MAYA

CALUSA
CIBONEY
LUCAYO
SUBTAINO
TAINO
CARIB

MEXICAN AND
CENTRAL AMERICAN FARMERS

CARIBBEAN FARMERS

MOSQUITO
LENCA
GUAYMI
CUNA
CHOCO
GOAJIRO
TAIRONA
MOTILONES
CHIBCHA
JIRAJARA
ARAWAK

ARAWAK
TAULIPANG

BARBACOA
CAYAPA
COLORADO
CAÑAR
JIVARO
TUCUNA
MOCHICA
CHIMU
INCA
CHAVÍN
AMAHUACA
CAMPA
MOJO
AYMARA
URU

OMAGUA
WITOTO
YAGUA
YAMAMADI
PANO

NAMBICUARA
SIRIONÓ
ZAMUCO GUATÓ
MBAYÁ
CHIRIGUANO

ARUA
TUPINAMBÁ
ARARA
TIMBIRA
CARAJÁ
MUNDURUCU
SHERENTE

CARIRI
TUPINA
CAMACAN
COROADO

RAIN FOREST FARMERS AND GATHERERS

ANDES MOUNTAIN FARMERS

TARAPACA
LIPE
ATACAMA
DIAGUITA
HUARPI
ASHLUSLAY
PAYAGUÁ
MATACO
ABIPÓN
BORORO
GUAYANÁ
GUARANÍ
CAINGANG

DRY LAND
HUNTERS
AND GATHERERS

ARAUCANIAN
CHARRUA
QUERANDI
PUELCHE

TEHUELCHE
CHONO

ALACALUF
ONA
YAHGAN

0   1000   2000 Miles
0   1000   2000 Kilometers

38

The First Peoples in the Americas

The explorers found people living in every environment in the Americas. The explorers called these people Indians. The Indians of the Americas spoke over 2,000 different languages and had almost as many different **cultures,** or ways of life. A culture includes all of the things a group of people do, value, and believe in.

Technology is a part of culture. Technology is all of the ideas and tools a group develops to meet its needs. In the desert, some groups had a technology suited to hunting rabbits and other animals. They also knew which desert plants were safe to eat.

Other Indian groups lived in the desert too. The Hopi, for example, were farmers who knew how to make the most of every drop of water. The Spanish called these Indians the Pueblo (pweb'lo) people. *Pueblo* means *village* in Spanish. Hopi villages looked like large apartment buildings.

The Indians who lived along the northwest coast of what is now the

◄ *Where did the Hopi live? Who were their neighbors?*

The Hopi irrigated their crops.

Fish was a major food in the Northwest.

United States also lived in villages. These Indians did not farm, however. Most of their food came from the ocean and the many rivers that crossed their lands. They developed many ways of using salmon, cod, and shellfish. They also hunted whale, seal, and porpoise.

In the eastern forests of North America, many Indians lived by hunting, fishing, and farming. Their way of life changed with the seasons. In the spring, they planted their crops and fished in rivers and streams. In the fall, after their crops were harvested, they went hunting.

Some Indians in the Americas lived in large cities. There people worked at many jobs. Some wove cloth. Others made jewelry. Still others worked as carpenters, miners, teachers, and priests. City people got their food by trading with farmers.

The Aztecs (az'teks) of Mexico built the largest city in the Americas. Tenochtitlán (te nok'tē tlän') was its

Woodland Indians hunted and farmed for their food.

The Plains Indians used the buffalo for food, clothing, tools, and shelter.

Over 100,000 people lived in the beautiful city of Tenochtitlán. The people traveled on roads and on canals.

name. Over 100,000 people lived there. In the 1400's, Tenochtitlán was also one of the largest and best-planned cities in the world.

These are only a few of the ways people lived in the Americas at the time the Europeans arrived. As more and more people came to the Americas, these cultures would change greatly. In the next chapter, you will see some of the changes the Spanish brought.

To Help You Remember

1. (a) List three ways environments in North and South America are alike. (b) Tell one way they are different.
2. Although the early explorers found no gold or silver, what other valuable resources did they find?
3. How many different cultures did the Americas have before the explorers came?
4. Describe two Indian technologies.

Chapter Review

Words to Know

Complete each of the sentences below.

1. Chrisopher Columbus' voyage in 1492 changed *history*. History is ___.
2. Marco Polo was a *merchant*. A merchant is ___.
3. Columbus *claimed* San Salvador for Spain. To claim lands is to ___.
4. Columbus *explored* Cuba. To explore is to ___.
5. The explorers traveled through many *environments*. An environment is ___.
6. The explorers found *resources* in the Americas. A resource is ___.
7. The Indians had many different *cultures*. A culture is ___.
8. Every group of people has its own *technology*. A technology is ___.

Reviewing Main Ideas

1. Why did interest in an all-water route to Asia grow in the 1400's?
2. (a) Describe Portugal's plan for reaching Asia. (b) Did it work? Why or why not?
3. (a) Describe Columbus' plan for reaching Asia. (b) Did it work? Why or why not?
4. Why did Columbus die a poor and unhappy man?
5. Explain how the two continents Columbus explored came to be called North and South America.
6. (a) Name two ways environments in North and South America are similar. (b) Identify two ways they differ from one another.
7. Give three examples of differences among Indian cultures.

In Your Own Words

Suppose you were a reporter who traveled with Columbus. Write the story of Columbus' first voyage to the Americas. A good newspaper story always answers the following questions.
   Who? (Who sailed to the Americas?)
   What? (What were the voyages like?)
   When? (When did the voyage take place?)
   Where? (Where did the sailors reach land?)
   Why? (Why did the voyage take place?)

Challenge!

How might history have been different if the Vikings had built lasting settlements in the Americas? Would Columbus still have sailed west to reach China and India? Would the Spanish still have started settlements in the Americas? Give reasons for your answers.

Things to Do

Find out when Columbus Day was first celebrated in the United States. What other countries celebrate the holiday? Compare celebrations in those countries with celebrations in the United States.

Keeping Skills Sharp

The map below may help explain why Columbus was confused about where he landed. Use the map to answer the following questions.

1. At about what latitude is India?
2. At about what latitude are the West Indies?
3. At what longitude is India?
4. At what longitude are the islands that make up the West Indies?
5. In Columbus' time, sailors knew how to measure latitude but not longitude. For what reasons did Columbus think the West Indies were islands near India?
6. Find a western route to Asia for Columbus. Use latitude and longitude to describe your route.

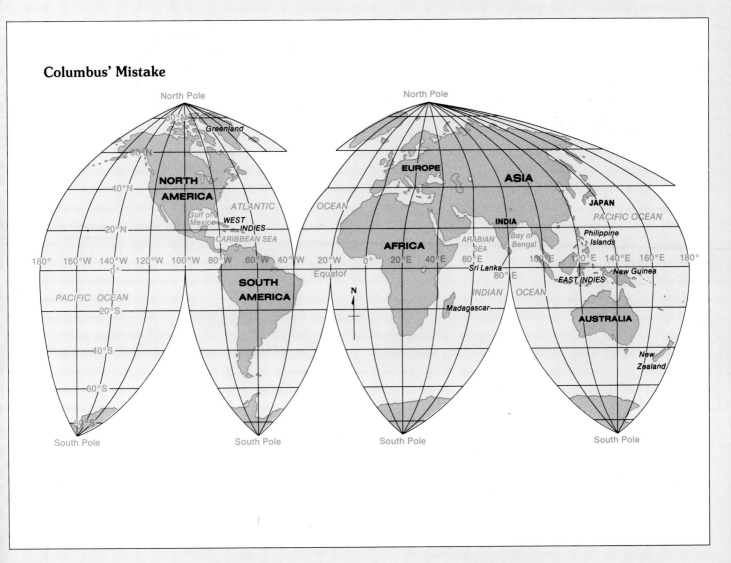

Columbus' Mistake

43

.SVR.

hornos donde quemã lamas.

2

Spain's Colonies in the Americas

In the years following Columbus' voyages, many people from Spain came to the Americas. They built the first Spanish **colonies** in the Americas. A colony is a settlement or group of settlements far from the home country. The people who live in a colony are called **colonists**. They are ruled by the home country.

At first, the Spanish spent most of their time searching for gold. When they found little gold, many turned to farming or ranching. A few Spaniards, however, refused to give up the search. They were excited by tales of rich Indian cities west of Cuba and Hispaniola. In the 1500's, some Spaniards set out to find those cities.

As You Read

This chapter is divided into four parts.

- Conquering Mexico
- Conquering Peru
- Seeking Gold North of Mexico
- Life in Spanish America

As you read the first three parts of the chapter, notice how the Spaniards won new lands. As you read the last part, find out what life was like in the lands the Spaniards won.

◀ *A silver mine in Spanish America in 1584*

Conquering Mexico

Hernando Cortés (är nän′dō kôr tez′) was one of the Spaniards who searched for gold and silver. He was just a boy when Columbus made his first voyage. Yet it started Cortés dreaming of adventure and wealth.

In 1504, at the age of 19, Cortés joined the Spanish army and sailed for Cuba. There he and the other Spanish soldiers fought the Indians. When the fighting was over, Cortés settled on the island. By the time he was 33, Cortés had made his first fortune by raising cattle in Cuba.

Even though he was now rich, Cortés was not happy. He missed the dangerous and exciting life he had led as a soldier. So when Cortés heard tales of gold and silver treasure in Mexico, he decided to set out in search of it.

Cortés Lands in Mexico

In the spring of 1519, Cortés sailed west from Cuba with 11 ships. With him were 700 men, 18 horses, many guns, and a few large cannons. They landed on the sandy shores of the Yucatán (yü′kə tan′) in Mexico.

A group of Indians gathered along the shore. They watched Cortés and his men carry their weapons off the ships. It was the first time the Indians had ever seen cannons or guns. They had never seen horses before, either. The huge beasts and large metal weapons terrified them.

In spite of their fears, the Indians fought the Spaniards. The Indians had no way to defend themselves against horses, guns, and cannons, so the Spanish won.

After the fighting, Cortés made peace with the Indians. They told him then about the rich and powerful Aztec Indians who were the rulers of all Mexico.

In the Land of the Aztecs

In August of 1519, Cortés and his army marched toward Tenochtitlán,

In which direction did Cortés travel from Cuba to Mexico? The voyage was slow and difficult. Why did he make the trip?

Cortés' Conquest of Mexico, 1519-1521

← Route to Tenochtitlán

NORTH AMERICA

ATLANTIC OCEAN

GULF OF MEXICO

MEXICO

CUBA

Tenochtitlán • Veracruz • Yucatán Peninsula

CARIBBEAN SEA

PACIFIC OCEAN

CENTRAL AMERICA

N

| 0 | 400 | 800 Miles |
| 0 | 400 | 800 Kilometers |

In Tenochtitlán's busy marketplace, people bought and sold many kinds of goods.

the Aztec capital. To get there, the army had to travel more than 275 miles (447 kilometers) from the coastal lowlands up into the mountains. The trip took two months.

When Cortés and his men finally reached the city, they could not believe their eyes. It was one of the most beautiful cities they had ever seen. Tenochtitlán was built on several islands in a shining lake. On the lake, brightly colored canoes carried goods and people around the city. Everywhere, the Aztecs were busy working.

In the marketplace, farmers sold brightly colored flowers and many kinds of foods the Spanish had never seen before. Other Aztecs worked at different crafts. There were people who wove cloth and people who made clay pots. Some made jewelry of gold and silver. Others fashioned feathers into fine capes.

To their surprise, no one stopped Cortés and his men as they walked around the city. The Aztecs thought Cortés might be their god Quetzalcoatl (ket′säl kō ä′tl). According to an old Aztec legend, Quetzalcoatl was supposed to return to Mexico from the east in 1519.

Cortés, with his fair skin and thick beard, looked like the Aztecs' drawings of Quetzalcoatl. Just like the god of the legend, Cortés too came from

Believing Cortés was a god, Montezuma treated the Spaniards as guests.

the east in 1519. For these reasons, the Aztec king, Montezuma, treated the Spaniards as honored guests.

Cortés was quick to take advantage of the Aztecs' mistake and his good luck. He tricked Montezuma into living with the Spanish in Tenochtitlán. He also got the king to give the Spanish gold and jewels.

The Spaniards and Aztecs lived together in peace until May of 1520. Then Cortés learned that the governor of Cuba had sent another army to Mexico. Cortés feared that the army would take the Aztec treasures away from him. So he rushed to the coast to meet the soldiers. He did not want to lose control of Mexico.

The Fight for Mexico

While Cortés was away, Spanish soldiers killed Montezuma and a number of other Aztec leaders. A great battle then began. From the start, the Spanish were hopelessly outnumbered. So they took as much gold as they could and fought their way out of the city.

In 1521, Cortés and his men returned to Tenochtitlán. With them were many Indians from lands along the coast. They too wanted the Aztecs defeated. After 75 days of bitter fighting, the war was over. The Spanish and their Indian friends had defeated the Aztecs.

Once the Spaniards had won the Aztecs' capital, they took over all the lands the Aztecs had ruled. The people in those lands now had to obey the Spanish. Also, the great wealth of the Aztecs belonged to Spain.

To Help You Remember

1. Why did Cortés decide to go to Mexico?
2. For what reason were the Indians along the coast fearful of Cortés and his men?
3. Why did the Aztecs treat Cortés and his men as honored guests?
4. What happened to the soldiers after Cortés left Tenochtitlán?
5. What did Spain gain by defeating the Aztecs?

48

Conquering Peru

Mexico was not the only place in the Americas rich in gold and silver. The Spanish heard stories of a rich Indian kingdom in South America called Peru. In 1531, ten years after Cortés had defeated the Aztecs, Francisco Pizarro (frän sēs′kō pi zär′ō) set out to win the kingdom of Peru. First, however, he had to find it.

Pizarro began his search for Peru by sailing south along the western coast of South America. From time to time, he stopped at Indian villages to gather more information. He soon learned that the people who ruled Peru were the Incas (ing′ kəz). They lived high in the Andes Mountains.

Pizarro immediately sailed back to Spain. There he got the king's permission to try to conquer Peru. He also gathered the men, supplies, and weapons he would need.

In the Land of the Incas

In 1531, Pizarro returned to South America with a small but powerful army. He and his men marched inland from the coast. After two months, the army reached the Incan city of Cajamarca (kä′hə mär′kə). Not knowing what to expect, the Spaniards approached the city carefully.

Around the city, the Spaniards found fields planted with potatoes,

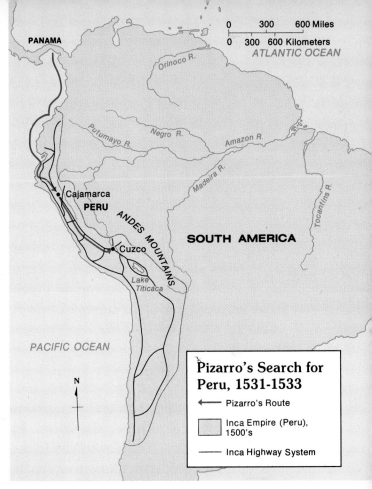

The Incas ruled the empire of Peru. In what part of South America was the Incan empire? Find Cajamarca on the map.

corn, and tobacco. Inside the city, they saw avenues lined with stone houses. In the center of town stood a large fort. Nowhere, however, did the Spanish see any people.

The people of Cajamarca and their king, Atahualpa (ä′tä wäl′pä), had fled to a camp three miles (4.8 kilometers) south of the city. There, thousands of Incas waited to see what the Spaniards would do.

49

This mask of gold is an example of work done by skilled Incan artists.

The Fight for Peru

Back in Cajamarca, the Spaniards made plans to conquer the Incas. Pizarro sent a few soldiers to the Incas' camp. The soldiers then invited the king to come to Cajamarca to meet Pizarro.

The Spaniards told Atahualpa that Pizarro, a priest, and a few others would be the only Spaniards in the city. The Incas did not know that the rest of the Spanish army and all of their horses remained hidden in the city. When Pizarro gave the signal, the army would attack and capture the Incas' king.

The next day, the Spaniards waited for Atahualpa to arrive. When he came, he did not walk into the city. Instead, with thousands of his people around him, Atahualpa was carried into the city on a golden throne.

Soon after the king reached the city square, Pizarro gave the signal to attack. The battle lasted barely half an hour. The Spaniards killed about 2,000 Indians. They also took Atahualpa prisoner.

Atahualpa offered to pay for his freedom. He promised the Spaniards a room full of gold and two smaller rooms full of silver. Pizarro's soldiers helped to gather the treasure. Once they had the treasure, however, the Spaniards did not free Atahualpa. Instead, they killed him.

Then Pizarro and his men headed for Cuzco (kü′skō), the capital city of the Incas. They destroyed it and marched on to other Incan cities. Even though the Indians fought long and hard, by 1533 the Spanish had conquered all of Peru. They had also won a fortune in gold, silver, and jewels.

To Help You Remember

1. Why did Pizarro search for Peru?
2. How did the Spaniards plan to conquer the Incas?
3. (a) What did Atahualpa promise to give the Spanish in order to gain his freedom? (b) Rather than free him, what did the Spanish do?
4. What did the Spanish gain by conquering the Incas?

So far in this chapter you have read about two people who explored the Americas for Spain. Their experiences were different. A chart can help you compare their experiences. Below is a chart that lists the names of the explorers, their reasons for exploration, the dates, the areas they explored, the personal gains, and the gains for Spain from their exploration. Copy the chart on a sheet of paper. Then fill in the blanks. You may need to look back through the chapter to find the information you need.

Explorer	Reason for Exploration	Dates of Exploration	Areas Explored	Personal Gains	Gains for Spain
1. Cortés			Mexico	Gold and silver	Gold, silver, jewels, and all Aztec lands
2. Pizarro	Searching for kingdom of Peru	1531–1533			

In the next section you will learn about two more explorers. As you read, add those explorers to the chart above.

Cortés (left) and Pizarro (right) added greatly to Spain's wealth.

51

Seeking Gold North of Mexico

Tales of still other rich cities to the north of Mexico encouraged more Spaniards to explore the Americas. Some of them searched for gold in the mountains, deserts, and forests of what is now the southern part of the United States.

De Soto's Journey

One of the Spaniards who searched for rich Indian cities in lands north of Mexico was Hernando De Soto

De Soto risked all of his money in hopes of finding gold north of Mexico.

(är nän'dō di sō'tō). De Soto was a soldier with Pizarro in Peru. His conquests there made him a rich man. Still, he decided to try his luck again rather than settle down to the quiet life of a rich gentleman.

De Soto got permission from the king of Spain to explore the lands north of Mexico. Hoping to find more gold, De Soto spent a fortune buying supplies for his journey.

In May 1539, De Soto and an army of about 600 men landed at what is today Tampa Bay, Florida. For the next two years, they traveled north and west searching for gold.

Dressed in heavy armor, the soldiers cut their way through swamps. They crossed rivers and walked through forests. Their journey took them through parts of what is now Georgia, South Carolina, Tennessee, and Alabama. Along the way, nearly half of the soldiers died from fever or were killed fighting Indians. Yet they found no gold.

By April of 1541, De Soto and his men had reached the Mississippi River. They may have been the first Europeans to see it. De Soto had not made the hard journey just to explore a river, however. So he and his men pushed on up the Mississippi and then along the Arkansas River as far as present-day Oklahoma. Still they found no gold.

Disappointed, the Spaniards then headed back across the Mississippi. There De Soto died of a fever. He had found no treasure. Yet his journey gave Spain a claim to a large area of land in the southern and eastern parts of what is now the United States.

Coronado's Journey

Even as De Soto and his men were exploring, yet another Spaniard set out in search of gold. His name was Francisco Coronado (frän sēs′ kō kôr′ə nä′dō). In 1540, Coronado led a group of men from Mexico through the southwestern part of North America.

Coronado's search took him through parts of what is today Arizona and New Mexico. He also journeyed across the Great Plains as far east as present-day Kansas. Along the way he saw cities built by the Pueblo and the Zuñi (zü′nyē) Indians. He also saw huge herds of buffalo grazing on the plains. Yet, like De Soto, he found no gold. Disappointed, Coronado returned to Mexico.

Coronado's journey gave Spain a claim to much of the southwestern part of what is now the United States. Although Coronado never knew it, that part of North America

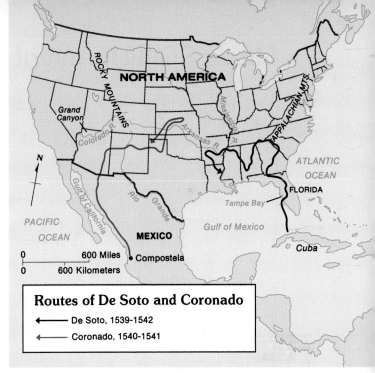

Where did Coronado explore? Where did De Soto explore? Neither found gold, but what did they achieve for Spain?

was rich in gold, silver, and other treasures. Those riches, however, were buried deep in the earth.

To Help You Remember

1. Why did the Spanish explore the land north of Mexico?
2. (a) What lands did De Soto journey through? (b) What did Spain gain as a result of De Soto's long journey?
3. (a) What lands did Coronado journey through? (b) What did Spain gain as a result of Coronado's journey?

Life in Spanish America

The land the Spaniards claimed in the Americas was twenty times the size of Spain and thousands of miles away. To govern the land, the king divided it into two large colonies. Each of these large colonies was called a **viceroyalty.** One was the viceroyalty of New Spain. The other was the viceroyalty of Peru.

Each viceroyalty had its own government and its own capital city. The capital of New Spain was Mexico City. The capital of Peru was Lima (lē′mə). Each viceroyalty had its own leader, called the **viceroy.**

On Farms and Ranches

Most of the first colonists were given land by the king of Spain. Many of these colonists owned huge pieces of land. Where the land was good for farming, they grew sugar cane, coffee, cacao, or wheat. Where the land was not so good, landowners raised cattle or sheep. Both farmers and ranchers **exported** food. That is they shipped food to Spain for sale.

Few of these farmers or ranchers did the hard work necessary to grow crops or to raise animals. Most thought of themselves as gentlemen. In those days, gentlemen did not work in the fields. In much of Spanish America, Indians did the work for them. The Indians were **slaves.** A slave is a person who is owned by another person and is forced to work for that person without pay.

Whether the Indians worked on farms or on ranches, the work was very hard. Many Indians died from overwork. Many more died from measles, smallpox, and other diseases brought from Spain. As the Indians died, the Spanish turned to Africa for more workers.

On which continent was the viceroyalty of New Spain? Of Peru? What was the capital of each?

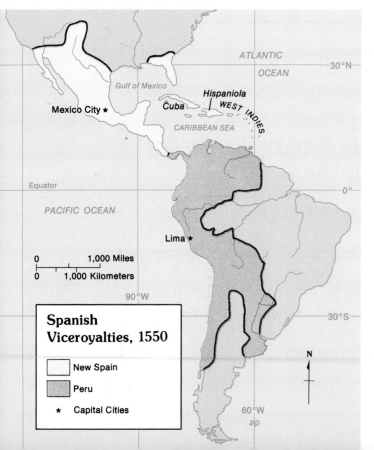

ATLANTIC OCEAN

30°N

Gulf of Mexico

Hispaniola

Cuba

WEST INDIES

Mexico City ★

CARIBBEAN SEA

Equator

PACIFIC OCEAN

0°

Lima ★

0   1,000 Miles

0   1,000 Kilometers

90°W

30°S

N

Spanish Viceroyalties, 1550

☐ New Spain

■ Peru

★ Capital Cities

60°W

This Spanish mission was built in California in the 1800's. At missions such as this, missionaries taught their religion and spread the Spanish way of life.

During the early 1500's, the Spanish began buying slaves from the west coast of Africa. The slaves were Africans who had been captured by other Africans in wars. These slaves were then taken to the Spanish colonies in chains. They were not free people.

The Spanish first brought slaves from Africa to work on large farms on the islands in the Caribbean Sea. This happened because by the early 1500's, almost all the Indians on those islands had died or been killed by the Spaniards. Yet landowners still needed many workers.

The Africans proved to be good farm workers. They were skilled farmers who were used to a warm climate. For these reasons, when landowners in Mexico and South America needed more workers, they too brought slaves from Africa.

Life in the Missions

One of Spain's goals in the Americas was to teach the Indians the Christian religion. Therefore, many priests came to the Americas. Unlike those hoping to get rich, the priests came as **missionaries.** Missionaries are

Labels on image: Cathedral · Homes of City Workers · Government Buildings · Central Square · Leather Workers · Marketplace · Blacksmith · Potters · Cabinetmakers · **A Spanish-American City, 1550's**

This is what a typical Spanish-American city looked like in the middle of the 1500's. What is at the center of the city? What buildings face the open plaza?

people who teach their religion to people of other faiths.

In the Americas, the priests did their work at settlements known as **missions.** A mission usually included a church, homes, and a fort. Later a school and workshops were added.

In the missions, the priests helped to spread the Spanish way of life. They taught the Indians to use plows, drive oxen, grow Spanish crops, and to raise sheep and cattle. In time, orchards of orange, lemon, and lime trees shaded the low stone buildings of mission towns. The missions became busy places for work and trade.

Life in Towns and Cities

Not every Spaniard who came to the Americas owned land or built a mission. Many settled in cities and towns.

Cities like Lima, Peru, were centers of trade and government. Mule trains from all over Peru came to Lima loaded with gold, silver, and other goods. They traveled the old Incan roads to the coast. At the harbor, the goods were exported to Spain. The mule trains then hauled goods **imported** from Spain back to Lima. These were tools and other goods shipped to the colonies for sale there.

Lima was built around a square, or plaza. The finest buildings, such as the church, government offices, and the mayor's house, faced the square. Just beyond the square were streets set aside for different crafts. The blacksmiths, cabinetmakers, glassblowers, leather workers, and other skilled laborers worked and lived along those streets.

Other cities were built on the ruins of Indian cities. The very stones of Tenochtitlán can still be seen in Mexico City today. The Spanish built government offices and churches with stones from the old Aztec city. They used those stones to show the Indians that the Spanish and their Christian religion had taken the place of the Aztecs and their religion.

Some cities, like Havana (hə van′ə) on the island of Cuba, were little more than forts. Behind thick walls that faced the ocean, Havana was alive with ship workers, sailors, and soldiers.

Spain's colonies in the Americas made Spain the richest country in the world, but only for a short time. In the 1600's, other European countries would begin building colonies of their own. Some countries built colonies in South America. Others built colonies in North America. The next chapter looks at those that England started in North America.

Lima in the 1500's bustled with activity just as cities do today.

To Help You Remember

1. (a) Why were the viceroyalties of New Spain and Peru formed? (b) Name the capital of each.
2. How did the Spanish use their land in the Americas?
3. What work did Indians do in the Spanish colonies?
4. (a) Why were Africans brought to the Americas? (b) Why did the Spanish continue to use African workers?
5. (a) Why did many priests come to the Americas? (b) What work did they do at a mission?
6. (a) What did Peru export to Spain?
7. (a) Name three cities the Spanish built in the Americas. (b) Which was the center of trade and government? (c) Which was built on the ruins of an old Aztec city? (d) Which was mostly a fort?

Chapter Review

Words to Know

Read the sentences below and explain what the *italicized words* mean.

1. Why are you likely to find a *missionary* at a *mission*?
2. What kinds of jobs does a *viceroy* do in a *viceroyalty*?
3. Why will you find many *colonists* in a *colony*?
4. Why can you not have *slavery* without *slaves*?
5. Food was both *exported* from Peru and *imported* into Spain. Explain.

Reviewing Main Ideas

1. Why did Spanish soldiers want to explore the Americas?
2. Cortés, Pizzaro, De Soto, and Coronado were all explorers. Tell what each was searching for and what Spain gained as a result of his search.
3. (a) What crops did the Spanish landowners grow on their land? (b) What animals did they raise? (c) Who did most of the hard work on these farms and ranches? (d) What did the landowners do with the food they raised on their farms and ranches?
4. (a) Why did priests come to the Americas? (b) Where did they work? (c) What did they teach the Indians?
5. In many ways, Lima was a typical Spanish city. (a) What was in the center of the city? (b) What buildings surrounded the center?

In Your Own Words

Write a paragraph about one of the explorers in this chapter. The outline below will help you organize your ideas.

Explorer's Name
 I. Reasons for Exploring
 II. Places Explored
III. Results of Trip
   A. Personal Gains
   B. Gains for Spain

Challenge!

This poem was written after the Spanish defeated the Aztecs. What words show that the poet was an Aztec? What words suggest that he has given up hope of ever defeating the Spanish?

> We are crushed to the ground;
> We lie in ruins.
> There is nothing but grief and suffering in Mexico,
> Where once we saw beauty and valor.

Pretend you are a soldier in Cortés' army. Write a poem about your victory.

Things to Do

1. Make a map of North and South America showing Spanish claims in 1505 and 1545. The maps and other information in the chapter will help you.
2. Choose one of the explorers described in the chapter. Write a report telling about his life after his career as an explorer was over.

Keeping Skills Sharp

As the Spanish explored the Americas, they named many bodies of land and water. For example, Columbus named the island he landed at in 1492 San Salvador. Use the map below to find other bodies of land and water the Spanish explored. Then, on a separate sheet of paper, answer the following questions.

1. An *island* is a body of land surrounded by water. An island is smaller than a continent. Name two large islands that Columbus explored in the Caribbean Sea.

2. A *mountain range* is a row of connected mountains. Name three of the mountain ranges that the Spanish explored.

3. A *peninsula* is a body of land almost totally surrounded by water. Name two peninsulas the Spanish explored.

4. An *isthmus* is a narrow body of land that connects two larger bodies of land. Name an isthmus that the Spanish explored.

5. A *gulf* is a part of a body of water that extends into land. A gulf is often larger than a bay. Name the largest gulf in the Caribbean Sea.

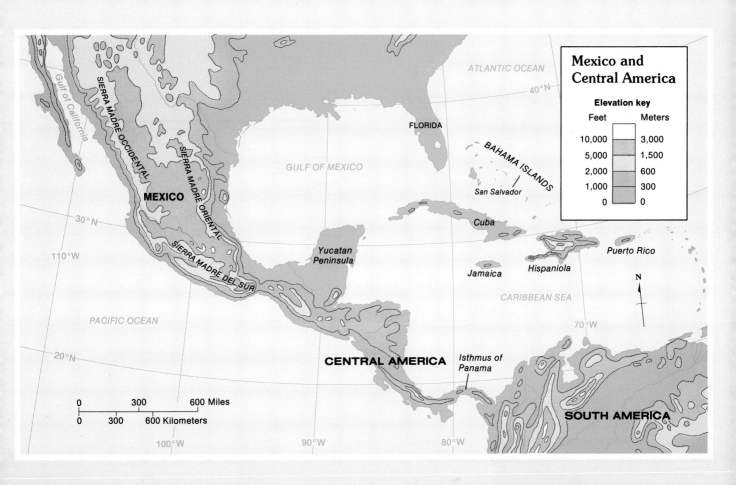

3

England's First Colonies

In 1497, John Cabot sailed west across the Atlantic. He was an Italian sailor who had been hired by the king of England. Like Christopher Columbus, Cabot hoped to find an all-water route to Asia. He never found such a route, but he did claim the northeast coast of North America for England.

When Cabot returned to England, he bragged that the waters off the coast of North America were so thick with fish that his ships could hardly push through them.

Throughout the 1500's, dozens of English fishermen crossed the Atlantic. They too came home with tales of all they had seen. Many Englishmen eager for adventure heard the fishermen's stories. They also crossed the Atlantic in the 1500's. Some returned to England with new stories of Spanish colonies rich in gold and silver.

As You Read

By the end of the 1500's, many people in England wanted to start colonies in the Americas. In this chapter, you will learn about the first colonies they built. As you read, look for reasons some colonies were more successful than others.

- Plans for Building Colonies
- England's First Colony
- England's Second Colony
- New English Colonies

◀ *Part of the Atlantic seacoast drawn by an European artist*

Plans for Building Colonies

Like Spain, England expected to get rich in the Americas. Unlike Spain's rulers, however, England's rulers did not supply the money needed to start colonies. Instead, they gave the right to start colonies to individuals and to groups of people. These people were willing to risk their money in hopes of making a **profit**. A profit is the money left over after paying all of the costs of doing business. If the Americas were rich in gold and silver, then building colonies would be a good way to make money.

All anyone needed to start a colony was a **charter** from the king or queen. A charter was a legal paper. In it, the English ruler gave people permission to explore, settle, and govern in the land claimed by England. Those who received charters promised that their colony would obey English laws.

A Colony at Roanoke

Among the first to get a charter was Sir Walter Raleigh, a wealthy English gentleman. Raleigh decided to build his colony on a small island off the coast of North Carolina. He called the island Roanoke.

In the spring of 1585, Raleigh sent 100 colonists to Roanoke Island. Within a year the hungry and unhappy settlers had returned home to England.

In 1586, Raleigh tried again. This time, he sent 117 people to Roanoke Island. Several families were among those colonists.

John White, who was among the first settlers of Roanoke, made this drawing of an Indian village. Find Roanoke Island on the map. Use longitude and latitude to describe its location.

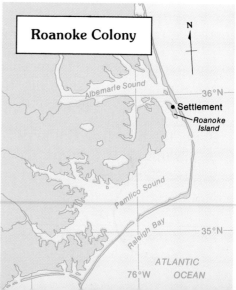

Roanoke Colony

About the time the colonists landed at Roanoke, England went to war with Spain. Because of the war, no one in England was able to check on the tiny settlement. An English ship finally returned to the island in 1591.

When the sailors went ashore, they found no sign of the colonists. The only thing the sailors found was the word *Croatan* (krō'ä tän') carved on a tree. The Croatan were a group of Indians who lived on a nearby island. To this day, no one knows what happened to the colonists.

A New Way of Paying for Colonies

Raleigh lost a fortune in his efforts to start a colony. Few other people in England had that kind of money to lose. Even the wealthy were not eager to risk all their money. Yet many people wanted to get rich in the Americas. So they looked for ways to start a colony without risking everything they owned.

To solve the problem, the English formed **joint-stock companies.** A joint-stock company is a business owned by many people. Each person puts money into the company by buying stock. People who buy stock own a part of the business. The stockowners share the costs of doing business. They also share the risks and the profits.

NOVA BRITANNIA.
OFFERING MOST
Excellent fruites by Planting in VIRGINIA.

Exciting all such as be well affected to further the same.

LONDON
Printed for SAMVEL MACHAM, and are to be sold at his Shop in Pauls Church-yard, at the Signe of the Bul-head.
1609.

The London Company wrote this pamphlet encouraging people to settle in Virginia.

During the 1600's, the English planned to use joint-stock companies to build colonies. Rich nobles, farmers, church leaders, and shopkeepers all bought stock. Then the companies hired people who wanted to live and work in the Americas. These were the colonists.

Colonists agreed to work for a company for a certain number of years. During that time, they had to make a profit for the company. If the colonists failed to make a profit, the company might no longer send help or supplies.

In 1606, King James granted a charter to a joint-stock company called the London Company. The charter gave the company the right to build a colony in a part of North America called Virginia. Hoping to get rich quickly, the company's owners told the colonists to look for gold in Virginia.

To Help You Remember

1. (a) Why did England want to start colonies in the Americas?
   (b) Who paid the cost of starting a colony?
2. (a) What is a charter? (b) What did people receiving a charter promise to do?
3. (a) Who started England's first colony in the Americas? (b) What happened to that colony?
4. (a) What are joint-stock companies? (b) Why were they started? (c) Where did a joint-stock company get the money needed to start a colony?
5. (a) How did the owners of a joint-stock company get people to come to North America? (b) What did these people agree to do for the company?

England's First Colony

In December of 1606, the London Company sent 144 men and boys to North America. They sailed on three small ships, the *Susan Constant*, the *Godspeed*, and the *Discovery*. They planned to start a colony in Virginia.

The voyage was long and hard for everyone. Then, on April 26, after 18 weeks at sea, the colonists entered Chesapeake Bay. From there, they sailed up a deep river. They called it the James in honor of King James I.

Within a few days, the colonists came to a small stretch of land surrounded on three sides by water. To the weary travelers, it looked like a good place to build a settlement. The grassy meadows were bright with spring flowers. The bushes nearby were thick with wild strawberries. The woods were filled with deer, beaver, and other animals.

Settling Down in Jamestown

As soon as the settlers went ashore, they built a settlement. They called

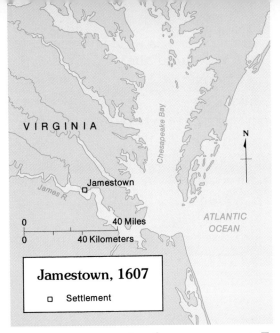

Jamestown was the first permanent English settlement. Find it on the map. What present-day state is it part of?

it Jamestown. At the time it seemed a good place to live. The settlers were wrong. The land they had chosen for the settlement was low and swampy. When summer came, mosquitoes and other insects spread sickness and disease. Within six months, half of their number had died.

To add to the settlers' troubles, the food they had brought with them was nearly gone. Everyone had been so busy searching for gold that no one had bothered to plant crops. In fact, few settlers even knew how to farm, hunt, or fish. Most of them had lived in cities in England. Even though there was lots of game in the woods and plenty of fish in the rivers, the people of Jamestown were starving.

A Leader for Jamestown

Jamestown needed a strong leader. The colonists found that leader in John Smith. He took charge of the colony. He ordered the settlers to clear land and plant crops. While waiting for the crops to grow, he traded with the Algonquin (al gong′kē ən) Indians. The colonists were living in the land of the Algonquin.

On one of his trading trips, Smith was captured by a group of Algonquin. According to Smith's own story, they were about to kill him when their leader's young daughter, Pocahontas (pō′kə hon′təs), saved his life. She pleaded with her father to allow Smith to return to Jamestown

Pocahontas convinced her father to save John Smith's life.

This diagram of Jamestown shows what the settlement looked like in the early 1600's.

unharmed. Her father let him go.

After Smith returned safely to the colony, Pocahontas visited him there many times. She often brought food to the starving colonists.

New Hope for Jamestown

In 1609, John Smith was injured by a gunpowder explosion. He returned to England to recover from his wounds. While he was gone, the colony suffered. Sickness and hunger killed dozens of colonists. Indians killed others.

By spring only 60 settlers were still alive. They were at the point of giving up and returning to England when two supply ships arrived. The ships carried 300 new settlers, food, tools, and a new leader. Lord Delaware, the new leader, ordered the earlier settlers to stay. They joined the new settlers and the little colony began again.

The people of Jamestown began to grow more of their own food. They also exported furs, wood, and some plants used for medicine to England. Yet Jamestown was still not making a profit. Many settlers wondered how much longer the company would support the colony.

In 1611, John Rolfe arrived in Jamestown. He was an experienced farmer. Rolfe knew that Spanish colonists were growing an Indian crop called tobacco. It sold for high prices in Europe. Rolfe thought that it might make a profit for Jamestown.

Rolfe experimented with different kinds of tobacco until he produced a mild-tasting tobacco. He sent his first shipment of the new tobacco to England in 1614. It was a great success. Within a few years, everyone in Jamestown was growing tobacco.

Rolfe helped the colony in another way too. In 1614, he married Pocahontas. Their marriage brought eight years of peace between the settlers and their Algonquin neighbors.

New Settlers for Jamestown

Yet even with peace and the success of the tobacco crop, few new settlers came to Jamestown. To encourage people to come, the London Company gave land free to people who paid their own way to Virginia.

By 1618, farms stretched for 20 miles (32 kilometers) or more along the James River. The colony had over a thousand people. Most of them were men. There were only a few women and children. If Virginia was to be a lasting colony, it had to be a place where families lived. In 1619, the company sent 90 women to Virginia. They married and started families there.

The year 1619 was important for another reason. That year a Dutch ship arrived in Jamestown with 20 Africans on board. The Dutch sold the Africans to several farmers in Jamestown.

The Africans were set free as soon as they had worked long enough to pay off their purchase price. Within a few years, the colonists were buying more and more people from Africa. These Africans were never set free. Instead, they were kept as slaves for life. So were their children.

The year 1619 also marked a change in the government of Virginia. In the past, the people who lived in Virginia had had no say in the way their colony was run.

Then, in 1619, the London Company gave colonists the right to choose people to **represent** them. A person who represents others has the right to speak or act in their name. The group who represented Virginians made laws for the colony. It was called the House of Burgesses.

To Help You Remember

1. Why were the colonists starving when the forest was filled with animals and the rivers filled with fish?
2. (a) Who was the first leader of Jamestown? (b) How did he help the colony survive?
3. Tell two ways John Rolfe helped Jamestown.
4. List three important events that took place in Virginia in 1619.

You have read how tobacco made it possible for the colonists of Jamestown, Virginia, to prosper. The first shipment of Virginian tobacco arrived in England in 1614. From that time on, more and more colonists in Virginia started raising tobacco.

One way to see how much tobacco was shipped to England between 1615 and 1630 is by studying a graph. Look carefully at the graph below. Notice the numbers along the bottom of the graph. They show the years the graph covers. The numbers along the side of the graph show the number of pounds of tobacco shipped to England. Use the graph to answer the following questions. Write your answers on a separate sheet of paper.

1. About how much tobacco was shipped to England in 1615?
2. About how much tobacco was shipped to England in 1620?
3. About how much tobacco was shipped to England in 1625?
4. (a) In what year was the largest amount of tobacco shipped to England?   (b) About how much was shipped?
5. (a) In the years between 1615 and 1630, what was the smallest amount of tobacco shipped?
   (b) About how much was shipped?
   (c) In what year was it shipped?
6. A **decade** is any ten-year period of time. In which decade did Virginians sell the most tobacco?

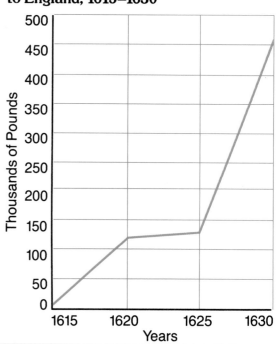

Tobacco Shipped From Jamestown to England, 1615–1630

England's Second Colony

While Virginia was being settled, new ideas about religion were spreading in England. Some people wanted to start their own churches. However, everyone in England was supposed to belong to their ruler's church, which was called the Church of England.

In 1608, a group of people who wanted their own church left England. They moved to the Netherlands in Europe. These people were called **Pilgrims.** A pilgrim is a person who makes a journey for religious reasons. The Pilgrims traveled to the Netherlands so they could be free to follow their religious beliefs.

Seeking a New Home

The Pilgrims lived in the Netherlands for about 12 years. Although the people there were kind to them, the Pilgrims were not happy. They wanted to remain English. Yet they saw their children becoming more and more like the people of the Netherlands. So the Pilgrims decided to look for a place where they could have their own church and also live as English men and women.

After thinking about a number of places, the Pilgrims decided to go to North America. The London Company was still looking for settlers. So it was willing to pay the cost of starting a new settlement.

The Pilgrims agreed to start a settlement in Virginia, just north of Jamestown. There they would be free to govern themselves. They could even have their own church. In return for the money the London Company spent, the Pilgrims were to send food, furs, and other goods to the company for seven years.

A Change in Plans

In September of 1620, about a hundred people crowded onto a small

Pilgrims sailed for Virginia. Blown off course, they landed at Cape Cod. In which direction is Cape Cod from Virginia?

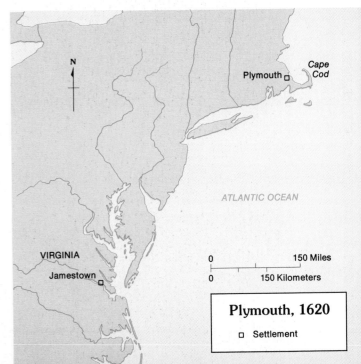

Plymouth, 1620

□ Settlement

ship called the *Mayflower*. It was bound for Virginia.

On November 9, after more than 60 days at sea, the *Mayflower* reached the sandy beaches of Cape Cod in what is now Massachusetts. Storms and high winds had blown the tiny ship hundreds of miles off course.

The Pilgrims did not have permission to settle in Massachusetts. The London Company did not own land that far north. Yet it was too late in the year to turn back or to try to reach Virginia. Winter was coming. Already there was snow on the ground. So they decided to stay.

Before anyone left the ship, the Pilgrim leaders drew up a **compact,** or agreement. It was called the Mayflower Compact. It set up the first government for the colony. That government had the power to make laws for the good of all. The 41 men on board ship signed the agreement. Then they chose John Carver to be governor of the colony.

Building Plymouth Colony

Once the Mayflower Compact was signed, the Pilgrims looked for a good place to settle. They found one just a little west of Cape Cod. They called the place they chose Plymouth. It had

The Pilgrims drew up the Mayflower Compact before leaving their ship. The Mayflower Compact set up a government for their new colony.

a good harbor. Also, much of the land around Plymouth had already been cleared by the Indians.

In spite of Plymouth's good location, the first winter was a hard one. The settlers were not prepared for the cold. Moreover, they did not have enough food. By March, over half of the colonists had died, including Governor Carver. Yet none of the survivors were willing to return to England. They were determined to build a lasting colony.

The colonists found a new leader in William Bradford. They elected him governor of the colony. Much of what we know about the Pilgrims' early years comes from a book Bradford wrote. The book is the *History of Plimoth Plantation*.

In his book, Bradford tells of an important event that took place soon after he became governor. One day in March, a tall Indian walked into Plymouth. His name was Samoset. He greeted Bradford and the other Pilgrims with the words, "Much welcome, Englishmen! Much welcome." Samoset had learned to speak English from English fishermen who had come to North America.

Samoset introduced the Pilgrims to the Indians who lived in New England. The Indians wanted to make friends with the English. The leader of the Indians, Massasoit (mas'ə soit), worked out a treaty with Governor Bradford. It was so successful that it kept peace in the area for about 50 years.

Samoset also introduced the Pilgrims to an Indian named Squanto. He spoke even better English than Samoset. He stayed on to live at Plymouth. Squanto taught the settlers many things. From him, they learned to rake clams at low tide. They also learned how to tap the sap of the maple tree and make maple syrup. Squanto showed the settlers which wild plants were good to eat and which were not. He taught them how to grow corn, a grain the English had never seen before. Squanto also showed the Pilgrims the best places to hunt deer and beaver.

Because of Squanto's help, the settlers did not starve while they waited for their crops to grow. William Bradford wrote that Squanto's coming was a sign of God's concern for the Pilgrims.

A Time of Thanksgiving

There was almost no rain that first summer in 1621. The young corn plants started to dry out in the sun. Everyone worried. The Pilgrims set aside a day of prayer to ask God for help. The answer was "gracious and speedy," Bradford wrote. "Sweet and gentle showers" began to fall that same evening.

Thankful for a good harvest, the Pilgrims held a feast to celebrate.
The custom of giving thanks continues today. It is called Thanksgiving.

In the autumn, the harvest was good after all. The Pilgrims knew they would have plenty of food to get them through the long winter. They were also happy because the *Mayflower* had returned to England with a small load of beaver skins. The beaver skins were sold in England. The money the Pilgrims earned from the sale helped to pay back their debt to the London Company.

The grateful colonists decided it was time to give thanks to God for their good fortune. They invited Massasoit to join them. He came with about 90 more Indians. Together they gave thanks for the good harvest.

For three days the colonists and the Indians feasted on lobsters, clams, eels, wild turkey, duck, geese, cornbread, fruit, berries, and other foods. The colonists thanked God for helping them. To be alive, to have good food, and to have the friendship of their Indian neighbors—these were their blessings. There was one more. They had begun to build the community of their dreams. It was a place where they could worship God as they pleased.

To Help You Remember

1. (a) Why did the Pilgrims leave England? (b) Why did the Pilgrims leave the Netherlands? (c) Where did they decide to go next?

2. What was the Mayflower Compact?
3. In what ways did Samoset help the Pilgrims?
4. How did Squanto help them?
5. Why did the Pilgrims celebrate Thanksgiving?

New English Colonies

Over the years, still other people came from England to live in North America. Some came for the freedom to worship the way they wanted. Others dreamed of wealth and power. Still others came dreaming of a better life in a new land.

The Puritans and Massachusetts

Even as the Pilgrims were building Plymouth, a group known as the Puritans came to North America. The Puritans had beliefs similar to those of the Pilgrims. The Puritans, however, did not want their own church. Instead, they tried to change the Church of England. Their efforts got them into a lot of trouble. So they were eager to find a place where they could worship as they pleased.

In the summer of 1629, a group of Puritans in England formed a joint-stock company. They called it the Massachusetts Bay Company. The king gave the company a charter for land near Plymouth Colony. The Massachusetts Bay Company had the right to make rules for all the people who lived on its land.

In 1630, one thousand Puritans came to what is now Massachusetts. They built their main settlement on a harbor. They called that settlement

Name the first three English colonies. What was the first settlement in each? What do these locations have in common?

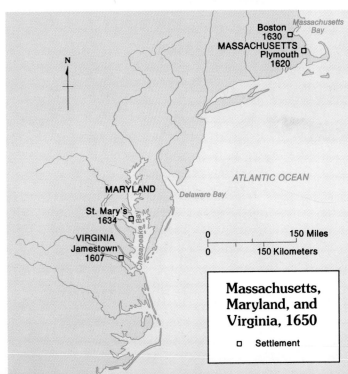

Massachusetts, Maryland, and Virginia, 1650

□ Settlement

Boston. They also started several other settlements nearby.

Over the years, many more Puritans left England. In the years between 1630 and 1643, more than 20,000 people came to Massachusetts. As more and more colonists arrived, new settlements were started in Massachusetts. Then, in 1691, the Plymouth colony and the settlements in Massachusetts Bay united to form the colony called Massachusetts.

The Catholics and Maryland

Like the Puritans, Catholics were not free to practice their religion in England. A Catholic named Sir George Calvert decided to start a colony in North America where Catholics could worship freely.

In 1632, the king gave Calvert a charter to settle land north of Virginia along Chesapeake Bay. Calvert named his colony Maryland in honor of the English queen. Before he could do much more, however, he died. His son, Cecilius Calvert, took over the work of building the colony.

Calvert knew that there were too few Catholics in England to start a separate colony. So he encouraged people of many religions to settle in Maryland. He promised that all of the colonists would be free to worship as they wished.

In 1634, the first colonists arrived in Maryland. They had good luck

This famous painting shows the Puritans on their way to church. They walked in groups to protect themselves from the Indians.

Baltimore was founded in 1729. Located on Patapsco River, it was a trading center for nearby tobacco growers.

from the start. Soon after they arrived, they noticed a group of Indians moving out of a small village. The newcomers bought the village and named it St. Mary's. The Indians also sold their extra corn to the colonists.

The colonists got help from their neighbors in Virginia, too. The Virginians sold supplies to the new settlers and showed them how to grow tobacco. It quickly became the most important crop in Maryland.

By 1650, England had three colonies in North America: Virginia, Massachusetts, and Maryland. At the same time, other countries were also building colonies nearby. These colonies were very different from the

ones the English started. In the next chapter you will read about two of those colonies.

To Help You Remember

1. (a) Why did the Puritans come to North America? (b) Where did they settle?
2. (a) When was the colony of Massachusetts formed? (b) Name the settlements that were included in Massachusetts.
3. (a) Why did Sir George Calvert decide to start a colony in North America? (b) What was the name of his colony? (c) How did he encourage people to come to the colony?

Chapter Review

Words to Know

1. What is a *pilgrim?*
2. What kind of legal paper is known as a *charter?*
3. When does a person or group make a *profit?*
4. What does a person who *represents* others do?
5. How long a period of time is a *decade?*
6. What kind of agreement is known as a *compact?*

Reviewing Main Ideas

Copy the chart below. Then fill in the blanks.

In Your Own Words

William Bradford wrote a history of Plymouth. That is, he told the story of the colony. You can write a history too. Use your chart to write a short history of one of the colonies you read about in this chapter. Be sure your history tells the following:

Who started the colony.
Where the colony was started.
When the colony was founded.
Why the colony was started.
How the colonists were able to succeed or how their efforts failed.

England's First Colonies

Colony	Where Started	Date Started	Why started	First Settlers	Explain Success or Failure
Roanoke					
Virginia					
Plymouth					
Massachusetts Bay					
Maryland					

Challenge!

For several years, the colonists at Roanoke were cut off from England. When an English ship finally returned to the island in 1591, the sailors found that the colonists had disappeared. If you had been aboard the ship, how would you have solved the mystery? What evidence would you have liked to study? For what clues would you have looked? To whom would you have liked to talk? Why?

Detectives often have theories, or ideas, about the mystery they are investigating. What is your theory about what happened to the settlers? Be sure to explain the reasons for your theory. (Keep in mind that the sailors found no sign of a battle.)

Things to Do

1. Choose one of England's first colonies—Plymouth, Jamestown, or Maryland. Imagine that you want to attract settlers to that colony. Make a poster that shows why you think people should come. Use words on your poster that would encourage settlers. What words might discourage people from coming to the colony?

2. Each of the people listed below contributed to the success of England's first colonies. Choose one person from the list. Find out more about that person. Share what you learned with your class.

John Smith   John Rolfe
Pocahontas   William Bradford
Squanto   Cecilius Calvert

Keeping Skills Sharp

Use the graph below to answer the following questions. Write your answers on a separate sheet of paper.

1. In what year was Plymouth's population the largest?
2. How many people lived in Plymouth in 1620?
3. (a) In the years between 1620 and 1630, did the population increase or decrease? (b) By how much?
4. How many decades did it take for Plymouth's population to go from 100 to 1000?
5. By how much did the population increase between 1630 and 1640?

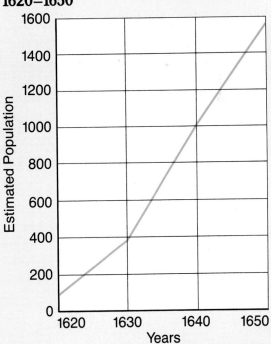

Estimated Population of Plymouth, 1620–1650

77

4

French and Dutch Colonies

People from Spain and England were not the only Europeans to explore the Americas. People from France came as well. So did the Dutch, as people from the Netherlands are sometimes called.

Both French and Dutch explorers searched for a route through North America to Asia. Like the English, they never found that route. They did, however, find riches in North America. The waters off the coast of North America were filled with fish. Forests were thick with furbearing animals.

During the 1600's, people in France and the Netherlands were eager to take advantage of those riches. They saw North America as a place where they could make money. In time, those people built colonies on the continent.

As You Read

This chapter is divided into four parts.

- The French in North America
- Building New France
- The Dutch in North America
- Building New Netherland

The first two parts focus on the French in North America. In the last two parts, you will learn how a Dutch trading company built a colony for the Netherlands. As you read, compare the two colonies.

◀ *The Dutch explore the Hudson River*

The French in North America

In 1524, the king of France hired a seaman named Giovanni da Verrazano (jō vä′ nē dä vär′ä zä nō) to find a route through North America to Asia. In his search, Verrazano sailed along the coast of North America from what is now North Carolina to what is now Newfoundland.

Verrazano never found a water route to Asia. However, as he sailed along the shores of North America, he saw forests rich in furbearing animals and waters filled with fish. He took news of what he saw back to France. Verrazano's tales excited many people in France. They came to North America to see for themselves. Among the first to come were French fishermen.

What part of North America did Verrazano explore for France? What river did Cartier explore?

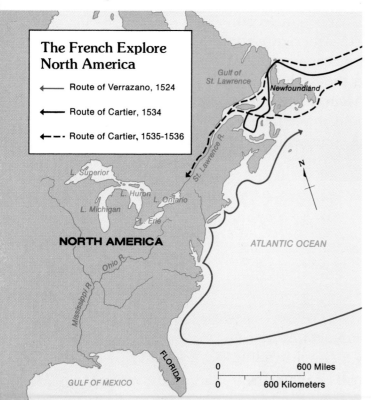

The French Explore North America

← Route of Verrazano, 1524

← Route of Cartier, 1534

←-- Route of Cartier, 1535-1536

Cartier's Voyage

One French fisherman was especially curious about North America. He hoped to find a route through it to Asia. The fisherman's name was Jacques Cartier (zhäk kär tyā′). In 1534, just ten years after Verrazano's voyage, Cartier received permission from the king of France to search for a route through North America to Asia.

On his first trip, Cartier made his way into a large gulf, which he named the Gulf of St. Lawrence. Cartier thought it might be the beginning of the water route through North America to Asia. He rushed back to France and reported his discovery to the king. The king ordered Cartier to explore that part of North America further.

The next year Cartier sailed once again into the Gulf of St. Lawrence. This time he traveled up a river that

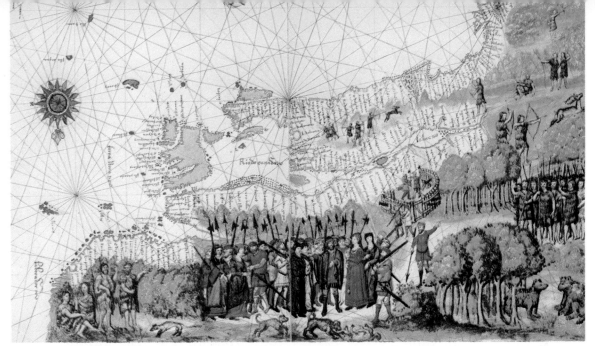

Printed in 1546, this is the earliest known map of Cartier's explorations. It pictures Cartier landing in North America.

he also named the St. Lawrence. He went ashore where the city of Quebec is today. After leaving some of his men there to build a fort, Cartier pushed on.

Far up the St. Lawrence River, Cartier found rapids leading west. Hopeful that this might be the way to China, Cartier called the bubbling white water the Lachine (China) Rapids. However, when he tried to sail farther up the river, the rapids blocked his way. So Cartier turned around and headed back to the fort at Quebec.

When Cartier arrived at the fort, he was shocked to discover that only a few of his men were still alive. Most had died from the cold or from **scurvy.** Scurvy is a sickness caused by the lack of fresh fruits and vegetables. However, in Cartier's day, no one knew its cause.

The men who were still alive wanted to return to France. However, by now it was winter and the river had frozen over. So the group had to stay until the ice melted the following spring.

Cartier claimed the land around the St. Lawrence for France. He named it New France. Other French explorers also came to New France. Some tried to start settlements there, but they were not successful. Still these early French explorers helped establish France's claims to the land around the St. Lawrence River.

The Start of the Fur Trade

Between 1550 and 1600, only French fishermen continued to come to North America. Many of them dried their fish on the shores of the Gaspé (ga spā') Peninsula. They discovered that the Indians there were willing to **barter,** or trade for goods, with them.

The French exchanged metal goods such as kettles, knives, and axes for furs caught by the Indians. The fishermen knew they could sell the furs for high prices back in France, where furs were in great demand.

Several French merchants were eager to make money from the fur trade. One of these merchants was Pierre (pē är'), lord of De Monts (də mon). In 1604, he asked the king for permission to build a trading post in New France. He planned to trade with the Indians there. The king agreed.

De Monts then asked Samuel de Champlain (də sham plān'), the king's mapmaker, to join him. Champlain jumped at the chance to go. This was his chance to look for a route through North America to Asia.

Champlain and De Monts, along with their crew and some settlers, set

Like many other explorers, Champlain was looking for an all-water route through North America to Asia. Why was he unable to sail across North America?

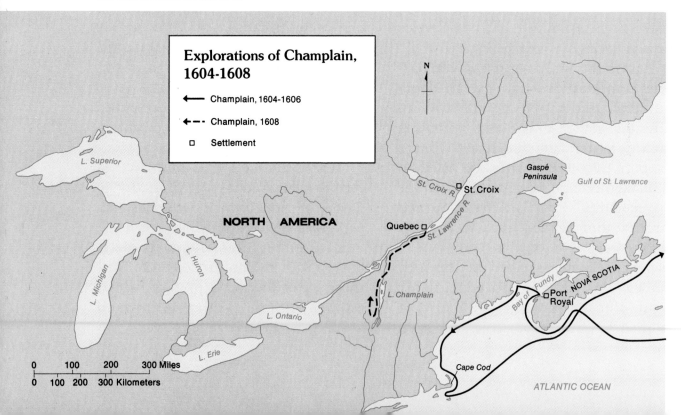

sail for North America in 1604. They sailed into the St. Croix (sānt kroi') River near present-day Maine. The men built a small trading post on an island near the mouth of the St. Croix. Before long, they were trading with the Indians.

Champlain left settlers at the trading post and sailed up the rushing rivers Cartier had seen earlier. Champlain also explored the coast of North America from what is now Nova Scotia in the north to Cape Cod in the south. Yet he did not find a waterway leading through North America to Asia.

Champlain in Charge

When winter came, Champlain returned to the settlement on the St. Croix River. The settlers there were miserable. The river was frozen solid. The settlers found themselves locked in a prison of snow and ice. They had nothing to eat but salted meat and dried vegetables. By spring, almost half of the settlers had died from the cold or from scurvy.

When additional supplies arrived from France, the settlers moved across the Bay of Fundy to Port Royal, Nova Scotia. There they built a new settlement.

This time Champlain took charge of the settlement. Every day he sent some of the men hunting and fishing to bring in fresh food. At almost every meal, they ate cabbage or potato. Today we know that the vitamin C in these foods kept the men from getting scurvy. At that time, however, no one knew that scurvy could be prevented by eating foods containing vitamin C. Champlain and his men were lucky to have chosen the right kinds of food to eat.

Just as the French were learning how to survive in North America, the king took away their right to trade. He ordered the settlers of Port Royal back to France.

To Help You Remember

1. What riches did Verrazano find in the lands he explored for France?
2. (a) What parts of North America did Cartier explore? (b) What did he call the land he claimed for France?
3. (a) What did the Indians living on the Gaspé Peninsula have that the French wanted? (b) Why did the French want to barter for it?
4. (a) When did De Monts come to North America? (b) What did he hope to find there?
5. What lands in North America did Champlain explore?
6. How did Champlain help the Port Royal settlers survive?
7. Why was the settlement at Port Royal abandoned?

Building New France

Although the king broke up the Port Royal settlement, he knew it was time for France to build permanent settlements in North America. After all, Spain had grown rich from its American colonies. So the king asked Samuel de Champlain to build a colony in North America. The colony was to be called New France.

In 1608, Champlain left again for North America. Once he arrived, he sailed up the St. Lawrence River. He reached the same place where Cartier had built a fort 73 years before. The Indians called this place Kebec. In their language, it meant the narrowing of the waters. In French, the Indian word became Quebec. Here, Champlain decided to build the first settlement in New France.

The People of New France

Champlain brought many people with him to New France. Some were farmers. Most, however, were traders who hoped to get rich in the fur trade. A few were priests. They wanted to bring their religion to the Indians living there.

Champlain founded Quebec in 1608. This diagram shows what Quebec may have looked like more than 250 years ago.

Quebec
1720

Farmers. The king gave land along the St. Lawrence River to a handful of wealthy men. They did not plan to do the farm work themselves. Instead, they brought over people to work their land. Those who did the work were **tenant farmers**. Tenant farmers rent small farms from a large landowner. They give the landowner a share of the crops they grow.

Fur traders. A tenant farmer had no chance of getting rich. A fur trader did. Fur traders were supposed to work for the wealthy merchants who controlled the fur trade. However, many of them set out on their own even though they knew they were breaking the law.

The fur traders traveled far from Quebec in their search for furbearing animals, especially beaver. For the most part, traders worked alone. They hunted, set traps, and traded with Indian hunters and trappers. Traders saw one another only once a year. Every spring they loaded their furs on canoes and headed for Quebec. There they sold furs and bought supplies for the coming year.

Priests. The priests also traveled from Quebec. They made their way deep into the forests. They were not looking for furs, however. They were seeking Indian villages. The priests stayed with the Indians and learned

Champlain made this drawing of a battle between the Algonquin and Iroquois.

their languages. The priests helped the French to gain the friendship and trust of the Indians.

Making Friends with the Algonquin

Champlain knew that the success of New France depended on winning the friendship of the Indians. After all, they controlled the rivers. The Indians also knew the best places to trap beaver and furbearing animals.

Most of the Indians who lived near Quebec were Algonquin. To gain their friendship, Champlain agreed to help them fight their lifelong enemies, the Iroquois (ir′ə kwoi).

In the summer of 1609, the French fought the Iroquois for the first time. In that battle, Champlain raised his gun and fired at three Iroquois leaders. Two were killed immediately. The third died soon after.

The Iroquois had never seen guns before. They were frightened. So they fled into the woods. Champlain's action pleased the Algonquin. At the same time, however, it earned the French the hatred of the Iroquois.

With the help of his Algonquin friends, Champlain explored the lands around Quebec. He was still looking for a water route through North America. His search took him up many rivers and on to the Great Lakes. Champlain traveled as far west as Lake Huron and the eastern end of Lake Ontario.

Champlain made a map showing all of the land he explored. He also sent carefully written reports to the king. Even though Champlain never found a route to Asia, his work greatly added to France's knowledge of the geography of North America.

Exploring the Mississippi Valley

A priest and a fur trapper also added to France's knowledge of North America. The priest was Father Jacques Marquette (zhäk mär ket'). He was a mapmaker who knew many Indian languages. Louis Joliet (lü'ē jō'lē et), the fur trapper, was born in Quebec. He had spent years working in the fur trade around the Great Lakes.

Both men had heard Indian stories about a great river to the south and west of Lake Michigan. They thought that the river might be the water route through North America to Asia. So they made plans to explore it.

In the spring of 1673, Marquette and Joliet set out with five other men to find the great river. They paddled two birch bark canoes into the wide waters of Lake Michigan, through Green Bay and up the Fox River. Then they carried their canoes across miles of land until they reached the Wisconsin River. They found that it flowed into an even wider river, the Mississippi.

Marquette and Joliet sailed down the Mississippi to the Arkansas River. The Indians living there told them that the Mississippi flowed south, not west. Now certain that the Mississippi was not a water route to Asia, the men returned to Lake Michigan.

Another French explorer, Robert Cavalier (kav' ə lir'), lord of La Salle (lə sal'), continued the exploration begun by Marquette and Joliet. In 1682, with a party of 54, La Salle sailed down the Mississippi River all the way to the Gulf of Mexico. There he planted a cross. He then claimed all the lands surrounding the Mississippi and the rivers that flowed into it for France.

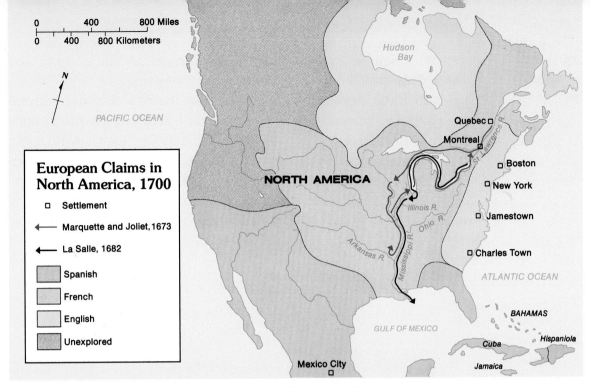

Trace La Salle's route on the map. Where did it start? Where did it end? By 1700, who claimed more land in North America, the English or the French?

The area La Salle claimed was many times larger than France itself. He named the area Louisiana in honor of the French king, Louis XIV.

By 1700, New France included much of present-day Canada and about two-thirds of what is now the United States. In spite of its size, New France did not have many settlers. By 1700, after nearly a hundred years of settlement, fewer than 100,000 French people lived in New France. The English colonies, on the other hand, had more than 250,000 colonists in North America, over twice as many as in New France.

To Help You Remember

1. (a) Where did Champlain build France's first permanent settlement? (b) What did he call it?
2. Name three groups who came to New France.
3. (a) Why did Champlain want the friendship of the Algonquin? (b) How did he win their friendship?
4. (a) What were Marquette and Joliet looking for? (b) What parts of North America did the two men explore?
5. What land did La Salle claim?
6. What lands were included in New France by 1700?

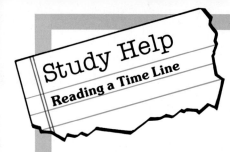

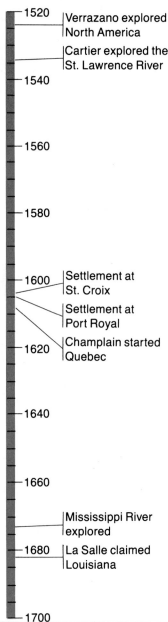

1520 — Verrazano explored North America

Cartier explored the St. Lawrence River

1540 —

1560 —

1580 —

1600 — Settlement at St. Croix

Settlement at Port Royal

1620 — Champlain started Quebec

1640 —

1660 —

Mississippi River explored

1680 — La Salle claimed Louisiana

1700 —

You have been reading about the history of New France from 1524 to 1700. Many important events took place during those years. One way to keep track of those events is by making a time line. A time line is a diagram that shows the order in which events happened. A time line is read from left to right or from top to bottom. Use the time line on this page to answer the following questions.

1. (a) How many years does each marker on the time line measure? (b) How many markers equal one **century**? A century is a period of one hundred years.
2. (a) When did Verrazano explore North America? (b) Who was the next French explorer to arrive? (c) When did that explorer come?
3. Who explored the Mississippi River first, Marquette and Joliet or La Salle?
4. How many years passed between the time Verrazano explored North America and the first French settlement on the continent?
5. Was Quebec built before or after Cartier's voyage?
6. Which was built first, the settlement at St. Croix or the one at Port Royal?
7. How many years passed between the time Columbus first reached the Americas and Verrazano's voyage for France?
8. How many years passed between the founding of Quebec and the exploration of the Mississippi River?
9. (a) The English founded Jamestown in 1607. Was that before or after the founding of Quebec? (b) Plymouth was founded in 1620. How old was Quebec that year?
10. In 1541, De Soto explored the Mississippi River and claimed it for Spain. How many years later did the French explore and claim that same river?

Copy the time line on a separate sheet of paper. As you read the rest of the chapter, add important events to it.

The Dutch in North America

During the 1600's, the Netherlands was the center of trade in Europe. Dutch trading ships could be found in ports all over Europe. Those ships also sailed around Africa to Asia. They returned to Europe loaded with spices, jewels, and other treasures.

The trip to Asia around Africa was long and costly. If a shorter route through North America could be found, the length of the trip would be cut in half. The search for such a route brought the Dutch to North America too.

Hudson's Voyage

In 1609, a group of Dutch merchants hired an Englishman named Henry Hudson to find a route through North America to Asia. They chose Hudson for the job because he had already made two voyages to North America in search of an all-water route to Asia. On each of those voyages he had sailed for the king of England. Perhaps this time, sailing for the Dutch, he would have better luck.

In the autumn of 1609, Hudson steered a small, stout ship named the *Half Moon* across the Atlantic and up a wide, deep river in North America. Surely, Hudson thought, this was the waterway that led to Asia. However,

as he sailed farther upstream near what is now the city of Albany, the river became shallow. With a few of his men, Hudson paddled a smaller boat northward to see what lay ahead. They found that the water only grew more shallow.

Finally Hudson realized that the river was not a route to Asia. Disappointed, he turned back, leaving what he called the Great River of the Mountains. Later, it was renamed the Hudson River in his honor.

In 1609, Henry Hudson sailed to North America on the Half Moon.

Based on Hudson's voyage, the Dutch claimed land in North America. Along what river did they build settlements?

From Trading Posts to Colony

While Hudson was exploring the river, some of his sailors traded with the Indians who lived along it. The fine furs Hudson and his men brought back to the Netherlands caused much excitement among Dutch merchants.

Before long, many merchants were sending ships across the Atlantic Ocean and up the Hudson River. The ships were loaded with metal goods, fishhooks, guns, and other goods that the Indians of the region would want to barter for.

In exchange for the Dutch goods, the Indians traded furs. The Dutch ships returned to the Netherlands stuffed with those furs. The fur trade was so profitable that the Dutch quickly claimed the Hudson Valley for the Netherlands.

The Dutch were not the only people interested in the Hudson Valley. The English also claimed that land. To protect their claims to land along the Hudson River, the Netherlanders decided to build a colony there. The colony was called New Netherland.

In 1621, the king of the Netherlands gave the right to settle, govern, and trade in North America to the Dutch West India Company. The company was given all of the land along the Hudson River as well as some land in what is now New Jersey and Connecticut.

The Dutch West India Company sent over its first boatload of settlers in 1624. Thirty families came. They were told to spread out so they could claim as much land as possible for the Netherlands. They built several trading posts along the Hudson and Delaware rivers.

The following year the company built a fort on the island of Manhattan. It was to serve as the center of the Dutch fur trade in North America. The fort was named New Amsterdam. New Amsterdam and the other Dutch trading posts made up the colony of New Netherland.

To Help You Remember

1. What first brought the Dutch to North America?
2. (a) In what year did Henry Hudson sail to North America for the Netherlands? (b) What body of water did he find?
3. What did Hudson's sailors do while he continued to explore?
4. (a) Why were the Dutch interested in the Hudson Valley? (b) Why did they build a colony there?
5. (a) Who was given permission to settle and trade in the new Dutch colony? (b) In what year?

Building New Netherland

In 1626, the Dutch West India Company sent Peter Minuit (min′yü it) to govern New Netherland. Minuit saw at once that the island of Manhattan, with its great harbor, should be the center of the colony. So he bought the whole island from the Indians.

Minuit ordered the Dutch families on the island to move closer to New Amsterdam. Fur traders, fishermen, and families from Europe also came to live there. By 1628 about 270 people lived in the small Dutch fort.

Finding New Settlers

The people of New Amsterdam worked very hard and their settlement slowly began to grow. Yet the other settlements in New Netherland

This early view of New Amsterdam was painted in the 1600's. It shows a windmill in the background and the Dutch-style buildings.

This diagram of New Amsterdam shows what the city looked like about 35 years after it was founded.

remained little more than trading posts. To get more people to come to New Netherland, the Dutch West India Company came up with a plan.

The company offered huge pieces of land along the Hudson River to anyone who brought 50 people to the colony. The wealthy Dutchmen who took advantage of the offer were called **patroons.**

The patroons agreed to pay for the settlers' passage from the Netherlands to the colony. In return, the settlers agreed to farm or trade for the landowners. A number of wealthy patroons built large estates along the Hudson River. Few of them turned out to be successful, however. When the settlers saw how much land was available, many left to start their own farms. Others moved farther west and worked in the fur trade.

Since the patroons failed to bring many people to New Netherland, the Dutch West India Company tried another plan. They offered land or the right to work in the fur trade to anyone who came to the colony. The new plan was more successful in attracting settlers to New Netherland.

Trouble in New Netherland

Even though the new plan pleased many colonists, trouble was brewing in the Dutch colony. The colonists did not like the way they were being treated by the Dutch West India

Company. The company would not allow colonists to trade with merchants from other countries. It also made the colonists pay a tax.

Because the colonists believed those laws made it harder for them to make money, some did not obey the laws. Before long, New Amsterdam became well-known for its smugglers and pirates.

The colonists also had trouble with their neighbors, the Algonquin. The Algonquin believed that the Dutch traders were not giving them a fair price for beaver skins and animal furs. Nor did the Algonquin like it when the Dutch governor told them they had to pay a tax. So they attacked the Dutch. Fighting between the Dutch and the Algonquin broke out again and again.

Finally, in 1647, the Dutch West India Company sent a new leader to New Amsterdam. His name was Peter Stuyvesant (stī′və sənt). He had been the governor of a Dutch colony in the West Indies and was well-known for his strong will.

During his 17 years as governor of New Netherland, Stuyvesant brought order to the colony. He made the settlers obey strict laws. He also made peace with the Algonquin. Moreover, in 1655, Stuyvesant took control of a small Swedish colony on the Delaware River. The Dutch claimed that land as well.

The English Capture New Netherland

Even Stuyvesant's leadership was not enough to save New Netherland from the English. England wanted to control the busy harbor at New Amsterdam. So in 1664, the English king sent 4 ships and 900 soldiers to take over the Dutch colony. The people of New Netherland gave up without a fight because they did not like Stuyvesant's strict rules.

When the Dutch gave up, 40 years of Dutch rule came to an end. The Dutch colony of New Netherland was renamed New York in honor of the English king's brother, the Duke of York. The settlement at New Amsterdam was renamed too. It became New York City.

To Help You Remember

1. Tell two ways the Dutch West India Company tried to get people to come to New Netherland.
2. What problems did the Dutch West India Company cause?
3. Why did the colonists have trouble with the Algonquin?
4. (a) When did Peter Stuyvesant come to New Netherland? (b) How did he help the colony?
5. (a) When did the English take over New Netherland? (b) Why did they want New Amsterdam?

Chapter Review

Words to Know

Choose the letter of the answer that best completes each sentence. Write your answers on a separate sheet of paper.

1. *Scurvy* is (a) a kind of food, (b) a disease caused by lack of fresh fruits and vegetables, (c) a disease caused by cold weather.
2. *Tenant farmers* are (a) landowners, (b) slaves, (c) renters.
3. *Patroons* are (a) landowners, (b) slaves, (c) renters.
4. To *barter* is to (a) travel to new places, (b) trap furs, (c) trade one kind of good for another.
5. A *century* is a period of (a) 10 years, (b) 100 years, (c) 20 years.

Reviewing Main Ideas

Copy the chart below on a separate sheet of paper. Then fill in the information that is missing.

In Your Own Words

Use the chart to write a paragraph that tells how French and Dutch colonies in North America were alike. Then write a second paragraph that tells how the two colonies were different.

Challenge!

A French explorer told this story of his first week on a famous river. Guess which river it was.

Here then we are on this famous river. It has its source in several lakes in the country of the nations to the north. Its current, which runs south, is slow and gentle. On the right is a chain of very high mountains and on the left fine lands. The river is studded with islands in many places. We gently follow its course, which bears south and southeast until latitude 42° north. Here we see the whole face is changed. There is almost no wood or mountain.

New France and New Netherland

Colony	Who Came	Why They Came	Date Started	Ways of Earning a Living	Relations with the Indians	Was the Colony a Success? Why?
New France				Fishing, farming, and fur trading		
New Netherland	Dutch families, fur traders, fishermen, and other families from Europe		1624			The colony was not a success. It was taken over by the English in 1664.

Unit Review

Take Another Look

1. Why did Europeans seek an all-water route to Asia?
2. (a) Who were the first Europeans to reach the Americas?
   (b) Who built the first lasting colony in the Americas?
3. Choose one of the Indian groups you read about in the unit. Write a paragraph telling the following:
   Who the group was.
   Where the group lived.
   What the group's way of life was like.
4. Choose two of the colonies you read about in the unit. Write a paragraph telling in what ways the colonies were similar. Write another paragraph telling how they differed.

You and the Past

1. Use the map on page 38 to find out which Indian groups lived in your state long ago. Write a report about one of those groups. Describe its culture. Include information about where members of that group live today.
2. Who were the first Europeans to explore and settle your state? Make a map showing where they explored and where their early settlements were located. Be sure your map has a title and legend.
3. As a result of European exploration and settlement of the Americas, people in the Eastern Hemisphere learned about many new foods. So did the Indians, the people of the Western Hemisphere. A few of those foods are listed below. How many of these foods do you and your family eat regularly? How would your meals be different if one group or the other was not available?

Western Hemisphere Foods
cacao (cocoa)
corn
turkey
potatoes
pumpkins

Eastern Hemisphere Foods
sugar
wheat
chicken
beef
milk and milk products

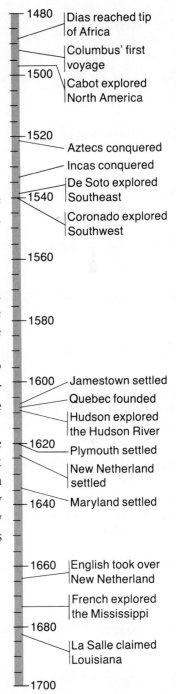

1480 — Dias reached tip of Africa
Columbus' first voyage
1500 — Cabot explored North America
1520
Aztecs conquered
Incas conquered
De Soto explored Southeast
1540
Coronado explored Southwest
1560
1580
1600 — Jamestown settled
Quebec founded
Hudson explored the Hudson River
1620 — Plymouth settled
New Netherland settled
1640 — Maryland settled
1660 — English took over New Netherland
French explored the Mississippi
1680
La Salle claimed Louisiana
1700

95

An early view of the settlements along Boston Harbor

Unit Two

Thirteen English Colonies

Starting in 1607 and continuing for the next 125 years, people from Great Britain built settlements along the Atlantic coast of North America. As time passed, they divided those settlements into 13 colonies. A new country, the United States of America, grew out of those colonies.

5

The New England Colonies

From the 1600's on, thousands of people left England to come to North America. Many of them settled in New England. Massachusetts was the first colony in New England. Three other colonies were started nearby. They were Rhode Island, Connecticut, and New Hampshire. Today, New England includes Vermont and Maine. In colonial times, however, both were part of Massachusetts.

The land and climate of New England presented colonists with both problems and opportunities. Much of the land was hilly and rocky. The climate was also much colder than the colonists were used to. Yet New England had thick forests full of valuable lumber and furs. In addition, the waters off the New England coast were filled with fish.

As You Read

Look for ways colonists solved the problems presented by the land and climate of New England. Look, too, for opportunities the colonists found in New England. This chapter is divided into three parts.

- The Growth of New England
- The Villages of New England
- Making a Living from the Ocean

◀ *A New England farming village in the 1700's*

The Growth of New England

During the 1600's, thousands of people came to Massachusetts. At first, most of them settled near the ocean. They started towns like Boston and Salem. As land along the coast was taken up, however, more and more people moved to other parts of New England. Many were children of the early settlers. Others were newly arrived settlers from Europe.

Some settlers cleared land along the borders of the forest and built new towns west of Boston. These included Lexington, Concord, Springfield, and Worcester. Other settlers left Massachusetts and started new colonies nearby.

New Towns in Massachusetts

People in Massachusetts usually settled near one another. Twenty or thirty families would join together and build a new town. They would get a grant of land for their town from the **elders,** or leaders, of the colony. Then the elders would divide the land among the families.

First, the elders set aside land for a meetinghouse. Here the Puritans held church services and had town meetings. Next, they set aside land for a **common,** a field where townspeople could graze their cows and sheep. Then the elders chose a place nearby to build a school.

Which Massachusetts towns on the map are on the coast? The building on the right is an old New England meetinghouse.

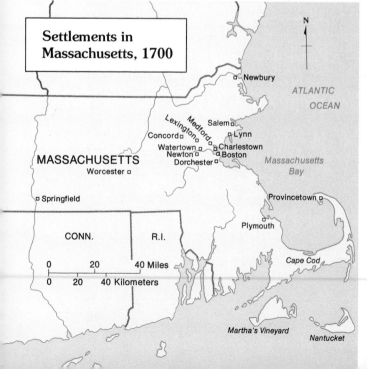

Settlements in Massachusetts, 1700

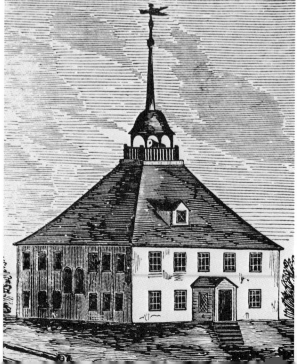

The minister and other important citizens had first choice of the remaining land. Often they would choose to build their homes near the meetinghouse. Then all the other settlers drew lots to determine where their houses would stand. Finally, each family received land outside the village for farming.

The Puritans built most of their early towns close to one another. This made it easier for the settlers to protect themselves in case of war with the Indians. It was also easier for the Puritan leaders in Boston to keep a watchful eye on life in the growing towns. Throughout Massachusetts, people were expected to follow the laws of the Puritan church.

Rhode Island

Some people in Massachusetts did not agree with the Puritan church. Two of those people started settlements that in time became a new colony called Rhode Island.

One of the people who disagreed with the Massachusetts government was Roger Williams. He was a Puritan minister who came to Massachusetts in 1631. From the start, he spoke out against many church rules. He did not think that people should be fined for not going to church. He also felt that the church should be separate from the government.

For disagreeing with church rules, Roger Williams had to leave Massachusetts.

In spite of warnings from the leaders of the colony, Roger Williams continued to voice his ideas. Finally, the elders met and decided that Williams had to be stopped. In 1635, they ordered him to leave the colony.

On a bitterly cold January day in 1636, Williams began a long and difficult journey. He left his wife and children in Massachusetts and set out into the forest alone, on foot, in the middle of a heavy snowstorm. He walked for miles before stopping to rest at an Indian village. There the Indians welcomed him and invited him to stay through the winter.

When spring came, Williams' family and a few followers joined him at the village. The small group then

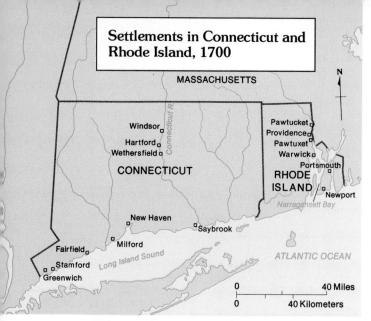

Settlements in Connecticut and Rhode Island, 1700

MASSACHUSETTS

N

Windsor
Hartford
Wethersfield
CONNECTICUT

Connecticut R.

Pawtucket
Providence
Pawtuxet
Warwick
Portsmouth
RHODE
ISLAND
Newport
Narragansett Bay

New Haven
Saybrook
Fairfield
Milford
Stamford
Greenwich
Long Island Sound

ATLANTIC OCEAN

0   40 Miles
0   40 Kilometers

What colonies are shown on this map? What river is located near Hartford? What bay is located near Providence?

headed south until they came to the shores of Narragansett Bay in what is today Rhode Island. There Williams bought land from the Narragansett Indians for a settlement he called Providence.

A year after Roger Williams left Massachusetts, the Puritans forced still another outspoken settler to leave the colony. Her name was Anne Hutchinson. Today her crime does not seem serious. She questioned a few Puritan rules. In those days, however, no one could challenge any rule of the Puritan church.

In the spring of 1638, Anne Hutchinson left Massachusetts with her husband, their 11 children, and 73 of their friends. They, too, went south

to what is today Rhode Island. There they started the town of Portsmouth.

In time, the towns begun by Roger Williams and Anne Hutchinson grew into the colony of Rhode Island. Unlike Massachusetts, people of all religions were free to worship in Rhode Island.

Connecticut

Rhode Island was not the only colony started by people unhappy with the rules of the Puritan church. So was Connecticut. Its leader was Thomas Hooker, the minister of a church near Boston. He too questioned the Puritan leaders of Massachusetts. Hooker believed that every man, no matter

Anne Hutchinson was put on trial for disobeying church rules.

Thomas Hooker led a group of settlers from Massachusetts to the fertile Connecticut River Valley. There they founded Connecticut.

what his religion, should take part in town government. The colony's leaders, however, would only allow Puritan men the right to vote.

Hooker and his followers decided to leave Massachusetts and start a new colony. They decided to go to the Connecticut River Valley, where the land was very fertile.

In June of 1636, about a hundred men, women, and children left Massachusetts for Connecticut. They walked into the forest, driving their cattle and sheep before them. After two weeks of walking, they reached a good place for a settlement, on the Connecticut River. The settlers called their settlement Hartford.

About the time that Hartford was being settled, several other settlements were started nearby. By 1638, there were about 800 people living in the Connecticut River Valley. Since they had settled far from the other colonies, the people in these settlements decided to form a new colony. They called it Connecticut.

Within a few years, the people of Connecticut drew up a set of rules for governing themselves. The plan of government was called the Fundamental Orders of Connecticut. It gave

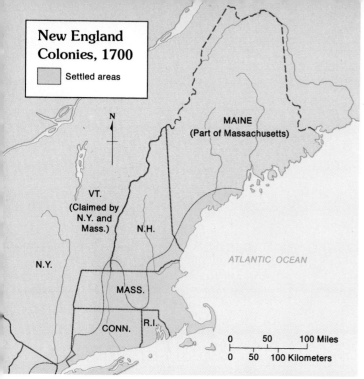

How many New England colonies are shown on the map? Which colony covers the greatest area? The smallest area?

men of all religions the right to vote. The Fundamental Orders were the first written plan of government in an English colony. They were also an important step toward the idea that all people should have the right to rule themselves.

New Hampshire and Maine

Many people who left Massachusetts did not move south. Some headed north to what is today Maine and New Hampshire. Many of these settlers left Massachusetts because they too wanted to get away from strict Puritan rules. Others left to find better farm land and fishing grounds. Still others left to work in the fur trade in the forests farther north.

At first, Maine and New Hampshire were part of Massachusetts. So was a part of Vermont. The rest of Vermont belonged to New York. Then, in 1679, the king of England gave settlers in New Hampshire a separate charter. New Hampshire became a colony like Connecticut and Rhode Island. Vermont stayed divided between New York and Massachusetts until 1791. Maine was part of Massachusetts until 1820.

To Help You Remember

1. Why did the Puritans build their early towns close together?
2. (a) Why did Roger Williams leave Massachusetts? (b) What colony did he start?
3. (a) Why did Anne Hutchinson leave Massachusetts? (b) Where did she go?
4. (a) Why did Thomas Hooker leave Massachusetts? (b) What colony did he start?
5. (a) What are the Fundamental Orders of Connecticut? (b) Why are they important?
6. (a) Why did people go to Maine and New Hampshire? (b) When did New Hampshire become a separate colony?

The Villages of New England

By the end of the 1600's, dozens of small villages and towns dotted New England. They all looked much the same. Each had a common where livestock grazed. Along the edges of the common stood a meetinghouse and a school. The streets around the common were lined with houses and a few shops. The fields the villagers farmed lay just outside of town.

Farming in a Hard Land

New England farmers were hardworking people. They had to be. New England's rocky soil and long, cold winters made farming difficult. New Englanders learned to take advantage of all they found on the land.

To clear their land, farmers had to cut down trees. They used the wood to build houses, barns, furniture, and tools. They saved some to feed the fire in the kitchen fireplace.

Farmers also had to remove many stones from their land. They used them to build walls around their farms. These stone walls are found today throughout New England.

Once their fields were cleared, farmers planted a variety of crops. They grew pumpkins, squash, beans,

This is what a typical New England village looked like in 1700. Find the meetinghouse and the common. Where is the farm land?

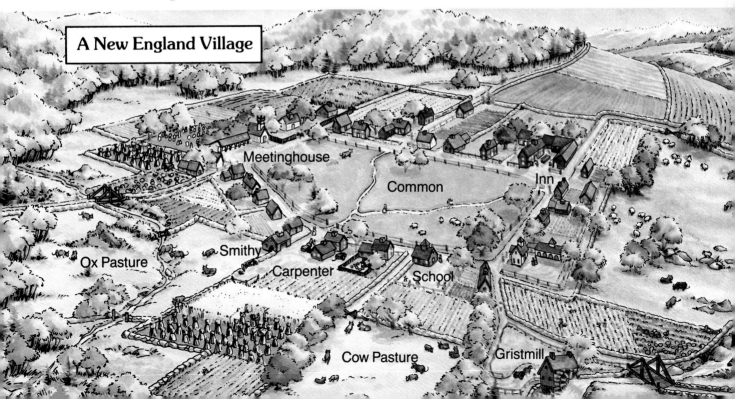

A New England Village

Meetinghouse

Common

Inn

Ox Pasture

Smithy

Carpenter

School

Cow Pasture

Gristmill

peas, carrots, and turnips. Wheat did not grow well in New England. So the settlers planted rye and corn instead.

Farmers in New England also kept cows, sheep, pigs, and chickens. The cows gave them a steady supply of milk, butter, and cheese. Sheep were raised for their meat and their wool. The women spun and wove the wool into cloth. Then they made blankets and clothing for their families. The hides from cows and pigs were made into leather for shoes, coats, and even hats. Nothing was wasted.

Every member of the family had to help with the work. Both men and women farmed. The men also added to the family's food supply by hunting and fishing. They made and repaired farm tools. The women pounded corn into meal, dried fruits and vegetables, and preserved meat.

Children worked hard too. They shelled corn, made brooms, and took care of the smaller farm animals. In late summer, they went into the forest to gather strawberries and blueberries. In late winter, the children tapped maple trees. The maple sap was used to make syrup.

Village Life

Just as the members of a family worked together, so did the families

This painting, done by a famous colonial artist, shows a well-to-do New England family.

in a village. When times were hard, villagers helped one another. If a family lost its crops, those with extra food shared with their less fortunate neighbors. If someone's barn burned down, neighbors got together to help put up a new one.

The men in the village also got together to talk over problems they all shared. They might talk over where to build a new road or whether to dig a new well. Sometimes they met to decide how the land outside the village should be divided. The men also voted on taxes. They elected judges and village officers. Working together helped to unite the village.

Religion also united the villagers. Since most were Puritans, they attended the same church. On Sundays, Puritan families walked to church, bringing along their afternoon meals.

Church services lasted all day. Breaks were needed, since even the shortest sermon was two hours long. During these breaks, villagers gathered together in noon houses. These were sheds near the church. Here families ate with their neighbors. As they shared food, they also exchanged news and information.

Village children got together even more often. Because the Puritans thought everyone should be able to read the Bible, every child was sent to school for at least a few years.

Children read their first lessons from hornbooks like the one shown above.

Children learned to read rhymes about good behavior and hard work. They also read the Bible. Villages with over a hundred families had grammar schools too. Puritan grammar schools were like today's high schools.

To Help You Remember

1. (a) Why was farming difficult in New England? (b) What crops did farmers grow? (c) What animals did they raise?
2. (a) Besides farming, what other jobs did men do? (b) What work did women do? (c) What work did children do?
3. In what ways did villagers help one another?
4. (a) Why did Puritans send their children to school? (b) What did the children learn at school?

Headings can help you figure out the main idea of each section of a chapter. One way to find the main idea is to turn the headings into questions. Below are the headings and subheadings from the two sections you have just read. Each has been turned into a question. Answer those questions. If you need help in doing so, the page numbers will tell you where to look in the text.

I. What caused the growth of New England? (page 100)
  A. How were new towns started in Massachusetts? (pages 100–101)
  B. How was Rhode Island founded? (pages 101–102)
  C. How was Connecticut founded? (pages 102–104)
  D. What led to the founding of New Hampshire and Maine? (page 104)
II. What were the villages of New England like? (page 105)
  A. How did New Englanders farm in a hard land? (pages 105–106)
  B. What was village life like? (pages 106–107)

As you complete the rest of the chapter, continue to turn headings into questions.

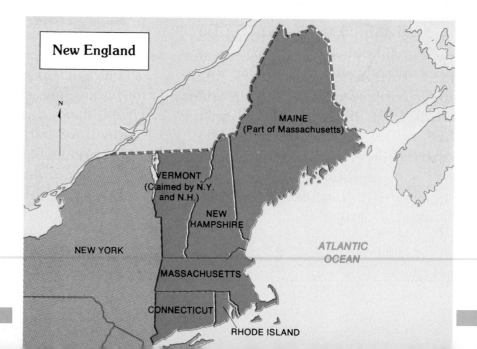

New England

MAINE
(Part of Massachusetts)

N

VERMONT
(Claimed by N.Y. and N.H.)

NEW HAMPSHIRE

NEW YORK

ATLANTIC OCEAN

MASSACHUSETTS

CONNECTICUT

RHODE ISLAND

Making a Living from the Ocean

The ocean was important to New England's **economy.** An economy is the way a group of people produces goods and services. It also includes their methods for getting those goods and services to the right people. Many New Englanders made their living from the ocean. They fished, built ships, and traded with people in other lands.

Fishing, Whaling, and Shipbuilding

In many towns along the New England coast, colonists made extra money by fishing. They went out in small boats to catch cod and nearly 200 other kinds of fish.

When the men returned home, there was still work to be done. Very little of their catch would be eaten fresh. Most of it was dried or salted before it was shipped to England or to other colonies. Before the days of refrigerators, fish had to be dried or salted to keep from spoiling.

Around 1700, some New England fishermen began to hunt whales instead of fish. In those days, whales were very valuable animals. Whale oil was used in lamps. Whales also

This sailor is carrying an instrument used to find a ship's location at sea.

Shipbuilding became an important job in the New England colonies.

provided whalebone (baleen) for women's corsets, buggy whips, and fishing rods.

At first, whalers hunted in the waters off the New England coast. As time passed, it became harder to find many whales there. Soon, New Englanders were sailing far from home in their search for whales. Some whaling crews made voyages that lasted three or four years.

As fishing and whaling grew more and more important to the economy of New England, another industry grew up. That industry was shipbuilding. The first to build ships were probably farmers who were eager to earn extra money in the winter months. As the demand for small boats and sailing ships grew, shipbuilding became a full-time job.

By the middle of the 1700's, many wealthy traders were ordering fleets of sturdy New England–built ships.

Sailors often carved beautiful pictures like the one below on whalebone.

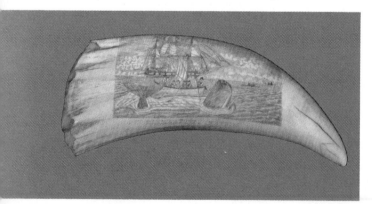

When Europeans saw those ships, traders in England began buying them too.

In New England Trading Towns

By the 1700's, trading ships from Boston, Newport, and other important cities along the coast were making regular trips to England. They carried lumber, furs, and tons of salted codfish. They returned home with furniture, glass, iron tools, and other goods made in England.

Before long, New England merchants were also trading with people in other countries and with other English colonies. On their trading trips, the merchants often made at least two stops before they returned home. Because the routes they took looked like triangles, this kind of trade is known as **triangular trade.**

One such trade route began in Newport, Rhode Island. Rhode Island merchants loaded rum made from maple syrup or molasses onto trading ships. The ships then sailed to Africa. The merchants sold the rum to African traders. With part of the money the merchants got for the rum, they bought African slaves.

Next the merchants loaded the slaves onto their ships and sailed to the West Indies. There, they sold the

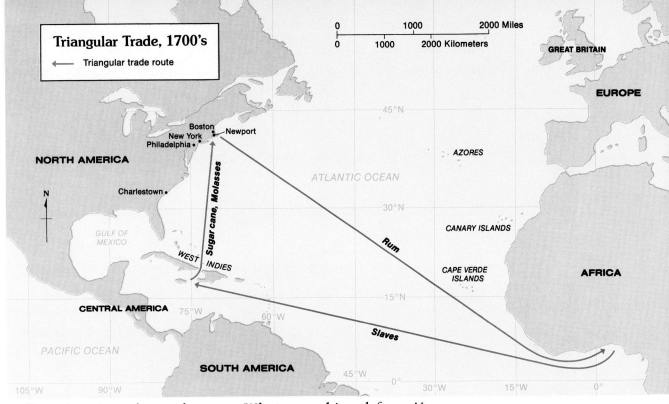

0   1000   2000 Miles
0   1000   2000 Kilometers

GREAT BRITAIN

EUROPE

45°N

Boston
New York Newport
Philadelphia

NORTH AMERICA

AZORES

ATLANTIC OCEAN

N

Charlestown

30°N

Sugar cane, Molasses

CANARY ISLANDS

Rum

GULF OF
MEXICO

CAPE VERDE
ISLANDS

AFRICA

WEST INDIES

15°N

CENTRAL AMERICA   75°W

60°W

Slaves

PACIFIC OCEAN

SOUTH AMERICA

45°W

0°

105°W   90°W

30°W   15°W   0°

Follow the triangular trade route. What was shipped from New England to Africa? From Africa to the West Indies? From the West Indies to New England?

slaves to West Indian farmers. The farmers used the slaves to work in their sugarcane fields. With part of the money from the sale of the slaves, the merchants bought sugarcane and molasses. People in New England used the molasses and sugarcane to make rum.

As trade grew, towns along the Atlantic coast became lively, crowded places where many people lived and worked. During the daytime, farmers and fish peddlers pushed their carts through the cities calling out the foods they sold. Knife sharpeners and

chimney sweeps were among those who offered their services too.

Colonial cities were not like modern cities, however. The narrow main streets were little more than dusty roads. Pigs roamed these streets eating garbage. Cows sometimes wandered through the city streets as well.

Houses lined the city streets. Candles and lamps placed in windows lighted the streets at night. Although most of the houses were small, they usually had enough land around them for a small vegetable garden.

The main streets of the cities were

The picture shows Boston in the late 1700's. Imagine the clatter of hooves and wheels on the cobblestone streets.

also lined with shops where people made and sold clothing, furniture, jewelry, and books. Many also had coffee houses or inns where people visited with friends or discussed business. The cities along New England's coast were becoming important centers of trade and business.

The settlers of New England overcame many hardships in a land new to them. In doing so they changed New England. At the same time, settlers much farther south were also changing the land. The next chapter looks at life in the Southern colonies.

To Help You Remember

1. Give three reasons why the ocean was important to the people of New England.
2. What did fishermen do to keep the fish from spoiling?
3. Why were whales such valuable animals?
4. (a) What is a triangular trade route? (b) Describe one triangular trade route.
5. Why were colonial cities busy places?
6. How were colonial cities different from modern cities?

Chapter Review

Words to Know

1. (a) Who were *elders?* (b) How did they divide land?
2. What is a *common?*
3. What is an *economy?*
4. (a) What does *triangular trade* mean? (b) Describe a triangular trade route.

Reviewing Main Ideas

1. Name the New England colonies and tell when each was founded.
2. List at least three ways people earned a living in New England.
3. What crops did farmers in New England raise?
4. Name at least one important city in New England.
5. (a) Why did Roger Williams and Anne Hutchinson leave Massachusetts? (b) What colony did they start? (c) How was their colony different from Massachusetts?
6. (a) Why did Thomas Hooker leave Massachusetts (b) What colony did he start? (c) How was his colony different from Massachusetts?
7. Why did people move from Massachusetts to places like Maine and New Hampshire?
8. What things brought people in a village together?

In Your Own Words

Below is a list of *topic sentences*. A topic sentence tells the main idea of a paragraph. Use one of the topic sentences to write a paragraph about the New England colonies.

1. People in New England earned their living in many different ways.
2. As land along the coast of Massachusetts filled up, more people moved to other parts of Massachusetts.
3. People in a New England village were united in many ways.

Challenge!

Anne Bradstreet was a poet who settled in Massachusetts in 1630. She wrote not only poems but also epigrams. An epigram is a wise or clever saying. What do the epigrams below suggest about the kind of people who built New England? Give reasons for your answer.

If we had no winter, would spring be so pleasant? If we did not have hard times, good times would not be so welcome.

Sweet words are like honey. A little may refresh, but too much gives you a stomachache.

Try writing your own epigram.

Things to Do

New Englanders learned to take advantage of everything they owned or found around them. Make a poster that shows the ways New Englanders used the following: trees, stones, and animals.

6

The Southern Colonies

Virginia was the first English colony in the Southern part of North America. Between 1634 and 1733, the English started four more. They were Maryland, North Carolina, South Carolina, and Georgia. These colonies were alike in many ways. All had plenty of good land. They all had a warm climate too.

The people who settled the five Southern colonies were alike in some ways too. Most had come to North America because they had a hard time making a living in England. These people came to the Southern colonies hoping to build a better life in the new land.

Unlike New Englanders, the people who settled in the Southern colonies settled far away from one another. They spread out to farm as much of the good land as they could. They thought farming was a good way to get rich. Indeed, some Southern farmers became very wealthy.

As You Read

Look for the ways in which the Southern colonies grew. Also look for the different ways of life in the Southern colonies. This chapter is divided into three parts.

- Growth of the Southern Colonies
- Life along the Coast
- Settlements Inland

◀ *A Southern plantation in the 1700's*

Growth of the Southern Colonies

The first two Southern colonies were Virginia and Maryland. Virginia was founded in 1607. The first colonists arrived in Maryland in 1634. Most of the people who settled the two colonies lived near the ocean.

By about the 1650's, many farms stretched along the coasts of Virginia and Maryland. People who wanted to start new farms either had to move inland from the coast or had to settle farther south. Between 1650 and 1733, these newcomers built three new colonies for England.

Moving West in Virginia and Maryland

Virginia and Maryland grew in similar ways. At first, people in both colonies had small farms along the coast. Most of them grew tobacco. As the price of tobacco went up, however, many colonists added more land to their farms. Growing tobacco was very profitable. By the 1650's, some farms covered hundreds of acres. These very large farms were called **plantations.**

In both Virginia and Maryland, plantations lay along the **tidewater,** the plain that borders the Atlantic coast. Here the land was flat and the soil was rich. There was plenty of water too. Many of the rivers flowed across the tidewater to the Atlantic Ocean. Farmers used these rivers to ship their tobacco to the Atlantic and then on to England.

When new settlers came to Virginia and Maryland, they followed the rivers inland from the coast. By

Shown here is a river at the fall line. The river forms a waterfall as it descends from highland to lowland.

Piedmont

Fall Line

Fall Line

Rapids

Waterfall

Tidewater

River

Atlantic Ocean

the 1650's, a line of farms and plantations along rivers like the James and the Potomac stretched to the western edge of the tidewater.

The place where the tidewater ends is called the **fall line.** The fall line is where the rivers from the higher land farther west form rapids and waterfalls as they tumble down to the lower land along the coast.

By the end of the 1600's, people in Virginia and Maryland began buying land beyond the fall line. They were settling on the **Piedmont,** the hilly land just west of the tidewater. The newcomers found that even though the land on the Piedmont was not as flat as the tidewater, it was good to farm. The soil was richer than it was along the coast.

At first, most of the farms on the Piedmont were small. The people who built those farms lived in small cabins miles from their nearest neighbors. They grew just enough to feed their families. Yet, by the early 1700's, many farmers on the Virginia and Maryland Piedmont had farms as large as those along the coast. They too grew tobacco.

Some settlers on the Piedmont made money from the forests. They hunted deer, bear, beaver, and other animals. They cut trees for lumber. Then they shipped the animal skins, meat, and lumber to people living farther east in the tidewater.

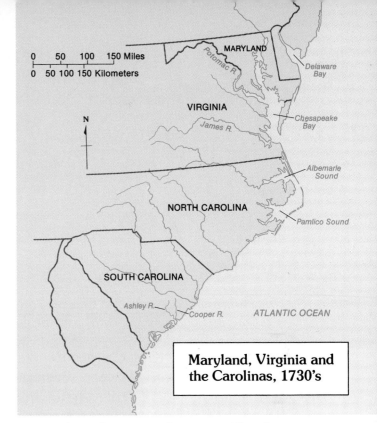

Maryland, Virginia and the Carolinas, 1730's

Name the colonies on this map. What bay lies near both Maryland and Virginia?

The Carolinas

Not everyone who wanted land headed west. Some people from Virginia moved south. Around 1650, a few built farms in what is now North Carolina. They settled along the fertile shores of Albemarle Sound.

Many of these early settlers were squatters. Squatters were settlers who did not buy their land. They simply cleared a part of the forest for their homes and fields. For a while, no one paid much attention to these settlers.

This painting of the harbor at Charles Town, South Carolina, shows what the busy harbor looked like in the early 1700's.

Then, in 1663, King Charles II gave a huge strip of land between Virginia and Spanish Florida to eight of his friends. The eight partners became **proprietors,** or owners of the new colony, which they named Carolina, in honor of King Charles.

The new colony included those settlements around the Albemarle Sound. Since the partners hoped to make money from their colony, they did not push out the squatters living there. Instead, they sent a governor to keep the colonists in line and to collect taxes from them.

At first, the colony grew slowly. The land around the Albemarle Sound was good for farming. Yet farmers there could not ship crops directly to England. The water in the Albemarle Sound is not **navigable.** That is, the water in Albemarle

Sound is not deep enough for ocean-going ships. For this reason, the men who owned Carolina decided to build new settlements farther south where there were harbors deep enough for ocean-going ships.

In 1670, the partners sent a group of colonists to Carolina. The group was to start a settlement on the west bank of the Ashley River. This settlement was named Charles Town in honor of the king. The settlers quickly discovered that the west bank was too swampy to be a healthy place to live. The swamps were breeding places for mosquitoes that carried a disease called malaria. Many settlers suffered and some even died from malaria.

In 1680, the colonists moved to a healthier spot, where the Ashley and Cooper rivers meet. This turned out to be an excellent location. It had one of the best harbors in the South.

People from many places settled in Carolina. Some moved to the colony from New England and Virginia. Others came from England, France, what is now Germany, and other European countries. Still others moved from islands in the West Indies.

The newcomers learned that tobacco did not grow as well in the southern part of Carolina as it did farther north. They looked for other crops that would grow in the warm, moist climate. They found that rice and **indigo,** a plant from which a blue dye was made, were well suited to the climate around Charles Town.

Thus, two groups of settlements grew up in Carolina. Those in the south centered around Charles Town, which is known as Charleston today. Settlements in the north lay along the Albemarle Sound.

For years, the partners **invested** in their colony. That is, they spent large sums of money on their colony in hopes of making more money. Failing to make a profit, they returned the land to the king in 1729. Then Carolina was divided into two colonies. One was North Carolina. The other became South Carolina.

Georgia

By 1700, some people in Carolina were moving even farther south to what is today Georgia. They wanted more land for their rice and indigo fields. Since the Spanish also claimed Georgia, Spanish soldiers in Florida attacked the English settlers. Fighting between the English and Spanish continued for many years.

When the king of England was told of the Spanish attacks, he decided to start a new colony south of the Carolinas. It would have forts and soldiers to protect English settlers from the Spanish.

A tough-minded general named James Oglethorpe saw the new colony as a place where people could get

The first English settlement in Georgia was Savannah. Find it on the map. What river lies on Georgia's northeast border?

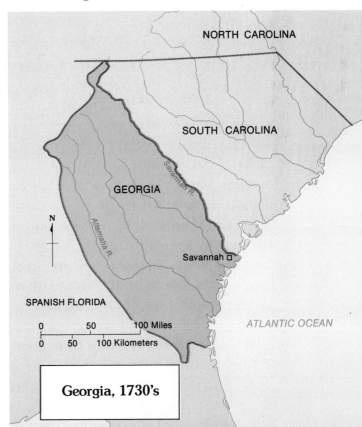

Georgia, 1730's

a fresh start. During the 1700's, people in England who could not pay their debts were put in jail. Oglethorpe wanted to take these people out of jail and put them to work building the colony.

Oglethorpe won the support of 20 businessmen. Together they persuaded the king to give them the new colony. The men were to serve as trustees. Trustees were given the right to rule a colony. They named their colony Georgia in honor of King George II of England.

In 1733, Oglethorpe arrived at Charles Town with more than a hundred settlers. South Carolinians welcomed their new neighbors. They gave the newcomers horses, sheep, pigs, rice, and money to help them get started.

Soon it was time for the new settlers to leave Charles Town. They sailed south to the Savannah River. There they built a settlement called Savannah. It was Georgia's first English settlement.

The trustees made very strict rules for the colony. No one was allowed to own more than 50 acres (20 hectares) of land. Settlers were to grow grapes for wine making. They were also supposed to raise silkworms. The settlers had to do the work themselves because the trustees had outlawed slavery in Georgia.

The settlers obeyed the rules. Yet the colony did not make money. Georgia did not have the right climate for growing grapes or for raising silkworms. Discouraged, the trustees gave up.

The king then took over the colony and made some changes. Settlers could own as much land as they could afford. They also could raise whatever they wanted to on their land. Before long, some settlers grew rich by planting rice and indigo. Georgia, the last of the Southern colonies, was becoming as successful as its neighbors to the north.

To Help You Remember

1. (a) Where did people first settle in Maryland and Virginia? (b) Where did people settle next?
2. (a) What is a plantation? (b) What crops were grown on plantations in Virginia and Maryland?
3. (a) Why did the early settlements around Albermarle Sound grow slowly? (b) Why did Charles Town grow quickly?
4. (a) Why did the proprietors of Carolina return it to the king? (b) What then happened to the Carolina colony?
5. (a) Why did King George II decide to start a new colony south of the Carolinas? (b) What was the colony called? (c) Who were its leaders?

Life along the Coast

By the 1750's, a number of large farms, or plantations, stretched all along the coast from Maryland in the north to Georgia in the south. Those who owned plantations were called planters. In addition to running their large farms, they played an important part in the government of the Southern colonies.

On Plantations

A plantation was much like a small village. At the center of the plantation was the planter's home. Nearby stood a kitchen, a blacksmith's shop, a sewing house, a flour mill, a cheese and butter house, a smokehouse, stables, barns, and the cabins of plantation workers.

Mount Vernon, in Fairfax County, Virginia, was in many ways a typical plantation. It was owned by George Washington's brother Lawrence. The family house stood on a hill overlooking the Potomac River. Over the years, Lawrence and later George added on to the house. The same was true of the plantation. In time, it covered 8,000 acres (3,238 hectares).

This diagram of George Washington's plantation in Fairfax County, Virginia, shows what a typical Southern plantation was like.

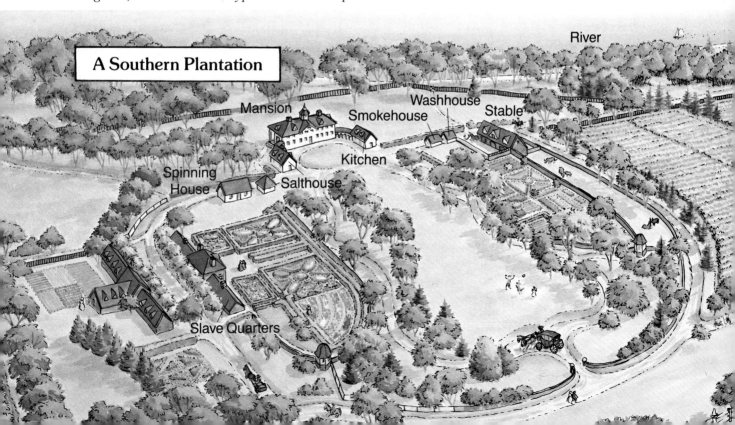

A Southern Plantation

River

Mansion
Washhouse
Smokehouse
Stable
Kitchen
Spinning House
Salthouse
Slave Quarters

The Washingtons made or grew almost everything they needed. They ordered from England the few things they could not make, such as fine furniture, books, silk, and some farm tools. They got the money by selling tobacco to English merchants. In addition to buying English-made goods, many wealthy planters also sent their sons to England to be educated.

George Washington planned to go to school in England. When he was 11 years old, however, his father died. Instead of going to school in England, he went to live with his brother Lawrence and his family. Lawrence taught him all he needed to know. In those days, Mount Vernon, like most Southern plantations, was far away from its nearest neighbor. Therefore, there were no local schools that George could attend.

Although plantations were sometimes separated by hundreds of miles, planters did visit one another from time to time. Mount Vernon was often filled with guests. George Washington once wrote that he and his family hardly ever had dinner alone.

When guests came for dinner, they did not go home the same night. The trip was too long. Most guests stayed at least a few days. During that time, there were parties, dances, fox hunts, and horse races. Planters and their families had a very comfortable life.

Plantation Workers

The comfortable life that Southern planters enjoyed was possible only because they had so many workers. Planters hired **indentured servants** to help with the work. Indentured servants were people from Europe who promised to work for a colonist for about seven years. In return, they were given the money for their passage to North America. When indentured servants finished their time of service, they were free to move on.

Many planters, however, did not want to hire new workers every seven years. They needed workers who would always remain on their plantations. During the 1700's, many planters started buying black slaves from Africa. At that time, people in many parts of the world owned slaves, and very few people then thought it was wrong to do so.

Slaves cost more than indentured servants, but slaves worked all their lives for their owners. In addition, the children of slaves also belonged to their parents' owners. As a result, planters found owning slaves more profitable than hiring indentured servants.

Slaves did not come to North America willingly. They were captured in West Africa and forced onto slave ships. There they were chained together and packed into the lower

On many plantations, slaves did the hard work. Here slaves are shown growing rice.

parts of the ship. Many Africans died on the long voyage to North America.

Once slaves reached the colonies, they were put to work. Most slaves on large plantations worked in the fields planting and harvesting crops. Some worked in the planter's house. They cooked, cleaned, and even cared for the children in the family. Still others were trained as carpenters, blacksmiths, and weavers and for other skilled jobs.

Since slaves were the property of their owners, they had no rights of their own. They had to do whatever they were told to do. Some were able to adjust to a lifetime of slavery. Others fought against slavery in quiet ways. They broke tools or worked very slowly. Many slaves also ran away.

Although there were slaves in every English colony, the Southern colonies had more than all of the others combined. In fact, in some Southern colonies, slaves made up more than half the population.

Communities along the Coast

Unlike New England, where people lived close together, people in the South lived far from one another. Since there were few villages or towns, local problems were not handled at town meetings. Instead, every

The Virginia House of Burgesses met here in the capitol at Williamsburg.

Southern colony was divided into **counties.** A county is a division, or part, of a colony. It has its own government. A county covers a much larger area than a town. It often includes several towns.

Each county had a courthouse where rich planters met from time to time to make laws. They decided what roads and bridges to build or repair. They voted on how tax money would be spent. They did not, however, choose county officers such as sheriffs and judges. These officials were chosen by a governor.

Since the men the governor selected for county offices had to own a certain amount of property, the men he chose were usually rich planters. In every Southern colony, planters became the leaders in county government.

Every colony also had an assembly like the Virginia House of Burgesses. Members of the assembly were chosen by voters in that colony. In the South, only free white men who owned property could vote or could be elected to the assemblies.

In South Carolina, for example, an assemblyman had to own 500 acres (200 hectares) and 10 slaves or have other property worth at least $5,000. That was a great deal of money in those days, so the men who could vote or hold office were often rich. Most were planters.

To Help You Remember

1. (a) What is a plantation?
   (b) What were owners of plantations called?
2. How did families like the Washingtons, who lived on plantations, get the things they needed?
3. Who did the work on a plantation?
4. (a) How did slaves come to North America? (b) Once in the colonies, what jobs did they do on plantations?
5. Where were local problems handled in the Southern colonies?
6. Who were the leaders of government in the Southern colonies?
7. Who was allowed to vote in the Southern colonies?

The first section of this chapter looks at the growth of the Southern colonies from the early 1600's to the late 1700's. Another way to show that information is on a map. Below are two maps of the Southern colonies. One shows the areas that were settled by 1700. The other shows the areas settled between 1700 and 1763. By comparing these maps, you can see how the Southern colonies grew. Study both maps. Then answer the questions that follow them.

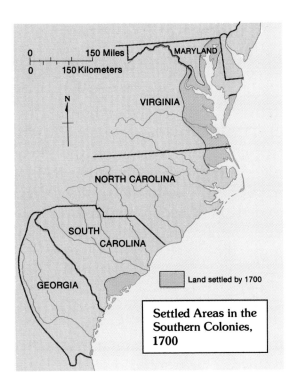

Settled Areas in the Southern Colonies, 1700

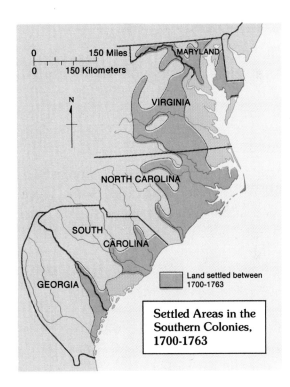

Settled Areas in the Southern Colonies, 1700-1763

1. Where was most of the settled land before 1700?
2. Which colony had the largest amount of settled land before 1700?
3. What colony was not settled before 1700?
4. Name the two colonies that had the largest growth in settlement between 1700 and 1763.

Settlements Inland

Only a small number of people in the Southern colonies were rich planters. Most people owned small farms. They could not afford to buy slaves or land along the coast. Therefore, many of them settled on land west of the tidewater. There, on the hilly Piedmont, they built farms.

Making a Living on Small Farms

Some of the settlers on the Piedmont came from colonies farther north. Others came from England and from what is now Germany, Switzerland, Ireland, and other countries in Europe. A small number of blacks settled on the Piedmont too. Some were freed slaves. Others were slaves who had run away.

The Piedmont settlers left the trunks of trees standing when they cleared land.

It took time and hard work to build a farm on the Piedmont. The land was covered by thick forests. Before settlers could even begin farming, they had to chop down enough trees to make a clearing. Then a family would build a small log cabin. As more and more trees were chopped down, the clearing slowly widened to become a farm.

On their newly cleared land, most families grew corn, peas, beans, tobacco, and other crops. Some also kept cattle and pigs. Those who had no livestock depended on hunting for all of their meat. Most people also did a little fishing. Farms on the Piedmont were far apart. Families had to make or grow almost everything they needed. Few people could afford to buy things that were made in England or in the other colonies.

Life on the Frontier

In the 1750's, the Piedmont was the **frontier.** The frontier was the land that lay just beyond the settled areas. Life on the frontier could be very dangerous. Bears and other wild animals lived in the forest. There were even dangers in gathering wild plants and berries. Some were good to eat. Others were poisonous.

Settlers also had to keep a lookout for Indians. As more and more people from Europe moved onto the Piedmont, the Indians who lived there watched in horror. The newcomers were destroying the forests. The Indians depended on the animals that lived in the forest for their food and clothing. Soon the Indians began to attack settlements along the frontier.

Some settlers banded together for protection. Instead of living far apart, they built forts. A fort was a group of cabins surrounded by a high fence called a stockade. At the corners of the stockade were two-story cabins called blockhouses. From there, the settlers could keep watch for Indians.

When there was peace, the fort served as a trading post where the Indians and settlers traded goods. In times of war, however, even families who lived miles from the fort left their farms for the stockade.

Making a Living in the Forest

Most people on the frontier were farmers, but some made their living from the forests. The Carolinas and Georgia had some of the finest pine forests in North America. From those pine trees people got turpentine, pitch, and tar.

Pitch, turpentine, and tar were in great demand. Shipbuilders and

Settlers on the frontier moved into forts in times of danger.

sailors used pitch and tar to seal the spaces between the wooden planks on ships. They used turpentine to thin paint. Since pitch, tar, and turpentine were used for and stored on ships, those products were often called **naval stores.**

The forests also had many animals. Some settlers made a living by hunting and trapping those animals. They hunted deer, bear, and other large animals. They also trapped smaller animals such as beaver and marten. These settlers lived for months at a time in the forest. A few times a year, they brought animal skins or furs to forts along the frontier.

127

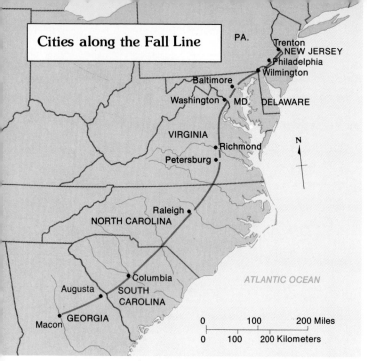

Cities along the Fall Line

Trace the path of the fall line. What do the locations of the cities on the fall line have in common?

At the forts, trappers traded the animal skins for guns, food, clothing, and other supplies. Merchants at the fort then took the furs to the nearest river. To reach the rivers of the tidewater, they had to travel just beyond the fall line. The furs could then be shipped by water to the trading cities along the coast.

By 1750, a number of small settlements had been built up along the fall line. The settlers used the power of the running water to grind their corn and to cut wood into logs.

In a short time, some of these small settlements grew into large cities. Baltimore, Maryland; Richmond,

Virginia; and Macon and Columbus in Georgia are a few of the cities that grew up along the fall line. These cities became important links between the settlers on the Piedmont and the people who lived in the tidewater. The fall line cities served as centers of trade for goods coming from the Piedmont as well as for goods coming from the tidewater.

Farming was the most important way of earning a living in the Southern colonies. In the next chapter, you will read about the Middle colonies. There, too, most people farmed. Yet the crops grown in the Middle colonies were very different from those grown in the South.

To Help You Remember

1. (a) Why was building a farm on the Piedmont difficult? (b) What crops did the settlers grow on those farms?
2. (a) What is a frontier? (b) How did settlers on the frontier protect themselves?
3. (a) Name three products people got from pine trees. (b) Why were those products called naval stores?
4. (a) Name four cities that grew from settlements along the fall line. (b) Why were those cities important to people living on the Piedmont and in the tidewater?

Chapter Review

Words to Know

1. What is a *plantation?*
2. How does land on the *tidewater* differ from land on the *Piedmont?*
3. What is a *fall line?*
4. Who is a *proprietor?*
5. Give an example of *naval stores.*
6. What is *indigo* used for?
7. Explain how *indentured servants* differ from other servants.
8. What kind of river is *navigable?*
9. What does a person who *invests* do?
10. What is a *county?*
11. Where is a *frontier?*

Reviewing Main Ideas

1. Name the Southern colonies and tell when each was founded.
2. List at least three ways people earned a living in the South.
3. What crops did farmers in the Southern colonies raise?
4. Name at least one important city in the Southern colonies.
5. How were early settlements in Virginia and Maryland alike?
6. How was a plantation like a small village?
7. Why did planters prefer slaves to indentured servants?
8. Why did planters become the leaders in county government?
9. Tell two ways in which forts were important on the frontier.
10. Why was the fall line important?

In Your Own Words

Write two paragraphs describing the way of life on the Piedmont and the way of life on the tidewater. The first paragraph should tell how life on a tidewater plantation was like life on a small farm in the Piedmont. The second should tell how life in the two places was different.

Challenge!

Savannah, Georgia, was laid out according to a plan. James Oglethorpe wanted the streets to form a grid. What are the advantages to his plan? Disadvantages?

Many other cities have streets that form a grid. Use a road atlas that has city maps to find at least five of those cities. What plan, if any, was used to lay out the streets in your town?

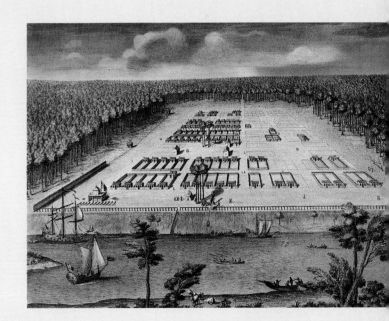

7

The Middle Colonies

Four colonies lay between New England and the South. Those colonies became known as the Middle colonies. They were New York, New Jersey, Pennsylvania, and Delaware. These colonies were settled later than those farther north and south.

New England and the Southern colonies were settled mostly by people from England. The Middle colonies were not. Settlers there came from many different countries. Yet their reasons for coming to North America were much the same. Some came in search of religious freedom. Others came hoping to make a fresh start in a new land. Still others saw a chance to get rich through farming or trade. Whatever their reasons, most of them found what they were looking for in the Middle colonies.

As You Read

In some ways, life in the Middle colonies was like life in New England. In other ways, it was like life in the South. As you read, look for those similarities. Look too for ways life in the Middle colonies was different. The chapter is divided into three parts.

- Growth of the Middle Colonies
- Farming in the Middle Colonies
- Philadelphia, the Leading City

◀ *A small farm in the Middle colonies in the 1700's*

Growth of the Middle Colonies

The story of the Middle colonies begins in 1664 when England took over the colony of New Netherland from the Dutch. At that time, England gained a huge stretch of land in North America. The king gave part of that land to his brother, the Duke of York. The Duke divided it into two colonies: New York and New Jersey. The king gave the rest of the land to the son of one of his friends, William Penn. That land became the colony of Pennsylvania. In those days, Delaware was part of Pennsylvania.

New York

New York was the oldest of the Middle colonies. The Dutch built a settlement there in 1624. Yet under both the Dutch and the English, New York grew unevenly. Throughout most of the colony there were very few settlers. Most settlers lived in the southeast corner of New York near the mouth of the Hudson River. Small farms and trading posts dotted Manhattan Island, Long Island, and the lower Hudson River Valley.

There were several reasons why more people did not settle in the colony of New York. One reason was that much of the land in the Hudson River Valley was owned by a few wealthy Dutch families. They owned huge estates along the river. Although these families did not farm all of their land, they were not willing to sell any of it. Instead, they chose to rent parts of it. Therefore,

By 1750, New York City, at the mouth of the Hudson River, had become one of the largest cities in the colonies.

people who wanted to own their own farms had to settle somewhere else.

Another reason northern and western New York grew slowly was because of the fur trade. Many beaver, deer, and other animals lived in the forests. The fur trade there was very profitable. Trappers and traders discouraged farmers from settling in northern New York. They knew that once the farmers started clearing parts of the forest for their fields, the animals would move away from that part of New York.

Northern New York also grew slowly because of fighting along the borders there. The French claimed much of that land and they were willing to fight to keep it. The Iroquois also lived in this part of New York. They too were willing to fight to keep their lands. These people made northern New York a very dangerous place to settle.

New Jersey

In 1664, New York included all the land from the west bank of the Connecticut River south to Delaware Bay. The cost of governing such a large colony proved to be too great even for the brother of a king. After just three and a half months, the Duke of York gave the land between the Hudson and Delaware rivers to two friends, Lord Berkeley and Sir

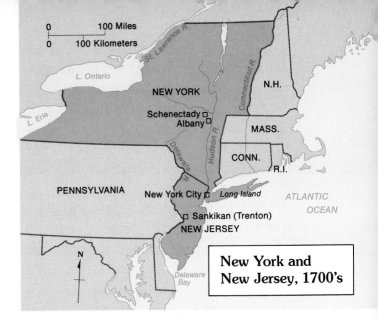

New York and New Jersey, 1700's

What river lies along the western boundary of New Jersey? What body of water lies at its southwestern end?

George Carteret. They named their colony New Jersey.

When the two men took over New Jersey, many people were already living there. Some of the settlers were Dutch. Others were from New England. Before long, these colonists were joined by many settlers from the West Indies, Scotland, France, and from what is now Germany. Berkeley and Carteret attracted the new colonists by offering land at low prices. They also promised the colonists the right to govern themselves. Thousands responded to their offer.

Some parts of New Jersey began to look much like New England. In those parts of the colony, groups of people built small towns and farming

133

villages like those in Connecticut and Massachusetts. In other places, people lived on widely scattered farms like those on the Piedmont in the Southern colonies.

Almost everyone in New Jersey farmed. The colony's fine soil and mild climate were well suited to such crops as wheat, corn, oats, and other grains. In fact, New Jersey grew so much grain that dozens of flour mills sprang up along the rivers. The mills used the power of running water to grind the grain into flour.

A few people made a living from the forests that covered the middle part of the colony. They chopped down trees and split the wood to make boards and shingles. These forest products, along with those of the farms, were shipped to New York City. There they were sold to people from other colonies or shipped to Europe and the West Indies.

New Jersey grew rapidly until 1674. That year Berkeley sold his share of the colony. Later Carteret did the same. As New Jersey changed hands again and again, many arguments took place over who owned what land. At times, New Jersey was divided into two separate colonies. Finally, in 1702, the king took over all of New Jersey and made it one colony again.

Pennsylvania

In 1681, King Charles II gave a huge piece of land in North America to William Penn. The king owed a large sum of money to Penn's father. When the elder Penn died, the debt came due. The land was the king's way of paying off that debt. The king named the new colony after William Penn's father. He called it Pennsylvania, or "Penn's Woods."

Unlike his father, William Penn was not a friend of the king. Indeed, he belonged to a religious group that the king was trying to outlaw. The group was called the Society of Friends. Its members were known as Quakers because they were said to quake before God.

In the 1600's, the Quakers suffered greatly in England. Many were even

What bay borders Delaware on the north? What river flows from Pennsylvania into the bay?

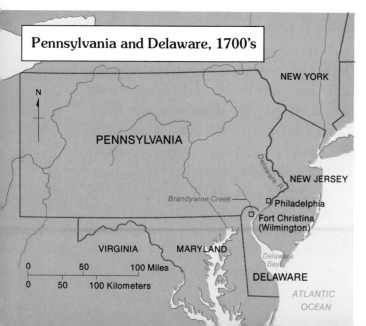

Pennsylvania and Delaware, 1700's

NEW YORK

PENNSYLVANIA

NEW JERSEY

Brandywine Creek

Philadelphia

Fort Christina (Wilmington)

VIRGINIA

MARYLAND

Delaware Bay

DELAWARE

ATLANTIC OCEAN

0   50   100 Miles

0   50   100 Kilometers

This painting shows William Penn buying land from the Indians.

sent to prison. Penn decided to use his land to start a colony where Quakers could worship freely without fear of punishment.

Penn realized that there were not enough Quakers in England to build a colony. He advertised for settlers in many other countries. He encouraged those who were willing to work hard to come. He warned dreamers looking for easy riches to stay away.

Penn promised religious freedom to all who came. He also sold or rented land at lower prices than in any other North American colony.

In September 1682, Penn left England with a hundred colonists. Two months later, they sailed up the mouth of the Delaware River. Penn chose a spot on the northern side of the river for the colony's first settlement. He named the settlement Philadelphia, which in Greek means "the city of brotherly love."

Penn and other Quakers believed that all people were equal in the eyes of God. Therefore, they treated all people fairly and with respect. As a result, Penn was careful to buy the land the king had given him from its real owners—the Indians.

Thousands of settlers flocked to Pennsylvania. At first, most of them built homes and farms in and around

Swedish settlers were the first to build log cabins in the colonies.

Philadelphia. Later, people began moving north and west of the city. Some moved in groups and built villages like those in New England. Many started small farms far away from other settlers. These farms were similar to the farms on the Piedmont in the Southern colonies.

Pennsylvania grew quickly because it had plenty of rich farm land. It also grew because of the hard work of the people who moved there.

Delaware

William Penn believed that Pennsylvania would grow even faster if it included the land south of the Delaware River. Then ships from England could sail directly up the Delaware River to Philadelphia. At the time, the land belonged to the Duke of York, so Penn asked him for it. When the duke became king of England in 1685, he granted Penn's request. From 1685 until 1776, that land remained part of Pennsylvania. After 1776, it became Delaware.

People from Sweden, Finland, and The Netherlands were living in Delaware long before Penn was given the land. Penn allowed them to stay. Before long, many more people were moving there. Because Delaware has good soil and few hills, it is easy land to farm. Its rivers also make it easy for farmers to ship their wheat and other crops to market.

To Help You Remember

1. (a) Where did most of the settlers in New York live? (b) Give three reasons why the rest of the colony had few settlers.
2. (a) How did Berkeley and Carteret get people to come to New Jersey? (b) How did the settlers there make a living?
3. (a) How did William Penn get his colony? (b) Why did he want to start a colony? (c) How did he get people to come to his colony?
4. (a) Why did William Penn want the land south of the Delaware River? (b) What people were already living there? (c) What attracted people to Delaware?

The first section in this chapter describes how the land in each of the Middle colonies was settled. As more land was settled, the number of people in each colony grew.

One way to show the growth in population is on a table. A table is a list of facts that have been arranged in rows and columns for easy reference.

Study the table below. Then use the information on the table to answer the questions on this page.

Estimated Population of the Middle Colonies, 1680–1760

Year	New York	New Jersey	Pennsylvania	Delaware
1680	9,830	3,400	680	1,005
1700	19,107	14,010	17,950	2,470
1720	36,919	29,818	30,962	5,385
1740	63,665	51,373	85,637	19,870
1760	117,138	93,813	183,703	33,250

1. Which colony had the most people in 1680?
2. Which colony had the smallest population in 1680?
3. Which colony had the largest population in 1740?
4. Which colony had the fewest people in 1740?
5. Between 1680 and 1700, which increased more, the population of Delaware or of New Jersey?
6. Between 1700 and 1720, which increased more, the population of New York or of Pennsylvania?
7. Which colony grew fastest between 1740 and 1760?
8. List the colonies by population, from largest to smallest, for the year 1680.
9. List the colonies from largest to smallest, for 1760.
10. How do you explain the differences between the two lists? If you need help, look back in the chapter.

Farming in the Middle Colonies

The Middle colonies produced more food than New England or the Southern colonies. People there grew so much food, especially wheat, that the Middle colonies were sometimes called the breadbasket colonies.

On Large and Small Farms

New York had a few large estates that were similar to the plantations in the South. However, most people in the Middle colonies owned small farms.

These farms were often far apart. Families usually saw their neighbors only at church on Sunday. Otherwise, neighbors got together for events like weddings or in times of trouble. If a barn burned down, everyone in the area helped rebuild it.

A typical farm in the Middle colonies was 50 to 150 acres (20 to 61 hectares). It had a house and a barn, a fenced-in yard for animals, a garden, and fields. Many farmers also had apple and peach orchards.

Most families were able to grow more food than they needed. For example, 2 or 3 bushels (70 to 106 liters) of grain seed planted in one acre

This diagram shows what a typical farm in the Middle colonies looked like in the 1700's.

A Middle Colony Farm

Smoke house · Barn · Fields · Garden · Well · Farm house · Chicken coop · Tool shed · Apple orchard

(.4 hectare) produced 25 or 30 bushels (881 to 1,057 liters) of grain. Farmers also grew many kinds of fruits and vegetables. Some raised cattle and pigs.

On a farm, everyone had many jobs. Men in the family did the plowing and the planting. They herded cattle and sheep as well. Men often hunted squirrel, wild turkey, and deer. They also made and repaired farm tools. They made furniture too.

The women spent much of their time preparing food for the long winter. They tended the family garden, pickled vegetables, and dried and preserved fruits. They turned apples into cider and apple butter. They also spun sheep's wool, from which they knit socks and wove cloth. From the cloth they made shirts, dresses, and pants. Both soapmaking and candlemaking were women's jobs too.

Children helped in many ways. The boys worked in the fields with their fathers. They also learned how to make tools and furniture. The girls helped their mothers. They also helped care for the babies in the family.

Industries along the Brandywine Creek

Since most farmers grew more food than their families needed, they were eager to sell their extra food to people

This mill on the Brandywine Creek was used to make gun powder.

in England. Yet wheat, the crop that grew best in the Middle colonies, often spoiled on the long voyage to England. Therefore, some people in the Middle colonies built flour mills along the fast-running rivers. Wheat was ground into flour at these mills. Flour did not spoil on the long trip across the ocean.

Nowhere on the east coast of North America was there as much water power as on the Brandywine Creek in Delaware. At the fall line, the creek rushes over a rock almost a thousand feet (304 meters) high. Because of its height, it is called the Great Falls. The Great Falls is an excellent source

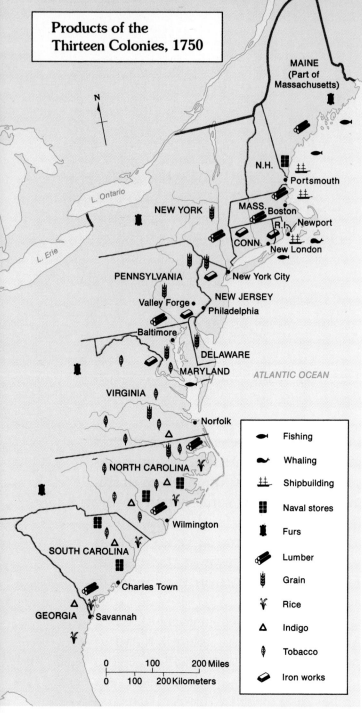

Products of the Thirteen Colonies, 1750

MAINE
(Part of
Massachusetts)

L. Ontario

N.H.
Portsmouth

NEW YORK

MASS. Boston
R.I. Newport
CONN.
New London

L. Erie

PENNSYLVANIA
New York City

Valley Forge
NEW JERSEY
Philadelphia

Baltimore

DELAWARE
MARYLAND

ATLANTIC OCEAN

VIRGINIA

Norfolk

NORTH CAROLINA

Wilmington

SOUTH CAROLINA

Charles Town

GEORGIA
Savannah

Symbol	Product
	Fishing
	Whaling
	Shipbuilding
	Naval stores
	Furs
	Lumber
	Grain
	Rice
	Indigo
	Tobacco
	Iron works

0   100   200 Miles
0   100   200 Kilometers

The map shows the major products of the colonies. What goods were produced in Georgia? Virginia? Rhode Island?

of water power. As early as 1687, a group of Swedish settlers used it to power a barley mill. As time passed, more mills sprang up along the Brandywine. Then, around 1730, the town of Wilmington formed around these mills.

Farmers in Delaware, Pennsylvania, and Maryland brought their wheat, rye, and barley to the mills in Wilmington. Wilmington's grain mills ground some of the best wheat and rye in the colonies. After the grain was ground into flour, it was shipped from Wilmington down the Brandywine to the Delaware River. From there, it could be shipped directly to England, the West Indies, or to the other colonies.

Flour milling was not the only industry to grow up along the Brandywine. Other industries that used large amounts of water also developed there. One such industry was tanning. A **tanner** is a person who turns the skin of cows, sheep, horses, and other animals into leather. Since water was used in almost every step of the tanning process, it is not surprising that a tannery was started along the banks of the Brandywine.

Papermaking was another industry that grew up along the Brandywine. Like tanning, it too used large amounts of water. The Brandywine could supply all of the water needed to run both the paper mill and the tannery. In addition, its fast-running falls powered the nearby grain mills. As time passed, these industries helped Wilmington grow into an important **industrial** city. That is, it became a city with much manufacturing and trade.

To Help You Remember

1. Why were the Middle colonies called the breadbasket colonies?

2. (a) How large was a typical farm in the Middle colonies? (b) What crops did farmers there raise?
3. (a) List four jobs men did on a typical farm. (b) List four jobs women did. (c) List three jobs children did.
4. (a) Name three industries that grew up along the Brandywine. (b) Why were those industries started there? (c) What industrial city grew up on the Brandywine?

Philadelphia, the Leading City

In addition to Wilmington, two other major cities grew up in the Middle colonies—New York and Philadelphia. New York lay at the mouth of the Hudson River. Philadelphia grew up along the shores of the Delaware. Both cities became important centers of trade. Philadelphia, however, grew much faster than New York. By 1750, Philadelphia had become the largest and busiest city in the colonies.

Working in a Busy City

Like most port cities, Philadelphia's waterfront was often crowded with ships from different countries. They lay anchored at **docks** waiting to be loaded or unloaded. A dock is a wooden platform built over the water. Philadelphia had many docks along its waterfront.

The docks were crowded, busy places. Strong men worked at the docks loading and unloading ships. Some carried crates of cloth, fine furniture, tools, and other goods off English ships. Then they reloaded the ships with tall stacks of tobacco from Virginia. Others were busy hauling barrels of molasses, wine, and salt off ships from the West Indies. Then goods from the Middle colonies such as lumber, wheat, beef, and pork were packed onto those ships.

Farther down the waterfront stood huge wooden frameworks. They were the skeletons of ships that were still being built. Philadelphia had four shipyards. There shipwrights worked

Shipbuilding was a major industry along Philadelphia's busy waterfront.

on boats and sailing ships of many kinds and sizes. People all along the waterfront could hear the clanging and banging of their hammers.

Philadelphia's busy marketplace was located near the waterfront too. The street where it stood was called Market Street. Wednesdays and Saturdays were market days. The market opened to the sound of a bell. The bell rang out at 6 A.M. in summer and 8 A.M. in winter. From the time the bell sounded, Market Street was crowded with people. Farmers and fur traders formed long lines as they waited to unload their wagons. People from the city stood by watching. The goods were unloaded and put in the large stalls that lined the middle of Market Street.

All kinds of goods were sold in the market. Farmers sold fruit, vegetables, grains, and meat. They also sold fresh eggs and freshly made butter and cheese. Merchants sold lumber, furs, and tobacco. Fishermen sold the fish, eels, and other seafood they had caught early in the day. Indians came to the market too. They sold corn, beans, pumpkins, and squash.

People went from stall to stall looking at and feeling the peaches, apples, squash, and other goods. Nearby, the city butcher slaughtered the animals that farmers wanted to sell. People in Philadelphia found plenty of fresh food at the market.

The streets beyond the market were lined with all kinds of shops. There were many silversmiths, clockmakers, gunsmiths, blacksmiths, printers, bookbinders, carpenters, and other skilled craftworkers as well. Farmers brought broken tools to the blacksmith for repair. Fur traders ordered new rifles from the gunsmith.

Before long, people throughout the colonies learned that Philadelphians could make crafted objects as fine as or even finer than those made in England. By 1750, many of these skilled craftworkers, or **artisans,** had become well known for their skill. Wealthy people from other colonial cities traveled to Philadelphia to order fine furniture, silverware, glassware, and other crafted objects.

Ben Franklin in Philadelphia

Philadelphians were proud of their city. They had every right to be. People visiting the city for the first time were impressed with its wide, well-planned, and well-lighted streets. In 1747, a Swedish visitor wrote that the city had "risen so suddenly from nothing into such grandeur and perfection." Other Europeans also spoke in glowing terms about Philadelphia. No other colonial city received such high praise from Europeans as Philadelphia did.

One of the city's greatest admirers was Benjamin Franklin. Franklin was not born in Philadelphia. He came to the city as a young man from Boston, Massachusetts. In Boston, he had worked in his brother James' printing shop.

Ben Franklin was an **apprentice.** An apprentice is a person who learns a trade from a master artisan. Ben's brother was teaching him how to be a printer. In colonial times, many young boys learned a trade from a skilled artisan. They lived and studied with the artisan from the age of 11 to about 21. Then they were ready to work on their own.

Young Ben did not like working for his brother. He and James often quarreled. Finally, when Ben was 17, he ran away from home. He boarded a boat to New York. From there, he walked across New Jersey and then hitchhiked a boat ride down the Delaware to Philadelphia.

Franklin arrived in Philadelphia in 1723. He soon found work as a printer. Before long, he printed the best-selling newspaper in the city. He also became famous for his **almanac.** An almanac is a book published yearly with daily weather forecasts and interesting facts. Franklin's was called *Poor Richard's Almanac.*

Poor Richard's Almanac contained weather forecasts for every day of the year, riddles, jokes, poems, proverbs, recipes, and all kinds of interesting or odd facts. From the first printing, it became the most popular almanac in the colonies. The leaders of Pennsylvania were so impressed with the quality of Franklin's newspaper and almanac that they made him the official printer for the colony.

Below is an example of one of the famous sayings Ben Franklin published.

Improving City Life

Franklin was able to make a good living in Philadelphia. During the many years he lived there, he grew to love the city and its people. Grateful for what Philadelphia had done for him, Franklin set out to make the city a good place to live for everyone.

Franklin saw the people of Philadelphia wading through mud and dirt as they walked around the city. He thought it would be a good idea to have the streets paved. He wrote about his idea in his newspaper and talked about it to anyone who would listen. Before long, most of the city streets were paved with stones.

Franklin helped the people of Philadelphia in other ways too. Like most colonial cities, Philadelphia had many wooden buildings. If one caught fire, the building just burned up. Sometimes the fire spread to nearby buildings as well. Franklin suggested that people in Philadelphia organize a volunteer fire company. He helped to start the Union Fire Company. In a short time, Philadelphia had a network of volunteer fire companies. They helped to make

Thanks to Ben Franklin's efforts, Philadelphia's streets were paved with cobblestones and had lamps to light them at night.

Ben Franklin helped to organize the first fire department in the colonies.

Philadelphia a much safer place for people to live.

Franklin wanted Philadelphians protected in other ways too. When he walked around the city at night, he noticed that the night watchmen were more interested in drinking whiskey than in protecting the people. He suggested that the citizens of Philadelphia hire people to patrol the city. He also got people to protect themselves by joining together to form a **militia**. A militia is a group of citizens who have been trained as soldiers. In times of trouble, its members could be called on to defend the city.

Franklin not only helped to bring the people of Philadelphia together, he also helped to bring people throughout the colonies together. He did this by improving mail service.

Franklin rode over every postal route in the colonies. Along the way, he stopped to talk with the local postmasters. He offered them advice on how to improve mail service along their routes. Before long, news and ideas began to travel faster and more easily throughout the colonies.

People from many different countries settled in the Middle colonies. As they worked together and traded with one another, they slowly changed. Before long, they were borrowing words from each other's languages, sharing ideas, and learning new ways of doing things. Gradually, they started to become more alike. They were no longer English or Dutch or Swedish—they were, in fact, becoming American.

To Help You Remember

1. Why was Philadelphia the leading city in the colonies in 1750?
2. What type of work did people do along Philadelphia's waterfront?
3. What kinds of goods were sold in the marketplace in Philadelphia?
4. List three ways Franklin helped to improve life in Philadelphia.
5. How did Franklin help to bring the people throughout the colonies together?

Chapter Review

Words to Know

Match each term with its definition

(a) dock   (e) apprentice
(b) militia   (f) tanner
(c) artisan   (g) industrial
(d) almanac

_____ 1. citizens trained as soldiers
_____ 2. a book with weather forecasts and with many facts
_____ 3. a person who is learning a trade
_____ 4. a person who turns skins into leather
_____ 5. a wooden platform built over water
_____ 6. a skilled worker
_____ 7. much manufacturing

Reviewing Main Ideas

1. Name the Middle colonies. Tell when each became an English colony.
2. How did the fur trade affect the growth of New York?
3. What did William Penn do to encourage settlers?
4. List three ways people earned a living in the Middle colonies.
5. Why were the Middle colonies known as the breadbasket colonies?
6. Name the leading city in the Middle colonies.
7. What industries were started in the Middle colonies?
8. What did Ben Franklin do to improve life in Philadelphia?

In Your Own Words

Write two paragraphs. In the first, tell how the Middle colonies were similar to the New England and Southern colonies. In the second paragraph, tell how the Middle colonies were different from the others.

Keeping Skills Sharp

Use the graph to answer the following questions.

1. (a) Rank the colonies by size in 1680. (b) In 1720. (c) In 1760.
2. (a) Which group of colonies grew fastest between 1680 and 1700? (b) Between 1740 and 1760?

Challenge!

Use the graph to make a prediction. How do you think the colonies will rank in population by 1780? Give reasons for your answer.

Population Growth in the Thirteen Colonies

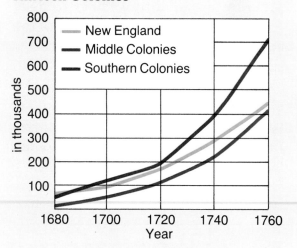

Unit Review

Take Another Look

Tell whether each of the following statements is true for the **New England colonies,** the **Middle colonies,** or the **Southern colonies.** Some statements may be true for two groups of colonies. Others may be true of all three groups.

1. Between 1636 and 1679, three colonies were started here.
2. These colonies had representative assemblies like the House of Burgesses.
3. The first and last English colonies were started here.
4. The first towns grew up along the coast.
5. Most of the settlers came from England.
6. By the 1700's, merchants in these colonies made regular trips to England.
7. These colonies were known as the breadbasket colonies.
8. People in these colonies had the largest number of slaves.
9. By 1750, Philadelphia had become the largest and busiest trading center in these colonies.
10. Fishing, whaling, and shipbuilding were very important industries in these colonies.
11. People came to these colonies from many different countries.
12. Beginning in 1664, English colonies were started here.
13. People in these colonies got naval stores from pine forests.
14. The promise of religious freedom brought many people to these colonies.
15. Tobacco was an important crop in these colonies.

You and the Past

Every colony was divided into counties. In the Southern colonies, county governments did many of the jobs that cities and towns handled in the New England colonies. Today every state is divided into counties. (In Louisiana, a county is called a parish.) Which county do you live in? Find out what your county government does. How is the county organized? Report your findings to the class.

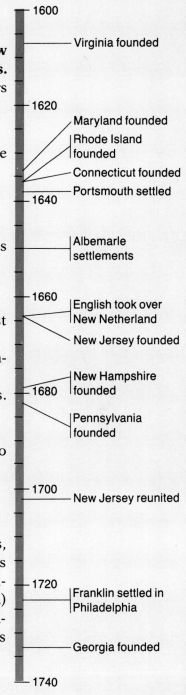

1600

Virginia founded

1620

Maryland founded
Rhode Island founded
Connecticut founded
Portsmouth settled

1640

Albemarle settlements

1660

English took over New Netherland
New Jersey founded

New Hampshire founded

1680

Pennsylvania founded

1700

New Jersey reunited

1720

Franklin settled in Philadelphia

Georgia founded

1740

Angry colonists in New York before independence

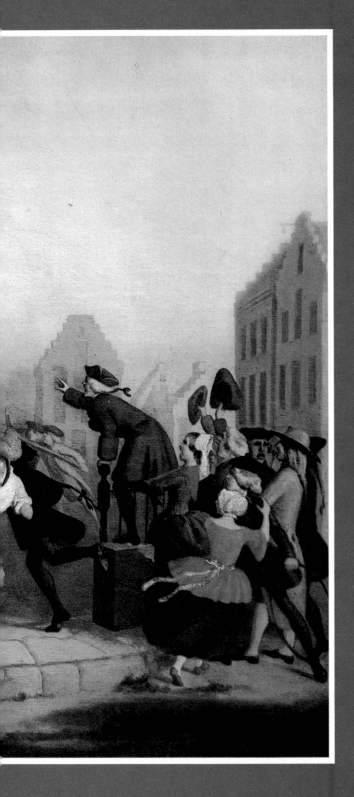

Unit Three

Building a Nation

By the 1700's, a new way of life was growing up in the colonies. Colonists were becoming less European and more American. Soon many colonists were eager to break away from Great Britain and build their own nation. In 1776, a war for independence began.

8

Becoming American

The people who came to North America as colonists hoped to build villages and towns just like the ones they had known in Europe. They wanted to keep alive their **heritage.** A heritage includes the values, beliefs, and other parts of a culture that are passed from parent to child. The newcomers dreamed of building a *new* England, a *new* Netherlands, or a *new* Sweden. It was hard work, but the colonists were successful. By the 1700's, dozens of European-looking towns dotted the Atlantic coast.

Yet even as the colonies came to look more and more European, the colonists were becoming less and less European. Many no longer thought of themselves as English, Dutch, or Swedish. Instead, they began thinking of themselves as Americans. As Americans, they had more opportunities and more freedom than most Europeans.

As You Read

In this chapter, you will find out how and why the colonists changed. You will also find out the reasons for those changes. The chapter is divided into four parts.

- In a Land of Opportunity
- The Growth of Education
- The Spread of Ideas
- Taking Part in Government

◀ *A portrait of an American family in the 1700's*

In a Land of Opportunity

The colonies offered Europeans many opportunities to improve their lives. Newcomers found endless acres of good land available at bargain prices. Also, there were many more jobs than workers to fill them. As a result, the colonists earned more money and lived better than most people in Europe did in the 1700's.

Many Jobs, Few Workers

Throughout the colonies, there was much work to be done and few people to do it. Many workers were needed to build farms, villages, and towns. The most important work was clearing land for farms. The colonists chopped down trees, pulled up bushes, and burned the underbrush. Day after day, they worked. Finally, they changed patches of dark forests into sunlit farm land.

As time passed, the colonists also built many villages and towns. Here too, many colonists also found jobs. Some were carpenters, printers, shipbuilders, or blacksmiths. Others worked in mills, inns, and the many different shops that sprang up in the colonies.

So many workers were needed that almost anyone could get a job in the colonies. Even a person with few skills could find many ways to earn a living. A writer in Virginia called

The woman working at a loom (left) is weaving yarn to make linen. What kind of work is the worker at the right doing?

On a colonial farm, everyone had to help with the work. What jobs are the members of this farm family doing?

that colony "the best poor man's country in the world" because it was so easy to find work there. The same was true of the other colonies.

Because there were so many jobs and so few workers, people in the colonies were well paid for their labor. For example, dockworkers in Boston were paid twice as much as those who loaded and unloaded ships in London, England. Many colonists were able to save some of their pay. Then they used their savings to buy land or to start a business.

Plenty of Land

In Europe, only a few rich families owned land. Land was so expensive in Europe that owning a farm was an impossible dream for most people. Families usually rented the fields

they farmed. In the colonies, however, almost everyone could afford to buy land. Prices were very low. Sometimes the owners of a colony even gave settlers land free.

Even people who came to the colonies as indentured servants had the chance to own land. Many were given a few acres when they finished their terms as indentured servants. Others began saving to buy land once they finished their terms.

The opportunity to own land brought many people to the colonies. Much of North America was settled by people eager to own their own land. Everywhere families worked to make that land prosper.

In the 1700's, a Frenchman who settled in New York bragged that his fellow colonists worked much harder than people in other places. What was the reason? "We have no princes for whom we toil, starve, and bleed," he wrote. "Here man is free as he ought to be." Most of his neighbors would have agreed. Throughout the colonies, people believed that their future was in their own hands. If they worked hard, there was no limit to what they could achieve.

To Help You Remember

1. Why were the colonists able to live better than most Europeans?
2. In Europe, only a few rich families owned land. Who owned land in the colonies?
3. Why were the colonists willing to work hard?

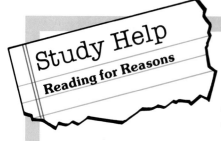

Study Help
Reading for Reasons

At the beginning of this chapter, you were asked to look for ways the colonists changed and the reasons for those changes. One way to do these things is to list each change and then look for reasons it happened. The *cause* is the reason *why* something happened.

Below are some changes and their causes described in the first section of the chapter. Copy the changes on a sheet of paper. Then next to each, write the letter of the reason that caused it to happen.

Changes	Causes
1. Colonists were willing to work harder than people in other places.	a. There were more jobs than people in the colonies.
2. The colonists were well paid for their labor.	b. There was plenty of land in the colonies.
3. Many people in the colonies were able to buy land.	c. The colonists were free to work for themselves.

As you read the rest of the chapter, continue to list ways the colonists changed. For each change, find at least one cause, or reason, it took place.

The Growth of Education

Americans believed in hard work. They also believed in education. Many saw it as a way of getting ahead in life. Parents also wanted their children to be able to read the Bible. As more and more children learned to read and write, schools in the colonies began to grow and change.

Learning to Read and Write

In Europe, most people did not have the chance to get an education in the 1700's. Only the rich could afford to send their children to school. In the colonies, however, even poor families were able to get some schooling for their children.

Kitchen Classrooms. The Puritans started the first schools in the English colonies. Classes met in the kitchen of one of the village families. Between household tasks, the woman of the house taught her own children and the children of her neighbors how to read and count. In colonial times, women were called dames. So these kitchen classrooms were known as **dame schools.**

The Start of Public Schools. Few children in dame schools learned much more than how to read the Bible and to count. Yet many people in New England wanted their children to know more than that. So in 1647, Massachusetts passed a law ordering all villages with at least 50 families to hire someone to teach reading and writing.

To support these schools, each family had to pay a **tax**. A tax is the money people must pay for government services. The money raised by this tax was used to build schools and to hire teachers.

The first public schools in the colonies were started in New England. Children learned to read and count at school.

Church Schools. There were few public schools in the Middle colonies or in the South. Some children in the Southern colonies studied at home with tutors. A tutor became part of the household. Many children in the Middle colonies went to church schools. The Quakers, for example, started many schools for children of their faith. So did members of other religious groups.

The church schools were private schools. They were not supported by taxes. So the parents of students at these schools had to pay a fee. Some families paid in goods or work instead of money. They paid in bushels of wheat, in hogs, or in shoes. A few parents worked several days each month at the school to pay for their children's schooling.

Fees for most church schools were so low that most families could afford to send their children to school for at least a few years. Some church schools even allowed children to attend free if their parents were too poor to pay the fee.

Getting a Higher Education

In colonial times, very few people went beyond grade school. Yet many colonists wanted their children to have every chance of getting ahead. So they began to build high schools and colleges.

The First High Schools. In the 1600's, high schools were called grammar or Latin schools. There boys were prepared for college. They studied Latin, Greek, mathematics, ancient history, and, of course, grammar. Girls were not allowed to go to college. So they did not attend these grammar schools.

The first grammar school in the colonies was the Boston Latin School. When it opened in 1635, it served the whole colony of Massachusetts. By the 1650's, every town in Massachusetts with more than 100 families had its own grammar school. By the 1700's, there were dozens of grammar schools in every colony.

Also by the 1700's, grammar schools were no longer just for boys interested in going to college. They taught many subjects that helped both boys and girls get good jobs. Students studied bookkeeping, geography, and languages used in trade, such as Spanish and French. There were even night schools for students who worked during the day.

Going to College. In colonial times, the main purpose of a college was to train ministers. So it is not surprising that the oldest colleges in the colonies were founded by religious groups.

The Puritans built Harvard, the first college in the English colonies.

This engraving shows how Harvard College looked nearly 100 years after it was founded in 1636.

It was founded in Cambridge, Massachusetts, in 1636, just six years after the first settlers arrived. The first college in the Southern colonies was founded in 1693. Named for the king and queen of England, it was called William and Mary College. It was located in Williamsburg, which was then the capital of Virginia.

There were no colleges in the Middle colonies until the 1750's. In 1754, King's College was built in New York City. Today it is known as Columbia University. In 1755, Benjamin Franklin started the College of Philadelphia in Pennsylvania. It later became the University of Pennsylvania.

To Help You Remember

1. Why was education important to the colonists?
2. (a) Who started the first schools in the English colonies? (b) How was money raised to build those schools?
3. In the Middle colonies, students went to church schools. How were the church schools different from public schools?
4. What did high schools teach in the 1600's and in the 1700's?
5. (a) Why were colleges started? (b) Name four and tell where each was founded.

157

The Spread of Ideas

As education grew in the colonies, so did interest in reading. Most families could afford only one or two books. In those days, most books had to be brought to the colonies from Europe. So they were very expensive.

Almost everyone owned a Bible, but few colonists could afford to buy other books. Yet many people could afford to buy a newspaper. They were eager to read about ideas and events. They wanted to know what was happening in the rest of the world.

Zenger reports on the outcome of his trial in the New York Weekly Journal.

THE

New-York Weekly JOURNAL

Containing the freshest Advices, Foreign, and Domestick.

MUNDAY August 18th, 1735.

To my Subscribers and Benefactors.

Gentlemen;

I Think my self in Duty bound to to make publick Acknowledgment for the many Favours received at your Hands, which I do in this Manner return you my hearty Thanks for. I very soon intend to print my Tryal at Length, that the World may see how unjust my Sufferings have been, so will only at this Time give this short Account of it.

On Munday the 4th Instant my Tryal for Printing Parts of my Journal No. 13. and 23. came on, in the Supreme Court of this Province, before the most numerous Auditory of People; I may with Justice say, that ever were seen in that Place at once; my Jury sworn were,

1 *Harmanus Rutgers,*
2 *Stanley Holms,*
3 *Edward Man,*
4 *John Bell,*
5 *Samuel Weaver,*
6 *Andrew Marschalk,*
7 *Egbert Van Borsen,*
8 *Thomas Hunt,*
9 *Benjamin Hildrith,*
10 *Abraham Kitcltass,*
11 *John Goelet,*
12 *Hercules Wendover,*

John Chambers, Esq; had been appointed the Term before by the Court as my Council, in the Place of *James Alexander* and *William Smith,* who were then silenced on my Account, and to Mr. *Chambers's* Assistance came *Andrew Hamilton,* Esq; of *Philadelphia* Barrester at Law; when Mr Attorney offered the Information and the Proofs, Mr. *Hamilton* told him, he would acknowledge my Printing and Publishing the Papers in the Information, and save him the Trouble of that Proof, and offered to prove the Facts of those Papers true, and had Witnesses ready to prove every Fact; he long insisted on the Liberty of Making Proof thereof, but was over-ruled therein. Mr. Attorney offered no Proofs of my Papers being *false, malicious* and *seditious,* as they were charged to be, but insisted that they were Lybels tho' true. There were many Arguments and Authorities on this point, and the Court were of Opinion with Mr. Attorney on that Head : But the Jury having taken the Information out with them, they returned in about Ten Minutes, and found me *Not Guilty*; upon which there were immediately three Hurra's of many Hundreds of People in the presence of the Court, before the Verdict was returned. The next Morning my Discharge was moved for and granted, and sufficient was

The Growth of Newspapers

In the 1600's, there were few newspapers in the colonies. Most contained little more than reports from Europe.

By the 1700's, however, every colony had at least one newspaper. Many colonies had several. Pennsylvania, for example, not only had a number of English newspapers but also had two German ones. These newspapers carried more than just news from Europe. They also told about life in the colonies.

Some newspapers criticized the actions of government officials. The idea that newspapers must be free to criticize as well as to praise government leaders was becoming more and more important to the colonists.

Freedom of the Press

Colonists won the right to print stories that criticized the government in 1735. At that time, the *New York Weekly Journal* carried several stories about the governor of that colony. He was accused of being dishonest in his dealings with the people of New York.

When the governor read the stories, he was furious. He ordered John Peter Zenger, the owner of the newspaper, thrown in jail. The governor then took away the right to practice law from two lawyers who had offered to defend Zenger. In their place, the governor chose a lawyer who supported him to defend Zenger. Things did not look good for the printer.

Then, on the day of the trial, Zenger learned that another lawyer had offered to defend him. He was Andrew Hamilton of Philadelphia. At the age of 80, Hamilton was the most respected lawyer in the colonies. One of the men who supported Zenger had made a trip to Philadelphia to ask Hamilton to defend Zenger.

Zenger had a **trial by jury.** In a trial by jury, a group of citizens hear a case presented in court. Together they examine the charges and decide which side is in the right.

After much talk, it was time for Hamilton to address the jury. He said the question before the court was more than whether Zenger had the right to criticize the governor. The real question was whether English people everywhere were free to speak and write what they believed. The jury quickly returned a verdict of not

Zenger was found not guilty. The verdict was a victory for freedom of the press.

guilty, and Zenger was set free.

The trial made it clear that colonists had the right to speak out against the government. It was a right the colonists guarded carefully.

To Help You Remember

1. Why were newspapers so popular in the colonies?
2. In what ways were the newspapers of the 1600's different from those in the 1700's?
3. (a) Why was John Peter Zenger put on trial? (b) What did his trial prove?
4. What is a trial by jury?

Taking Part in Government

News of the Zenger trial spread quickly throughout the colonies. It made people aware of the importance of free speech and a free press. Many colonists also believed that they had the right to take part in government. It was a right colonists won very early.

The Growth of Self-Government

When Jamestown was founded in 1607, settlers there had no say about how they were governed. The London Company made all the laws and chose the leaders of the colony. Then, in 1619, the company decided to let

America's first representative assembly met at the Virginia House of Burgesses.

the colonists take part in government. They were told to select people to make laws for the colony. This group of lawmakers was called the Virginia House of Burgesses.

In 1620, just one year after the House of Burgesses held its first meeting, the Pilgrims arrived in New England. Before they left their ship, they agreed on a plan of government. They called the plan the Mayflower Compact.

The Mayflower Compact was based on the idea that people ought to have a say in the way they are governed. It was not a new idea. People in England had been fighting for that right for many years. The colonists did not want to lose it just because they were living in North America. When the English rulers prepared charters for new colonies, they included in them the right of the colonists to take part in their own government.

A Challenge to Self-Government

In 1686, the king of England decided that the colonists had too much freedom. He decided to take away some of the rights promised in the charters, including the right to elect lawmakers. His first step was to send a new governor to New England with orders to destroy the charters of all of the colonies there.

Throughout New England, people protested. When the new governor arrived in Connecticut and demanded that colony's charter, members of the assembly tried for hours to change his mind. By then, it was so dark that candles had to be lighted in the hall.

Tired of all the speeches, the governor demanded that the charter be brought to him. Just as the metal box containing the document was placed on the table, the candles went out. When they were lighted again, the charter was gone.

One of the men in the room had carried the charter off. He hid it in the hollow trunk of a great oak tree. The tree which stood for about 100 years was known afterward as the Charter Oak.

Even though the new governor never got the charter, he declared that the colony would no longer be governed by it. People in Connecticut did not give up. Nor did other New Englanders. They waited, and they watched for just the right time to move against the governor. It came in 1689, when England got a new king. That year an armed mob in Boston forced the governor to return to England. Soon after, New Englanders once again had the right to take part in their governments.

This scene shows a Connecticut assemblyman hiding the colony's charter.

Colonial Governments

By the 1700's, all 13 English colonies were governed in much the same way. Each had a governor who was appointed by the king or queen. The governor made sure that the laws were obeyed. He also chose judges for the colony. The judges made sure that the laws were enforced fairly.

Each colony also had a **legislature** similar to the Virginia House of Burgesses. The legislature was the group of people who made laws for the colony. In most colonies, the legislature was divided into two parts, or houses. Members to the upper house

161

Although Mercy Otis Warren was a well-known writer, she could not vote.

were chosen by the governor. Members of the lower house were elected by the voters of the colonies.

Not everyone in the colonies had the right to vote. In most colonies, only men who owned a certain amount of land or goods could vote. In some colonies, a voter also had to belong to a certain church. For example, in Massachusetts, only members of the Puritan Church had the right to vote. In other colonies, such as Connecticut and Rhode Island, all adult men were allowed to vote.

Women were not allowed to vote anywhere, no matter what church they joined or how much property they owned. Americans, like Europeans, believed that women were not capable of taking part in government. A few women challenged that idea. In Virginia, for example, one woman fought for and won the right to vote as a property owner.

Americans took their rights very seriously. They were more than willing to fight to protect them. In the next chapter, you will see how the need to protect their rights drew Americans more closely together than ever before. You will also see how that need led to serious trouble with people in England.

To Help You Remember

1. (a) Who made the laws and chose the leaders for Jamestown in 1607? (b) What change took place in 1619?
2. On what idea was the Mayflower Compact based?
3. Why were the charters issued by the English rulers important to the colonists?
4. (a) What did the king of England do to challenge self-government in 1686? (b) How did the colonists react to his challenge?
5. How were the colonies governed in the 1700's?
6. Who had the right to vote in the colonies?

Chapter Review

Words to Know

Choose the answer which best completes each sentence.

1. A *heritage* is (a) jobs, (b) freedom of speech, (c) values, beliefs, and other parts of a culture passed from parent to child.
2. A *dame school* was a school where children learned (a) Latin and Greek, (b) reading and counting, (c) bookkeeping and geography.
3. A *tax* is (a) money people pay for government services, (b) money loaned to government, (c) money people save to buy land or to start a business.
4. In a *trial by jury*, a person accused of a crime is tried in court before (a) a judge, (b) a group of citizens, (c) the governor.
5. A *legislature* is a group of people who (a) see to it that laws are obeyed, (b) make sure that laws are enforced fairly, (c) make laws.

Reviewing Main Ideas

Complete each of the following sentences. They will help you to review the main ideas in the chapter. The page numbers will help you.

1. Because there were so many jobs and so few people, the colonists ____. (page 153)
2. Because land was plentiful in the colonies, ____. (page 153)
3. Colonists were willing to work hard because ____. (pages 153-154)
4. Most of the colonies had schools because ____. (page 155)
5. Because the colonists wanted to know what was happening in the world, they ____. (page 158)
6. Because of the Zenger trial, ____. (page 159)
7. Charters were important to colonists because ____. (page 160)
8. Because colonists took their rights seriously, they ____. (page 162)

In Your Own Words

In this chapter, you learned that the colonists fought hard for the things they believed in. Write a paragraph that tells *why* some colonists were willing to fight for free speech and a free press.

Challenge!

Many of the jobs people did in colonial times have almost disappeared today. Can you guess what a cooper did? What work did a chandler do? A blacksmith? Check your answers in a dictionary.

Things to Do

Find out more about colonial schools. Write a report comparing them to your school. How are they alike? Different?

9
Quarrels with England

By the middle of the 1700's, people had been living in England's colonies in North America for over 150 years. For most of that time, people in England paid little attention to events in North America. So the colonists were free to run their own affairs.

After 1763, however, things began to change. The English took a much greater interest in what was going on in North America. They quickly discovered that the colonists were not pleased by this new interest. The colonists wanted to do things their own way. They did not want outsiders telling them what to do. As a result, England and its North American colonies had one quarrel after another. In time, those quarrels led to war.

As You Read

As you read the chapter, look for events that caused quarrels between England and the colonies. Look too for changes that resulted from those quarrels. This chapter is divided into four parts.

- War Brings Changes
- One Quarrel Leads to Others
- The Colonies Drift toward War
- Fighting Begins

◀ *British soldiers on the Boston Common in 1768*

War Brings Changes

In the 1700's, England, or Great Britain as it is now known, claimed much of North America. British claims in North America stretched from the Atlantic Ocean to the Pacific. Much of that land was also claimed by France. The countries went to war over the claims.

Trouble with France

In 1754, more than a million and a half people lived in British colonies

This painting shows George Washington as a colonel in the Virginia militia.

in North America. These people could be called on to protect Great Britain's claims to land there. However, there were only about 100,000 people in all of New France. So the French, to protect their claims, built a chain of forts along the St. Lawrence, Mississippi, and Ohio rivers.

British colonists had already begun to settle in the Ohio Valley. So they were especially alarmed by new French forts there. Feelings ran particularly high in Virginia because that colony claimed most of the land along the Ohio River.

The governor of Virginia decided to give the French a choice. They could either leave the Ohio Valley or risk a war. He chose a 21-year-old Virginian named George Washington to deliver the message.

After eight days of hiking through miles of woodland, Washington reached the commander of the French troops in the Ohio Valley in October 1753. The meeting was a polite one. Still the French general made it clear that he would not leave the valley.

The governor of Virginia responded by sending a group of soldiers under the command of George Washington to the Ohio Valley in June 1754. Their orders were to build a fort where the Allegheny and Monongahela rivers met. The soldiers were at work when French troops arrived. The battle that followed marked the start of a war that lasted seven years. The British called it the French and Indian War because they fought not only the French but also Indian groups that helped France.

Peace with France

Together colonial soldiers and British troops won the war. In 1763, Great Britain and France signed a peace **treaty.** A treaty is a formal agreement between countries stating the terms upon which fighting ends.

In the treaty, France agreed to give up its claims to land in North America. Great Britain took control of all the land east of the Mississippi River as well the area known today as Canada. A few months earlier, the French had secretly given Spain their lands west of the Mississippi and the city of New Orleans. The land was France's way of rewarding Spain for siding with the French in their war against Great Britain.

Trouble with the Indians

The terms of the peace treaty pleased many British colonists. With the French no longer a threat to their

The maps show changes in land claims in North America. Which country gained the most land in 1763? Which lost the most? What countries were left with large areas of land in North America?

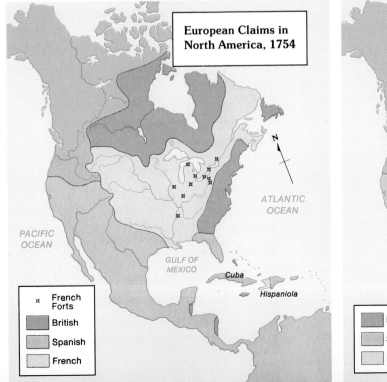

safety, many colonists looked forward to moving west of the Appalachian Mountains. Some had already moved there. However, they were not prepared for the reaction of the Indians who lived in the Ohio Valley.

Many groups of Indians lived west of the Appalachian Mountains. Some had been living in the Ohio Valley for hundreds of years. It was their homeland, and they had no intention of letting the colonists take it away

Find the proclamation line. What land was set aside for the Indians? What land was set aside for the colonists?

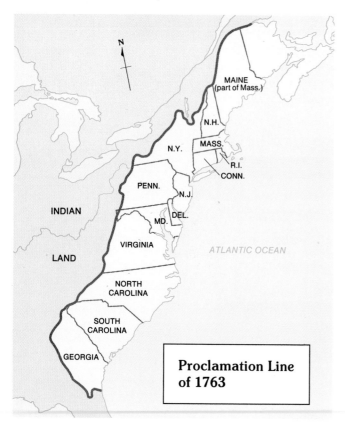

Proclamation Line of 1763

from them. Other groups of Indians had once lived along the Atlantic coast. As more colonists settled in North America, those Indians were pushed into the Ohio Valley. They did not want to move again.

Fearful and angry, the Indians decided to make a stand. In 1763, more than 40 different groups banded together under a leader named Pontiac. Together, they attacked one British settlement after another.

British soldiers stepped in to protect the colonists. Facing heavy British gunfire, the Indians were forced to end the fighting for a while.

Peace with the Indians

The British knew that the Indians would attack again unless their lands were protected. So in 1763 King George III issued a **proclamation,** or an order.

The Proclamation of 1763, as the king's order was known, set aside for the Indians all the land west of the line shown on the map. Colonists were no longer allowed to settle there. Those already living in the valley were ordered to leave.

Many colonists refused to go. In the end, they were forced to move out by British soldiers who burned the settlers' cabins. Even though the strong-willed colonists fought back, they were no match for the British army.

To Help You Remember

1. Why was it more difficult for the French to protect their claims to land in North American than for the British?
2. How did the French try to protect New France?
3. What caused the French and Indian War?
4. What is a peace treaty?
5. What lands did Great Britain gain in the war?
6. Why did Indian groups band together to attack the British colonists in the Ohio Valley?
7. (a) What was the Proclamation of 1763? (b) What effect did it have on the colonists?

Study Help
Putting Things in Order

In the first section of this chapter, you learned that several important events took place in 1754 and in 1763. One way to keep track of key events is to remember *when* the events happened.

Below is a list of key events taken from the first section of the chapter. Look back in the text to find out *when* each took place. The page numbers listed next to the events tell you where to look in the text. Then, on a separate sheet of paper, put the events in the order in which they occurred.

1. Groups of Indians attack British settlements in the Ohio Valley. (page 168)
2. The French and Indian War begins. (pages 166-167)
3. George Washington is sent to talk to the French soldiers in the Ohio Valley. (page 166)
4. A treaty is signed ending the French and Indian War. (page 167)
5. King George III issues a proclamation. (page 168)

In the next two parts of this chapter, you will find several more key dates. As you read, make a list of those dates and tell why each was important.

One Quarrel Leads to Others

With so much unrest in the colonies, the British government decided to keep an army in North America. The soldiers were to keep the peace with the Indians in the Ohio Valley. The soldiers would also protect colonists from the Spanish to the south.

During the French and Indian War, the British government had taxed people in Britain to pay the soldiers. The government decided the colonists should pay the cost of keeping soldiers in North America.

Parliament, Britain's legislature, decided to raise the money in two ways. First, they would make the colonists obey the old tax laws. These earlier laws had taxed goods the colonists bought or sold. Second, they planned to pass a new tax law. The new law would require that colonists buy special stamps.

Disagreements over Taxes

When the colonists heard about Parliament's plans for a new tax, they united as they never had before. In many colonies, angry citizens forced tax collectors out of town. Everywhere people wrote letters of protest to members of Parliament. These letters pointed out that the American colonists were not represented in Parliament. Therefore, Parliament had no right to tax the colonists. Only colonial legislatures had that right.

The British disagreed. They argued that Parliament represented everyone in the British colonies, even those who could not vote. Neither side was willing to give in.

In spite of the protests, Parliament passed a Stamp Act in 1765. According to the Stamp Act, the colonists had to buy stamps and place them on everything from marriage licenses to calendars. The list of papers that had to have stamps was nearly six pages long.

To protest England's Stamp Act, angry colonists burned the hated stamps.

People throughout the colonies were angry. Among those who spoke out against the Stamp Act was a rough frontier lawyer named Patrick Henry. He was the youngest member of the Virginia House of Burgesses.

In May 1765, Patrick Henry addressed the House of Burgesses. He argued that never before had Virginians been taxed without the agreement of their elected lawmakers. Clearly then, anyone who told the colonists to obey the Stamp Act was an enemy of **liberty,** or freedom. He ended his speech by saying. "If this be treason, make the most of it. Give me liberty or give me death."

Many of the people who gathered to hear the speech were shocked by Henry's fiery words. Others stood in silent thought. Among them was a young college student who would later become an important leader in the struggle with Great Britain. His name was Thomas Jefferson.

Patrick Henry gave his most famous speech against the Stamp Act.

Organizing for Protest

People in every colony voiced anger. Sam Adams, one of the leaders in Boston, decided the colonists would be more effective if they worked as a group.

Secret Clubs. In 1765, Adams started a chain of secret clubs in the colonies. Members were known as the Sons of Liberty. They worked together to fight the new taxes. Women started a group called the Daughters

These are examples of stamps the colonists were required to use.

The Daughters of Liberty were among those who protested the Stamp Act.

of Liberty. They too vowed to fight the Stamp Act.

Sam Adams united colonists in another way. He formed Committees of Correspondence. Members exchanged information through letters. The letters let people know what was happening in other colonies.

A Stamp Act Congress. In 1765, just a month before the Stamp Act was to go into effect, **representatives,** or delegates, from nine colonies met to protest the new law. The meeting was known as the Stamp Act Congress.

For the first time, colonists were acting together as a group.

At the meeting, the representatives promised that their colonies would not trade with Great Britain until the tax was removed. They sent a formal request or **petition,** to the British. In it, they argued that as English people they could not be taxed without the agreement of their elected representatives. The cry of "no taxation without representation" was heard throughout the colonies.

An End to the Stamp Act. These protests finally convinced Parliament that people in the colonies would never accept the Stamp Act. So in 1766, they **repealed,** or did away with, the law. Colonists celebrated with bonfires and parades. Many believed the colonies' quarrels with Great Britain were finally over.

To Help You Remember

1. (a) Why did Great Britain decide to keep soldiers in North America? (b) How did Parliament plan to raise money to pay the soldiers? (c) How did the colonists react to Parliament's plans?
2. (a) What was the Stamp Act? (b) List three ways the colonists organized to protest the Stamp Act. (c) What effect did these protests have on Parliament?

The Colonies Drift toward War

The colonists' joy over the end of the Stamp Act did not last very long. Parliament still believed that it had the right to tax colonists. The colonists, of course, disagreed. Before long, quarrels between Parliament and the colonists broke out again.

Trouble over Taxes

In 1767, Parliament voted to tax all tea, glass, paint, and lead sold in the colonies. When the news reached North America, people there were outraged. This time, so many colonists **boycotted,** or stopped buying, the taxed goods that merchants and manufacturers in Great Britain began to lose money. In the end, it was they who persuaded Parliament to do away with the new taxes.

In 1770, Parliament got rid of all the taxes except for the one on tea. Parliament left the tax on tea to show the colonists that it still had the right to tax them.

Violence in Boston

On the very day Parliament did away with most of the taxes, there was trouble in Boston. For months, feelings against the British had been running high in the city. Much of that anger was directed against British soldiers stationed in Boston. On the night of March 5, 1770, that anger led to bloodshed.

The streets of Boston were white with newly-fallen snow. A soldier stood guard in front of the place where the taxes were collected. A group of townspeople gathered around him. Some shouted and jeered at the soldier. A few threw snowballs, rocks, and ice. Frightened, the soldier called for help.

Study Paul Revere's print of what became known as the Boston Massacre. How does it differ from the account in your text?

In an act known as the Boston Tea Party, colonists dumped tea into Boston Harbor.

As other soldiers rushed to the scene, so too did more townspeople. In the confusion, shots rang out. Five people died. Six were wounded.

Fearing the violence would spread, the governor talked to the crowd. He promised that if the soldiers were guilty of a **massacre,** as some of the colonists said, they would be punished. A massacre is the killing of people who have no way of defending themselves.

John Adams was one of three lawyers who agreed to defend the soldiers. Like his cousin Sam Adams, John had taken part in many protests against the British. Why then did he defend the soldiers? He believed that everyone should have the right to a fair trial. To Adams, it was a right as important as the right to vote or to speak freely. He made a strong case in favor of the soldiers. In the end, the jury found all but two of the soldiers not guilty.

Trouble over Tea

For the next few years, the colonies were calm. Americans once again traded with Great Britain. They bought everything except for the taxed tea.

When the colonists stopped buying tea, British merchants lost money. They appealed to Parliament for help. Parliament promptly came up with a plan to tempt the colonists into buying British tea again. In May 1773, Parliament passed a law making the price of tea so low that even with the tax it was far cheaper than the tea the colonists had been buying from the Netherlands. Parliament believed this would tempt the colonists into buying British tea again.

Parliament was wrong. In every colony, there were protests. Ships loaded with tea were not even allowed to dock at some ports.

In Boston, the ships were allowed to enter the harbor. However, on the night of December 16, 1773, a group of colonists dressed like Indians rushed to the place where the ships were docked. They boarded the ships and dumped more than 300 chests of tea into the ocean. Colonists called this action the Boston Tea Party.

Parliament Takes Action

When news of the Boston Tea Party reached London, members of Parliament were furious. They decided to punish the people of Boston. They closed Boston Harbor to all trade until the colonists paid for the tea. In addition, Parliament made the head of the British army in the colonies governor of Massachusetts.

Committees of Correspondence throughout Massachusetts wrote letters to other colonies. Before long, food and money poured into Boston.

Protests over the tax on tea also continued. In october 1775, in Edenton, North Carolina, nearly 50 women from 5 counties signed a promise to boycott English tea.

To Help You Remember

1. (a) What new taxes were placed on the colonists in 1767?   (b) How did the colonists react to the new taxes?   (c) How were British merchants affected?
2. What happened in Boston in 1770 to anger the colonists further?
3. (a) How did Parliament try to get the colonists to buy British tea?   (b) What was the reaction of the colonists?   (c) How did Parliament react to the colonists?

Fighting Begins

News of events in Massachusetts spread quickly. Many wondered if their colony would be next to suffer from Great Britain's **tyranny,** or unjust use of power. George Washington wrote to a friend saying that all of the colonies must stand together. If they did not, he feared, each colony would fall alone. Many shared that fear. As a result, the colonies once again organized a meeting known as the First Continental Congress.

A Meeting in Philadelphia

On September 5, 1774, representatives from every colony except Georgia gathered in Philadelphia. Among those who attended this First Continental Congress were Patrick Henry, Benjamin Franklin, George Washington, Sam Adams, and his cousin John Adams.

The meeting was called not just to protest the way Massachusetts had been treated. The group also wanted to find a way of avoiding a war with Britain. After much discussion, the group sent their complaints to the king. They also agreed to meet in May. However, in April the first shots were fired in the war known as the American Revolution. A **revolution** is a great change. The American Revolution would bring very great changes to North America.

The Battles of Lexington and Concord

Few colonists wanted a war with Britain, but many believed it was only a question of time before the fighting would begin. So farmers and townspeople in every colony trained for battle. They called themselves **minutemen** because they could be ready to fight at a moment's notice.

As the minutemen prepared for war, so too did the British. General

This cartoon urges the colonies to unite. What do the letters stand for?

Thomas Gage, the new governor of Massachusetts, decided to capture two leaders of the Sons of Liberty—John Hancock and Sam Adams. The two men were believed to be in Lexington, a village about 20 miles (32 kilometers) northwest of Boston. After taking Hancock and Adams prisoners, the soldiers were supposed to go on to nearby Concord. They had orders to find and destroy the guns and gunpowder the minutemen had hidden there.

A Midnight Ride. On the night of April 18, 1775, about 700 British soldiers moved toward Lexington. The Sons of Liberty, having learned of the general's plan, wanted to make sure it failed. Paul Revere and William Dawes were chosen to ride by different routes to Lexington and Concord to warn people of the danger.

Throughout the night, Revere and Dawes rode through the colony. Along the way, they stopped at every village and farm to let people know that the British were coming.

A Meeting at Dawn. When the redcoats, as the British soldiers were called, arrived at the Lexington village green, a group of colonists were waiting for them. The colonists were armed with muskets.

John Parker, the leader of the minutemen, told his men to hold their

This painting shows the fighting at the Battle of Lexington. Who appears to be winning the battle?

ground but to allow the British to pass. "Don't fire," he warned, "unless fired upon; but if they mean to have war, let it begin here." The British too were under orders not to shoot. Someone opened fire. To this day, no one knows who it was. When the smoke finally cleared on Lexington green, eight minutemen were dead and ten were wounded.

The battle at Lexington gave Hancock and Adams time to get away. So the British soldiers marched directly to Concord. There they destroyed the weapons the colonists had not been able to move to a safe place. Then the soldiers headed back to Boston. Hundreds of minutemen waited for them along the road. Hiding behind stone fences, barns, and farmhouses, they fired at the British soldiers. Many soldiers were killed or wounded.

Fighting Spreads

By the time the news of the fighting at Lexington and Concord reached the other colonies, it was May. The Second Continental Congress was meeting in Philadelphia. The representatives to that Congress had to try to find a way of dealing with the growing violence. Yet even as they talked about the problem, the fighting spread.

A group of soldiers from Vermont known as the Green Mountain Boys attacked Fort Ticonderoga, near Lake Champlain, in New York. After capturing that fort, they took two other British forts in Canada.

More fighting also took place in Massachusetts. After the battles of Lexington and Concord, minutemen from every part of the colony poured into Boston. They had come to fight the British.

In what section of the colonies did the early battles take place? Find the Battle of Bunker Hill on the map.

The Americans decided to make their stand on Bunker Hill just outside Boston. Knowing that the British were watching the hill carefully, the Americans changed their plans at the last minute. Instead of setting up their guns on Bunker Hill, they put them on nearby Breed's Hill.

When the British realized what had happened, they attacked. On June 17, 1775, line after line of redcoats marched straight up the hill. Again and again the colonists drove the British back. Then the Americans ran out of gunpowder. So in the end, they were forced to give up the hill. The British had won the Battle of Bunker Hill, but it was a costly victory. They lost over 225 men.

Preparing for Battle

Even before the Battle of Bunker Hill, the Second Continental Congress had decided it was time to set up a colonial army. The man chosen to lead that army was George Washington, the most respected soldier in the colonies.

On July 3, 1775, two weeks after the Battle of Bunker Hill, Washington arrived in Cambridge, Massachusetts, near Boston. For the next few months, he tried to turn a group of volunteers into an army.

Americans were going to need that army in the months ahead. While

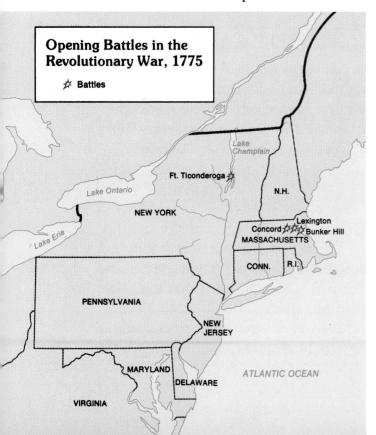

Opening Battles in the Revolutionary War, 1775

✗ Battles

Lake Champlain

Ft. Ticonderoga

Lake Ontario

N.H.

NEW YORK

Lake Erie

Lexington
Concord Bunker Hill
MASSACHUSETTS

CONN.   R.I.

PENNSYLVANIA

NEW JERSEY

MARYLAND
DELAWARE

ATLANTIC OCEAN

VIRGINIA

Although called the Battle of Bunker Hill, the battle was actually fought on Breed's Hill. This painting of the battle is thought to have been done by an eyewitness.

some hoped to patch up differences, more and more people were talking about becoming **independent.** To be independent means to be free to rule oneself. Everyone knew that the British would fight hard to keep their American colonies. Therefore, a declaration of independence would mean a long difficult war against the most powerful country in the world.

To Help You Remember

1. (a) Why did representatives from the colonies meet in Philadelphia? (b) What did they decide to do at that meeting?

2. What did the colonists do to get ready for war?

3. (a) How did the British plan to stop the minutemen? (b) What did the Sons of Liberty do to warn the minutemen?

4. (a) Why did General Gage send soldiers to Lexington and Concord? (b) What happened in Lexington? (c) What happened to Gage's soldiers when they left Concord?

5. (a) Where did the fighting spread to after the battles of Lexington and Concord? (b) How did the Second Continental Congress react to the fighting?

Chapter Review

Words to Know

Match each term with its definition.

a. proclamation
b. repeal
c. representative
d. independent
e. minuteman
f. revolution
g. treaty
h. liberty
i. massacre
j. petition
k. tyranny

_____ 1. an order issued by a ruler
_____ 2. a colonist ready to fight at a moment's notice
_____ 3. the killing of people who cannot defend themselves
_____ 4. free to rule oneself
_____ 5. freedom
_____ 6. a very great change
_____ 7. a formal request made to a government
_____ 8. unjust rule
_____ 9. an agreement made between countries
_____10. a delegate
_____11. to do away with a law

Reviewing Main Ideas

Tell why each date was important.

1. 1754 (pages 166–167)
2. 1763 (pages 167–168)
3. 1765 (pages 170–172)
4. 1766 (page 172)
5. 1767 (pages 173–174)
6. 1770 (pages 173–174)
7. 1773 (pages 174–175)
8. 1775 (pages 176–178)

In Your Own Words

Write a paragraph explaining how one of the quarrels listed below brought the British and the colonists closer to war.

1. the quarrel over taxes
2. the quarrel over the Ohio Valley
3. the quarrel over tea

Challenge!

The cartoon shown here is a political cartoon. It expresses an opinion, or point of view. Study the cartoon and then answer the questions.

1. What law does the cartoon describe?
2. How does the cartoonist feel about that law?
3. (a) What does a skull and crossbones stand for? (b) What does it stand for in this cartoon?

Draw your own political cartoon. It might show the Boston Tea Party from a British point of view. Or it might urge the colonists to unite against the British.

Keeping Skills Sharp

When British soldiers reached Lexington green in the early morning hours of April 19, 1775, they were met by a band of minutemen. Paul Revere and William Dawes had ridden all night to warn the colonists that the British were coming.

The map below shows the routes taken by Revere, Dawes, and the British. Use the legend on the map to answer the following questions:

1. (a) Where did Paul Revere begin his famous ride?   (b) Where did it end?

2. How far did Paul Revere ride? Use the scale to figure out the distance he traveled.

3. (a) Where did William Dawes begin his ride?   (b) Where did it end?

4. What distance did William Dawes' route cover?

5. What body of water did William Dawes have to cross?

6. (a) What body of water did Paul Revere cross at the beginning of his ride?   (b) Who else crossed the same body of water?

7. Who traveled the farther west?

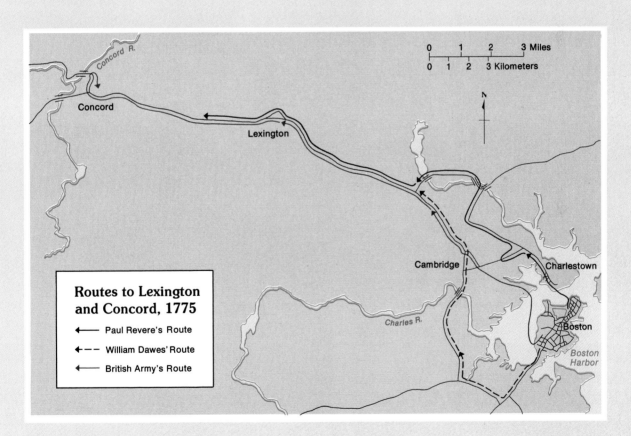

Routes to Lexington and Concord, 1775

◄—— Paul Revere's Route

◄– – William Dawes' Route

◄—— British Army's Route

181

10

The Fight for Independence

In June of 1776, the colonies decided to declare their independence. A group of colonists prepared a document telling the world exactly why they were breaking away from Great Britain. Most of the work was done by Thomas Jefferson, a young lawyer from Virginia.

In the Declaration of Independence, Jefferson expressed two important ideas. One was that all people are created equal. They have the right to life, liberty, and the pursuit of, or search for, happiness. The second idea was that when a government fails to protect those rights, the people have a duty to change that government.

On July 4, 1776, the Continental Congress approved the Declaration of Independence. The colonies now had to fight a war, the American Revolution, to win their independence.

As You Read

As you read this chapter, look for reasons 13 small, poorly-equipped states were able to defeat one of the strongest countries in the world. The chapter is divided into four parts.

- The Will to Win
- Fighting in the North
- The War Spreads South and West
- The End of the War

◄*The signing of the Declaration of Independence*

The Will to Win

At the time independence was declared, Americans were divided over the war. About one third of the colonists were **Loyalists.** They supported Great Britain. Many of these Americans even fought in the British army. Other Loyalists moved to Canada or England during the fighting.

Another third were what John Adams called Halfway men and women. They did not really care which side won. Yet as the war continued, many of these Americans took sides and joined the fighting.

The rest of the people in the newly-independent states were **Patriots.** They were determined to fight for their freedom. It was the Patriots who won the fight for independence.

The Patriots

The Patriots were shopkeepers and farmers, artisans and dockworkers. They included the richest people in the colonies and the poorest. They were Protestants, Catholics, and Jews. In their numbers were free people and slaves, men and women.

The Role of Black Americans. In every colony, black Americans were

Caught spying, Nathan Hale (left) was sentenced to death by the British. Deborah Sampson (center) brings a message to General Washington. Peter Salem (right) fought at the Battle of Bunker Hill.

denied the rights most other Americans enjoyed. Most blacks were slaves. Yet even those who were free could not vote or hold office in any colony. Still, many blacks became Patriots. They took part in every protest and battle. A runaway slave named Crispus Attucks was among those who died in the Boston Massacre. One of the heroes of the Battle of Bunker Hill was a free black named Peter Salem.

At first, Washington refused to let blacks serve in the army. Many people were afraid to give guns to their slaves. So blacks did other jobs. They built sandbank defenses, repaired roads, and cared for the sick. Many also served as guides or carried messages for the army. Later in the war, blacks were once again allowed to fight. Over 5,000 signed up.

The Role of Women. Women too were not supposed to fight. Yet a few managed to find a way. Perhaps the most famous of these women was Deborah Sampson. Disguised as a man, she fought in the war for over a year. Then she was wounded. The doctor who treated her was shocked to find that the soldier was a woman.

Other women cooked and cared for the wounded. Still others carried messages and served as spies. Many made weapons or sewed clothing for the soldiers.

Refusing to Give In. Women were not the only Americans who did things they had never done before. Shopkeepers and lawyers learned to fire cannons. Farmers and dockworkers mounted guns on the decks of ships. Yet no matter how difficult things became, and they became very difficult, most Patriots refused to give in. Many showed great courage.

Among those brave Americans was a young Connecticut man named Nathan Hale. When George Washington needed a spy, Hale volunteered. Dressed as a teacher, he visited several British army camps. As he was returning with the information he had gathered about the British, a Loyalist recognized him. Hale was promptly arrested by the British and sentenced to hang. His last words were, "I only regret that I have but one life to lose for my country." Many Patriots felt as Hale did.

Supplying the Troops

The Patriots knew they had a tough job ahead of them. British soldiers were well trained and well equipped. By 1778, Great Britain had over 50,000 British soldiers in North America. In addition, Parliament had hired 30,000 German soldiers. They too would fight on American battlefields. Besides its large army, Great Britain also had a huge navy.

The Patriots, on the other hand, had an army made of volunteers who served for only six months at a time. They had little if any training. Many expected to go home as soon as a battle was over.

At the beginning of the war, the Patriots had no navy. However, they did have a few trading ships that had been armed for war. These ships were called **privateers.** They were used to hunt down British ships. It was dangerous work but very necessary.

The Patriots had very few cannons, guns, or other equipment. The Continental Congress did not have the money to buy more. All of its money came from the state governments. The Continental Congress did not have the power to tax Americans directly. Only the states had that power, and they were short of money. So the Patriots looked to their supporters for help.

Many farmers shared their crops with the soldiers. The townspeople housed and fed as many troops as they could. They built weapons and made gunpowder and cannonballs too. Some Americans also raised money for the army. Still other Americans helped the war effort by sharing what they knew of the land. They acted as guides, showing soldiers

These are some of the uniforms worn by soldiers and sailors during the American Revolution.

| German Soldier | British Soldier | American Soldier | American Sailor | American Rifleman | American Soldier |

shortcuts, places for campgrounds, and good hiding places.

To Help You Remember

1. Describe the different feelings of Americans toward the revolution at the time the colonies declared their independence.
2. (a) What roles did black Americans play before the war began? (b) How did those roles change during the war?
3. What roles did women have in the American Revolution?
4. (a) Who was Nathan Hale? (b) How did he help the Patriots?
5. (a) What advantages did the British have early in the war? (b) From what country did the British hire soldiers?
6. (a) Who fought in the Patriots' army? (b) How did the Patriots get money and supplies to fight the revolution?

Fighting in the North

In March of 1776, the British decided to change generals. General William Howe replaced General Gage as head of the British army in North America. It proved to be a good change from the Patriots' point of view.

Howe was often slow to act. In New England, the Patriots were helped by Howe's failure to move quickly. Washington was even able to force British troops out of Massachusetts. The war then shifted to New York, Pennsylvania, and New Jersey.

The Struggle for New York

In June of 1776, just before the Declaration of Independence was signed, General Howe landed in New York City with a large army. Washington rushed to defend the city. His men fought bravely, yet they were driven off by Howe's army.

By the end of 1776, the Patriots were in trouble. They had not only lost New York City but also two forts on the Hudson River. Both had been filled with guns and other war supplies. When British soldiers captured several thousand cattle, the Patriots suffered still another loss. The animals had been herded all the way from Pennsylvania to feed Washington's army.

Badly beaten, the Patriots headed south for safety. After crossing the Delaware River, they camped in Pennsylvania. The British did not chase after them. Instead, General Howe divided his army and settled them in several towns in northern New Jersey.

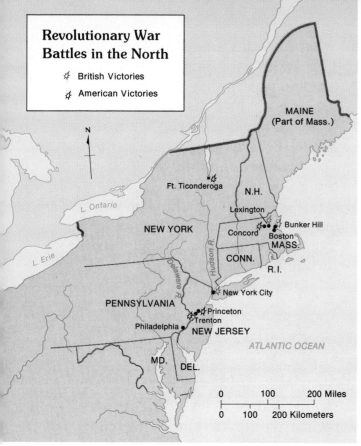

MAINE
(Part of Mass.)

N

Ft. Ticonderoga

N.H.

L. Ontario

Lexington

NEW YORK

Bunker Hill

Concord

Boston
MASS.

L. Erie

CONN.

R.I.

Hudson R.

Delaware R.

New York City

PENNSYLVANIA

Princeton
Trenton

Philadelphia

NEW JERSEY

ATLANTIC OCEAN

MD.

DEL.

0   100   200 Miles
0   100   200 Kilometers

Which of the battles shown on the map were won by the British? Which were won by the Americans?

The Struggle for New Jersey

When winter came, Washington's troubles grew. Many of his soldiers would soon be going home. They had signed up for only a few months. If they were going to fight at all, Washington had to act quickly. He decided to attack a group of German soldiers stationed in Trenton, New Jersey.

On Christmas night, 2,400 American soldiers ferried across the icy Delaware River to New Jersey. They were joined by local farmers who supported the Patriots. The group made its way to Trenton along nine miles (14 kilometers) of rough roads.

Just outside Trenton, the American forces divided into two. Then both sides closed in together. The Germans were completely surprised. Many were still sleeping soundly after their Christmas celebration. Dazed by the sudden attack, they quickly surrendered.

When the news reached Lord Cornwallis, a British general stationed in New York, he quickly marched toward Trenton. He was determined to wipe out Washington's army.

At the same time, Washington made plans for his army. All through the night, the fires in the Patriot camp blazed brightly. When Cornwallis and his men arrived there early the next morning, the fires were still burning. However, the soldiers were gone. During the night, Washington and his army had silently slipped away.

Before long, the British heard the sound of distant cannon fire. It was coming from nearby Princeton. Washington's army was attacking British soldiers stationed there. Cornwallis rushed to the scene, but he was too late. Fearful of being cut off from his supplies, he returned to New York.

This famous painting shows George Washington and his troops crossing the icy Delaware River Christmas night, 1776.

Help for the Patriots

The Patriots had finally begun to prove themselves. Their victories in New Jersey convinced more and more people to help them. By spring, the army had over 9,000 soldiers.

By March 1777, the Americans were secretly getting help from France, Spain, and the Netherlands. These countries sent thousands of guns and other supplies to the Patriots. For example, Bernardo de Gálvez (Gäl bäth), the governor of Spanish Louisiana, sent supplies up the Mississippi River. He also attacked British ports along the Gulf of Mexico.

Many Europeans were also eager to help the Americans. Among them was the Marquis de Lafayette (mär kēz′ də laf′i et′). He became one of Washington's most trusted advisors.

A Turning Point in the War

Even before the American victory at Trenton, British generals were planning their next move. Their plan called for three armies. The main one, under General John Burgoyne, would fight its way south from Canada along the Hudson River. Another army, under Colonel Barry St. Leger, would push east from Oswego through the Mohawk Valley. A third army, under General Howe, would press north from New York City.

The three armies would meet near Albany. There they would wipe out the Patriots in New York and cut off New England from other colonies.

Luckily for the Patriots, the plan failed. It failed in part because General Howe never reached the Hudson Valley. He had decided to capture Philadelphia first. It was the richest city in the colonies and the place where the Continental Congress met. Howe captured Philadelphia, but the fighting there kept his soldiers from joining Burgoyne's army.

In the meantime, Burgoyne's army was marching toward Saratoga. As Burgoyne's army moved south, the Patriots prepared to fight. Nearly 15,000 soldiers gathered near Saratoga. The Americans set up their battle lines along a narrow pass that was protected by a thick forest on one side and the Hudson River on the other. The Patriots fought the British to a standstill.

Faced with heavy losses, Burgoyne decided to return to Canada. Yet before he could move his army, Patriot soldiers blocked his path. Burgoyne had no choice but to surrender. On October 17, 1777, over 5,000 British laid down their guns.

The Battle of Saratoga was a turning point in the war. It was the greatest American victory up to that time. When news of the British defeat finally reached Paris, no one was more delighted than Benjamin Franklin. He had been sent to Paris to get help from France. He was not having much luck until the French government heard about Saratoga. Only then did France decide to enter the war openly on the Patriots' side.

A Winter at Valley Forge

While talks were still going on in Paris, Washington's army was building its winter camp at Valley Forge. Washington had chosen the campsite. From the wooded hill, he could observe the British in Philadelphia, 20 miles (32 kilometers) away. The location had few other advantages.

People in much of the surrounding area supported the British. Even those who did not favor Great Britain in the war refused to sell food to the Americans. These farmers feared that they might not ever be paid. So American soldiers went hungry.

Not only did the soldiers have little food, but also many were without coats or shoes. In the quick moves between battles, the army had lost many supplies. So the 2,898 Americans stationed at Valley Forge spent the winter wrapped in dirty rags.

Washington's hungry, ragged army spent a difficult winter at Valley Forge in Pennsylvania.

Many soldiers became sick and died. Yet somehow Washington managed to keep his army together through this terrible time.

Then, late in the winter, help came from Europe. A German soldier named Baron von Steuben (stü′bən) came to Valley Forge to help the Americans. He planned to teach them everything he knew about warfare.

Day after day Baron von Steuben drilled the Americans. They learned to fight the way Europeans did. By spring, the ragged American army was becoming a hard-hitting fighting force.

To Help You Remember

1. How did the change in British generals from Gage to Howe help the Patriots?
2. What were the results of the struggle for New York?
3. (a) How did the Patriots capture New Jersey? (b) Why was the victory important?
4. Why was the Battle of Saratoga a turning point in the war?
5. Why was the winter at Valley Forge so difficult for the Patriots?
6. How did Baron von Steuben help the Patriots?

The British plan to cut the colonies in two and capture New York failed at Saratoga. The plan failed because the three British armies never reached Albany. The Battle of Saratoga was an important victory for the Patriots. It was also a heavy blow to the British.

One way to see why the British plan failed is to look at a map of the battle. Use the map below to answer the following questions.

1. General Burgoyne led the main British army. (a) Where did the soldiers set out from? (b) In what direction did they travel? (c) They never reached Albany. Why not?
2. (a) Where did Colonel St. Leger and his men set out from? (b) In what direction did they travel? (c) They never reached Albany. Why not?
3. (a) Where did General Howe and his army set out from? (b) In what direction did they travel? (c) They never reached Albany. Why not?

The Battle of Saratoga, 1777

General Howe's Route
Colonel St. Leger's Route
General Burgoyne's Route

The War Spreads South and West

Even as Washington and his men were fighting in the North, battles were also taking place in other parts of the country. Many of these battles were fought in the South and the West. Others took place at sea.

The War in the West

Throughout the West, British soldiers stirred up the Indians against the American settlers. Washington's army was too far away to help the settlers. So Virginia sent soldiers to protect the Americans. In those days, Kentucky was part of Virginia.

The soldiers were led by a young Virginian who lived in Kentucky. His name was George Rogers Clark. To force the British out, Clark would have to capture British forts throughout the West. He began by attacking the one at Kaskaskia on the Mississippi River.

In the spring of 1778, Clark arrived in Kaskaskia with about 200 soldiers. The group hid in the woods until dark. Then they surrounded the fort. As they crept closer and closer to the fort, they heard music and laughter. The British were having a party. Clark walked boldly into the hall and

George Rogers Clark (right) captured Vincennes and Kaskaskia, two British supply forts. Find Vincennes and Kaskaskia on the map. Near what river is each fort?

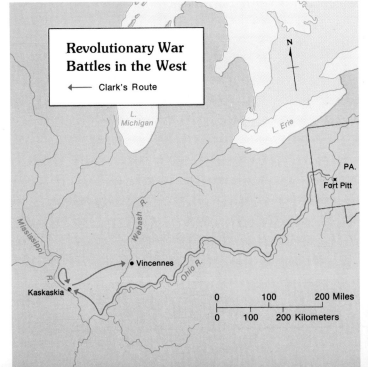

announced, "Go on with your dance. But remember that henceforth you dance under the American flag." Without firing a shot, Clark had taken over the fort.

After the capture of Kaskaskia, Clark headed for Vincennes on the Wabash River. There too he won an easy victory. The British made several attempts to recapture the two forts, but Clark was able to hold them. His victories gave Americans control of much of the land east of the Mississippi.

The War at Sea

Several important battles were also fought at sea. At the beginning of the war, the colonists used privateers to stop British supply ships. Then, as time passed, the Patriots built a navy. They even found enough money to pay for several warships.

The commander of one of those warships became a hero overnight. His name was John Paul Jones. A skilled seaman, he came to the colonies from Scotland at the beginning of the revolution to help Americans win their freedom.

In 1779, Jones took command of the ship *Bonhomme Richard*. It was neither swift nor strong, but Jones and his brave crew made up for its shortcomings.

On September 23, 1779, Jones and his men overtook the British warship *Serapis* off the northwest coast of England. The 44 guns on board the *Serapis* tore into the American ship. Within a few minutes, the deck was

This painting shows the battle between the British ship Serapis *(left) and the American ship* Bonhomme Richard *(right).*

in flames. The captain of the *Serapis*, sure of victory, asked the Americans to surrender. Jones replied, "No! I have not yet begun to fight."

After three hours of hard fighting, a Patriot threw a grenade onto the British ship. By chance, it landed on loose gunpowder. There was an explosion. When the air cleared, the battle was over. The Americans had won after all.

The War in the South

By 1779, the war had already lasted for four years. The Americans had lost more battles than they had won, and yet they refused to give up.

Hoping to end the war, the British generals decided to try yet another plan. This time they chose to move the fighting to the South. Many Loyalists lived there. The British hoped to get help from them.

For a time, the British plan seemed to work. By 1780, they had captured Savannah, the capital of Georgia, and much of the surrounding countryside. The Americans, even with the help of the French, were unable to retake the city.

Early in 1780, the British gathered around Charles Town, South Carolina. It was the most important port in the South. Things went badly for the Americans. British ships broke through Patriot defenses around the

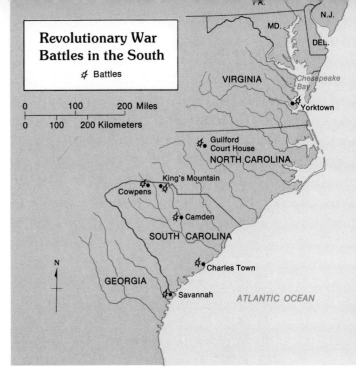

Where were battles fought in North Carolina? Where were battles fought in South Carolina? In Georgia?

harbor. Then British guns began to pound the city. The Americans were defeated. The fall of Charles Town was a heavy blow to the Patriots.

To Help You Remember

1. (a) Why were soldiers sent to protect the Americans in the West? (b) Why were Clark's victories there important?
2. (a) How did John Paul Jones help the patriots? (b) What did he say when asked to surrender?
3. (a) Why did the British decide to move the fighting south? (b) Who won the major battles there?

The End of the War

By 1780, the British had overrun the South. Many now believed that Great Britain would soon defeat the Americans and win the war.

Still, Americans refused to give up. In the Southern colonies, bands of Patriots hounded the British. These bands would attack a group of soldiers and then escape into nearby woods or swamps. They were gone before the British knew what had happened. The most famous of these bands was the one led by Francis Marion, a colonel in South Carolina's army.

A New Patriot Plan

In 1780, Washington sent his best general, Nathaniel Greene, to take charge of the American forces in the South. Greene gathered together the scattered Patriot soldiers in the South. Then he made plans to attack the British army.

Greene trained his soldiers to fight in much the same way Marion's men fought. Greene's soldiers learned to hit and then run. In this way, Greene hoped to force the British to follow his retreating soldiers.

The plan worked. As the British chased after the Americans, the British moved farther and farther from their supply bases. When the British realized what Greene was doing, they moved back to the coast. However, in doing so, they left most of Georgia and the Carolinas in American hands.

Yorktown: The Last Battle

In 1781, General Cornwallis had become the head of all British troops in North America. That August, he decided to set up his army on the banks of the York River near Yorktown, Virginia. The men built sandbanks and ditches. These were built to protect the camp from an inland attack. Cornwallis counted on British warships in the Chesapeake Bay to guard the side of the camp by the river.

Even as Cornwallis was preparing for battle at Yorktown, French troops were on their way to the colonies. An army of 8,000 French soldiers joined the American army in New York.

The two armies then marched to Yorktown. They arrived in Virginia before Cornwallis even knew they had left New York. On October 13, 1781, they attacked. The battle of Yorktown had begun. Musket balls streamed through the air. Bombs burst. The American flag fluttered in the dusty wind of battle as the people of Yorktown ran from their homes.

While the American and French soldiers fought on land, a fleet of

This famous painting shows General Benjamin Lincoln (on horseback) accepting the surrender of the British at Yorktown.

French warships entered Chesapeake Bay. The fleet kept the British navy from helping Cornwallis.

After six days of fighting, on October 20, 1781, Cornwallis surrendered to the Americans. Thousands of British soldiers silently laid down their guns. The Patriots had won the war.

Making Peace

From New Hampshire to Georgia, the news spread quickly. The British army had finally been defeated. Bells rang out, cannons roared, and people danced in the streets. The Continental Congress met at dawn to hear Washington's report of the victory. Members of Congress then went to a nearby church to give thanks to God.

Soon after, peace talks began in Paris. A treaty was finally signed on September 3, 1783. In it, Britain recognized the colonies as "free and independent states," to be known as the United States of America.

To Help You Remember

1. How did General Greene win Georgia and Carolina?
2. (a) What was the last battle of the war? (b) How was it won?
3. (a) In what year was the peace treaty signed in Paris? (b) What did the treaty state?

Chapter Review

Words to Know

1. Look up the word *patriot* in a dictionary. Why were the Patriots well named?
2. Look up the word *loyal*. Why were the Loyalists well named?
3. What is a *privateer*?

Reviewing Main Ideas

For each topic below, list at least two facts that add to or describe the topic. The page numbers tell you where to look in the chapter.

1. The Way the War Divided Americans (page 184)
2. The Role of Black Americans in the War (pages 184–185)
3. The Role of Women in the War (page 185)
4. Ways the Patriots Supplied the Troops (pages 185–187)
5. Fighting in the North (pages 187–191)
6. Fighting in the West (pages 193–194)
7. The War at Sea (pages 194–195)
8. Fighting the South (page 195)
9. The End of the War (pages 196–197)

In Your Own Words

Write a paragraph about one of the topics under Reviewing Main Ideas. Write a topic sentence that tells the main idea of the paragraph. Then write a sentence for each fact on your list. Organize your sentences into a paragraph. Be sure the order makes sense.

Challenge!

The words below are from the Declaration of Independence. They explain the ideas upon which our government is based. Read the words carefully and then answer the questions. Look up the meaning of any word that is unfamiliar to you.

We hold these truths to be self-evident: that all men are created equal; that they are endowed by their Creator with certain inalienable rights; that among these are life, liberty, and the pursuit of happiness . . .

1. A self-evident truth is one that is obvious to everyone. The Declaration lists a number of obvious truths. What is the first of these truths? Why do you think it was placed first?
2. An inalienable right is one that no one has the right to take away. What rights are inalienable?

The Declaration goes on to say.

to secure these rights governments are instituted among men, deriving their just powers from the consent of the governed . . .

3. (a) Why do people form governments? (b) Where do governments get their power?
4. Do you think the word *men* means men only or all people? Why?

Unit Review

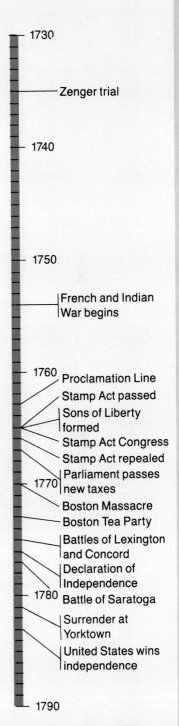

Take Another Look

Use the time line on this page to put the following events in the order in which they occurred. Tell why each was important. The page numbers tell you where to look in the text.

a. Start of Virginia House of Burgesses (page 160)
b. Declaration of Independence (page 183)
c. Boston Tea Party (pages 174–175)
d. Mayflower Compact (page 160)
e. Beginning of French and Indian War (pages 166–167)
f. Proclamation of 1763 (page 168)
g. Stamp Act (page 170)
h. Boston Massacre (pages 173–174)
i. Zenger Trial (pages 158–159)
j. Battles of Lexington and Concord (pages 176–177)

You and the Past

1. Soon after the signing of the Declaration of Independence, the Continental Congress began to look for symbols for the new nation. The first symbol chosen was a flag. On June 14, 1777, Congress voted on the design for that flag. It was to be red, white, and blue. The red on the flag was to stand for courage and bravery, the white for purity, and the blue for truth and loyalty. Why are these colors good symbols for a nation? What do the 13 stripes stand for? What does each star on the flag mean? Use an encyclopedia to find out our country's flag code—the rules for displaying and honoring the flag. Then make a poster showing how the flag is to be treated.

2. Some symbols of the United States have become important because they are connected with great events in the nation's history. One of those symbols is the Liberty Bell in Philadelphia. It announced the first reading of the Declaration of Independence. It rang out on the day a peace treaty was signed with Britain. Find out more about the Liberty Bell. On what other happy occasions did the bell ring out? On what sad occasions has the bell tolled? How was the bell cracked?

Timeline:
- 1730
- Zenger trial
- 1740
- 1750
- French and Indian War begins
- 1760
- Proclamation Line
- Stamp Act passed
- Sons of Liberty formed
- Stamp Act Congress
- Stamp Act repealed
- Parliament passes new taxes
- 1770
- Boston Massacre
- Boston Tea Party
- Battles of Lexington and Concord
- Declaration of Independence
- 1780
- Battle of Saratoga
- Surrender at Yorktown
- United States wins independence
- 1790

Washington receiving naval salute after his inauguration

Unit Four

The United States: A New Nation

April 30, 1789, George Washington became the first president of the United States. Over the next 25 years, the new nation would face many challenges. Each challenge helped the nation grow stronger.

11

Forming New Governments

In 1783, two years after the Revolution had ended, Americans finally heard the news they had waited so long for. At a special meeting in Paris, France, Great Britain gave up all rights to its 13 colonies in North America. The colonies were now truly independent states.

During the war, each state had set up its own government. The states had also joined together to form a nation, the United States of America. The United States was a **republic.** A republic is a government that is not headed by a king or queen. It is a government in which the right to rule comes from the people.

In 1783, most countries were ruled by kings or queens. For that reason, many Americans wondered whether their republic would be a success. During the war, the states had often quarreled. Now that the war was over, many wondered whether the states would remain united.

As You Read

In this chapter, you will learn more about the first governments Americans formed. As you read, look for ways Americans tried to keep those governments strong enough to protect their freedom. The chapter is divided into three parts.

- First Governments
- Planning a Stronger Government
- Under the New Government

◀ *Washington on Inauguration Day*

First Governments

Even while Americans were fighting for their freedom, they were also organizing governments. Americans tried to learn from the past in planning these governments.

State Governments

By 1776, ten states had working governments. The other three completed theirs by 1780. In every state people

Most of the states divided government into three branches.

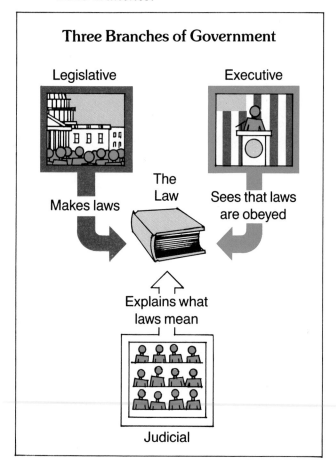

Three Branches of Government

Legislative

Makes laws

Executive

Sees that laws are obeyed

The Law

Explains what laws mean

Judicial

demanded written **constitutions.** A constitution is a plan for a government. It tells exactly what the government can and cannot do.

Three Branches of Government. Most state constitutions divided the work of government into three parts, or branches. Each branch had a special job. The job of the **legislative branch** was to make the laws. The people who served in the legislature were called representatives. They represented, or spoke for, the people who elected them.

The governor was the head of the **executive branch.** His job was to make sure that laws were obeyed.

The job of the **judicial branch** was to explain the meaning of laws in court. This branch of government was made up of judges who ensured **justice,** or fairness.

By dividing the work of the government among three groups, no branch could become too powerful. Still many Americans were worried about giving any power at all to the governor. They remembered what had happened to their rights under British governors.

Some people also worried that their lawmakers might become too powerful. Therefore, most states divided their legislatures into two parts. They called these parts houses. Neither house of the legislature could pass a law on its own. Members of both houses had to agree on all laws.

A Bill of Rights. Most state constitutions also had a **bill of rights.** A bill of rights is a list of the freedoms and liberties Americans were most eager to protect. Among them was the right to a trial by jury. This right is one that English people had had for many years. Americans did not want to lose this right.

Other rights, like freedom of religion and freedom of speech, were rights that Americans had come to value in their new land. Now they wanted their governments to protect these rights too.

Not Everyone Votes

The state constitutions gave more Americans the right to take part in government than people had in any other country at that time. Yet even in the United States, many people did not have the right to vote.

The Rights of Women. Not one of the state constitutions gave women a voice in government. Most people believed that protecting property was the main purpose of government. Most states only gave men who owned property or paid taxes the vote.

Abigail Adams wanted the new governments to protect women's rights.

At that time, most women did not own property. When a woman married, all her possessions became the property of her husband. As a result, very few women owned a business, a farm, or even a house. That was the law. Only a few people at that time thought it should be changed. Abigail Adams of Massachusetts was one of them. She often spoke out against the law and argued for women's rights.

Abigail Adams was married to John Adams. During the war he served in the Continental Congress. Since he was away from home for months at a time, Abigail ran the family farm. She was a very good businesswoman and the family farm made a good profit. Yet if John had wanted to, he could have kept all the money she made. He could also have sold the farm without even telling her. By law, the farm belonged to him.

In 1776, Abigail Adams wrote a letter to her husband. He was in Philadelphia at the time working on the Declaration of Independence. In the letter, she said, "If particular care and attention are not paid to the ladies, we will not hold ourselves bound to obey any laws in which we have no voice or representation."

Abigail Adams was not worried about herself. She had a husband who valued her ideas. However, many women were not as lucky. Nearly 100 years would pass before married women were allowed to own land. It would take another 50 years before women won the right to vote.

In Pennsylvania, Reverend Absalom Jones tried to win blacks the right to vote.

The Rights of Black Americans. Black Americans also wanted a say in government. Yet they were denied the right to vote in every state. Even blacks who owned property could not vote.

Many of the new constitutions did give black Americans their freedom from slavery, however. Vermont was the first to do so. Before long, slavery was also ended in Pennsylvania, Massachusetts, New York, New Jersey, Connecticut, and Rhode Island.

Many slave owners in other states decided on their own to free their slaves. Between 1782 and 1790, more than 10,000 slaves were freed in Virginia alone. At the same time, nearly every state stopped the slave trade.

The new state constitutions were not perfect. Still they gave Americans a greater voice in government than people had anywhere else.

The First National Government

While each state worked out its constitution, members of the Second Continental Congress worked out a plan for a national government. They called it the Articles of Confederation. It was finished in 1777. Copies were sent to the states for approval. By 1779, the plan was accepted by 12 states. Maryland did not approve it until March 1, 1781. On that day the Articles of Confederation went into effect.

The articles set up a **federal system** of government. In a federal system, power is divided between the national government and the state governments. However, the articles granted most of the power to the states. The national, or federal, government had very little power. It was run by Congress. Each state had one vote in Congress. Nine states had to vote in favor of a law before it could be passed.

Congress did not even have the power to tax Americans. Instead, it had to ask the states for money. Many were slow to pay. So Congress could not ever count on having enough money to pay for army supplies or to pay the soldiers' salaries.

Congress was weak in other ways too. It had no say over trade. Each state could tax goods from other states and many did. These taxes caused many conflicts between the states, but Congress was unable to do anything about them.

The Nation's Money Troubles

Taxes often led to bitter arguments because people had little cash. Much of the nation's wealth had been drained by the war. Many merchants had been forced out of business when the fighting cut off overseas trade.

Each of the original 13 states printed its own money.

Farmers and traders suffered too. Many were never paid for the goods they supplied to the army. State and national governments were even slow to pay their troops. Many soldiers never received pay for their service during the war.

To pay off their debts, some states printed their own money. Many people refused to accept it. They said it was not worth the paper it was printed on. Lawmakers in other states refused to pay their war debts. In still others, like Massachusetts, they taxed landowners to raise money. Those taxes were very high. Many people were forced to sell their land in order to pay the government the taxes they owed.

Hundreds of farmers in western Massachusetts protested. When the state ignored their cries for a change in the tax laws, they decided to fight. They were led by Daniel Shays, an army captain during the war.

Throughout the fall of 1786, the farmers tried to keep the courts from taking land away from those people who could not pay their taxes. That winter, they even marched on Springfield, a town in western Massachusetts where guns were stored. The governor sent troops to stop the farmers.

The uprising alarmed people throughout the country, even though no blood was shed. Massachusetts had asked for help from Congress, but Congress did not have the power to help. Many Americans were outraged. Was the national government so weak that angry people could just take over? More and more people now believed it was time to strengthen the national government.

To Help You Remember

1. Why did many Americans want written constitutions?
2. How did state constitutions divide the work of government?
3. (a) What is a bill of rights? (b) List three rights it protected.
4. According to the new constitutions, who had the right to vote?
5. How is power divided in a federal system of government?
6. (a) What was the new national constitution called? (b) How did it divide power? (c) Who had the most power?
7. Why were there bitter arguments in many states over taxes?

Planning a Stronger Government

Early in May of 1787, Congress asked each state to send delegates to a meeting in Philadelphia. The purpose of the meeting was to change the Articles of Confederation so that the national government had more power. People came to Philadelphia from every state except Rhode Island. Rhode Islanders did not want a stronger national government.

A Meeting in Philadelphia

The meeting, which became known as the Constitutional Convention, was set for May 25, a rainy Friday. Fifty-five men from twelve states came. Nearly all had taken a leading role in the fight for independence. Twenty-eight had served in Congress. Most of the rest were members of state legislatures.

Washington was president of the Constitutional Convention. He and other delegates worked out the new plan of government.

The meeting began with much agreement. Everyone thought that George Washington should be president of the convention. The delegates also agreed that what was said should be kept secret. They wanted to be able to talk freely.

We only know what happened at the convention because James Madison and a few other delegates kept notes that were later published. At the time, even the people of Philadelphia did not know what was taking place. Guards stood at the doors. They made sure that only members of the convention entered the building. The windows around the big hall were tightly closed so that no one outside could hear what was going on inside.

Working Out the Plan

Soon after the convention started, the delegates decided to do away with the Articles of Confederation and write a new constitution. After much debate, the new government began to take shape. Like the state governments, the national government would be divided into three branches. Each would have separate duties and powers.

A **president** and a **vice-president** would take charge of the executive branch. The vice-president would head the government in the president's absence. The judicial branch was to be headed by the **Supreme Court** made up of **justices,** or judges. **Congress** would make laws for the nation.

Making Compromises. Then the arguments began. How many votes should each state have in Congress? The smaller states wanted every state to have the same number of representatives in Congress. The larger states argued that the number of votes a state had should be based on the number of people living there.

After much debate, members of the convention reached a **compromise.** A compromise is an agreement in which both sides give up certain things in order to get something they both value more. This compromise divided Congress into the **Senate** and the **House of Representatives.**

In the Senate, every state was to have two **senators** no matter how many people lived there. This pleased people from New Jersey,

This engraving shows people celebrating the ratification of the Constitution.

Connecticut, and other small states. However, in the House of Representatives, the number of **representatives** would be based on the number of people living in a state. This pleased people who lived in large states like Virginia and New York.

The compromise over how many votes a state could have in Congress was only one of many compromises the delegates made. Some men wanted a strong national government. Others did not like that idea. Members argued each point.

Finally, on September 17, 1787, the Constitution was finished. Few members were completely happy with their work. Many believed the new Constitution was far more practical than the old Articles of Confederation. The delegates had even provided a good way of changing, or **amending,** the document. Under the articles every state had to agree to a change. Now an **amendment,** or change, went into effect as soon as two thirds of the states approved it.

The delegates had done a far better job than they had dreamed. In the past 200 years, the Constitution has been changed only 26 times. Yet none of those amendments has changed the basic plan of government.

Getting the Constitution Approved.
After the delegates signed the Constitution, they took copies of it back to

their states. Each state had to approve, or **ratify,** the document. It would become the law of the land as soon as nine states had approved it. Yet if the country was to remain united, the support of all 13 states was needed.

In many states, the debates were as bitter and heated as those at the convention itself. Much of the fighting arose because the Constitution did not have a bill of rights. When the writers of the Constitution agreed to add one, state after state voted yes.

By November of 1788, Rhode Island was the only state that had not yet approved the Constitution. It did not do so until 1790. Then it was clear that the 13 states would remain united. In 1791, the first ten amendments, the Bill of Rights, were added to the Constitution.

To Help You Remember

1. Why did the Constitutional Convention meet in Philadelphia?
2. (a) Under the new Constitution, who headed the executive branch? (b) The judicial branch? (c) The legislative branch?
3. Explain the compromise that determined how many votes each state would have in Congress.
4. What did some states want added to the Constitution?

The Bill of Rights

1. **Basic Freedoms**
   People have a right to freedom of religion, speech, and press. They also have the right to have meetings and to ask the government to make changes.
2. **Right to Bear Arms**
   People have the right to have weapons to protect themselves.
3. **Quartering Troops**
   People do not have to quarter (give food or shelter to) soldiers in peacetime.
4. **Search and Arrest**
   No person, home, or property can be searched without an order from a court. People cannot be arrested without being told why.
5. **Rights of the Accused**
   People accused of a crime are safe from unfair trials and unjust punishments.
6. **Protection in Criminal Trials**
   People accused of a crime have the right to a speedy trial by jury.
7. **Right to Trial by Jury**
   In cases involving more than $20, people have the right to a jury trial.
8. **Bails, Fines, and Punishments**
   People are protected from cruel and unusual punishments.
9. **Other Rights**
   People have more rights than those listed in the Constitution.
10. **Rights of the States and the People**
    All rights not given to the federal government by the Constitution belong to the states or to the people.

The Bill of Rights protected people's basic rights and freedoms.

The new government of the United States was divided into three branches. Americans did not want any one of those branches to become too powerful. So they made sure that each branch would have a way of checking the power of the other two branches. That is, each branch could keep the other branches from acting too quickly or becoming too powerful. We call this system **checks and balances.** The diagram below can help you understand how the system works.

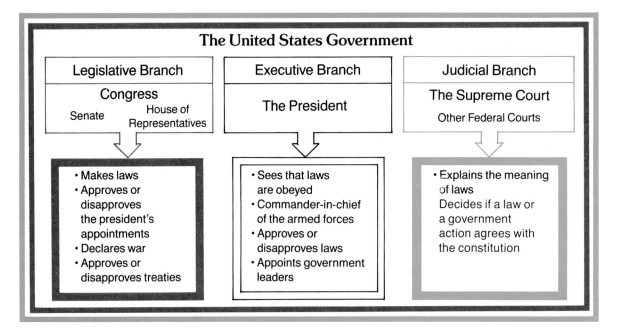

The United States Government

Legislative Branch	Executive Branch	Judicial Branch
Congress Senate House of Representatives	**The President**	**The Supreme Court** Other Federal Courts
• Makes laws • Approves or disapproves the president's appointments • Declares war • Approves or disapproves treaties	• Sees that laws are obeyed • Commander-in-chief of the armed forces • Approves or disapproves laws • Appoints government leaders	• Explains the meaning of laws Decides if a law or a government action agrees with the constitution

1. (a) Congress makes the laws. How does the president check that power? (b) How does the Supreme Court?
2. The president is commander in chief of the armed forces. How can Congress check that power?
3. Judges are not elected. They are appointed. (a) Who appoints them? (b) Who must approve the appointment of judges?
4. (a) The president enforces the nation's laws. Who sees to it that the president enforces those laws fairly? (b) How does that check the power of the president?

Under the New Government

As the world watched, Americans organized a new government. Many wondered if that government would work. Could people with so many different interests unite under one government? The early years would tell.

Getting Started

Under the Constitution, voters in every state chose people called **electors** to decide who the nation's president would be. There was little doubt in anyone's mind who should have the honor. The electors quickly agreed. They chose George Washington as the first president of the United States. John Adams received the second largest number of votes. He became the first vice-president.

Taking Office.   April 30, 1789, was the country's first **inauguration** day. On that day in New York City, which was then the nation's capital, George Washington took the oath of office. It is the same oath that every president since has spoken.

Americans cheered Washington's inauguration. They felt good knowing that he was in charge. Yet Washington was fearful of his ability to run the country. "Integrity and firmness are all I can promise," he wrote a friend. In the end, they proved to be what was needed.

Martha Washington stands on a platform at an inaugural reception in her honor. Find George Washington in the painting.

Members of President Washington's (far right) first Cabinet were (from left) Randolph, Knox, Hamilton, and Jefferson.

Advising the President. The Constitution said that President Washington could choose people to help him run the country. For that reason, Washington selected four men to serve as his advisors. They made up what came to be called the president's **Cabinet.**

Each member of the Cabinet is the secretary, or head, of a department in the federal government. Thomas Jefferson was secretary of state. The Department of State handles the country's dealings with other nations. Henry Knox was named secretary of war. Knox had been in charge of the army since the war ended. Washington appointed Edmund Randolph of Virginia attorney general. His job was to serve as the nation's lawyer.

Alexander Hamilton was the first secretary of the treasury. The Department of the Treasury handles the nation's money. It collects taxes and pays bills. Hamilton had been a member of the Constitutional Convention. There he had argued for a strong, national government.

The New Government at Work

The first problem facing the president was the nation's growing debt. Somehow those debts had to be paid. The government set up under the Articles of Confederation had not been able to solve the problem.

Hamilton's Money Plan. Alexander Hamilton studied the problem and then came up with a plan to pay off not only the nation's debt but also the debts of the states. The government would tax a variety of goods.

Jefferson and Madison did not like the plan. They were from Virginia. Virginia had paid off most of its debts. People there did not want to be taxed to pay other states' debts.

The Start of Political Parties. The disagreements over Hamilton's money plan led to the rise of **political parties.** A political party is a group of people who have similar ideas about how the government should be run. These people then join together

Since 1782, the bald eagle has appeared on the Great Seal of the United States.

to elect other people who will carry out those ideas. The supporters of Hamilton called themselves Federalists. Jefferson's supporters were known as Democratic-Republicans.

Raising Money. The members of Congress accepted Hamilton's plan. They agreed to place a tax on a number of goods, including whiskey.

The tax on whiskey brought trouble. Many farmers along the frontier made their corn into whiskey, which they sold. It was easier to get whiskey to markets in the East than wagonloads of corn. In some places, whiskey was even used in place of money. Many frontier farmers were angry about the tax.

In 1794, a group of farmers in western Pennsylvania banded together and attacked the tax collectors. This event was called the Whiskey Rebellion. It was the first test of the new government, and Hamilton was eager to meet the challenge.

With Washington's approval, Hamilton led a group of soldiers into Pennsylvania. When the farmers heard that the secretary of the treasury was coming to enforce the law, they put down their guns. The Whiskey Rebellion was over. The government had shown it was strong enough to enforce its laws.

During its first years, the new government had been tested and had met the challenge. The nation was off to a good start.

To Help You Remember

1. What does an elector do?
2. What is an inauguration?
3. What did members of the first Cabinet do?
4. (a) What was the first problem facing President Washington?
   (b) How did Alexander Hamilton want to solve the problem?
   (c) How did his solution lead to the growth of political parties?
5. (a) What caused the Whiskey Rebellion? (b) How did Hamilton put down the rebellion? (c) How did his actions strengthen the power of the government?

Chapter Review

Words to Know

1. How is power divided in a *federal system?*
2. What does a *bill of rights* protect?
3. What is a *compromise?*
4. What do people do when they *ratify* an agreement?
5. What is the president's *Cabinet?*
6. Explain the difference between the *legislative branch*, the *executive branch*, and the *judicial branch*.
7. What is a *political party?*
8. (a) What two groups make up *Congress?* (b) What are members of each group called?
9. How does the *vice-president* help the *president?*
10. (a) When people *amend* the Constitution, what are they doing? (b) What is an *amendment?*
11. (a) What is *justice?* (b) What government official is known as a *justice?* (c) What is that official's connection to the *Supreme Court?*
12. What is a *constitution?*
13. What does a system of *checks and balances* check and balance?
14. How do *electors* help bring about an *inauguration?*

Reviewing Main Ideas

Give at least one reason for each of the following events.

1. States divide the work of government into three parts. (page 204)
2. Farmers in western Massachusetts rebel. (page 207)
3. States send delegates to a meeting in Philadelphia. (page 208)
4. Delegates divide Congress into two lawmaking groups. (page 210)
5. States refuse to approve the Constitution until a bill of rights is added. (page 211)

In Your Own Words

Choose one event from *Reviewing Main Ideas* and write a paragraph about it. Explain the *causes*, or reasons, the event took place and one *outcome*, or result, of the event. The model below will help you. It describes an event not included in *Reviewing Main Ideas*. The event is the Whiskey Rebellion.

When Congress tried to raise money by putting a tax on whiskey, it ran into trouble with farmers along the frontier. Many of these farmers made whiskey from their corn and then sold it for profit. Some people used whiskey as money. For these reasons, they attacked the tax collectors in what has been called the Whiskey Rebellion. That rebellion resulted in Hamilton's leading troops into western Pennsylvania. When the farmers saw that the new federal government was going to enforce its laws, the farmers backed down. As a result, the rebellion ended peacefully.

Keeping Skills Sharp

The Constitution set up a system for passing laws. The diagram shows how the system works. Study the diagram carefully. (Note: A law that has not yet been passed is called a bill.)

1. After someone in Congress suggests a new law, what happens to the idea?
2. After the House of Representatives approves a bill, where does the bill go?
3. What happens if the House and Senate do not agree on a bill?
4. When does the president get the bill?
5. What happens if the president rejects the bill?
6. What happens if the president signs the bill?

Challenge!

Look carefully at the diagram. Why do you think the people who wrote the Constitution made it so difficult for a bill to become a law?

Find out how a bill becomes a law in your state. How is it like the system set up in the Constitution? What are the main differences?

Things to Do

1. The day the president takes office is called Inauguration Day. Use the library to find out how it is celebrated today. Then compare it to the way it was celebrated in Washington's time.
2. Find out how a representative or Senator takes office. What oath does each take? How are these oaths like the one presidents take? How do they differ?

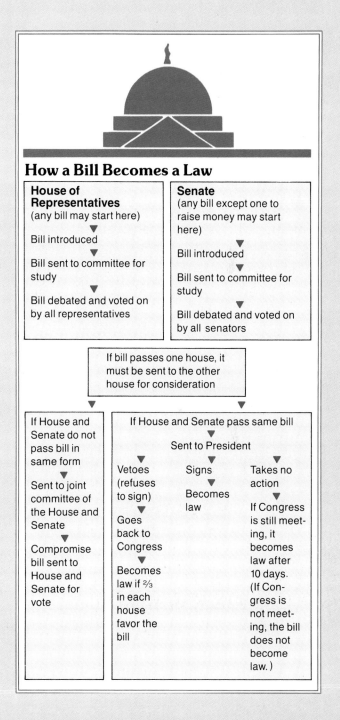

How a Bill Becomes a Law

House of Representatives
(any bill may start here)
▼
Bill introduced
▼
Bill sent to committee for study
▼
Bill debated and voted on by all representatives

Senate
(any bill except one to raise money may start here)
▼
Bill introduced
▼
Bill sent to committee for study
▼
Bill debated and voted on by all senators

If bill passes one house, it must be sent to the other house for consideration

If House and Senate do not pass bill in same form
▼
Sent to joint committee of the House and Senate
▼
Compromise bill sent to House and Senate for vote

If House and Senate pass same bill
▼
Sent to President
▼

Vetoes (refuses to sign)
▼
Goes back to Congress
▼
Becomes law if ⅔ in each house favor the bill

Signs
▼
Becomes law

Takes no action
▼
If Congress is still meeting, it becomes law after 10 days. (If Congress is not meeting, the bill does not become law.)

12

The Nation Grows Stronger

In 1790, Americans decided to build a capital for the nation. Maryland and Virginia each gave up some of their land so that the city would belong to all the people of the United States. It would not be a part of any state.

Americans named their capital Washington after the first president. They also gave him the honor of choosing an architect to design the city. The architect promised to build a capital "magnificent enough to grace a great nation." It would have many parks and broad avenues. Work on the city began almost immediately, but it took many years to complete.

When the government finally moved to Washington, D.C., ten years later, the city was little more than a swampy village. It takes time for a city to grow. It takes even longer for a nation to grow. In 1800, Americans were just beginning to build their nation.

As You Read

This chapter is divided into four parts. In each, look for signs that the nation was beginning to prosper and grow.

- Opportunities across the Oceans
- Opportunities at Home
- Moving West
- Protecting the Nation

◄ *The Capitol, in Washington, D.C., in the early 1800's*

Opportunities across the Oceans

In colonial times, Americans were supposed to do business only with Great Britain. However, after the Revolution, Americans were free to trade with any country in the world. American merchants sent ships to all parts of the world in search of new **markets,** or places to sell American products. Seaports from Boston, Massachusetts, to Charleston, South Carolina, bustled with activity.

Trading with China

In 1784, the first American trading ship reached China. Many Americans were eager to buy silk, tea, and other Chinese goods. At first, the Chinese had little interest in buying American goods. So merchants began to look for products that would appeal to the Chinese.

The first product American merchants found that the Chinese wanted was ginseng. Ginseng is a root the Chinese used as a medicine. It was hard to find in China, but it grew wild in New England. Then, in 1787, a sea captain named Robert Gray left Boston on a trading voyage that would take him around the world. On the trip, he discovered

How did ships from the United States reach the west coast of North America? Where did they stop next? What country was their last stop before heading home?

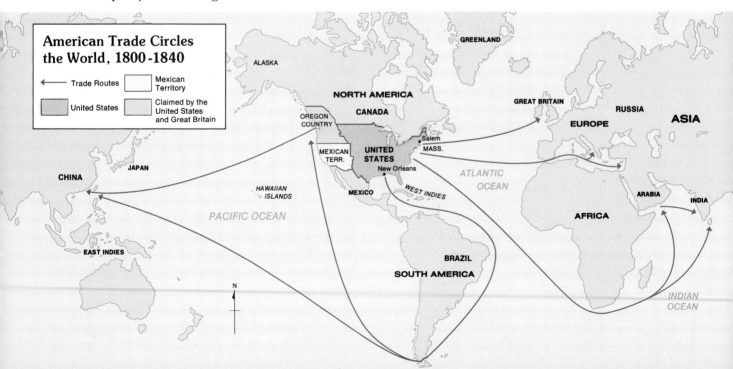

American Trade Circles the World, 1800-1840

← Trade Routes

☐ United States

☐ Mexican Territory

☐ Claimed by the United States and Great Britain

something the Chinese were even more eager to buy than ginseng.

In what is now the state of Oregon, Gray had bought seals, beavers, and other furs from the Indians who lived along the coast. In China, he found he could sell the furs for high prices. By 1806, fur trade between Boston and China was worth $5 million.

At that time, Boston merchants were not just stopping in Oregon. They were also making regular visits to the Hawaiian Islands in the Pacific. There they traded for sandalwood. They then sold it to the Chinese who used the wood to make furniture.

Markets around the World

Merchants in other cities also looked for new markets. Some found business in Europe and the West Indies. Others traded with people in India, Africa, Russia, Brazil, and any other place a profit could be made.

Like the merchants of Boston, these traders also bought and sold goods at every stop. Merchants from Salem, Massachusetts, for example, sailed around Africa to India and the East Indies. (The East Indies are the islands Columbus was looking for when he reached the Americas.) They brought home ivory from Africa, spices from the Indies, and jewels from India.

Trading ships traveling west in 1821 stopped in the Hawaiian Islands.

Trading with distant lands could be risky. Many ships were lost at sea or threatened by pirates. However, merchants felt that the risks were worth taking. If their ships made it through, they made huge profits.

To Help You Remember

1. After the Revolution, why did Americans send ships to all parts of the world?
2. (a) What goods did Americans buy from people in China? (b) What goods did the Chinese buy from Americans?
3. (a) What goods did Americans buy in Africa? (b) In India? (c) In the Indies?
4. (a) Why was trading in distant lands risky? (b) Why were people willing to take the risk?

221

Opportunities at Home

Some Americans preferred to do business closer to home. Yet they too found opportunities to get ahead after the War for Independence.

A New Cash Crop

Before the Revolution, Southern farmers sold most of their crops to people in Great Britain. During the war, that trade was cut off. So the British found other places to buy rice, tobacco, and indigo. In the years after the war, Southerners had to find new places to sell their crops.

How did Eli Whitney's cotton gin (short for engine) clean seeds from cotton?

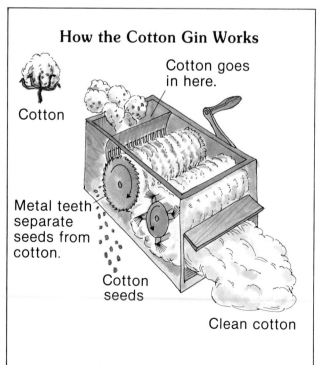

How the Cotton Gin Works

Cotton

Cotton goes in here.

Metal teeth separate seeds from cotton.

Cotton seeds

Clean cotton

Finding new markets for Southern goods was difficult. Therefore, many Southerners were eager to find a new **cash crop.** A cash crop is a product that is grown for sale rather than for use by the farmer. At the time, cotton seemed to be the best choice.

In the 1700's, the British invented machines that spun cotton into thread and then wove the thread into cloth faster than ever before. Thanks to the new machines, British cotton mills were booming. British factory owners began buying as much cotton as they could get.

Yet few Southerners planted the crop. Why? The kind of cotton that grew best in the South was covered with many sticky seeds. At best a worker could clean only a pound or two a day. So cotton would not be profitable until someone found a faster way of cleaning the seeds from the cotton. That person turned out to be a young man from Massachusetts named Eli Whitney.

In the fall of 1792, Whitney took a year off from college to work on a plantation in Georgia. Catherine Greene, the owner of a nearby plantation, learned that Whitney liked to invent things. She asked him if he could design a machine that could clean cotton.

By the spring of 1793, Whitney's invention was ready. He called it the cotton gin. A worker could clean 1,000 pounds (450 kilograms) of cotton in a day with the new machine.

Soon farmers throughout the South planted cotton. In 1791, they had sold less than 190,000 pounds (85,000 kilograms) of cotton. In 1800, only 7 years after Whitney invented the cotton gin, Southerners sold over 41 million pounds (about 18 million kilograms). Cotton was becoming the South's most valuable crop.

As cotton became more and more important to the South, so too did slavery. Many workers were needed to grow, pick, and clean the crop. Just as it seemed that slavery might soon end everywhere in the country, the invention of the cotton gin changed things.

The Growth of Factories

Some Americans were interested in starting their own cotton mills. They could not, however, buy the machines they needed. It was against the law for anyone in Great Britain to sell the machines or to take plans for them out of the country.

Then, in 1789, a young British factory worker named Samuel Slater found a way to get the plans out of Great Britain. He memorized them. Then he disguised himself as a

Samuel Slater's cotton mill used water power to run its machines.

farmer and boarded a ship headed for the United States.

Shortly after Slater arrived in the United States, a group of business people asked him to build a cotton mill with machines like those in Great Britain. Slater spent months building the machines from memory. By 1793, he was ready. That year the first cotton factory in the nation opened its doors in Pawtucket, Rhode Island.

Speeding Up Factory Work. A few years later, Eli Whitney came up with an idea that helped to speed up factory work. In 1798, he got an order from the government for 10,000 muskets. Whitney decided to make the guns in a new way.

The factory workers are welding the metal parts of guns and rifles.

In the past, each worker made a gun from start to finish. As a result, no two guns were exactly alike. Now Whitney planned to build machines that would make each trigger exactly like every other trigger. The same was true of every other part. When all parts of a product are alike and can fit together with the other parts, they are **interchangeable**.

With interchangeable parts, workers could put together guns quickly and easily. Other factory owners in the United States used Whitney's idea. So did Europeans. They called it the American method.

Factories Begin to Boom. Yet even with Whitney's invention, it was still cheaper to buy manufactured goods from Great Britain than to make them in the United States. However, when war broke out between Britain and France in 1803, the fighting cut off trade. Therefore, it became necessary for Americans to build more factories of their own.

Cotton mills, like the one Slater built, were among the first factories in the United States. Yet before the war was over, Americans were also making paper, leather goods, iron tools, and many other products in factories. Most of these factories were in the Northeast. Places there had the rushing streams and waterfalls. They provided the water power needed to run the new machines.

To Help You Remember

1. Why did Southern farmers have to find new markets for their crops after the Revolution?
2. (a) What new cash crop did Southerners try to grow? (b) Why did they choose it?
3. What invention made raising cotton profitable?
4. (a) Who built the first factory in the United States? (b) What did he have to do to get it started?
5. How did Eli Whitney speed up the work done in factories?
6. How did the war in Europe help to speed up the growth of factories in the United States?

In the early 1800's, the United States began to prosper and grow in many ways. One way to keep track of the way it changed is by taking notes as you read. The headings and subheadings in the chapter can help you organize those notes into an outline.

Below are headings and subheadings from the first two sections of this chapter. Copy them on a separate sheet of paper. Then, under each subheading, fill in the missing information. The page numbers tell you where to look in the text.

  I. Opportunities across the Oceans
    A. Trading with China (pages 220-221)
      1. _____
      2. _____
    B. Markets around the World (page 221)
      1. _____
      2. _____
 II. Opportunities at Home
    A. A New Cash Crop (pages 222-223)
      1. _____
      2. _____
    B. The Growth of Factories (pages 223-224)
      1. _____
      2. _____
        a. Speeding Up Factory Work
          1. _____
          2. _____
        b. Factories Begin to Boom
          1. _____
          2. _____

Continue the outline as you read the rest of the chapter.

Daniel Boone and his companions look out over Kentucky.

Moving West

At the same time factories spread in the Northeast and cotton farming grew in the South, changes were also taking place in the West. Great Britain had promised the land west of the Appalachian Mountains to the Indians. Yet even before the American Revolution, settlers had crossed the mountains. They settled first on the land east of the Mississippi River and south of the Ohio River. It was later known as the Old Southwest.

Moving to the Old Southwest

One of the first Americans to explore the Old Southwest was Daniel Boone.

He had liked growing up on the frontier, first in Pennsylvania and then in North Carolina. By 1770, both places had many farms, villages, and towns. Daniel Boone was eager to move on.

In the 1770's, Boone heard that just beyond the Appalachian Mountains there were "deer at every salt lick, birds in every bush, and herds of buffalo on every meadow." Daniel Boone decided to see this land for himself.

In 1772, Boone and six other men crossed the mountains. They followed an old Indian trail through the Cumberland Gap—a narrow valley, or pass, in the mountains. In years to come, thousands of people would travel through it.

On his trip, Daniel Boone explored much of what later became the state of Kentucky. He liked what he saw there so well that he brought his family and friends to the area. In 1775, they built the town of Boonesboro. Other settlements quickly followed. By 1792, Kentucky had enough people to become a state. Other settlers built settlements in what is today Tennessee. By 1976, Tennessee had also become a state.

Settling the Old Northwest

Americans were also eager to settle the land north of the Ohio River. They called this land the Old Northwest. So, soon after the war ended, the government began buying land there from the Indians.

Congress passed a law in 1787 called the Northwest Ordinance. The law said that as soon as any part of the Old Northwest had enough voters, it could become a **territory** of the United States. A territory is an organized part of the nation whose land is not included within the borders of any state. People in a territory could choose representatives to make laws for their territory.

When a territory had enough people, voters could write a state constitution. Then the territory could ask Congress to make it a state.

Less than a year after the law was passed, many Americans moved to the Northwest. In 1788, they founded the towns of Marietta and Cincinnati in Ohio. George Washington was president at the time. As a young man, he had explored parts of the Old Northwest. Now he feared that Americans might lose this land if they did not settle it. Even though the war was over, the British still had soldiers stationed in the West.

The Indians' Reaction

The Indians watched as Americans moved west. Many of the Indians were alarmed at how quickly the newcomers cleared the woodlands.

These Indians had been living in the forests of the Old Northwest and Old Southwest for thousands of years. They farmed along the rivers and lakes. They gathered berries and nuts in the forests and used the wood from trees for homes and tools. They hunted deer and beavers there too. It was a way of life they valued and were willing to fight for.

Other Indians in the West were newcomers. They had lost their lands in the East to the white settlers. They did not want to have to move again.

By the 1790's, American settlers had taken over most of the Indians' land in Kentucky and Tennessee. Now they were moving north of the Ohio River. Many Indians there refused to sell their lands.

What river divides the Old Northwest and the Old Southwest? What were the first three states in these territories?

These Indians did not want to give up their way of life so they united against the newcomers. Such groups as the Miami, the Shawnee, the Ojibwa, the Ottawa, and the Pottawatomi fought side by side to protect their homelands.

In 1794, the Indians made a stand at a place in Ohio called Fallen Timbers. It got its name after a storm blew down thousands of trees. Fighting among the tangled tree trunks and branches suited the Indians. Yet in the end, the Indians could not stop the American army that was sent to protect the settlers.

The following summer, the Indians were forced to give up most of their lands in Ohio. One group after another packed up and moved farther west. Even as the Indians were heading west, thousands of easterners were moving to Ohio.

The Indians Unite

Among the Indians who left Ohio were the Shawnee. They settled in what is now Indiana. Yet in 1810, the United States demanded that they sell their lands once again. By now Ohio was a state, and some Americans were eager to move farther west into the Shawnee's land and beyond.

Tecumseh, the leader of the Shawnee, was outraged. He had been a young warrior at the Battle of Fallen Timbers. He remembered how painful it had been to leave his home in Ohio. He did not want to move again.

Tecumseh traveled about, urging Indian groups west of the Appalachian Mountains to unite. Everywhere he reminded people how strong the Delaware, the Narraganset, and other eastern Indians had once been. Now their forests were gone, and these Indians were scattered as leaves in the wind.

Tecumseh argued that the Indians would keep their lands only if they united against the settlers. Many Indians agreed. They joined Tecumseh and the Shawnee to fight against the Americans.

In July of 1811, Tecumseh told the governor of the Indiana Territory, William Henry Harrison, of his plans to unite the Indians. Tecumseh had hoped that his plan would frighten the Americans. Instead, Harrison led an army to Prophetstown, the main Shawnee village on the Wabash River in Indiana. The army attacked and a bloody battle broke out. In the end, Harrison's soldiers defeated the Indians and burned the Shawnee's village to the ground.

Tecumseh was away from home at the time along with most of his best warriors. They returned to find their village in ruins. Tecumseh vowed he would get even. He kept his word.

Under the leadership of Tecumseh, the Indians attacked one settlement after another. By the spring of 1812, many American families were leaving the Northwest.

Many Americans in the Northwest were convinced that Tecumseh was getting help from the British. They believed that as long as Great Britain ruled Canada, the Indians would continue to attack. Therefore, they wanted the United States to invade Canada and force the British out. Representatives in Congress from the new Western states pushed so hard for war that they became known as the War Hawks.

Tecumseh was a Shawnee leader. A strong warrior and gifted speaker, he worked to unite Indians throughout the West.

To Help You Remember

1. How did Daniel Boone help to start settlements in the area known as the Old Southwest?
2. How did Congress encourage settlement of the Old Northwest?
3. How did the Indians react to the first American settlers in the Old Northwest?
4. (a) What did Tecumseh try to do to help the Indians keep their land? (b) What happened to ruin his plans?

Protecting the Nation

The War Hawks were not the only Americans who wanted to go to war in the early 1800's. From time to time, other Americans also favored war. The United States government wanted all Americans to feel that their country would protect them no matter where they settled. However, it did not want to risk a war. Yet finding peaceful ways of settling disagreements was not an easy task.

Protecting American Trade

In the early 1800's, many American merchants were doing business on

How much bigger was the United States after the Louisiana Purchase? What river did the nation gain control of?

The Louisiana Purchase, 1803

almost every continent. Even Western farmers sold wheat, corn, and hogs to people in distant lands. So the nation's leaders kept a close watch on events in other parts of the world.

The Country Doubles in Size. In 1803, for example, President Thomas Jefferson learned France was about to take control of New Orleans and the Louisiana Territory. For years, that land had belonged to Spain.

Jefferson feared the French might close New Orleans to Americans. Settlers needed the port to get goods to market, so Jefferson decided to buy New Orleans from France. He sent two representatives to Europe.

The Americans were in for a big surprise. France was willing to sell not only New Orleans but also all of Louisiana. The Americans quickly agreed, and the Louisiana Territory became part of the United States.

A War in Europe. A war broke out between France and Great Britain the same year that the United States purchased the Louisiana Territory. The United States tried to stay out of the war. Yet many American trading ships made regular stops in Europe. The British captured any ship heading for France. The French, in turn, stopped all ships bound for Britain.

Great Britain needed sailors. In those days life in the British navy was so bad that few men joined. Many of those who did ran away as soon as they could. So British officers began taking sailors off American ships. They claimed those sailors were British citizens who had deserted their country.

No More Trade. Many Americans were outraged. They demanded that President Jefferson take action, so he asked Congress to put a stop to all overseas trade. He hoped that by doing so he would force Great Britain and France to respect the rights of American sailors and merchants.

Lost trade, however, caused hardship in the United States. There was less work for the shipbuilders, sailmakers, sailors, and merchants. Without overseas markets, much of the harvest of 1808 was wasted.

Just before Jefferson left office, Congress once again allowed Americans to trade with Great Britain and France. Still, the problem that had led to the ban on trade had not been solved. The British and the French still stopped American ships. The British, however, had the stronger navy. They captured more American ships than the French did.

American settlers west of the Appalachian Mountains were angry with the British for another reason.

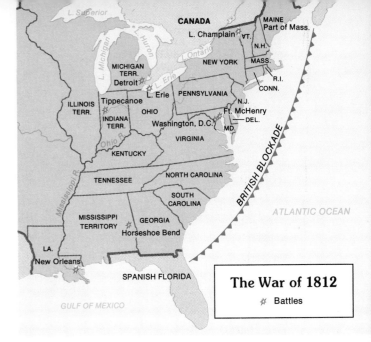

The War of 1812

⚔ Battles

Where did most of the fighting of the War of 1812 take place? On what lake did a major battle take place?

The settlers believed that British soldiers were helping the Indians in the Northwest attack American settlers.

The War of 1812

By 1812, more and more Americans were calling for war with Great Britain. Finally, on June 18, 1812, President James Madison asked Congress to declare war. People in the western part of the country cheered at the news. Those who lived in the Northeast were less pleased. Many of them had business ties with Great Britain that would now be broken. Some Americans also feared the United States was not ready for war.

The British attacked Washington, D.C., in 1814 and burned many buildings, including the White House.

Fighting in the West. From the start, the United States had trouble holding its own against the British in the West. Many Indian leaders there, including Tecumseh, supported the British. By the end of 1812, the British held both Detroit, Michigan, and the city later known as Chicago.

Then, in September of 1813, a naval captain named Oliver Hazard Perry won an important victory on Lake Erie. He did it even though many of his men had never been on a ship before. Their success gave the Americans control of Lake Erie. However, the Americans were not strong enough to follow up with similar victories on land. So the war in the West dragged on.

Fighting in the East. Then, in the spring of 1814, Great Britain defeated France. The war in Europe was over. The British gave their full attention to fighting in the United States. They began to move troops from Europe to North America.

In August of the same year, the British attacked Washington, D.C. After setting fire to the White House, the Capitol, and other public buildings, they moved north toward Baltimore. Outside that city stood Fort McHenry. On September 13, British cannons began pounding the fort from Chesapeake Bay. Luck was with the Americans. The heavy British ships could not get close enough to do much damage. So early the next morning, the British soldiers and the British ships left.

Francis Scott Key, a prisoner on one of the British warships, watched the fighting. In the early morning he looked out and saw that the United States flag was still waving in the dim light of dawn. He was so moved by what he saw that he wrote a poem. Later, the words of his poem were set to the music of an old song. That song, "The Star-Spangled Banner," has become our national anthem.

Fighting in the South. The last part of the war was fought in the Louisiana Territory. Americans learned that British soldiers were heading for

New Orleans, so they moved quickly to protect it. The general in charge was Andrew Jackson, a tough soldier from Tennessee.

Jackson's men were as tough as he was. Many had lived on the frontier all their lives, and most of them were keen marksmen. With these able sharpshooters, the Americans won a smashing victory at New Orleans. Britain lost more than 1,500 soldiers in the battle.

The Battle of New Orleans took place two weeks after the United States and Great Britain had signed a peace treaty in Europe. News moved slowly in those days. Neither side knew it at the time, but the war was over. However, Jackson's victory made Americans proud. It showed once again that Americans could stand up to the British and win.

The War of 1812 was finally over. No one gained anything from the war. Yet it helped Americans feel more confident about the future of their country. The nation was strong enough to protect itself.

Independence brought many changes to the United States in the early 1800's. Many of those changes helped the country to prosper and to grow stronger. Americans were beginning to show the world they could take care of themselves. They felt great pride for their young country.

What song was written in honor of this scene at Fort McHenry? Who wrote it?

To Help You Remember

1. (a) Why did President Jefferson offer to buy New Orleans from France? (b) How did the United States increase its size in 1803?
2. (a) How were Americans affected by the war between Great Britain and France? (b) What did President Jefferson do to keep Americans out of that war? (c) Why did the United States finally declare war on Great Britain?
3. (a) During the war, what victories did the United States win in the East? (b) In the West? (c) In the South?

Chapter Review

Words to Know

1. Why did Americans look for new *markets* when war broke out in Europe?
2. During the war, why did Southerners look for a new *cash crop?*
3. How did *interchangeable* parts speed up factory work?
4. How is a *territory* different from a state?

Reviewing Main Ideas

Below is a list of topics that were discussed in this chapter. For each topic, list at least *two* details that add to or describe the topic. Use the outline that you made for this chapter. It should have the information you need.

a. Opportunities Americans Found across the Oceans
b. Opportunities for Americans at Home
c. Opportunities Americans Had in the West
d. Ways Americans Protected the United States

In Your Own Words

Choose one of the topics listed in *Reviewing Main Ideas*. Then write a paragraph telling how your topic helped the United States to prosper and grow.

Challenge!

1. During the War of 1812, a president's wife became a hero. Find out her name and what she did. Here is a clue to help you. The woman's husband was the fourth president of the United States.
2. The saying, "Don't give up the ship" came out of the War of 1812. Find out the story behind this famous motto. These clues will help you find the information you need. The man who said it fought under Oliver Hazard Perry and took part in the battle for control of Lake Erie.
3. The use of the name Uncle Sam to mean the United States started during the War of 1812. Find out who the real Uncle Sam was.

Unit Review

Take Another Look

The following is a list of key events described in Unit Four. Put the events in the order in which they occurred. Then tell how each event helped the nation to prosper or grow stronger.

a. Eli Whitney invents the cotton gin.
b. The United States opens trade with China.
c. The Constitution of the United States is ratified.
d. Congress passes the Northwest Ordinance.
e. George Washington becomes president.
f. Samuel Slater builds the first factory in the United States.
g. Eli Whitney invents the American method.
h. Congress declares a second war with Great Britain.
i. Jefferson buys the Louisiana Territory from France.
j. William Henry Harrison defeats the Indians of the Old Northwest.
k. Tennessee becomes a state.
l. Kentucky becomes a state.

You and the Past

1. Every year, thousands of people visit Washington, D.C. Some go to see the White House, the Capitol, the Supreme Court building, or the monuments that honor some of the nation's presidents. Use the library to find out more about these and other interesting places in the nation's capital. Then make a poster showing the places you would most like to visit. Write captions explaining the reason for each of your choices.
2. Washington is not laid out on a grid. Find out what pattern was used to lay out the city's streets. Why do you think the city was laid out in this way?
3. Use an encyclopedia to find out how the "Star Spangled Banner" by Francis Scott Key became the national anthem. Who wrote the music?
4. George Washington appointed the first Cabinet. It had four members. How many members are there today? What are the duties of each member of the Cabinet?

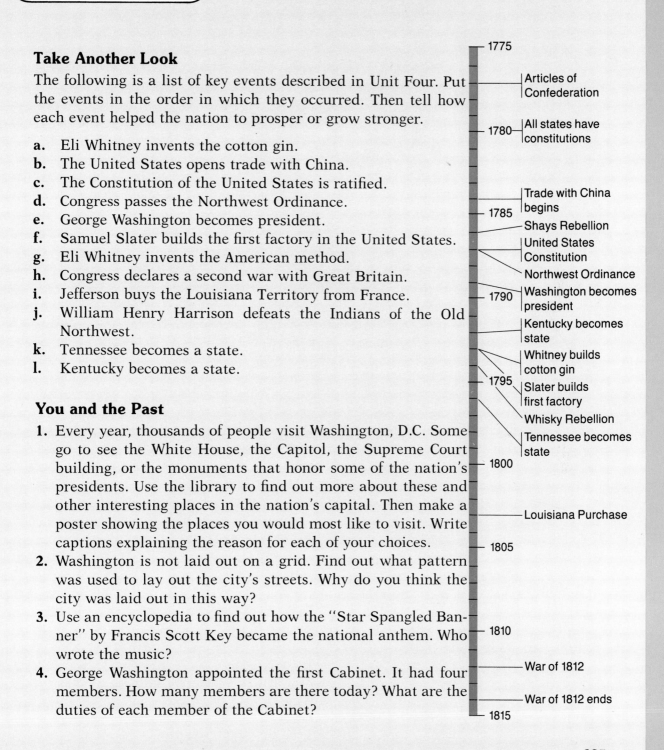

1775
Articles of Confederation
1780 — All states have constitutions
Trade with China begins
1785
Shays Rebellion
United States Constitution
Northwest Ordinance
1790 Washington becomes president
Kentucky becomes state
Whitney builds cotton gin
1795 Slater builds first factory
Whisky Rebellion
Tennessee becomes state
1800
Louisiana Purchase
1805
1810
War of 1812
War of 1812 ends
1815

A wagon train along the Oregon Trail in the early 1800's

Unit Five

Moving West

In 1783, the United States was made up of 13 small states along the Atlantic coast. Over the next 70 years, the country continued to grow. By 1853, the United States was made up of 31 states and several large territories stretching from the Atlantic Ocean to the Pacific Ocean.

13

Across the Appalachians

In the early 1800's, many families packed their belongings onto wagons or mules and moved west. They headed for the Ohio River Valley and other lands beyond the Appalachian Mountains. They went west hoping to make a fresh start in a new land.

Most families came from states along the Atlantic coast. Others were **immigrants.** Immigrants are people who leave their homelands to settle in another country. By the early 1800's, more and more immigrants were arriving in the United States each year. Thousands settled in the West. In 1783, only a handful of Americans lived west of the Appalachian Mountains. By 1840, one third of all the people in the United States lived there.

As You Read

This chapter is divided into three parts.

- Routes West
- Moving into Frontier Lands
- Beyond the Mississippi

In the first part, you will find out how improvements in transportation helped the West to grow. The second part tells what it was like to live in the West in the early 1800's. The last part tells about a new frontier. As you read each part, look for ways the West was changing.

◄ *Daniel Boone leading settlers through Cumberland Gap*

Routes West

During the early 1800's, routes through the Appalachian Mountains were crowded with travelers. As one writer put it, "They come in crowds a mile long; they come with wagon loads of household fixings, with droves of cattle and flocks of sheep. They come from every land."

Traveling over Land

The first families to move west of the Appalachian Mountains scrambled over rough Indian trails. Others followed paths made by buffalo herds. Still others made their own trails.

After a toll was paid, a pike or post was turned aside to allow a wagon to pass.

No matter what trails they took, travel was difficult. The trails were thick with dust during the dry summer months. During the wet months, rain turned the trails to mud. People and horses slipped. Wagons and stagecoaches got stuck.

Then, in the early 1800's, people began building roads covered with gravel or stone. Such roads would not turn to mud when it rained. These roads were toll roads. Every ten miles (16 kilometers) or so, travelers would come to a pike or pole across the road. They paid a toll to have the pike turned aside. This is why many people called toll roads turnpikes.

In 1811, the United States began building a freeway, or highway without tolls, to the West. It was called the National Road. It began in Cumberland, Maryland. By 1852, it reached Vandalia, Illinois, about 500 miles (800 kilometers) from Cumberland.

Many of the people who traveled west on the National Road or on turnpikes traveled in covered wagons. The covered wagons were known as Conestoga wagons because they were first made in the Conestoga Valley of Pennsylvania. German immigrants there used the wagons to haul furs and crops to market. Later people heading west used them to

Above is a painting of Fulton's steamboat, the Clermont. *Unlike other riverboats, it could go upstream as easily as downstream.*

carry their tools, furniture, clothing, and other belongings with them.

Traveling by Water

Even with better roads, traveling over land was slow and difficult. Most people preferred to travel on rivers and lakes whenever they could. Traveling by water was much faster than traveling over land.

Floating Downriver. Many families traveled at least part of the way west on large rafts called flatboats. Later they used flatboats to ship their corn and wheat to market. These boats drifted down the Ohio and Mississippi rivers to New Orleans.

While flatboats were good for traveling downstream, they could not move upstream against the current of a river. So after the farmers reached New Orleans, they broke up their boats and sold the lumber.

To get back home, the farmers traveled on keelboats. These were long narrow boats with sharp pointed ends. Strong men used long poles to force these boats upstream against the current of the river. It was slow, hard work at best.

Steaming Upriver and Down. Then, in 1807, an American inventor named Robert Fulton developed a boat that could move upstream as easily as downstream. His boat was

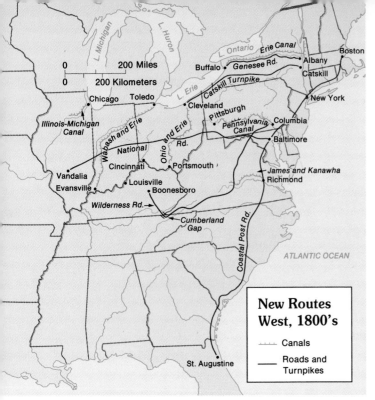

The map shows some of the canals and roads people took west. Name three canals and two roads they traveled on.

powered by a steam engine. On August 19, his steamboat the *Clermont* was ready for its trial run on the Hudson River. It was to travel from New York City to Albany, New York.

As the huge boat made its way up the river, hundreds gathered to watch. When the boat finally came into view, people ran in terror. It creaked and rumbled as huge paddle wheels on each side of the boat sprayed water high into the air. A smokestack in the middle of the boat set off a shower of fiery sparks.

In spite of the way it looked, the

Clermont was a success. It made the 150-mile (240-kilometers) journey in just 32 hours. The return trip was even faster. It took only 30 hours.

Before long, steamboats were a common sight on the Ohio, Missouri, and Mississippi rivers too. Steamboats were also used on the Great Lakes. Every year they were improved. By 1840, a 150-mile (240-kilometers) trip took just 8 hours.

Building Canals. In the early 1800's, people began to dig **canals**. A canal is a narrow waterway made by people rather than by nature. Canals are made deep enough for large boats to travel on. They link two rivers together or a river to a lake.

At first, most canals in the United States were less than 30 miles (48 kilometers) long. Then, in 1817, the state of New York began work on the Erie Canal. It was to join the Hudson River with Lake Erie. Workers using picks and shovels dug a ditch 4 feet deep (120 centimeters), 40 feet wide (1,200 centimeters), and 362 miles (579 kilometers) long.

Eight years later, on October 26, 1825, the Erie Canal was finally finished. It was an instant success. The cost of shipping a ton (1 metric ton) of wheat from Buffalo, New York, to New York City dropped from $100 to $5. Soon canals were built in other states too.

242

Many people traveled all or part of the way west on the Erie and other canals. Later they used those same canals to get their goods to market. For example, thousands of farmers brought their wheat, hogs, and other goods to towns along the Great Lakes. From there, they were shipped to New York by way of the Erie Canal. The canal made New York City the trading center of the nation.

The Coming of the Railroad

In 1825, the same year the Erie Canal opened for business, the British built the first railroad in the world. It was a steam engine on wheels that pulled a line of railroad cars.

Two years later, a group of business people in Baltimore, Maryland, started their own railroad. It was to connect the city of Baltimore with the Ohio River. At first, the railroad cars were pulled by horses. Then, in 1830, a young inventor named Peter Cooper talked the owners into using his steam locomotive to pull the train. He called his engine the Tom Thumb. Everyone else called it a teakettle on wheels.

On August 25, 1830, Cooper's engine made its first trip. The little engine raced along at the amazing speed of 18 miles (29 kilometers) an hour. Soon people all over the country were building railroads. By the

The Tom Thumb raced a horse-drawn carriage. The horse won the race.

1850's, hundreds of miles of railroad track connected cities in the East with places as far west as Cincinnati, Ohio, and Chattanooga, Tennessee.

To Help You Remember

1. Why were toll roads also called turnpikes?
2. Why did Western farmers break up their flatboats?
3. What was so special about Robert Fulton's steamboat?
4. (a) Why did New Yorkers build a canal? (b) How did it help them make money?
5. How did Peter Cooper help to speed up travel over land?

You have just read about many improvements that took place in transportation during the 1800's. Americans were very excited about them. One way to keep track of the improvements in transportation and other important facts is to take notes as you read. A chart can help you organize the notes.

Below is a chart that lists improvements in transportation. Copy it on a separate sheet of paper. Look back in the chapter to find the missing facts and add them to the chart.

Improvements in Transportation

Event	Date	Improvement	Importance
Building of the National Road			
Building of the Erie Canal			
Trial run of the *Clermont*			
Trial run of Cooper's steam locomotive			

As you continue to read the rest of the chapter, look for ways Americans used improvements in transportation to move west.

Moving into Frontier Lands

Improved transportation made it easier for people to move west. As more people headed for the lands beyond the Appalachians, they pushed the frontier—the land just beyond settled communities—farther and farther west.

In 1796, there were only two states west of the mountains: Kentucky and Tennessee. By 1812, there were four states. Ohio became a state in 1803 and Louisiana in 1812. By 1819, the United States was made up of 22 states. Eight of them were west of the Appalachian Mountains. Also in 1819, the United States bought Florida from Spain. Then Americans began moving south to Florida as well.

The Pioneers

The first families to move west are known as **pioneers.** Pioneers are people who are the first to try something new. The early pioneers prepared the way for others who followed later.

Among the pioneers who settled west of the Appalachians were the grandparents of Abraham Lincoln. They left the Shenandoah Valley of Virginia in 1782. They settled in Kentucky. There they helped turn the wilderness into a settled community.

Lincoln's father was also a pioneer. In 1816, he moved his family to a place called Pigeon Creek in southern Indiana. Abraham Lincoln was just seven years old at the time.

During the Lincoln family's first year in Pigeon Creek, they cleared their land and planted crops. They also built a log cabin. While the Lincolns waited for their crops to ripen in the fields, they hunted and fished for food. They also gathered nuts and berries in the forest.

Everyone in a family had many jobs to do, including the children. At the age of seven, Abraham Lincoln was already learning how to chop

The map shows the original 13 states and the new states formed between 1781 and 1819. Name the new states.

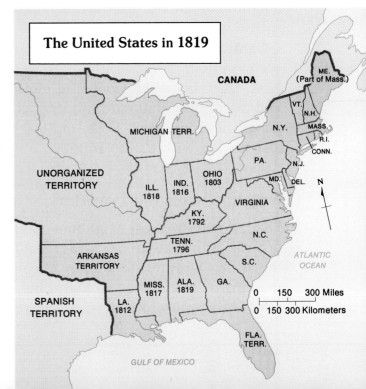

The United States in 1819

Building the roof

Making shingles

Squaring logs

Rock for doorstep

Mud

Sharpening tools

The diagram above shows how a log cabin was built. Notice the ways neighbors worked together at a "house-raising."

wood. When he was older, he became known for his skill with an ax. His neighbors claimed that no one could split logs faster than Abe Lincoln.

Sarah, Abe's older sister, helped their mother prepare the family's food. She also wove wool into cloth and then sewed that cloth into shirts, pants, and dresses. Both children also helped with the farming.

Neighbors on the Frontier

The Lincolns' nearest neighbors lived several miles away. Yet they and the other families in Pigeon Creek thought of themselves as a community. The people of Pigeon Creek were always willing to pitch in and help one another in many ways.

For example, when a new family was ready to build a cabin, neighbors gathered to help chop the trees and saw them into logs. By working together, several strong men could raise a cabin in a day. Working alone, one person would have taken weeks.

House-raising was hard work, but it was also fun. While the men built the cabin, the women prepared a feast of wild turkey, roasted deer and bear meat, fresh vegetables, and corn bread. The children played games and held shooting contests. Toward evening, someone usually brought out a fiddle for dancing.

Neighbors also helped each other in times of trouble. On the frontier, people had to depend on their neighbors. Few of the families could have survived without that help.

From Frontier to Settled Land

In spite of hardships, many pioneers liked the frontier life. They grew restless when the wilderness began to disappear. Abe Lincoln's father was such a pioneer. As he watched more and more people move to Indiana, he decided it was time to move on. In 1830, he sold his farm and took his family farther west. This time they moved to Illinois.

Changes in Pigeon Creek. The people who bought the family's farm had a much easier time than the Lincolns did. They did not have to clear the land or build a cabin in the wilderness. They were not as lonely either. They saw their neighbors every Sunday. Pigeon Creek had a church now. Abe Lincoln's father had helped to build it.

The newcomers could also travel to the nearby town of Gentryville. It had a store that served as a meeting place for families from miles around. People came there not only to buy supplies but also to visit with friends. The store even had newspapers so that people could find out what was happening back East.

Gentryville also had a mill. Farmers gathered there to grind their wheat into flour. Some of that flour was shipped to New Orleans. People in Indiana no longer grew crops just to feed their families. Many farmers were also planting cash crops. They used the rivers and canals to get their crops to market.

In Gentryville and other places along the Ohio River, wheat and corn were cash crops. Both were in great demand in Eastern cities such as New York and Philadelphia. People in the East also bought Western beef and pork.

Those who settled farther south planted cotton and tobacco. They

Many frontier villages like the one shown below grew into settled communities.

built plantations on the rich, black soil of Alabama and Mississippi. By the 1840's, most of the nation's cotton was grown west of the Appalachian Mountains.

The Growth of Towns and Cities. As farms and plantations grew, so did towns and cities. Mobile, Alabama, became a center for the cotton trade. In other states, towns like Chicago, St. Louis, and Cincinnati were becoming centers for the trade of wheat, corn, and meat products. These towns had many flour mills and stockyards. People there were building factories too. Those factories turned out everything from farm tools to sausages.

This painting shows election day in a western town in the 1800's. Voters gathered around to hear who won.

The Pioneer Spirit

A special feeling developed among the people who lived in the West. Many called it the pioneer spirit. A willingness to pitch in and help others was part of that spirit.

Democratic Ideas. **Democracy** was also a part of the pioneer spirit. In a democracy, citizens have the right to take part in government. From the start, Westerners demanded the right to take part in the government of their communities, their states, and their country.

In many Western states, all white men could vote whether they owned property or not. Slowly that idea spread east. By 1860, all white men over the age of 21 could vote almost anywhere in the United States. However, many Americans still could not take part in government. Black men were allowed to vote in only five states. Women could not vote anywhere at all.

The First Western President. Westerners also believed that there was no limit to what a person might become if he or she worked hard. Some even claimed that a poor boy from the frontier could grow up to become president of the United States.

That dream came true in 1828 when Andrew Jackson became president of the United States. He was the same Andrew Jackson who won the Battle of New Orleans during the War of 1812.

Jackson lived on the frontier all of his life, first in the wilderness of South Carolina and later in Tennessee. He was always a fighter. A long-time friend of Jackson's once said, "I could throw him three times out of four, but he would never stay *throwed*. He would never give up."

Unlike the early presidents, Jackson did not come from a wealthy family. He had to make his own way. He did not get much schooling, yet he did study to become a lawyer. In those days a person did not have to go to college to study law. Instead, they learned about the law from someone who was already a lawyer.

After Jackson became a lawyer, he moved to Tennessee. There he served as a soldier, a judge, and a lawmaker. Over the years, he also bought land in Tennessee and became a wealthy cotton planter.

Westerners were proud of Jackson, and they often bragged about him. They told how he fought in the Revolutionary War at the age of 13. During his first battle, he was captured by the British and sent to prison. When a British officer demanded that the boy shine his boots, Jackson refused. He told the officer, "I may be your prisoner, but I am not your servant." The soldier then slashed his

Andrew Jackson posed for this portrait five years after the War of 1812.

hand with a sword. Jackson carried the scar for the rest of his life.

Westerners nicknamed Jackson Old Hickory after the strongest, toughest tree in Tennessee. When he was sworn in as president, thousands of Westerners came to Washington, D.C., to watch. After all, they felt that Andrew Jackson was one of them.

To Help You Remember

1. In what ways did frontier families help one another?
2. Why was life easier for the family that bought the Lincolns' farm?
3. List two beliefs that are part of the pioneer spirit.
4. Name two men who were raised on the frontier and later became president.

Beyond the Mississippi

Even as Americans were settling the land between the Appalachian Mountains and the Mississippi River, a few people were looking farther west. They had their eyes on the lands that lay beyond the Mississippi River.

Back in 1803, President Thomas Jefferson had bought Louisiana from France. News of the purchase had excited many Americans. They knew that there was plenty of rich farm land along the Mississippi River. However, they knew very little about the rest of Louisiana. So in 1804, Jefferson decided to send a group of explorers west.

The Adventures of Lewis and Clark

President Jefferson asked his secretary Meriwether Lewis to lead the group. Lewis had grown up on the frontier. He had served in the army there. Lewis invited a friend to join him on the trip. The friend's name was William Clark, a younger brother of Revolutionary War general George Rogers Clark. He too had lived in the West for many years.

The two men were asked to explore the northwestern part of the Louisiana Purchase. They were to follow the Missouri River to its **source.** The source of a river is the place where it begins. The explorers were also told to cross the Western mountains to find out what rivers flowed into the Pacific Ocean. Jefferson asked the two to record everything they saw.

Up the Missouri. In May of 1804, Lewis and Clark began their journey. They left from St. Louis, Missouri, with about 50 men. They traveled from St. Louis up the Missouri River on one large keelboat and two smaller boats. It was hard going from the start. Rain fell day after day as the group fought its way upstream. High winds tossed the boats. Some days the group was only able to travel three miles (5 kilometers).

As the group pushed its way farther and farther north and west, the forests began to disappear. In their place was a huge grassland. In some places the grass was taller than they were. The only trees the group saw were those that lined the river.

In the Land of the Mandans. By fall, the group had reached what is now North Dakota. They spent the winter there living among the Mandan Indians. During their stay, they met a Shoshoni (shō shō'nē) woman named Sacajawea (sak'ə jə wē'ə). Her people lived in the land the explorers planned to travel through.

This Mandan village is much like the one Lewis and Clark visited. It too lies on the grasslands of North Dakota.

Lewis and Clark asked Sacajawea to join them and act as their guide. Sacajawea was about to have a baby. Still she agreed to come. She brought along her husband, a French trapper. Their baby was born along the trail.

As soon as the ice on the river broke in the spring, the group continued up the Missouri River. As the explorers came closer to its source, the river changed. It was no longer slow moving. It had become a narrow, fast-moving mountain stream. So the group had to leave the boats and travel over land.

In the Land of the Shoshoni. By August of 1805, the group had reached the land of the Shoshoni in what is now western Montana. There Sacajawea was reunited with her family. Yet she decided to leave them in order to help the explorers reach the Pacific Ocean. She even persuaded her people to give them horses, canoes, and guides.

Slowly the group made its way through deep forests, over steep hills, and through the highest mountains they had ever seen. The land was so rugged that the group lost several horses.

By October, the explorers had finally reached the top of the Rocky Mountains. Below them lay rivers that emptied into both the Atlantic and the Pacific oceans. They had come to the **continental divide.** It is

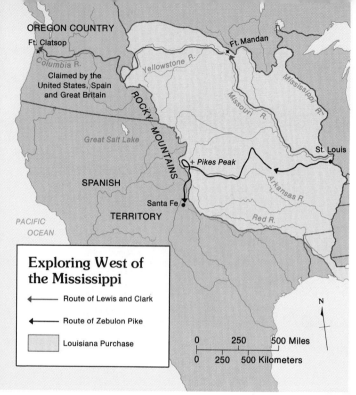

The map shows Lewis and Clark's route to the Northwest and Pike's route to the Southwest. Where did each begin and end?

the place where rivers flow east to the Atlantic Ocean and west to the Pacific Ocean.

Reaching the Pacific. The explorers put the canoes they had carried into the Snake River. They took the Snake River to the Columbia River. Then they floated down the Columbia. The trip took many days. They reached the Pacific on November 7, 1805. "Great joy in camp," wrote Captain Clark in his journal. "We are in view of this great Pacific Ocean, which we have been so anxious to see."

The explorers built a fort near the ocean and camped there until spring. In March of 1806, they began the long journey home. The following September, they returned to St. Louis. They brought back important information about the land, people, plants, and animals they had seen.

The Adventures of Zebulon Pike

Soon after Lewis and Clark arrived home, another explorer set out to explore the southwestern part of the Louisiana Territory. President Jefferson wanted to know about the land there too. He asked an army captain named Zebulon Pike to lead a group of explorers.

Pike and his men left from St. Louis in July 1806. They were to search for the source of the Arkansas and Red rivers. At the time, the Red River was the southwestern boundary of the Louisiana Territory.

Pike and his men traveled from St. Louis through what is now Missouri, Kansas, and Colorado. They too saw mile after mile of tall grasslands. They also made their way over steep mountain trails. In Colorado, Pike climbed a tall mountain that was later named Pikes Peak after him. Then he turned southward. Finally he came to a river. "At last," he wrote, "I have found the Red River."

He was mistaken. The river was actually the Rio Grande. Pike never found the Red River.

When Pike crossed the Rio Grande, he was in Spanish territory. He visited Santa Fe, a small town in what is now New Mexico. There he learned that New Mexico was rich in gold and silver. He also found that people there were eager to trade that gold and silver for American goods.

Plans for the Louisiana Territory

The stories about Pike's adventures in the Southwest and those of Lewis and Clark in the Northwest captured the imagination of many Americans. Some Americans were eager to trade with Mexico. Others set out to trap furs in the thick forests of what is today Washington and Oregon.

Few Americans, however, were interested in the vast grasslands in the middle of the country in what is today Kansas, Nebraska, Oklahoma, and the Dakotas. They called those grasslands the Great American Desert. Most Americans believed that the land there was much too dry for farming.

As more and more Americans settled beyond the Mississippi River, many groups of Indians were pushed onto the grasslands. Some Westerners, including Andrew Jackson, even wanted the United States government to move all the Indians in the United States there. These Westerners wanted to take over whatever land the Indians still owned east of the Mississippi. When Jackson became president, he ordered one group of Indians after another to sell their lands and move farther west.

Among those forced to move were the Cherokee (cher'ə kē'). They had lived in western Georgia and in Tennessee for hundreds of years. Unlike most other Indians, the Cherokee chose to live the way United States citizens did. They had a constitution modeled after the United States Constitution. Many grew cash crops like cotton and tobacco.

Zebulon Pike was only 26 years old when he explored the Southwest.

The Cherokee were forced to leave lands they had lived on for years.
They called the long, hard march the Trail of Tears.

In 1838, the United States army rounded up over 15,000 Cherokee men, women, and children. The soldiers led them across the Mississippi River to what is now Oklahoma. It was a long, hard journey. About 4,000 people died along the way. The Cherokee called the journey the Trail of Tears.

By the 1840's, there were few Indians east of the Mississippi. Most Indians lived in the Louisiana Territory. Many of these Indians wondered how long they would be able to keep their new lands. They feared United States citizens would soon settle in the Louisiana Territory too.

To Help You Remember

1. Why did President Jefferson send Lewis and Clark to explore the northwestern part of the Louisiana Territory?
2. How did Sacajawea help the two explorers?
3. (a) Who did Jefferson send to explore the southwestern part of the Louisiana Territory? (b) What did that explorer learn when he visited New Mexico?
4. (a) Why did President Jackson want all the Indians living east of the Mississippi River to move farther west? (b) Where did most Indians live by the 1840's?

Chapter Review

Words to Know

On a separate sheet of paper, complete each sentence with the correct term from the list below.

a. source   d. democracy
b. canal   e. immigrants
c. pioneers   f. continental
                   divide

1. ____ are people who leave their homelands and make a new life in another country.
2. A ____ is a waterway made by people.
3. In a ____ every citizen has the right to take part in government.
4. The ____ is the place where rivers flow west to the Pacific Ocean and east to the Atlantic Ocean.
5. The ____ of a river is the place where a river begins.
6. ____ are people who are the first to try something new.

Reviewing Main Ideas

The following is a list of key events from the chapter. For each event, tell *when* it took place and *why* it was important.

1. Fulton's *Clermont* makes its trial run. (page 241–242)
2. The Erie Canal is completed. (pages 242–243)
3. Cooper's engine makes its first trip. (page 243)
4. Lincoln's grandparents settle in Kentucky. (page 245)
5. Andrew Jackson is elected president. (pages 248–249)
6. Lewis and Clark explore the northwestern part of the Louisiana Territory. (pages 250–252)
7. Zebulon Pike explores the southwestern part of the Louisiana Territory. (pages 252–253)
8. The Cherokee follow the Trail of Tears. (pages 253–254)

In Your Own Words

Write a paragraph about one of the people mentioned in the exercise above. Tell:
Who the person was.
What the person did.
When the person did it.
Why it was important.

Challenge!

There are many stories, legends, and even songs about the pioneers of the Old Northwest and the Old Southwest. Look in the library for songs about the Erie Canal, the riverboatmen, and pioneer life. Look too for legends and tales about Abe Lincoln's early years, Daniel Boone, and riverboatmen like Mike Fink. Share your findings with your classmates. Then find similarities and differences in these legends and songs. What qualities do the heroes have? What do those qualities suggest about the things the pioneers valued and believed in?

14

On to the Pacific

Until 1803, the Mississippi River marked the western boundary of the United States. Then, in 1803, President Thomas Jefferson bought the Louisiana Territory from France. This purchase moved the nation's western borders to the Rocky Mountains. The border remained there for over 40 years.

Then Americans began to open new frontiers in the 1840's. The trails to the West were clogged with wagons heading for Oregon, California, Texas, and even the dry deserts of Utah. As Americans moved farther and farther west, the nation's borders moved west as well. By 1848, the United States stretched across the continent of North America. The nation now reached from the Atlantic Ocean to the Pacific Ocean.

As You Read

This chapter tells how the United States grew in the 1840's. As you read, look for reasons the country added so much land during those years. The chapter is divided into three parts.

- Moving into New Frontiers
- Winning the Southwest
- A Rush to California

◀ *A wagon train slowly making its way west*

Moving into New Frontiers

Until the 1840's, only a few Americans journeyed beyond the Rocky Mountains. Some were traders. Every spring they loaded their wagons with goods made in the United States and headed west for New Mexico. Mexicans there were eager to buy goods from the American traders. Other Americans headed north and west to look for furs in the thick forests that lay beyond the mountains. In their search, they explored much of the Northwest.

Some traders and trappers made maps showing rivers, streams, and passes through the steep mountains.

Others wrote books about the rich green valleys of Oregon and other places along the Pacific coast.

Wagons West

As the land east of the Mississippi became more settled, many Americans longed to see the land the trappers wrote about. By the 1840's, some people were ready to head farther west. Many of them dreamed of starting life over as pioneers. Others were drawn by the thought of owning their own land. The best land in the East was already taken.

The diagram below shows the inside of a Conestoga wagon. The wagon had to be packed carefully to make use of every inch of space.

The trip across the Rockies was too long and too dangerous to make alone. So each spring pioneers gathered at Independence, Missouri. There they formed wagon trains.

Getting Started. The pioneers quickly learned that early spring was the best time to start. Ice and snow in the western mountains blocked trails in winter.

When the group was ready to leave, the pioneers hired a guide. The guide rode ahead of the wagons to search for the safest routes. He also kept a lookout for Indians. The pioneers would be traveling over land that belonged to the Indians. Many Indian groups did not want the settlers traveling through their land.

A Day on the Trail. Once the pioneers were on the road, each wagon train followed the same routine. Every day the travelers woke at about four o'clock in the morning. They fixed breakfast, packed up their bedding, and rounded up their animals. By seven o'clock, the wagons began to move out.

The guide and half a dozen men went ahead with picks and shovels. Their job was to smooth the way for the wagons. They removed stones from the path and cleared away brush. Several other men left the wagon train to hunt for buffalo and deer.

The rest of the group stayed with the wagon train.

Wagon trains moved very slowly. The pace was so slow that the children were able to walk much of the way. They often stopped to play games and pick flowers.

At noon, the pioneers stopped for a light meal. Then they moved on. At dusk, they pulled the wagons into a tight circle. It served as a corral for the tired animals. Fires were lighted, and the women cooked the evening meal. Before bedding down for the night, the travelers talked about the problems of the day.

On the Road. Day after day the wagon train slowly pushed west. A good day's journey was 20 or 25 miles (32 or 40 kilometers). Often travelers went far less. Many became tired and bored. Others complained of the hardships of travel on the trail. When it rained, the wagons got stuck in the mud. When the weather was hot and dry, clouds of dust hung over the trail. The travel was not easy.

When the wagon train finally reached the continental divide, the group cheered up. They could see the rivers that flowed west as well as east. So they thought the Pacific Ocean could not be far away. They were wrong. They still had to travel another 600 miles before they would reach the Pacific Ocean.

The United States Claims Oregon

Most of the families who went west in the early 1840's settled in Oregon. At that time, Oregon included all of the present-day states of Oregon, Washington, and Idaho as well as parts of Montana.

Ever since the United States had claimed Oregon in the early 1800's, the government encouraged Americans to settle there. So did the many American missionaries who lived in the territory. They had come to Oregon in the 1830's to teach the Indians the Christian religion.

The first missionary to arrive was Jason Lee. In 1834, he started a Methodist mission in the Willamette Valley. It was the first permanent American settlement in Oregon. Two years later Marcus and Narcissa Whitman built a mission in what is today the state of Washington.

Missionaries like Lee and the Whitmans wrote letters to friends and relatives urging them to move west. Marcus Whitman even led a group of settlers across the continent.

Between 1843 and 1845, 5,000 Americans arrived in Oregon. They helped to strengthen the United States' claim to the territory. At the time, the United States was not the only country that wanted Oregon. Great Britain claimed it too.

In 1846, the two countries solved the problem. They agreed to divide Oregon along latitude 40 degrees north. The land north of that line would belong to Great Britain. The land south of the line would belong to the United States.

Moving into Utah

While Oregon's boundary was being settled, a group of people moved into another part of the West. They did not settle in a green valley with good soil. They chose a sun-baked desert near the Great Salt Lake instead.

These settlers were Mormons. They belonged to the Church of Jesus Christ of the Latter-Day Saints. Like the Pilgrims more than 200 years before, the Mormons were seeking a safe place to live, a place where they could freely follow their religion.

A man named Joseph Smith had started the Mormon Church in western New York in 1830. Under his leadership, the church won many followers. However, some people did not agree with the teachings of the new church. They forced the Mormons to leave New York.

The Mormons moved to Ohio. They were not any more welcome there than they had been in New York. So they moved to Missouri and later to Illinois. Trouble developed there too. Smith and his brother were killed by an angry mob.

Unable to afford wagons and oxen, Mormons pulled two-wheeled handcarts on their journey to the Great Salt Lake.

A new leader named Brigham Young took charge of the group. Young decided that the Mormons should leave the United States. He planned to bring them to a part of the West claimed by Mexico. There they could live in peace.

In the spring of 1847, one group of Mormons after another headed for what is now the state of Utah. Over 15,000 men, women, and children made the long, hard journey.

The first group arrived in the valley of the Great Salt Lake in July of 1847. They found themselves in the middle of a dry, empty land. Many people might have given up and returned home, but not the Mormons. Instead, they dug ditches to carry water from mountain streams to their fields. By the end of the 1840's, they were growing crops where only a desert had once been.

To Help You Remember

1. List three problems the settlers moving west in the 1840's faced.
2. (a) Who were the first Americans to settle in the Oregon Territory? (b) Why did they go there?
3. How did the Oregon Territory become part of the United States?
4. (a) Why did the Mormons move so many times? (b) Where did they finally settle in 1847?

You have just read about some of the settlers who moved west during the 1840's. One way to see how far they had to travel is to look at a map that shows their routes.

The scale on a map can help you figure out distances. Use the scale on the map below to answer the questions.

1. Find the Oregon Trail. (a) How far did the settlers travel from Independence to Fort Laramie? (b) How far was it from Fort Laramie to Fort William?
2. Find the Mormon Trail. (a) How far did the Mormons travel from Nauvoo to Fort Laramie? (b) How far was it from South Pass to Salt Lake?
3. If settlers traveled 20 miles (32 kilometers) a day, how long would it take to travel (a) the length of the Oregon Trail? (b) The length of the Mormon Trail?

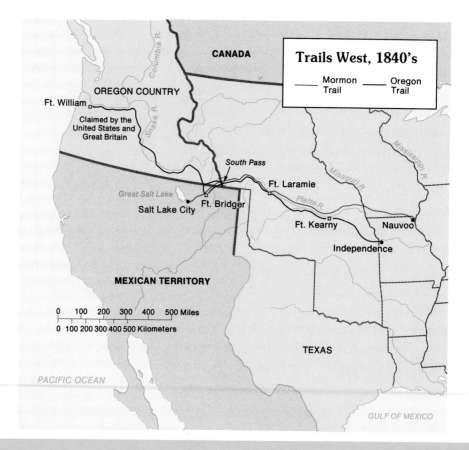

Winning the Southwest

The Mormons were not the only Americans to settle in Mexican territory. Americans were also moving to Texas. It too belonged to Mexico.

Americans in Texas

In 1823, an American named Stephen Austin received a huge grant of land from the Mexican government. So did several other Americans. Each had permission to start colonies on that land. The more people each brought to Texas, the more land Mexico would give them. The government wanted to build up Texas.

By 1830, over 20,000 Americans had settled in Texas. Many started small farms and ranches in southeastern Texas. Others built plantations. The mild climate and fertile soil there made it a good place to grow cotton. These settlers brought slaves to work on the plantations even though slavery was against Mexican law.

Trouble in Texas. At first, the Mexicans welcomed American settlers. However, as more and more Americans came, the government became alarmed. In some places, the newcomers outnumbered the Mexicans. The Mexican government was also angry because the Americans refused

to give up their slaves. In 1830, the Mexicans announced that Americans could no longer settle in Texas.

Many Americans living in Texas were outraged. They grew even angrier when Antonio Lopez de Santa Anna became president of Mexico in 1832. He quickly made himself president for life. As he took more and more power, people in every part of Texas protested. Among those who protested were Spanish-speaking Texans.

As the quarrel grew, many people in the United States rushed to help Texans free themselves from Mexican control. Among them were Davy Crockett and Jim Bowie. These men

The map shows American settlements in Texas. In what part of Texas were most of the settlements located?

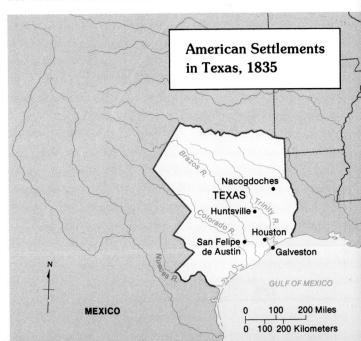

American Settlements in Texas, 1835

Brazos R.

Nacogdoches
TEXAS
Trinity R.
Huntsville
Colorado R.
Houston
San Felipe
de Austin
Galveston

Nueces R.

GULF OF MEXICO

N

MEXICO

0   100   200 Miles
0 100 200 Kilometers

had lived on the frontier all of their lives. Freedom was very important to them.

In 1836, Santa Anna decided to teach the Texans a lesson. He led 6,000 Mexican soldiers across the Rio Grande. They attacked an old mission near San Antonio called the Alamo. The Texans had been using the Alamo as a fort.

Fighting Begins. Inside the Alamo were 187 English-speaking and Spanish-speaking Texans. Davy Crockett and Jim Bowie were among them. The Texans' leader was a man named William B. Travis.

Soon after the Mexican soldiers attacked the fort, Travis sent a rider to get help for the small band of Texans.

This banner carried by the New Orleans volunteers is the only Texas flag to survive the Alamo.

The message the rider carried ended by saying "We have made up our minds: victory or death." The Texans tried to hang on until help came, but the United States army did not get there in time.

The battle raged for 13 days. The Mexican soldiers then forced their way into the fort. The Texans fought hard; yet when the battle was over, all 187 men were dead.

Other Texans were determined to fight back. An army led by Sam Houston, attacked Santa Anna at San Jacinto (san' jə sin'tō). With shouts of "Remember the Alamo," the Texans defeated the Mexicans and took Santa Anna prisoner. They forced him to sign a treaty giving Texas its independence.

Joining the United States. In September 1836, Sam Houston was elected president of the Republic of Texas. He and other Texans wanted Texas to become part of the United States.

Many Americans, however, were not sure that this was a good idea. Some feared that adding Texas to the United States would lead to war with Mexico. Others did not like the idea of having another slave state. They did not want slavery to spread farther west. The Texans finally won the argument. In 1845, Texas became part of the United States.

War with Mexico

Trouble with Mexico did not end in 1845. Texans claimed that the Rio Grande marked their southern border. Mexico said it was farther north and east at the Nueces (nü ā′səs) River. Both sides refused to give in. War seemed likely to follow.

War Begins. The United States made the first move. In 1846, President James Polk ordered the United States army under General Zachary Taylor to cross the Nueces River. When it did, Mexican soldiers attacked. The Mexican War had begun. By early 1847, General Taylor was pushing south into Mexico.

Meanwhile a United States army under General Winfield Scott made its way to Mexico from New Orleans. At the same time, Colonel Stephen Kearny headed west. He conquered New Mexico and then went on to California. By the time Kearny reached California, Americans there had already taken over the government.

The Fight for Mexico City. General Scott led his army to the capital of Mexico. As the army fought its way up the mountains toward Mexico City, it reached an ancient fort called Chapultepec (chə pul′tə pek).

One hundred young students from a military school were at the fort. When the Americans stormed the fort,

The United States army parades through Mexico City after defeating the Mexicans.

the boys fought to the end. Every one of the boys died in the battle.

On September 14, 1847, the United States army entered Mexico City. A fierce battle began. Over 1,000 American soldiers and 4,000 Mexican soldiers were wounded or killed in the fighting. Soon after the battle ended, Mexico surrendered.

Peace. The two countries signed a peace treaty in February 1848. Mexico gave up about half of its land. That land later became the states of California, Utah, Arizona, and Nevada. It also included a large part of

265

What was the western boundary of the United States in 1783? In 1803? When did the nation first reach the Pacific Ocean?

what is now New Mexico, Colorado, and Wyoming. In return, the United States paid Mexico $15 million.

The United States agreed to protect the rights of Mexicans who were living in the land Mexico gave up. It also promised that the Mexicans could keep their language, their religion, and their way of life.

Five years later the United States bought more Mexican land along the southern border of New Mexico and Arizona. The purchase was arranged by James Gadsden, the United States minister to Mexico. The Gadsden Purchase, as it was called, cost the United States $18 million. With the additional land, the United States reached its present boundary in the Southwest.

To Help You Remember

1. (a) Why did Americans settle in Texas? (b) Why did the Mexican government stop Americans from settling in Texas in 1830?
2. (a) What happened at the Alamo? (b) How did Texans get revenge for what happened at the Alamo?
3. (a) Why did the United States go to war with Mexico? (b) What did the United States gain as a result of the war?
4. (a) What was the Gadsden Purchase? (b) How much did it cost?

A Rush to California

On January 24, 1848, just two weeks before the peace treaty with Mexico was signed, a man named John Marshall made an important discovery. While building a sawmill in northern California, he spotted a shiny stone. He noticed a similar stone nearby. He stared at the two of them for a minute. Then he announced to the other workers nearby, "Boys, I believe I have found a gold mine." Rough tests showed he had, indeed, found gold.

The Word Spreads

The sawmill belonged to an American named John Sutter. At first, both he and Marshall tried to keep the discovery secret, but the news quickly spread. Thousands of people rushed to California. They came from every part of the United States and from many parts of the world. By 1849, a **gold rush** was in full swing.

Many people traveled to California over land in covered wagons. They followed the California Trail from Independence, Missouri, to Sacramento, California. Some people, eager to get to California, set out without taking along enough supplies for the long trip. Many of these people died along the way. Their graves served as grim reminders to travelers of the dangers of crossing a desert without taking along enough food or water.

People also came to California by water. In just one month, over sixty **clippers,** or fast sailing ships, sailed from Eastern seaports to San Francisco. Hundreds of ships also left ports in Europe, Asia, and South America. By the end of 1849, over 700 ships had pulled into the harbor at San Francisco. Altogether they carried over 45,000 passengers.

How does this advertiser persuade people to take clipper ships?

112 DAYS TO
SAN FRANCISCO.
MERCHANTS' EXPRESS LINE OF CLIPPER SHIPS.
Dispatching the Greatest Number of Vessels!
SMALLEST, CHEAPEST AND FASTEST VESSEL NOW UP!

THE MAGNIFICENT OUT-AND-OUT CLIPPER SHIP
WHITE SWALLOW
BUNKER, Commander, is now rapidly loading at PIER 16 E. R.
This splendid vessel, having made *very short passages,* and delivered her cargo in *unexceptionable order,* has established a reputation that will ensure *immediate dispatch.*
RANDOLPH M. COOLEY, 88 Wall Street,
Agents in San Francisco, Messrs. De Witt, Kittle & Co.

Sacramento started out as a small mining camp and quickly grew into a large city.

Some of these ships sailed around South America and then north along the Pacific coast. This route took six to eight months of travel. Therefore, many people tried a shorter route. They sailed to Panama. Then they crossed the Isthmus of Panama on foot or by wagon. The isthmus is a narrow strip of land that separates the Atlantic from the Pacific.

When the travelers reached the Pacific, they boarded a ship bound for San Francisco. It was a much shorter trip than sailing around South America but a far more dangerous one. Much of the isthmus was a breeding ground for mosquitoes, which carried dangerous diseases. Thousands of people died before they ever saw the Pacific.

Changes in California

As more and more people poured into California, San Francisco grew from a village of 1,000 people to a city of 25,000 in a few months. Mining camps grew even faster. The city of Sacramento started out as a mining camp on Sutter's land. Before the rush, there were only four houses there. A few months later more than 10,000 people were living in Sacramento.

The **boom,** or sudden growth, in California brought many changes. Eggs sold for $10 a dozen. Picks, shovels, and other tools cost 10 or even 20 times as much as they did back east. People turned their houses into hotels. At first, they charged from $7 to $14 a day for a room. Later they charged even more just for a bed in that same room. Many people earned more money in two months than they normally made in two or three years.

The gold seekers paid whatever was asked. They were too busy looking for gold to complain about prices. Besides, many were certain it was only a matter of time until they would become rich.

In the Mining Camps

The gold seekers rushed to the rivers and mountainsides near Sutter's mill. There each staked out a claim and began searching for gold. Many miners dug up the gravel from the bottoms of rivers and streams. Then they washed and sifted the gravel in hope of finding gold nuggets.

Within 10 years, the miners had found about $500 million worth of gold in California. Yet only a few people struck it rich. Most of the miners earned very little after months of backbreaking work.

In time, some people gave up their search for gold and returned home. Talk of gold in what is today Nevada and Colorado led others to rush there. They wanted to try their luck one more time. However, most people decided not to leave California. Instead, many of them built farms and ranches in California's fertile river valleys.

By the end of 1849, over 100,000 people were living in California. It became a state the following year. By 1860, the state's population had more than tripled. Many of the newcomers came for land, not to get rich quick.

By the end of the 1840's, the United States stretched from the Atlantic to the Pacific. It was one of the largest countries in the world. Some people wondered if such a big country could stay united. By 1860, many Americans shared that fear. The next unit tells why.

Thousands of people came by sea and over land to California to search for gold.

To Help You Remember

1. What did John Marshall discover that caused thousands of people to rush to California?
2. Describe three routes people took to California.
3. What changes took place in San Francisco and Sacramento as a result of the gold rush?
4. (a) Why did many people decide to stay in California after the gold rush? (b) What did they do there?
5. In 1850, the borders of the United States touched two oceans. Name them.

Chapter Review

Words to Know

1. Why was boarding a *clipper* a good way of getting to California?
2. How can a *gold rush* lead to a *boom?*

Reviewing Main Ideas

Below is a list of important events from the chapter. Find two facts from the chapter that describe each event.

1. In the 1840's, many Americans decide to move west of the Mississippi. (page 258)
2. The United States encourages people to settle Oregon. (page 260)
3. Mormons settle in Utah. (pages 260–261)
4. Americans settle in Texas. (pages 263–264)
5. Santa Anna attacks the Alamo. (page 264)
6. President Polk orders General Taylor to cross the Nueces River. (page 265)
7. In 1848, the United States and Mexico sign a peace treaty. (pages 265–266)
8. News of gold found in California spreads. (pages 267–269)

In Your Own Words

During the 1830's, Americans living in Texas quarreled with the Mexican government. Write a paragraph explaining the reasons for the quarrel from the American point of view. Write another paragraph explaining the Mexican side.

Keeping Skills Sharp

1. People moving west in the 1830's and 1840's traveled over many different routes. Make a map showing the routes people took to Oregon, Utah, and California. Be sure your map has a title and legend.
2. Draw a map of the United States. Do not include Alaska and Hawaii. On the map, show the territories the United States gained in the following years: 1845, 1846, 1848, and 1853. Be sure your map has a title and legend.

Challenge!

Suppose the year is 1840 and you and your family are getting ready to join a wagon train bound for Oregon. What supplies should you take with you? Make detailed lists of the food, clothing, weapons, household goods, farm equipment, and animals you will need. Do not forget it all has to fit in your wagon.

Things to Do

1. Write an article that might have appeared in newspapers of the day telling about one of the following events: war begins between the United States and Mexico, the Mormons change the desert, gold is discovered in California, a trip on the Oregon Trail.
2. Make a poster urging people to join a wagon train headed west. Use words that will make people eager to come.

Unit Review

Take Another Look

Below is a list of key events from the unit. On a separate sheet of paper, place the events in the order in which they occurred. Then tell why each was important to the country.

a. Lewis and Clark expedition begins.
b. California gold rush begins.
c. Texas joins the nation.
d. Jackson is elected president.
e. Oregon's boundary is settled.
f. The Erie Canal opens.
g. Mormons settle Utah.
h. The Cherokee take the Trail of Tears.
i. The United States and Mexico fight a war.
j. Pike explores the Southwest.
k. The National Road is started.
l. The first steamboat makes its way up the Hudson River.
m. Texas becomes a republic.

You and the Past

As people from the United States came into contact with people from the Spanish colonies and later from Mexico, many Spanish words found their way into the English language. In fact, the English that Americans speak has borrowed more words from Spanish than from any other language. Below are a few of those words. Try to explain how they became a part of the English language.

adobe	rodeo	corral	ranch
alligator	breeze	buffalo	canyon
mosquito	patio	pronto	tornado

See how many other words you can find that were borrowed from the Spanish language. Then study the map of the United States in the Atlas. How many Spanish place names can you find on the map? (Clue: Six states have names that come from Spanish.)

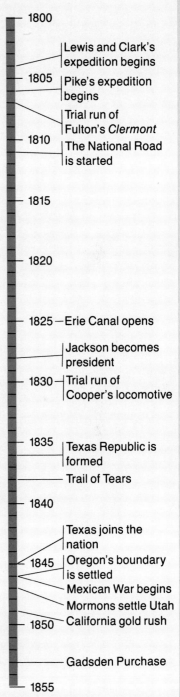

1800

Lewis and Clark's expedition begins

1805 Pike's expedition begins

Trial run of Fulton's *Clermont*

1810 The National Road is started

1815

1820

1825 — Erie Canal opens

Jackson becomes president

1830 — Trial run of Cooper's locomotive

1835 Texas Republic is formed

Trail of Tears

1840

Texas joins the nation

1845 Oregon's boundary is settled

Mexican War begins

Mormons settle Utah

1850 California gold rush

Gadsden Purchase

1855

271

The Union army at Cumberland Landing, Virginia, in 1864

Unit Six

A Time of Trouble

The early 1800's were a time of growth for the United States. The country gained much land during those years. The early 1800's were also a time when quarrels divided Americans. By 1861, these quarrels had led to a bitter war. When the war ended, Americans had to unite their country again.

15

The Nation Divides

In the early 1800's, thousands of Americans moved west. In their new homes, they developed ways of life similar to the ones they had left behind. By the 1840's, the Old Southwest looked much like the Southeast. Cotton fields lined the rivers much as they did in the East. At the same time, the Old Northwest was becoming more like the Northeast. It too was a land of small farms and bustling cities.

In the 1850's, Americans wondered how the land the United States won from Mexico would be settled. Many Southerners dreamed of the West covered with cotton plantations. Northerners saw the West covered by wheat fields, hog farms, and cattle ranches. Northerners and Southerners disagreed over far more than the future of the West, however. As arguments grew, many wondered whether the nation would survive. It seemed to be splitting apart.

As You Read

As you read this chapter, find out what caused the split that almost destroyed the nation. The chapter has three parts.

- Divisions in Congress
- The Fight for Freedom
- The Road to War

◀ *Henry Clay addressing the Senate in 1850*

Divisions in Congress

Soon after 1800, Americans began to talk about the United States as the Union. The word *union* reminded them of the way the nation had been formed. In 1776, the 13 original colonies formed a union of states.

As the nation grew, new states were admitted to the Union. The people living in those states sent senators and representatives to Congress. There they met with state leaders from other regions, or parts, of the country. Together they tried to agree on plans for the nation as a whole.

Different Concerns in Congress

From the start, people from different regions had very different concerns. Each region wanted to protect what was important to its own economy. Northerners wanted laws that would help trade and factories grow. Their needs were different from those of Southerners. Southerners owned very few factories. Most people in the South grew cotton. Some owned large plantations with many slaves. Therefore, Southerners wanted laws that protected slavery.

During the nation's first years, many Americans thought slavery would soon end in the United States. One Northern state after another outlawed slavery after the Revolution. Many believed that the South would some day do the same.

Then Southerners began to plant cotton. As the demand for the crop grew, so did the need for workers. After 1800, slavery became even more important to the Southern way of life. Few people in the South spoke of abolishing slavery anymore. Instead, they tried to defend it.

Senator John C. Calhoun of South Carolina argued that slavery was "a good." Slaves, he claimed, were much better off than free workers in the North. Northerners disagreed. If slaves were so happy, they asked, why did so many run away or attack their owners? No issue divided Northerners and Southerners more than the future of slavery in the United States.

As disagreements mounted, each section tried to keep the other from having too much power in Congress. At first, this was easy to do. For many years, the North and the South were about equal in size and population. Each had about the same number of representatives in Congress.

By 1819, more people lived in the North than in the South. Since the number of people in the House of Representatives from a state is based on the number of people living in

In the early 1800's, factories were growing in the North. At the same time, cotton plantations were booming in the South.

that state, the North had more representatives in Congress.

As the number of representatives from Northern states grew, the number of senators stayed the same. Each state had only two senators no matter how many people it had. So the Senate was still evenly divided between the North and the South.

The Missouri Compromise

Then, in 1819, Missouri asked to join the Union. Many people in Missouri owned slaves. So it would join the Union as a slave state. Southerners were delighted. They would now control the Senate. Many Northerners

were outraged. They did not want slavery to spread farther west.

For months, the two sides argued. Neither was willing to compromise or give in to reach an agreement. Then, in 1820, Maine, which was still part of Massachusetts, asked to become a separate state. It would be a free state, since the people of Maine did not favor slavery.

Senator Henry Clay of Kentucky saw a way to end the arguments over whether the West would be divided into free or slave states. His plan was known as the Missouri Compromise.

According to Clay's plan, Maine would enter the Union as a free state and Missouri as a slave state. To

Henry Clay served in the Senate for many years. During that time, he worked hard to keep the country united.

prevent future arguments, Congress drew an imaginary line at latitude 36°30′ north. The line followed the southern boundary of Missouri. Any new state north of the line would be a free state. Any state south of the line would be open to slavery.

Many Americans were pleased with the compromise. Only a few were not. Among them was Thomas Jefferson. He wrote that he had never been more worried about his country not even in the darkest days of the Revolution. Jefferson then went on to say, "I consider [the compromise] an

omen of death for the Union." Jefferson believed the compromise would quiet the fight over slavery for a while. Yet he feared it would not settle the problem forever.

The Debate over States' Rights

Jefferson was right. Arguments over the future of slavery in the United States were hushed for many years. During those years, the North continued to grow in population. Thousands of immigrants were moving to the United States each year. Almost all of them settled in the North.

Many Southerners feared the growing power of the national government. These Southerners looked

Senator John C. Calhoun spoke in favor of slavery in the new territories.

for ways to protect the rights of their states. They found an answer in the Tenth Amendment to the Constitution. It says that the powers that are not given to the national government belong to the states. Therefore, many Southerners believed that each state had the power to decide for itself whether a law passed by Congress was in keeping with the Constitution.

John Calhoun spoke for the Southerners in the United States Senate. He believed that a state could refuse to obey a law passed by Congress if the state thought the law went against the Constitution. Some carried that idea one step further. They said a state could even leave the Union if it wished to do so.

Other Senators were outraged. Most of them were Northerners. They were led by Daniel Webster of Massachusetts. He set forth the view held by most people in the North that the national government was the highest law in the land. He said no state had the right to refuse to obey any law made by Congress.

When Calhoun and other Southern senators claimed the nation was a union of states, Webster argued that it was a union of people. As he told one Southern senator, "It is, sir, the people's Constitution, the people's government, made for the people, made by the people, and answerable to the people."

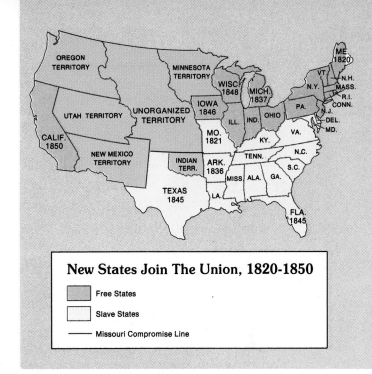

The number of free and slave states was equal until 1850. What happened that year to destroy the balance?

The Compromise of 1850

Over the years, Henry Clay found himself acting as peacemaker between Northerners and Southerners in Congress. Whenever the two sides could not agree, he would work out a compromise that both could accept. It became harder and harder for Congress to pass laws without making a compromise. Yet every year compromises were harder to reach.

In 1850, Clay faced his greatest challenge as a peacemaker. That year, California asked to join the Union as a free state. If it did, the

279

Black families were often split when they were sold at public auctions.

North would control not only the House of Representatives but the Senate as well. The South would surely object.

To satisfy both the North and the South, Clay came up with the Compromise of 1850. It included things that both the North and South wanted. To satisfy the North, California would be admitted to the Union as a free state. At the same time, Congress would outlaw the buying and selling of slaves in Washington, D.C., the nation's capital.

Clay also tried to satisfy the South. First, he suggested that the land the United States won from Mexico be divided into two new territories, New Mexico and Utah. The people of each territory would decide for themselves whether they would enter the Union as a free or a slave state. Second, Congress would pass a law that would make it easier for slave owners to get back **fugitive,** or runaway, slaves.

Calhoun, the senator from South Carolina, refused to accept the compromise. He argued that the South got too little and gave up too much.

Webster, on the other hand, favored the compromise. He made many speeches in favor of it. When his fellow Northerners angrily asked how he could speak for a law that would return people to slavery, Webster replied, "I speak not as a Massachusetts man, not as a Northern man, but as an American and a member of the Senate of the United States. I speak today because I do not want the Union broken up."

In the end, Clay's compromise was passed. However, it only settled the future of slavery for a few years.

To Help You Remember

1. People in the North and the South wanted different laws. What kinds of laws did each want?
2. What issue divided Northerners and Southerners more than any other?
3. How did Henry Clay solve the problem that came up when new states wanted to join the Union?
4. What was a fugitive slave?

Parallels of latitude tell how far north or south of the equator places are. Meridians of longitude tell how far east or west of the prime meridian places are. By the early 1800's, people were using these lines to draw state boundaries. For example, the Compromise of 1820 used 36°30′ north latitude to separate free states from slave states. (The 30′ stands for 30 minutes. There are 60 minutes in a degree of latitude or longitude. So 36°30′ north latitude is halfway between 36°N and 37°N.)

1. Name three states that have a border that lies along 36°30′ N.
2. (a) What line of latitude marked the Oregon Territory's northern border? (b) Its southern border?
3. Name four states that have 35°N as part of their borders.
4. (a) What state has 100°W part of its borders?
   (b) What state has 120°W as part of its borders?

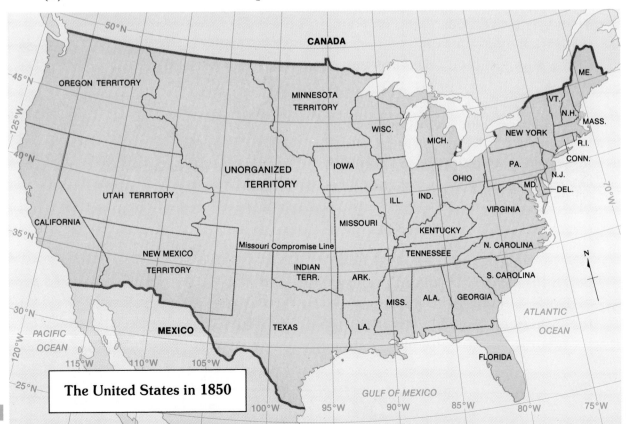

The United States in 1850

The Fight for Freedom

By 1850, few people in the United States could talk calmly about slavery. White Southerners, whether they owned slaves or not, saw slavery as important to their way of life. They argued that without slaves, the great cotton plantations would disappear.

Many Northerners, on the other hand, believed that it was wrong for one person to own another. Some even began to speak out against slavery. These men and women were called **abolitionists** because they wanted to abolish, or end, slavery.

The Abolitionists

William Lloyd Garrison, a young Boston printer, became one of the first leaders in the movement to free the slaves. In 1831, he started a newspaper called the *Liberator*. In the first issue, he called for an immediate end to slavery. It was a matter on which he would not compromise. "I am in earnest," he wrote. "I will not give up a single inch—and *I will be heard*." In following issues, Garrison told of the horrors of slavery. He also told of efforts being made to abolish it. He urged his readers to join in the fight.

Garrison started a group called the American Anti-Slavery Society. Its members spoke in churches and at town meetings. They also wrote articles about the evils of slavery.

Some of the leaders of the American Anti-Slavery Society were former slaves. The most famous of these leaders was Frederick Douglass. After escaping from slavery in Maryland, Douglass traveled through the North. He told people there what it was like to live in slavery. He also published an abolitionist newspaper called the *North Star*. He chose that name for his paper because the North Star helped runaway slaves find their way north to freedom.

Frederick Douglass, an ex-slave, spoke about the evils of slavery.

A few white Southerners also became abolitionists. Among them were Angelina and Sarah Grimke. They grew up in South Carolina. Although their parents owned many slaves, the sisters believed that slavery was wrong. They made speeches against slavery throughout the United States.

Many Americans were shocked by the Grimke sisters. In the 1800's, women were not supposed to speak in public. The Grimkes and other abolitionist women ignored the rule. They fought not only against slavery but also for women's rights.

The Slaves

Many slaves did not wait patiently for others to abolish slavery. They wanted their freedom and were willing to fight for it.

Some refused to work. They pretended to be sick. Others broke or hid tools to slow down work. A few attacked their owners, and countless others ran away. They escaped to the North or to Canada. Many abolitionists secretly banded together to form an underground railroad.

On the Underground Railroad. The underground railroad was neither underground nor a railroad. Instead, it was made up of barns, attics, and cellars, any place where slaves could

Harriet Tubman risked her life many times to lead slaves to freedom.

hide as they made their way north. The families who lived at each stop on the underground railroad acted as conductors. At night, they led the runaways to the next station where others hid them. Night after night, fugitive slaves continued the journey until they reached the North.

One of the most famous conductors on the underground railroad was Harriet Tubman. She was a former slave who had escaped from Maryland in 1849. For the next 15 years, she risked her life many times to lead more than 300 slaves to freedom. At

Many slaves escaped to freedom on the underground railroad. They hid during the day. At night, they traveled north.

one time, slave owners offered $40,000 to anyone who could capture Harriet Tubman. No one ever got the money because no one was able to catch her.

A Flight to Freedom. Not every slave had someone like Harriet Tubman to turn to. Some escaped on their own. A Kentucky woman named Eliza made one of the most daring escapes. When she heard that she was going to be sold, she decided to run away. She grabbed her baby and headed for the Ohio River. It was winter, and Eliza hoped the river would be frozen solid so that she could walk across it.

When Eliza saw that the river was only partly frozen, she decided to wait one more day. The next night, she could still see long jagged cracks in the ice. As Eliza debated what to do, she saw slave catchers coming toward her with bloodhounds. She quickly wrapped her baby around her in a shawl and leaped from one floating piece of ice to the next. In this way, she managed to cross the Ohio River.

In time, Eliza reached Canada and freedom. Yet she could not rest until her other five children were also free. The following June she returned to Kentucky and led the rest of her family to safety.

Harriet Beecher Stowe was an abolitionist who lived in Cincinnati, Ohio, just across the river from

Kentucky. When she heard Eliza's story, she decided to include it in a book she was writing about slavery.

The book was a novel about slavery called *Uncle Tom's Cabin*. It was published in 1851. It quickly became one of the most popular books ever written. Printing presses could not keep up with the demand for copies. The book helped many Americans see the evils of slavery for the first time. More and more people began to speak out against the system.

To Help You Remember

1. Who were the abolitionists?
2. How did the abolitionsts spread their ideas about slavery?
3. How did Frederick Douglass fight against slavery?
4. (a) How did Harriet Tubman help fugitive slaves find their way to freedom? (b) Explain how the underground railroad worked.
5. What effect did Harriet Beecher Stowe's book about slavery have on Americans?

The Road to War

The more some Americans spoke out against slavery, the louder others argued for it. Disagreements grew more heated. Arguments raged across the nation.

Trouble in Kansas and Nebraska

Many people in government did not realize how strongly Americans felt about slavery until 1854. That year Congress opened the Kansas and Nebraska territories for settlement. Stephen A. Douglas, a senator from Illinois, suggested that the people in the two territories decide for themselves whether they wanted slavery or not.

Many Northerners were against the idea. They pointed out that Kansas and Nebraska were north of the line drawn in the Missouri Compromise. So these territories should become free states. Douglas disagreed. He explained that the Compromise of 1850 had done away with the Missouri Compromise.

Douglas argued that the people in the territories should be given a chance to decide for themselves about slavery. At first, it seemed like a good idea. Southerners were happy because the territories would remain open to slavery. Both territories were so far north that most Northerners felt sure they would enter the Union as free states.

Nebraska did join the Union as a free state. That made Southerners more determined that Kansas must join as a slave state. Northerners were equally determined to keep slavery out of Kansas. Groups of people from both parts of the country rushed to Kansas. Northerners wanted to make sure Kansas became a free state. Southerners wanted to make it a slave state.

Kansas became a battleground. Groups of armed men from both the North and the South rode through the countryside attacking each other's towns and farms. In all, 200 people were killed in the fighting.

A New Political Party, A New Leader

Even as the fighting was spreading through Kansas, a group of men were meeting in Ripon, Wisconsin. They had come to start a new political party. They called it the Republican party.

Unlike other political parties, the Republican party took a strong stand on slavery. Republicans saw it as a great evil. They urged Congress to outlaw slavery in the territories.

Among those who joined the party was a lawyer from Illinois. His name was Abraham Lincoln. In 1858, he expressed the feelings of many Republicans.

The supporters of Stephen Douglas wore this campaign button.

In one of his speeches Lincoln said, "A house divided against itself cannot stand. I believe this government cannot last forever, half slave and half free. I do not expect the house to fall—but I do expect it will cease to be divided."

Lincoln was running for senator from Illinois when he made the speech. It did not help him win the election. Stephen Douglas defeated him. The speech and others like it did help to make Lincoln well known throughout the country. Two years later, in 1860, he became the Republican party's candidate for president of the United States. Once again, he ran against Stephen Douglas. This time, however, Abraham Lincoln won the election.

This campaign button showed support for Abraham Lincoln.

Abraham Lincoln and his running mate, Hannibal Hamlin, won the 1860 election.

Splitting Up

Long before the election, white Southerners had warned that they would **secede** from, or leave the Union if a Republican became president. When Lincoln was elected, they carried out their threat.

On December 20, 1860, South Carolina voted to secede. By February, 1861, Mississippi, Florida, Georgia, Louisiana, Texas, and Alabama also left the Union.

Representatives from the seven states met on February 4, 1861, in Montgomery, Alabama. They drew up a constitution for a new nation. The nation was called the Confederate States of America. Jefferson Davis of Mississippi was elected president.

Abraham Lincoln did not want a war, but soon he had no choice. On an island overlooking the harbor at Charleston, South Carolina, stood Fort Sumter. A few United States soldiers were stationed there. At dawn on April 12, 1861, Confederate soldiers attacked United States soldiers at the fort. War had begun.

To Help You Remember

1. Why did people from the North and the South rush to Kansas?
2. What stand did the Republican party take on slavery?
3. List the states that had seceded from the Union by February, 1861.
4. (a) What did the seceding states call their new nation? (b) Who was chosen to lead it?

Chapter Review

Words to Know

On a separate sheet of paper, complete the following sentences.

1. During the 1850's, many people in the North became *abolitionists*. An abolitionist is ____.
2. In February of 1861, seven states *seceded* from the Union. To secede from means to ____.
3. Harriet Tubman helped *fugitive slaves* escape. A fugitive slave is ____.

Reviewing Main Ideas

1. How did the Missouri Compromise balance the number of free states and slaves states?
2. (a) What did John Calhoun believe a state could do if it disagreed with a law passed by Congress? (b) How did Daniel Webster respond to Calhoun's argument?
3. (a) How did the Compromise of 1850 change the Missouri Compromise of 1820? (b) Who favored the compromise—and why? (c) Who was against it and why?
4. In what ways did the abolitionists fight against slavery?
5. In what ways did slaves fight against slavery?
6. What was the Republican party's view on slavery?
7. How did seven Southern states react to the news that Abraham Lincoln had won the election?

In Your Own Words

Pretend you are *one* of the following people living in the United States in 1860: a Southern planter, an abolitionist, a slave. Write a paragraph that tells how you feel about slavery. The page numbers tell you where to find the information in the chapter.

1. Southern planter—page 276
2. Abolitionist—pages 282–283
3. Slave—pages 283–284

Challenge!

Choose one of the candidates for president in the 1860 election. Make a poster or write a song urging people to vote for that candidate. Design a campaign button for your candidate. Be sure to put a slogan on it.

Things to Do

1. Senators John Calhoun and Daniel Webster both had strong views on whether or not a state had the right to leave the Union. Choose one of them and find out more about his point of view. Share what you learn with the class.
2. Prepare a report on Harriet Beecher Stowe. In your report, explain why Abraham Lincoln said she helped start the Civil War.
3. Find out more about the underground railroad. Through what states did it pass? Name a conductor.

Keeping Skills Sharp

The map shows the results of the 1860 election. Use the legend on the map to answer the questions.

1. Who ran for president in 1860?
2. (a) Which candidate won the largest number of states? (b) In what part of the country were most of those states located?
3. (a) How many states did Stephen Douglas win? (b) Where were the states he won located?
4. (a) Which candidate won most of the Southern states? (b) How many states did he win?
5. (a) Name the states John Bell won. (b) Which of those states were border states?
6. Which state gave its votes to two of the candidates?
7. People living in the territories were not allowed to vote. How do you think people in the Kansas and Nebraska territories might have voted? Give reasons for your answer.

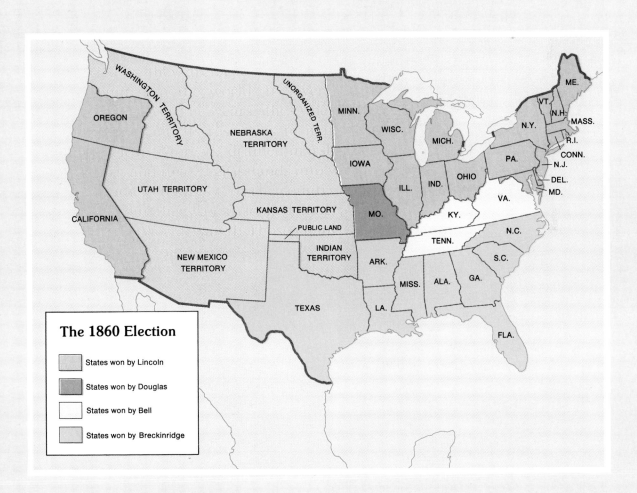

The 1860 Election

- States won by Lincoln
- States won by Douglas
- States won by Bell
- States won by Breckinridge

16
Civil War and Reunion

News of the attack on Fort Sumter rocked the nation. People who had never taken sides before chose one now. Americans believed that a war would settle the differences between the North and the South. Few expected the fighting to last more than a few weeks. No one was prepared for the long and bitter struggle that lay ahead.

A **civil war** had begun. This war was different from other wars in the nation's history. It was a war between people of the same country. Family members and friends often sided against each other on the battlefields. So a civil war is in many ways the most terrible kind of war a nation can fight.

As You Read

The chapter is divided into three parts.

- Preparing for War
- On the Battlefields
- A Troubled Peace

The first part of the chapter tells how the North and the South prepared for war. The next part describes the war itself. The last part tells how the nation struggled to unite after the fighting ended.

◀ *The attack on Fort Sumter, South Carolina, 1861*

Preparing for War

When the Civil War began, most people sided with their neighbors. Yet hundreds of Northerners fought in the Confederate army. Many Southerners supported the Union.

Choosing Sides

Hundreds of families were torn apart by the war. Among them was the Lee family of Virginia. When the war began, President Lincoln asked Robert E. Lee to take command of the Union army. He was one of the best officers in the nation.

Posters like the one below were used to encourage men to join the army.

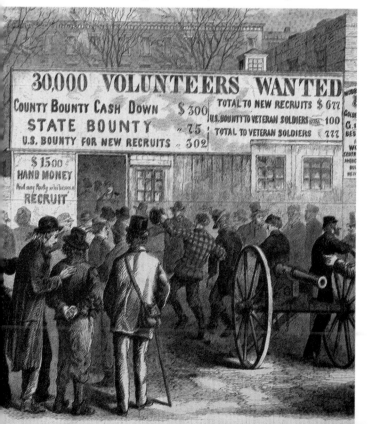

Lee was devoted to his country. Yet he also felt strong ties to Virginia, his home state. In the end, Lee decided his first loyalty was to Virginia. He resigned from the United States army to become a military advisor to Jefferson Davis, president of the Confederacy. Later he served as commander of the Confederate forces.

Lee's daughter Amy made a different choice. She left her family to support the Union. A nephew, Samuel P. Lee, also fought for the Union. He was a commander in the United States navy.

Abraham Lincoln's family was divided too. His wife, Mary Todd Lincoln, had three brothers. All three sided with the Confederacy.

Choosing sides was especially hard for those who lived in the border states. These were the eight states that lay between the North and the South. Although each allowed slavery, all had close ties with the North. Four of the states—North Carolina, Tennessee, Arkansas, and Virginia—joined the Confederacy. The others, Delaware, Maryland, Missouri, and Kentucky, stayed in the Union.

Yet even after such decisions had been made, arguments continued. Shortly after Virginia left the Union, the people in the northwestern part of the state protested. They did not

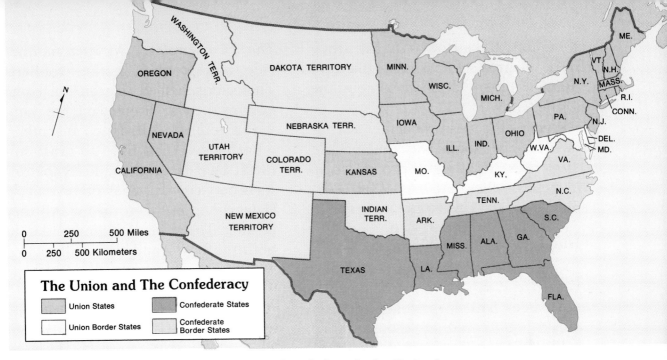

Find the border states on the map. Which sided with the Union? Which joined the Confederacy? How many states fought for the Confederacy? How many fought for the Union?

want to join the Confederacy. So they formed a new state called West Virginia. It joined the Union in 1863.

The Two Sides

At the start of the war, the Confederacy had 11 states. The other 22 states remained in the Union. Then Kansas became a state in 1861, West Virginia in 1863, and Nevada in 1864. They too fought for the Union.

The Union's Advantages. The Union not only had more states than the Confederacy, it also had more people. In 1861, the North had more than 22 million people. The South had only 9 1/2 million people.

The North also had over 90 percent of the nation's factories and mills. These factories kept the Union soldiers supplied with uniforms, tents, blankets, shoes, guns, and all of the other goods an army needs. The North had most of the railroads too.

Confederate Advantages. The North did not have all of the advantages. The South had the best generals. Over the years many young Southerners, eager for a career in government, attended the United States Military Academy at West Point,

New York. Like Robert E. Lee, they were talented soldiers. Also, like Lee, many of them decided to join the Confederacy.

Perhaps the most important advantage for the South was that people there were fighting to protect their homes, families, and way of life. People fight harder when the things they value most are threatened.

Soldiers and Volunteers

Both sides had to get ready for war quickly. They needed thousands of soldiers. They also needed people to keep the army supplied with food, weapons, and other goods. They needed people willing to scout, nurse the wounded, and even act as spies.

After 1863, many black Americans joined the Union army.

The Two Armies.
At first, neither side had trouble getting soldiers. Thousands rushed to sign up. However, as the war dragged on, the number of volunteers dropped sharply.

Both sides then tried to **draft** soldiers. That is, each required that all men between the ages of 18 and 35 (later 17 to 50) sign up for military service. The draft was unpopular in both the North and the South.

Southerners thought the draft was unfair because anyone who owned 15 or more slaves was excused from the draft. People in the South also believed that only the states had a right to draft citizens.

People in the North thought the draft was unfair too. Northerners did not have to go into the army if they paid the government $300. They were also excused if they had someone serve in their place. Poor people grumbled about a law that favored the rich.

Blacks in the War.
In spite of the need for soldiers, blacks were not allowed to join the Union army at the beginning of the war. Yet many found other ways to help. Some worked as cooks, scouts, and spies. Others drove supply wagons. About 250,000 blacks helped the Union during the first two years of the war.

Then, in 1863, Lincoln allowed blacks to join the army. More than

186,000 black Americans signed on as soldiers in the Union army. They had an outstanding war record. Twenty-two black soldiers received the Congressional Medal of Honor for acts of bravery.

Women in the War. Women too fought in the Civil War. As many as 400 women disguised themselves as men and went out on the battlefields. Others carried mail or served as spies. Harriet Tubman, the woman who led so many slaves to freedom, was the most daring Union spy. She made dozens of trips south.

Harriet Tubman also worked as a nurse. So did over 3,000 other women, both black and white. Some had the official backing of the Union or the Confederacy. Others set off on their own. Among them was a young woman named Clara Barton.

Clara Barton heard there was a shortage of doctors and nurses. So she loaded an ox cart with medicine and bandages and headed for the nearest battle. Her experiences in the war led her to start the American Red Cross. It still provides emergency help in times of war or when a natural disaster strikes.

Many women also helped out at home. They took their husbands' places on farms and plantations. Others worked in factories, offices, and shops.

Clara Barton spent her life helping others in times of trouble.

As the war continued, women in both the North and the South joined volunteer groups. Some of these groups sent food and medicine to wounded soldiers. Other volunteer groups ran military hospitals.

To Help You Remember

1. What is a civil war?
2. (a) List two advantages the North had in the war. (b) List two advantages of the South.
3. How did the North and the South get soldiers for their armies?
4. How did black Americans help the Union during the war?
5. How did women help during the Civil War?

On the Battlefields

The Civil War began in the spring of 1861. Few people expected it to last long. Southerners thought that the North would not be willing to fight long. Northerners were certain that the war would end as soon as the Union army captured Richmond, Virginia. It was the capital of the Confederacy.

On to Richmond

On July 21, Union soldiers marched south from Washington, D.C., to Richmond. Many people rode along in carriages to watch the battle. They were sure the Union would quickly win the battle and the war.

The Union army had its first defeat at the Battle of Bull Run.

At Bull Run in northern Virginia, the Union soldiers met the Confederate army. The untrained Northern troops fought bravely but they were no match for the Confederate army. In the end, the Union soldiers ran from the battlefield only to find the way blocked by frightened sightseers. Rushing to get away, the sightseers overturned wagons and carriages. Horses fell. People ran in fear for their lives. The road to Washington was jammed for hours.

Planning for Victory

The South's victory at the Battle of Bull Run shocked the North. People in the South were, of course, pleased by their success. However, the battle convinced leaders on both sides that the war would be long and bitter.

Many people in the South believed that a long war would help their side. They did not have to defeat the Union. They just had to keep the Union from conquering the South. Most Southerners believed Northerners would soon tire of fighting. Then the North would agree to let the South secede and form its own separate nation.

People in the North, on the other hand, knew they had to defeat the Confederacy. To do so, Union soldiers

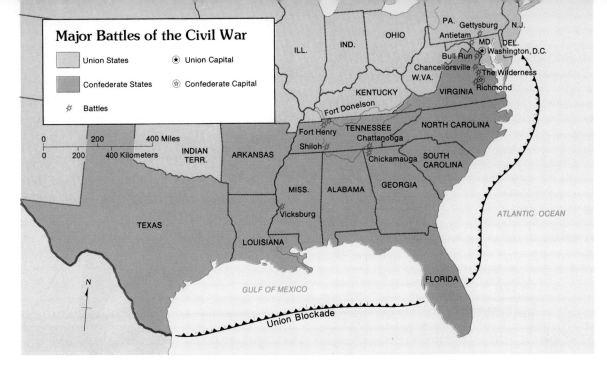

Major Battles of the Civil War

Union States

Confederate States

⭐ Union Capital

✪ Confederate Capital

✷ Battles

0   200   400 Miles

0   200   400 Kilometers

PA.   Gettysburg   N.J.
Antietam
MD.   DEL.
Washington, D.C.
Bull Run
Chancellorsville
W.VA.   The Wilderness
VIRGINIA   Richmond
Fort Donelson
NORTH CAROLINA
Fort Henry   TENNESSEE
Chattanooga
Shiloh
Chickamauga   SOUTH CAROLINA
INDIAN TERR.
ARKANSAS
MISS.   ALABAMA   GEORGIA
Vicksburg
TEXAS
LOUISIANA
FLORIDA
ATLANTIC OCEAN
N
GULF OF MEXICO
Union Blockade
OHIO
ILL.   IND.
KENTUCKY

Where in the Confederacy were most Civil War battles fought? Where in the Union did a major battle take place? How did the Union navy stop supplies from reaching Southern harbors?

had to divide and defeat the Confederate States. The North also had to keep the South from getting help from other countries. So the Union planned to **blockade** the Southern coast. It had to keep trading ships away from Southern harbors.

For the first two years of the war, the South did a better job of carrying out its plan than the Union did. Still it was impossible to tell which side would win the war until 1863.

1863, the Turning Point

In 1863, the Union blockade was beginning to work. Warehouses that lined the docks of New Orleans and other Southern cities stood empty. The South was running out of guns, ammunition, medicine, and other supplies. Three other important events also took place that year.

Freedom. The first event took place on New Year's Day. On January 1, 1863, President Lincoln signed the Emancipation Proclamation. To **emancipate** means to set free. The Emancipation Proclamation declared that all slaves in the Confederate States were forever free.

After the proclamation, the war took on new meaning for many

Americans. Some Northerners who were not willing to fight to save the Union were more than eager to fight to free the slaves. Europeans also welcomed the news. Before the proclamation, some Europeans wanted to help the South. After all, they bought a great deal of cotton from the South. However, when the war became a fight against slavery, people in Europe gave their support to the North.

Lee at Gettysburg.

The second event took place during the summer of 1863. That June, General Lee decided to invade the North. He believed the Union would be quicker to end the war if the fighting took place on Northern soil.

By the end of June, Lee's army was in Pennsylvania. Union soldiers watched nearby. On July 1, the battle began on a field west of Gettysburg. Lee attacked the Union army again and again but could not break through their lines. Then on July 3, 15,000 Confederate soldiers charged one more time. Soldiers on both sides fought bravely.

Thick smoke filled the air. When it finally cleared, thousands of Confederate soldiers lay dead. Lee had no choice but to return to Virginia with what was left of his army. He had lost more than one third of his men. Union losses were just as heavy.

Grant in the West.

One day after the Battle of Gettysburg, the Union had another victory. General Ulysses S. Grant and his Union army captured Vicksburg, Mississippi. Vicksburg was the last Confederate fort on the Mississippi River. The Union army now controlled the river. Time was running out for the South.

The End of the War

Early in 1864, General Grant took charge of all the Union forces. Then he rushed to Washington. From there, he led an army south toward Richmond, Virginia, to attack General Lee's army. At the same time, General William T. Sherman moved another Union army south and east from Chattanooga, Tennessee, to Richmond. There the two generals planned to surround Lee.

Sherman's March.

By May, Sherman's army was marching across Georgia to Atlanta. As the soldiers traveled, they blew up bridges and railroad tracks. They burned homes and farms. They destroyed everything that might help the South to continue to fight.

Sherman left Atlanta in flames. Then he headed east to Savannah, Georgia. Just before Christmas, the city fell. Then Sherman headed north into the Carolinas.

Wearing a new uniform, Lee surrenders to Grant at Appomattox. The Civil War was finally over.

Surrender. By the spring of 1865, Grant was pushing through Virginia. On April 3, he took Richmond. Six days later, on April 9, 1865, Lee surrendered at Appomattox, a small town in Virginia.

The defeated soldiers were allowed to return home as soon as they signed a pledge that they would not fight any longer. Lee's men wept as they said good-bye to their leader. Union soldiers started to cheer, but Grant stopped them. He told his men, "The war is over. The rebels are our countrymen again." Soon after Appomattox, other Confederate leaders also surrendered. After four long years, the Civil War was finally over.

To Help You Remember

1. When did the Civil War begin?
2. Why did the Southerners believe that a long war would favor their side?
3. What was the North's plan for winning the war?
4. (a) What was the Emancipation Proclamation? (b) Give two reasons why it was important.
5. How did the Civil War end?

299

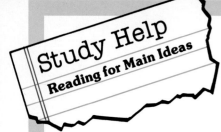
So far in this chapter, you have read about several events that took place during the Civil War. These events occurred in 1861, 1863, and 1865. Keeping track of important events can help you remember the main ideas in the chapter.

Below is a chart that lists the key dates from the first two lessons of the chapter. A few of the important events that took place in those years have been filled in. Look back in the chapter to find other important events. Then copy the chart on a sheet of paper and fill in the missing information.

Civil War and Reunion

1861: 1. _____
   2. Union soldiers are defeated at the Battle of Bull Run.

1863: 1. President Lincoln issues the Emancipation Proclamation.
   2. _____
   3. _____

1865: 1. _____
   2. The Civil War ends.

As you continue reading, look for other reasons 1865 was an important year. In the next lesson you will find out why 1866 and 1877 were important dates. Add them to the chart.

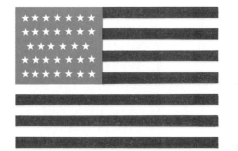

A Troubled Peace

Five days after the meeting at Appomattox, Abraham Lincoln was killed. On April 14, 1865, John Wilkes Booth, angry over the South's defeat, shot the president at Ford's Theater in Washington, D.C.

People in both the North and the South mourned his death. Americans also mourned the great losses they had suffered in the war. Many were eager to put the war behind them. However, the suffering was not yet over for the South. Much of the South was in ruins. Thousands of people, both black and white, were hungry and homeless.

Starting Over in the South

To help people in the South, Congress started the Freedmen's Bureau. It supplied food, medicine, and other emergency help to both white and black Southerners. The bureau also set up schools for free slaves throughout the South.

Many former slaves had dreamed of owning their own farms. They had hoped that the federal government would give them 40 acres (60 hectares) and a mule so that they could build a new life. The government did open some public land for farming. However, there was not enough land for everyone.

Many former slaves looked for work on plantations. Most planters needed help, but few had enough money to pay wages. So many divided up their land and rented it out. Because money was scarce, the land was rented for crops rather than cash. To pay the rent, farmers had to share their harvest with the landowner. The landowners took from one quarter to one half of the crop. This way of paying landowners became known as sharecropping, and the people who rented the land were called sharecroppers.

Richmond, Virginia, like many other Southern cities, lay in ruins after the war.

When the war ended, the Freedmen's Bureau built schools in the South.

In time, over 90 percent of all black farmers in the South became sharecroppers. Many white farmers who had lost their land during the war also became sharecroppers.

New Laws for the Southern States

While people were struggling to build a new life, the Southern states had no state governments. If they were to rejoin the Union, each had to form a new state government.

Lincoln's Plan. Lincoln had worked out a plan for the **reconstruction,** or the rebuilding, of the South. When he was killed, Andrew Johnson became president. Johnson tried to carry out Lincoln's plan.

As soon as ten percent of the voters in a state had sworn to be loyal to the Union, Johnson allowed them to form a new government. They could choose their own lawmakers. They could not elect anyone who had been a Confederate leader. However, Confederate soldiers could take part in government.

Each state also had to approve the Thirteenth Amendment to the Constitution. It outlawed slavery. Each of the Confederate States also had to write new state constitutions that outlawed slavery too.

Anger over Changes in the South. All of the Confederate States, except Texas, had outlawed slavery by December, 1865. However, many Republicans in Congress did not trust the new leaders of the South or the governments they set up. They pointed out that every one of the government leaders in the South had fought in the Confederate army.

Many Republicans were also angry at the way blacks were being treated in the South. The Southern states passed laws that kept blacks from enjoying the same rights as whites. Blacks could not change jobs or move from place to place. Those who did not have jobs could be arrested.

Republicans Offer a New Plan. Some Republicans in Congress decided

Johnson's plan did not force the South to change nearly enough. So they pushed for a more extreme, or radical, plan of reconstruction.

These Republicans got Congress to pass their plan for reconstruction in 1867. Under the plan, the South was divided into five parts. A general took charge of each part until the states in that district had written new constitutions. Black men took part in writing the new laws. However, people who had fought in the Southern army could not.

Congress also said that each state must agree to three amendments to the United States Constitution. One was the Thirteenth Amendment, which was passed in 1865. It ended slavery. The second was the Fourteenth Amendment, passed in 1868. It granted citizenship to black Americans. The third was the Fifteenth Amendment, passed in 1870. It gave black men the right to vote.

President Johnson on Trial. Johnson did not like the Republican plan. He argued against it. However, the Republicans had more than enough votes in Congress to pass it.

Johnson had lost the confidence of Congress. It began to pass laws that limited the president's power. When Johnson ignored those laws, the House of Representatives voted to **impeach** him. To impeach means to put the president on trial for not carrying out his duties.

The trial took place in the Senate. Two thirds of the Senate, 36 senators, had to find Johnson guilty before he could be removed from office. On May 16, 1868, the voting began. Only 35 senators thought Johnson was guilty. Congress was not able to come up with enough votes to remove him from office.

Newcomers in Government

Congress's plan for reconstruction brought many new people into government in the South. A few came

These citizens of South Carolina promise to remain loyal to the Union.

from the North. Most, however, were Southerners.

Northern Carpetbaggers. As new state governments were forming, some Northerners moved to the South. Because many of them carried suitcases made of carpeting, they were known as carpetbaggers. It was not a friendly nickname. Those who used it believed that the newcomers were getting rich at the South's expense. Some carpetbaggers did.

Most Northerners went south for other reasons. Some wanted to buy land or start a business. Others wanted to help the freed slaves.

Southern Scalawags. Some white Southerners also worked in the new state governments. They were known as scalawags. A scalawag is a dishonest person. Some Southerners believed that anyone who worked for the new governments was a crook or a traitor.

The people known as scalawags believed that the South would be better off if everyone worked together. They thought there had been more than enough fighting.

Blacks in Government. Many blacks took part in the new governments too. Many served in state legislatures. Two black men from Mississippi, Hiram Revels and Blanche K. Bruce, were elected to the United States Senate. There were black lieutenant governors in Louisiana, Mississippi, and South Carolina.

The Fight against Change

The new state governments brought many changes to the South. They started public schools. They also built roads, canals, and railroads.

Government in the South also became more democratic. Planters no longer controlled state government. Poor people, both black and white, had a larger role in government.

Many white Southerners did not like the changes the new governments made. State governments were spending a lot of money, so taxes went up. Southerners who had

These men are the first blacks to serve in the United States Congress.

served in the Confederate army resented the fact that they had no say in the new governments and blacks did. Many of these Southerners did not consider blacks equals.

A few people in the South used violence to show their views. In 1868, they started a secret society known as the Ku Klux Klan. Dressed in white hoods and robes, the Klan attacked and sometimes killed blacks. Federal soldiers tried to break up the Klan, but the group continued to make trouble.

An End to Reconstruction

In 1877, the last Union soldiers went home. Reconstruction was officially over. Soon after white Southerners took control of their state governments. Many passed laws that made it impossible for blacks to vote. Blacks who tried to vote lost their jobs. Some even lost their lives.

By 1877, Republicans had lost interest in helping blacks. The former slaves were on their own. Many moved North. Yet there too they were treated as if they were not equal to whites.

Many blacks began to fight against laws that **discriminated** against them. They believed that any law that treated black citizens differently from white citizens was unfair. Blacks struggled long and hard to

After the war, people in the South worked hard to rebuild their cities.

change such laws. Not until the 1960's, 100 years after the Civil War, did blacks begin to win that fight.

To Help You Remember

1. (a) What problems did the South face at the end of the war?
   (b) What did Congress do to help the South solve those problems?
2. What was the president's plan for reconstruction of the South?
3. What was Congress' plan for reconstruction?
4. What rights did blacks gain by the Thirteenth, Fourteenth, and Fifteenth amendments?

Chapter Review

Words to Know

1. In 1861, a *civil war* began. A civil war is ____.
2. During the Civil War, men between 17 and 50 faced a *draft*. A draft is ____.
3. The Union set up a *blockade*. A blockade is ____.
4. President Lincoln *emancipated* all slaves in the Confederate States. To emancipate is to ____.
5. After the war, black Americans faced *discrimination*. Discrimination is ____.
6. Radical Republicans wanted to *impeach* President Johnson. To impeach means to ____.
7. After the war, the South had to go through *reconstruction*. Reconstruction is ____.

Reviewing Main Ideas

1. List two important events that took place in 1861.
2. List three important events that took place in 1863.
3. List three important events that took place in 1865.
4. What important event took place in 1867?
5. Why was the year 1877 important to people in the South?
6. Why were the years 1865, 1868, and 1870 especially important to black Americans?

In Your Own Words

Choose a key event from the chapter. Then write a paragraph that gives the following information:

What happened.
When it happened.
Why it was important.

Keeping Skills Sharp

Make a bar graph showing exports of cotton for the following years:

1850— 635 million pounds
1855—1,008 million pounds
1860—1,768 million pounds

Do you think cotton exports rose or fell in 1865? Why?

Challenge!

Every victory for one side in a war is a defeat for the opposing side. Choose a battle in the Civil War and write a newspaper article that describes it from a Union point of view. Then rewrite the article as it might have appeared in a Confederate newspaper.

Things to Do

1. Many people took part in the Civil War. Make a poster that shows the various ways people helped out.
2. Write a report telling how Clara Barton's experience during the Civil War led to the founding of the Red Cross.

Unit Review

Take Another Look

Below is a list of key events from the unit. Look back through the unit to find out when they occurred. You will be able to find some of the events on the time line on this page. Then list the events in order. Tell why each was important.

a. Lee surrenders to Grant.
b. Fort Sumter is attacked.
c. President Lincoln is killed.
d. Lincoln issues the Emancipation Proclamation.
e. The Confederate States of America is formed.
f. Congress approves the Missouri Compromise.
g. The Republican plan for reconstruction is approved.
h. The Civil War begins.

You and the Past

1. After the Civil War, people in the South set aside a day to honor the men and women who had died fighting for the Confederacy. Not long after, Northerners decided to honor those who had died fighting for the Union. Today Americans set aside one day every year to honor all the men and women who died defending their country. That day is called Memorial Day. Find out how Memorial Day is celebrated where you live.
2. In 1862, Congress approved a new medal to honor Union heroes. It was called the Congressional Medal of Honor. It has been awarded to many men and women in the years since the Civil War. Find out who is eligible to win the medal. Find out, too, about Medal of Honor winners in your state.
3. On November 19, 1863, Abraham Lincoln came to Gettysburg, Pennsylvania to dedicate a part of the battlefield as a cemetery for those who had died in the battle there. In his speech, the President outlined the goals of the nation. He also explained why the nation was at war. His speech is known as the Gettysburg Address. Read the speech. Then discuss why the speech has become such an important part of our American heritage.

1850–Compromise of 1850

Uncle Tom's Cabin published

Republican party started

1855

South Carolina secedes

1860

Confederacy formed

Civil War starts

Emancipation Proclamation

Lee invades the North

1865 Grant's victory at Vicksburg

Lee surrenders to Grant

Thirteenth Amendment

Reconstruction begins

Fourteenth Amendment

1870

Fifteenth Amendment

1875

Reconstruction ends

1880

New York City's bright lights and elevated trains, 1895

Unit Seven

In an Age of Inventions

In the years following the Civil War, hundreds of new inventions changed life in every part of the United States. Many of those inventions brought Americans closer together. Others changed the ways Americans lived and worked.

17
The Last Frontier

Thousands of Americans on their way to Oregon or California crossed the Great Plains in the 1840's. Few thought of settling there. Most saw the plains as a dry, treeless, windswept land. They called it the last frontier.

The Indians, on the other hand, saw the plains as home. They hunted the great herds of buffalo that thundered across the grasslands. It was a way of life the Plains Indians valued greatly.

Then, in the late 1800's, the Indians' way of life suddenly ended. Over 5 million newcomers had moved on to the plains. They turned the plains into ranches, farms, cities, and towns. By 1890, the last frontier was gone.

As You Read

In this chapter, you will learn about the last frontier. As you read, find out why so many people settled there in the years after the Civil War. The chapter has four parts.

- The Indians' Last Stand
- Opening the Last Frontier
- The Days of the Cowboys
- Farmers on the Plains

◀ *A detail from a painting showing Indians on the plains*

The Indians' Last Stand

In the 1860's, over two thirds of all the Indians in the United States lived on the Great Plains. They did some farming, but they were mainly hunters who traveled the grasslands in search of buffalo.

The Indians' Way of Life

At first, the Plains Indians hunted buffalo on foot. Then, in the 1500's, the Spanish brought the first horses to the Americas. In time, some of the horses broke loose and began to wander freely on the plains. The Indians captured many of these horses. Over the years, the Plains Indians learned to tame and ride the wild animals. As the Indians learned to ride, their way of life began to change.

Many Indians gave up farming and hunted buffalo all year long. With horses, they could keep pace with the millions of buffalo that lived on the open grasslands.

The buffalo provided the Plains Indians with food. Its skin was used for clothing and for shelter. The Indians turned its bones into tools and its horns into spoons and cups. Even the stomach was put to use. The Indians cleaned it and made it into a bag for

The Indians who lived on the Plains traveled from place to place in search of buffalo.

carrying food and water. Sometimes they used it as a pot to cook their food in.

Hunting buffalo was exciting, but it was also dangerous. A successful hunt depended not only on the skill of the hunters but also on the skill of their horses. Even a small error could end in both the horse and its rider being trampled by herds of stampeding buffalo.

Hunting was usually a man's job. When the hunt ended, the women took over. They cut up the buffalo and loaded them on horses. Each animal supplied about 500 pounds (225 kilograms) of meat. Much of it was dried so that the Indians would have meat during the long winters.

Back at camp, everyone celebrated when the hunt was over. It was a time of feasting, dancing, and storytelling. It was also a time of thanksgiving. Many Indians prayed for a world in which there would always be buffalo.

The End of a Way of Life

Then, in 1861, telegraph companies strung telegraph wires across the plains. A few years later, railroad companies began to lay tracks across the plains too. At about the same time, more people began to settle on the Great Plains. Each of the newcomers presented a threat to the Indians' way of life.

The End of the Buffalo. Many of the newcomers killed buffalo. Some did so for sport, others for business. Passengers on trains shot the animals from train windows. Professional hunters like Buffalo Bill Cody shot them for their valuable skins.

Railroad companies also hired hunters to keep the buffalo away from the new rail lines. The hunters did their job well. Between 1870 and 1885, they killed over 10 million animals. For the first time, many Indians did not have enough to eat.

The Last Indian Wars. The Indians decided to fight to protect their way of life. Many were powerful warriors. Time and time again, they attacked anyone who crossed their land without permission. The United States government sent soldiers west to protect travelers and settlers. Within a short time, wars between the Indians and the newcomers began.

One war started in 1876 when thousands of miners rushed to the Black Hills of South Dakota to look for gold. That land belonged to the Sioux (sü), a powerful Indian nation. They fought to protect their homeland. Early in the war, a young colonel named George A. Custer was sent to the Black Hills to find out where the Indians were hiding. He found many of them camped beside the Little Big Horn River.

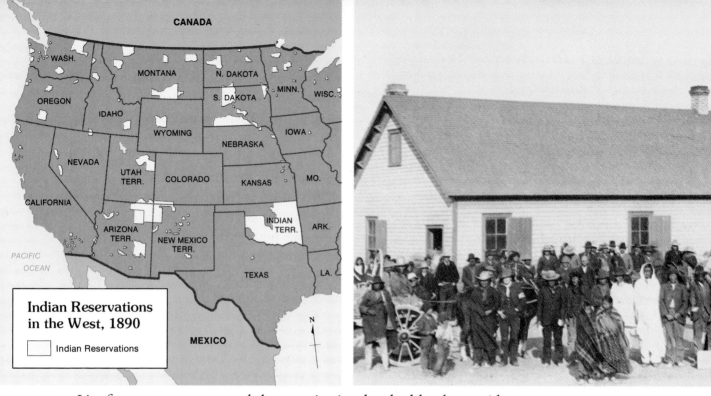

Indian Reservations in the West, 1890

☐ Indian Reservations

List five western states and three territories that had land set aside for Indian reservations. The picture on the right shows a group of Indians on a reservation in South Dakota.

Instead of waiting for help, Custer decided to attack. The Indians killed every soldier, including Custer. The United States sent more troops to fight the Sioux. Those troops hunted the Sioux and other Indian groups until the Indians finally gave up.

The Move to Reservations. By 1887, the government had moved most Indians on to **reservations.** A reservation is land that the government sets aside for a particular group of Indians. Most reservations were on land no one else wanted. It was often land that was too dry or rocky for farming.

In the past, most Indians who lived on the Great Plains did little or no farming. They depended mainly on the buffalo for food. By 1887, however, there were only a few hundred buffalo left anywhere on the Great Plains. The days of the great buffalo hunts were over. So was the way of life the Plains Indians had come to love. They began slowly to build a new way of life on the reservations. Some groups learned to farm. Others raised sheep and cattle.

314

To Help You Remember

1. (a) Who lived on the Great Plains before 1860? (b) Who moved there in the years after 1860?
2. (a) How did horses come to North America? (b) How did horses change the way the Plains Indians lived?
3. Why was the buffalo important to the Plains Indians?
4. (a) List three things that threatened the way of life of the Plains Indians. (b) What did the Indians do to protect their way of life?
5. By 1887, where did most Indians in the United States live?
6. (a) How many buffalo were on the Great Plains before 1860? (b) How many buffalo were killed between 1870 and 1885? (c) How many were left on the Great Plains by 1887?

Opening the Last Frontier

Until the 1860's, few newcomers settled on the Great Plains or in the mountains that lay beyond the plains. Then two events brought thousands of people west. Miners found valuable minerals in Colorado and Nevada, and the railroad finally crossed the continent.

Gold and Silver in the Mountains

The first event took place in 1858. That year gold was discovered in the foothills of the Rocky Mountains. Thousands of hopeful gold miners piled their belongings into covered wagons and headed for Colorado. Their wagons were painted with the slogan "Pikes Peak or Bust!" Pikes Peak is a mountain in Colorado.

A Gold Rush in Colorado. Nearly 50,000 prospectors rushed to the Cherry Creek River in Colorado. A few miners had found specks of gold. A mining camp quickly grew up nearby. Over the years it became the city of Denver.

Although some people found the gold they were looking for, they had no way of mining it. Colorado's gold lies deep in the mountains. Miners needed special machines that could tunnel through rock and stone. Very few, however, could afford such expensive equipment. So by the summer of 1859, many miners were on their way home. Their wagons had a new slogan, "Busted by Gosh!"

Some people stayed on in Colorado. A number of them took jobs with the large mining companies that were buying hundreds of small claims from miners. These companies could afford the costly machines needed to reach the gold. Others gave up mining completely. Some farmed in the mountain valleys. Others started businesses in Denver and other mining camps.

A Silver Strike in Nevada. A few miners refused to give up. They continued to search for gold. One of them was a prospector named Henry T. P. Comstock. In June of 1859, he teamed up with two prospectors digging along the eastern slopes of the Sierra Nevada Mountains in what is now the state of Nevada. The Sierra Nevadas are a mountain range to the west of the Rockies.

Comstock and his partners stake the first claim on the Comstock Lode.

As the three men dug, they found a little gold. They also uncovered a heavy blue-colored rock. They had no idea what it was. So they sent a sample to a nearby town to be analyzed. To their amazement, it turned out to be silver. In fact, they had stumbled upon one of the richest deposits of silver in the world. Their discovery was known as the Comstock Lode. Between 1860 and 1880, it produced over $500 million worth of silver.

As word of the discovery spread, hundreds of prospectors swarmed into Nevada. Reports of other strikes of gold and silver also brought thousands of miners to Montana, Idaho, Wyoming, and the Black Hills of South Dakota.

The Coming of the Railroad

The other event that changed the West took place on May 10, 1869, at Promontory Point, Utah. At 12:47 P.M., a telegraph operator tapped out three dots in Morse code. The dots stood for the word *done*. The message was flashed from coast to coast.

No one in 1869 had to ask what the message meant. Everyone knew it meant that the United States had a railroad that stretched all the way across North America. It was the nation's first **transcontinental** railroad.

The news that the railroad was completed triggered celebrations in

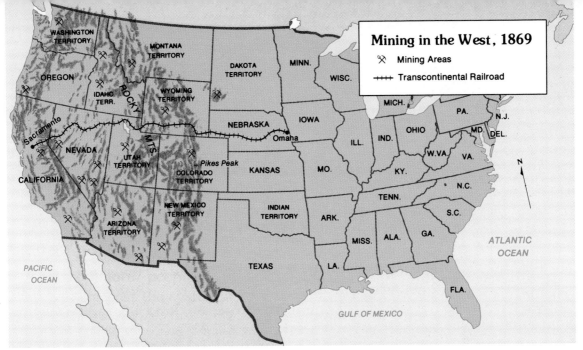

Find the transcontinental railroad. What states and territories did it pass through? Name two states that were important mining areas at the time the railroad was completed.

every large city in the nation. People had been calling for a transcontinental railroad since gold was discovered in California in 1848.

It took two companies six years to build the railroad. In 1863, the Central Pacific Railroad began laying track east from Sacramento, California, toward the Great Plains. The next year the Union Pacific began laying track. It worked west from Omaha, Nebraska.

Workers came from every state in the Union and many parts of the world. The Central Pacific hired many workers from China. The Union Pacific hired immigrants from Ireland. Both companies also hired Mormons, Indians, Mexicans, former slaves, and veterans of the Civil War.

Many workers stayed in the West after the railroad was completed. They were soon joined by many other Americans who took the railroad west.

To Help You Remember

1. (a) Why did many people rush to Colorado in the 1850's? (b) To Nevada in the 1860's?
2. What made it possible for thousands of Americans to move across the country after 1869?
3. Who helped to build the transcontinental railroad?

When the transcontinental railroad was completed, people along its route set their clocks differently. They had to ask, "Is the train arriving at 2:00 our time or their time?"

To end the confusion, railroad companies divided the United States into four standard time zones in 1883. Later, state and national governments made it official. Today the United States is divided into five time zones. Each time zone is centered on a meridian of longitude 15 degrees apart. Since Earth is a circle, it has 360 degrees. There are 24 hours in a day. Therefore, Earth rotates, or turns 15 degrees every hour. When it is 8 P.M. in the Eastern Time Zone, it is 7 P.M. in the Central Time Zone.

1. In what time zone is (a) New York City? (b) San Francisco? (c) Dallas? (d) The place you live?
2. When it is 12:00 noon in Chicago, what time is it in (a) Boston? (b) Denver? (c) Portland?

United States Time Zones

The Days of the Cowboys

As the railroad pushed farther and farther west, a number of Texans saw a chance to get rich. In Texas, huge herds of longhorn cattle were running wild on the grasslands. They were worth only about $4.00 a head in Texas. However, they could be sold for $40.00 a head in Chicago. Many saw a chance to get rich.

By 1866, many Texans were rounding up every animal they could find and taking their herds to Sedalia, Missouri. It was the nearest railroad town. From there, the animals were shipped to Chicago and other Eastern cities. This was the beginning of what came to be called the long drive.

The Long Drive

The long drive started in early spring before the grass had been burned dry by the hot summer sun. Rivers and water holes still had plenty of water. There were usually 6 cowboys for every 1,000 head of cattle. Two men rode at the head of the herd. Two watched on either side. The last two rode at the rear. They watched for strays.

A cowboy's job was always hard, often boring, and sometimes dangerous. Any sudden noise could frighten the animals and cause them to stampede. A Westerner wrote of one stampede, "By the time the clap of thunder reached us, the cattle were gone, the roar of their running mixed with the roar of the sky." It would take hours to round up the animals again.

The men also faced heavy rains that turned the prairies into lakes. Some animals drowned. Others got sick along the way and died. From time to time, Indians attacked. Still, those who made it through to the railroad earned a great deal of money.

Cowboys and cattle were a common sight on the Chisholm Trail in the 1860's.

Dodge City, Kansas, was an important cow town in the 1870's. Trains stopped along its main street to load cattle.

The Cow Towns

Despite the hardships of the long drive, raising cattle was a very profitable business. It was so profitable that a man named Joseph G. McCoy built a new town in Kansas called Abilene in 1867. It was the first **cow town.** It had everything a cowboy needed. There were pens, chutes, and stables for the cattle. There were also rooming houses for the cowboys.

The first year the town was open, only 3,500 animals came to Abilene. The following year the number skyrocketed and then continued to grow. Between 1868 and 1871, about 1,500,000 cattle were brought to Abilene and then shipped east.

Soon there were many other cow towns in the West. Each was more than just a shipping center for cattle. Each was also a place where cowboys could have a good time after the long, hard drive.

As herding cattle became more and more profitable, some people moved closer to the railroads. They started ranches on the central and northern plains. At about the same time, the railroad reached Texas. It soon had its own cow towns.

A Cattle Boom

Ranchers found it easier than ever to make money raising cattle. Since the

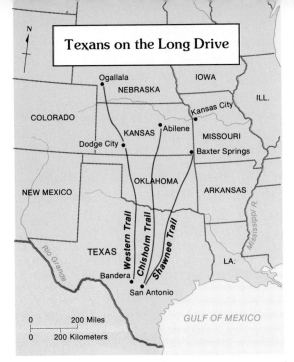

Texans on the Long Drive

Name three trails cowboys in Texas used on the long drive. Which trail led to Baxter Springs? To Abilene?

railroads were so close by, ranchers in Texas could easily send their cattle to market.

Many ranchers doubled the size of their herds. They could do so because they did not graze their cattle on their own land. Instead, they let their cattle roam on the **open range.** The open range was government-owned land. To make sure their herds did not get mixed with someone else's, ranchers branded each animal with a symbol that stood for the name of their ranch. Every ranch had its own symbol.

By the 1880's, the open range had become very crowded. Few worried until the summer of 1886 when hungry herds had grazed the grasslands bare. To make matters worse, the winter that followed was one of the worst ever. One blizzard after another swept across the plains. The hungry animals had no food at all.

When spring came, the plains were littered with dead and dying cattle. The small number of animals that survived were too scrawny to sell. Thousands of ranchers went broke.

Those who stayed in business changed their methods of grazing cattle. They no longer let their cattle roam freely on public land all winter. Instead, they kept them close to home. Some planted grain to feed their herds. Others just bred the cattle and then sold them to farmers in Kansas, Missouri, and Illinois for fattening. The days of the open range were over.

To Help You Remember

1. (a) What animals roamed freely on the Texas grasslands? (b) Why did Texans want to round them up?
2. (a) What was the long drive? (b) What did cowboys do on the long drive?
3. (a) What is a cow town? (b) Why were they built?
4. (a) How did ranchers use the open range? (b) Why did they stop using it after the winter of 1886–87?

Farmers on the Plains

Miners and ranchers were not the only people moving on to the Great Plains. Millions of farmers also settled there. They came because they could get land on the plains from the United States government for little or no money.

The Great Land Giveaway

The United States government gave away thousands of acres of land on the Great Plains in the late 1800's. The best land went to the companies that built railroads to the West. Each

Many former slaves packed up their families and moved to the Great Plains.

company got thousands of acres of land for every mile of track that was laid.

The government also gave land to settlers. In 1862, Congress passed the Homestead Act. It gave 160 acres (64 hectares) to any family willing to work the land for five years. Those who took advantage of the Homestead Act were called **homesteaders.** Many rushed to the Great Plains to claim the free land. Americans from both the North and South, black as well as white, came. Thousands of eager settlers also came from countries in northern and eastern Europe.

In the East, 160 acres (64 hectares) was a good-sized farm. Many farmers made a good living from farms half that size. On the Great Plains, however, there was far less rain. So each acre (0.4 hectares) produced less food. To produce as much food as a farmer with 160 acres (64 hectares) in the East, a plains farmer needed 4 times as much land.

Once people realized that 160 acres (64 hectares) was not enough, those who had money bought land from the railroads. The railroads put no limits on how much land a person could buy. This land was also more likely to be near a railroad. So it would be easy to get crops to market.

Living on the Plains

Whether farmers bought land or got it for free, they quickly found that life on the plains was not easy. In winter, deep snows blanketed the grasslands. In spring, the melting snow caused flooding. Then came summer. Hot, dry winds blew across the plains. Temperatures soared to 110°F (43°C).

Worst of all were the grasshoppers. The insects arrived in swarms so thick they blocked out the sun. They ate everything in sight from crops in the field to curtains in the windows.

Slowly the settlers learned to deal with the grasshoppers and the weather. They also found ways to solve many of the other problems of life on the plains.

A Shortage of Wood. There was little wood on the grasslands for homes or fences. So settlers learned to build cabins out of **sod.** Sod is a thick, tough layer of tightly tangled grass roots. It can be cut into blocks, and then one block can be stacked on top of another in much the way bricks are laid.

Finding a good fencing material to protect crops from animals was more difficult. Then, in 1873, an Illinois farmer came up with an idea. He twisted two strands of wire in such a way that there was a sharp barb every few inches. He called his invention barbed wire. It was an instant

South Dakota Memorial Art Center

Most of the settlers had a hard time farming on the dry grasslands.

success. In 1880, about 80 million pounds (3,600 thousand kilograms) of barbed wire were sold.

A Shortage of Water. Water was also in short supply on the plains. So farmers made good use of what little rain they did get. They plowed their fields a foot deep (30 centimeters) in the fall and again in the spring to keep the soil safe from the sun's heat and the drying winds. This way of farming is known as dry farming.

Many farmers also **irrigated** their land. That is, they dug ditches to bring water from nearby streams to their fields. Where there were no streams, farmers dug deep wells. Many were as much as 800 feet (240 meters) deep.

To reach water so far underground, settlers needed metal drills. They also needed windmills to pump the water to the surface. However, most people who owned small farms could not afford drills and windmills.

Farming by Machine

Farms on the plains were larger than farms in the East. So farmers needed plenty of help at planting and harvesting time. Yet many found it hard to find workers. Most people were busy on their own land. Those who could afford to do so bought machines to help with the work.

Dozens of new machines appeared in the late 1800's. One of the most valuable was a plow sharp enough to cut through the thick sod. Other machines helped with the planting or the harvesting. With these machines, a farmer could work thousands of acres of land with very little help. Many did.

Small farmers could not afford the new machines. So they found it harder and harder to work their lands. Many gave up. Others struggled on. A few moved from one part of the plains to another in hope of finding a place where they could make a go of it.

Then, in 1889, the government opened lands in Oklahoma for settlement. Thousands of settlers came on horseback and by covered wagon. Some jammed the trains. When a signal was fired on April 22, over 100,000 people raced to stake their claims. Within a few hours, the newcomers had claimed 2 million acres (800 thousand hectares) of land. These pioneers, like those who had come earlier, helped turn the dry lands of the plains into the breadbasket of the world.

By 1890, the last frontier was gone. The grasslands that had once stretched across the middle of the country were dotted with farms, villages, and busy towns. In the next chapter, you will learn how the United States continued to grow even after the last frontier was settled.

To Help You Remember

1. Why did many farmers move to the Great Plains in the late 1800's?
2. Why did a farm on the Great Plains need to be four times as large as a farm in the East?
3. List four reasons life was hard for farmers on the plains.
4. How did farmers on the plains build homes?
5. How did new machines help farmers on the plains?

Chapter Review

Words to Know

1. What is a *reservation?*
2. How does a *transcontinental railroad* differ from other railroads?
3. What is special about *sod?*
4. What do farmers do when they *irrigate* their land?
5. What was the *open range?*
6. What kind of town was a *cow town?*
7. What was a *homesteader?*

Reviewing Main Ideas

1. Name three events that affected the Plains Indians' way of life.
2. List two events that led more and more people to settle in the West.
3. (a) What caused a cattle boom in the late 1800's? (b) How did the winter of 1886–87 affect that boom?
4. Give four reasons farming was difficult on the plains.

In Your Own Words

Answer the following questions. Then use your answers to write a paragraph telling how the culture of the Plains Indians changed in the late 1800's.

1. Why were the buffalo important to the Plains Indians?
2. What happened to the buffalo in the late 1800's?
3. What did the Indians do to try to protect their way of life?
4. Where did most Indians live after 1887?

Challenge!

A teacher in Kansas in the late 1800's described her first school:

> The school building was a sod dugout, about fourteen feet long, with dirt floor, unplastered walls, two small windows in front, heated by a small fireplace about one yard across. It had neither blackboard, teacher's desk, nor chair. The seats were small logs split and supported by pegs and were placed at the sides of the room.

Another teacher wrote of her students:

> They had a few bare benches, flat, without backs, and so far off the floor that little legs, dangling high in the air, would ache cruelly before a change of position was possible. An extra-brave or desperate pupil might lie down a bit to relieve the strain, but the season of relief would be short lived. No charts, no maps, no pictures, no books but a speller. They would have "numbers" later, but some of the little fellows would never get that far. The miracle was that a love of "learning" ever survived the rigors of school days then. But it did in some cases.

Draw a picture of the kind of schoolroom the two teachers describe. Then write a paragraph telling what school was like from a pupil's point of view. What would you have liked about such a school? What would you have disliked?

18

The Industrial Revolution

While many Americans were moving to the last frontier, changes were taking place in the more settled parts of the United States. In the late 1800's, people invented machines that made many jobs easier and faster. These machines caused a revolution in the way people lived and worked. A revolution is a great and rapid change. People called the changes that took place in the late 1800's the **Industrial Revolution.**

Before the Industrial Revolution began, the United States was a nation of farmers. Most people lived on farms. By 1890, however, the United States was becoming a nation of factory workers. More and more people were moving to cities and towns.

As You Read

In this chapter, you will learn more about the changes the Industrial Revolution brought to the United States. As you read, notice the way one change led to many others. The chapter is divided into three parts.

- The Growth of Industry
- The Growth of Cities
- Improving American Life

◀ *Making steel in the late 1800's*

The Growth of Industry

After the Civil War, the number of factories grew rapidly. Their growth turned the United States into an industrial nation. What made this change possible?

The United States has coal, iron ore, wood, and thousands of other resources needed to build and run machines. The way the economy of the United States was organized also helped industry grow. The United States has a **free enterprise** system. That is, the United States has an economy in which people are free to own farms, mines, factories, stores, and other businesses. Each business tries to make a profit. To do so, it must compete with many other businesses for customers. Free enterprise therefore encourages people to try new ideas and new inventions.

The Inventors

In the years after the Civil War, there were thousands of new inventions. Some people tried out new ideas in their spare time. For others, inventing became a full-time job. The greatest of these inventors was Thomas Alva Edison. His ideas seemed so amazing to people that he was known as the Wizard of Menlo Park. A wizard does magic tricks.

Edison worked his magic in his laboratory at Menlo Park, New Jersey. Here he tried to turn out small inventions "every ten days and a big thing every six months or so." He came very close to making that many inventions. He and the 100 or more scientists and engineers he hired produced over 1,000 inventions.

Edison's most important invention was the electric light bulb. In 1879, Edison made a bulb that burned for 40 hours. Before long, he made an even better one. It stayed lighted for several hundred hours. To celebrate, Edison strung light bulbs on nearby houses. People came from miles around to see the bright lights.

By 1882, Edison had built a generator for New York City. A generator is a machine that makes electric power. Edison's generator supplied power for the first electric lighting system in the country. Within a few years, generators were built in other cities. Soon thousands of homes and businesses had electricity. People used electric power not only to get light but also to power machines.

A Daring Leader

Turning an invention into a business takes money. It also requires a person with a willingness to take chances, an ability to organize, and

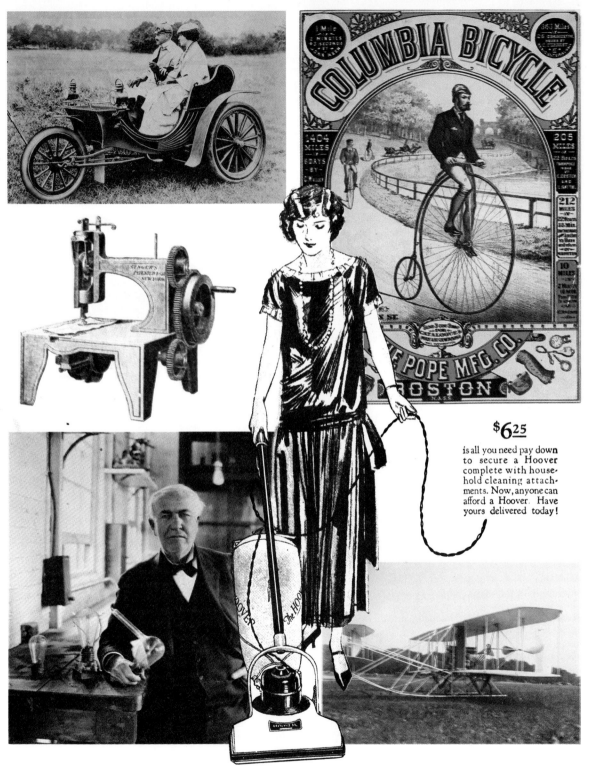

6^{25} is all you need pay down to secure a Hoover complete with household cleaning attachments. Now, anyone can afford a Hoover. Have yours delivered today!

Thanks to inventors like Thomas Edison (lower left), machines became a part of everyday life. People now used machines both at home and at work.

Andrew Carnegie helped the United States become a leader in industry.

a belief in the product and its future. The country had many people with those qualities. Andrew Carnegie was one of them.

Using Money to Make Money. Andrew Carnegie came to the United States from Scotland in 1848, at the age of 13. He went to work in a cloth factory. His family was too poor to send him to school. By the time he was 18, Carnegie found a better job. He became a clerk for the Pennsylvania Railroad. Carnegie learned much about business from his boss, Thomas Scott.

Scott showed Carnegie how to use his savings to make money. On Scott's advice, Carnegie bought **stocks** in various companies. A stock is a share, or part, of a business. The businesses in which Carnegie bought stocks were **corporations.** A corporation is a business that is owned by many people. The people who own stock in a corporation are called **stockholders.** If the business makes money, the stockholders get a **dividend.** A dividend is their share of the profits.

With his dividends, Carnegie bought more stock. Soon he had earned enough to start his own business. He decided to make steel.

Making Steel. Like iron, steel is a metal made from iron ore. However, steel is harder than iron and easier to shape. It was also more expensive. Then, in the 1850's, two people, working separately, invented a fast and less expensive way of making steel. One was an American named William Kelly. He was a kettle maker from Kentucky. The other was an Englishman named Henry Bessemer.

Andrew Carnegie was one of the first Americans to take an interest in the new method. He believed it would change the way all goods are made. He told a friend, "The days of iron have passed. Steel is king!"

In 1873, Carnegie sold all his stock and bought a steel mill outside of Pittsburgh, Pennsylvania. In time, he bought several other mills as well. At first, they used the Bessemer method. However, when a newer method was developed, Carnegie was one of the first to try it. He believed in keeping ahead of other steel makers.

Carnegie stayed ahead of steel makers in other ways as well. He bought coal mines in Pennsylvania and iron mines in Michigan. He also owned his own ships and trains to carry the coal and the ore. In this way, he controlled the cost of every step in the steel-making process.

By 1900, Carnegie was turning out about one fourth of all the steel made in the United States. The next year, he decided to retire. He sold his companies to the United States Steel Corporation for over $200 million.

Organizing Work

In the late 1800's, the steel industry was booming. It grew, in part, because of people like Carnegie. It also grew because Kelly and Bessemer had found a better way of making steel. People in other industries were also trying to turn out goods faster and cheaper. One of these people was Henry Ford, a young machinist from Detroit. He found a way to make automobiles more cheaply.

Automobiles were first invented in the 1890's. At first, only the rich could afford them. Then, in 1908,

Henry Ford discovered how to build a car that many people could afford. He called it the Model T.

To make his cars cheaper, Ford had to produce them faster. So he divided the job of making a car into hundreds of steps. Instead of one worker putting together a whole car, each would do just one job. A moving belt would bring workers the parts they needed. Another belt would carry the unfinished car to the next worker. This system is known as an **assembly line.**

In the days before the assembly line, it took 12 1/2 hours to make an automobile. After the moving

Workers on an assembly line are putting wheels together for Model T's.

assembly line, Ford's workers could put together a Model T in 1 1/2 hours. As a result, the Model T cost less than other cars. In 1912, a car cost $600. By 1916, the price had dropped to just $360.

Workers from Many Lands

Industry grew in the United States because of people like Carnegie, Edison, and Ford. It also grew because the nation was rich in resources. Yet there was still another reason for the growth of industry. Factories, mines, and mills need many workers. Without them, there can be no steel or electric lights or cars.

In the years just after the Civil War, many companies were desperate for workers. They advertised for workers both at home and abroad. Thousands of men, women, and children answered the call.

Americans on the Move. During the late 1800's, many Americans started moving into the cities. Families left their farms and headed for the nearest factory town. Most were farmers. They were finding it hard to make a living on small farms. They hoped to have better luck in the cities.

Other Americans were drawn to the cities by stories of people who went from rags to riches in just a few years there. Both Carnegie and Ford had come from poor families. Yet they both had become millionaires. Many Americans were sure they could get rich too.

Settlers from Other Lands. At the same time, many **immigrants** also came to the United States to work in factories and mines. Immigrants are people who leave their homelands to settle in another country.

Immigrants came for many of the same reasons people have always moved to the United States. Some came for religious freedom. In Russia, Jews were not protected under the law. Thousands were killed by mobs as soldiers watched.

Others came for the chance to build a new life in a new land. Times were hard in many places, especially in China and in southern and eastern Europe. So thousands of people from those parts of the world were eager to come to a country that needed workers. Between 1865 and 1900, over 12 million people settled in the United States. Another 18 million came between 1900 and 1930.

New Jobs, New Opportunities. The newcomers, whether they came from the United States or abroad, were mainly farmers. Only a few knew other trades. However, people who worked in factories did not need to know a trade. A child could learn to

The family on the left came from China. The picture on the right shows the kind of crowded neighborhood in which many immigrants lived.

run some of the new machines in just a few days. Many children worked in factories.

The immigrants found many opportunities to improve their lives. Although few became as rich as Carnegie or Ford, many learned skills that led to good paying jobs.

For example, the United States had 55,000 machinists in 1870. By 1900, there were over 280,000. They built reapers, sewing machines, and bicycles. Hundreds of other new jobs were also opening. Immigrants and people born in the United States used these jobs to get ahead.

To Help You Remember

1. (a) Name three resources important to the Industrial Revolution. (b) how did free enterprise encourage the Industrial Revolution?
2. What was Thomas Edison's most important invention?
3. How did Andrew Carnegie earn enough to start a business?
4. What made it possible for Henry Ford to produce cars cheaper than anyone else?
5. Why did many Americans move to the cities in the late 1800's?
6. Why did people from other countries come to the United States?

Graphs are one way of looking at information. They can answer many questions. They can also raise questions. Look carefully at the bar graph below. The numbers along the bottom of the graph show the years the graph covers. Notice they are grouped by decades. Every ten years is a decade. The numbers along the side of the graph show the number of Europeans who came to the United States during each ten-year period. Use the graph to answer the questions.

1. In what decade did the fewest people come?
2. In what decade did the most people come?

One question the graph raises is where in Europe did the immigrants come from. Look at the first circle graph. The circle stands for all European immigrants in the 1860's.

1. How many came from northern and western Europe?
2. How many came from southern and eastern Europe?

Now look at the second circle graph. It stands for all Europeans who came between 1900 and 1909.

1. How many came from northern and western Europe?
2. How many came from southern and eastern Europe?
3. What new questions do the two circle graphs raise?

European Immigration 1860–1869

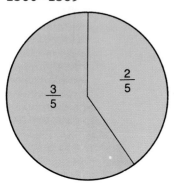

European Immigration 1900–1909

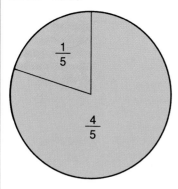

☐ Northern and Western Europe

☐ Southern and Eastern Europe

Immigrants Arriving in the United States, 1860–1909

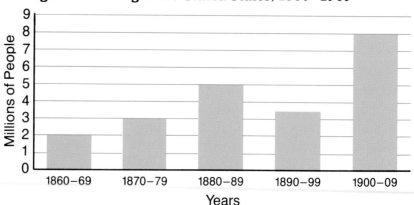

334

The Growth of Cities

At the start of the Civil War in 1861, eight out of ten Americans lived in the country. Most were farmers. By 1910, nearly half of all the people in the country lived in cities. Most of them worked in factories.

Making Room in Cities

As the number of people living in cities grew, more houses, shops, and offices were needed. Every bit of space was used. Buildings seemed crushed together. Before long, the only way left to build was up.

A building made of wood can only be a few stories high. However, a building with a steel frame can be much taller. In the late 1880's, people began using steel to build skyscrapers. The first was built in Chicago, Illinois, in 1884. It was ten stories tall.

Such a building would have been useless without an elevator. By the 1880's, several companies were making elevators.

Skyscrapers were one way of making better use of space. Buildings that had room for more than one family were another. As more people moved to cities, some property owners began dividing houses meant for just one family. In time, some houses held as many as 40 or 50 people.

In many cities, people tore down old houses and put up new ones called tenements. These buildings were from two to six stories high. Inside were many small apartments.

People who had a little money often wanted to buy their own homes. However, by the late 1800's, they had to leave the city to do so. Land in the city was too expensive. So some people began to move to the **suburbs.** These were small communities linked to a city by a railroad or streetcar line.

Workers put together the steel beams for a skyscraper.

City Life

Cities in the late 1800's were dark, dirty, noisy places. The lack of fresh water, the danger of fire, and crime were major problems. Yet nearly everyone wanted to live in the cities. Cities were very exciting places.

Cities had the latest fashions in clothes, shoes, hats, and even furniture. These goods were often sold in a new kind of store. It was called a department store. Shoppers could find everything from baby clothes to hardware all under one roof.

Cities also offered entertainment. There were circuses, concerts, plays, and variety shows. Some shows were in English. Others were in German, Yiddish, Italian, or one of dozens of other languages.

Cities had many schools and colleges. Some stayed open night and day. So even those who had jobs could get an education.

The cities also had public libraries. Here anyone could get a library card and borrow books. Until 1860, there were only a few libraries in the United States. However, during the 1900's, the number of libraries grew almost as fast as the size of cities.

To Help You Remember

1. (a) Where did most Americans live in 1861?   (b) In 1910?
2. Name two things that made skyscrapers possible.
3. What was a tenement house like?
4. (a) Why did people who wanted their own homes move out of the city?   (b) Where did these people move to?
5. List five problems associated with life in the city in the late 1800's.
6. List at least five ways people could have fun in the city.

Improving American Life

The growth of factories and cities brought many changes to the nation. Some of these changes made life better for everyone. Others caused many hardships and injustices. In the late 1800's, many Americans set out to make life better and to put an end to the injustices.

In Factories and Mines

Before the Industrial Revolution, most jobs required special training. It took many years to become a weaver or a printer. Many of these jobs were being done by machine in the 1890's. It took only a few days to learn how to run these machines.

As a result, workers could easily be replaced.

Factory owners often treated their workers poorly. One worker alone could do little to improve his or her wages or working conditions. So many workers united to form **labor unions.** A labor union is an organization of workers that helps its members get higher wages and better working conditions.

Workers Unite. Unions were not a new idea in the late 1800's. They started soon after the first factories were built. Workers would join together whenever they had a complaint. Then they went on strike, or refused to work, until their employer gave in to their demands. Once the strike was over, the union would often break up.

In the 1850's, a few workers formed more lasting unions. Some of these unions were made up of people from all parts of the country. Every member had the same kind of job. For example, there was a union for carpenters as well as one for railroad engineers.

Then, in 1886, the leaders of several of these unions decided to work together. They formed the American Federation of Labor, or A.F. of L. It was a union of unions.

In 1896, Samuel Gompers became president of the A.F. of L. Under his

Workers in New York City march in one of the first Labor Day parades.

leadership, the union took action to protect its members. Members pooled their money to help striking workers. In the past, strikes ended when workers had used up their savings. Gompers also tried to get companies to sign agreements that told workers their rights.

Still progress was slow. Many strikes turned into battles between workers and people the companies hired to break up the strike. City, state, and federal governments usually sided with employers. Many states outlawed strikes and unions. Judges said that workers had no right to shut down a factory. If they did not like their jobs, they could quit.

New Attitudes toward Unions. Ideas about unions changed slowly. People began to see that changing jobs was not the answer to poor working conditions and low wages. Still it was not until the 1930's that the federal government protected a worker's right to form a union.

Yet even earlier, some states passed laws that gave workers some protection. For example, by 1900, a few states set safety standards for factories and mines. At the same time, many states passed laws that made

These young girls worked long hours at sewing machines.

it illegal for children to work in mines. Some states also limited the number of hours a child could work.

Helping the Poor

The people who worked to get new laws passed were called **reformers.** They helped to reform, or improve, life for all Americans. Some of them were workers. Others were wealthy men and women who were eager to help the poor.

Helping Newcomers. The immigrants were often the poorest people in the cities. Few could speak much English. Many were confused by city life. Some Americans tried to help the immigrants. One of the most famous was a wealthy young woman from Cedarville, Illinois. Her name was Jane Addams. She and a friend founded Hull House in Chicago. It was one of the first **settlement houses** in the United States.

A settlement house is a kind of community center. People come to a settlement house to get help in finding a job, to get help for a sick child, or to get help in finding a place to live. They also come to learn. Hull House had a library. Workers at Hull House offered classes in English, child care, and dozens of different crafts. People came to Hull House to have fun as well. There were dances and clubs.

Jane Addams talks to a young visitor to Hull House.

Better City Services. Jane Addams did not think a settlement house could solve all the problems poor people in the city faced. She worried about overcrowded tenements, unhealthy living conditions, and the danger of fire. So she tried to get the city of Chicago to provide more police and fire protection, pick up garbage, and clean the streets. She and other reformers got help from writers like Jacob Riis, a Danish immigrant.

In 1890, Riis wrote a book describing the way poor people lived in New York City. It was called *How the Other Half Lives.* Riis told his story through photographs as well as words. His book led to new laws to help the poor.

Reforms in Government

In the early 1900's, many reformers worked for laws that would help the poor. They also worked for laws that would give everyone in the country what President Theodore Roosevelt called a square deal.

Roosevelt explained, "When I say that I am for a square deal, I mean not only that I stand for fair play under the present rules of the game but that I stand for having those rules changed to provide more equality of opportunity."

Controlling Big Business. Many reformers were worried about the giant companies that had been formed during the Industrial Revolution. One was Standard Oil founded by John D. Rockefeller in 1870. By 1890, it was a **monopoly.** A monopoly is a company that controls all sales of a product or service. It has little or no competition. By 1890, Standard Oil controlled over 95 percent of all the oil bought and sold in the United States.

In 1890, reformers persuaded Congress to pass a law that made it illegal for large companies like Standard Oil to control an entire industry. In

1911, the Supreme Court ordered Standard Oil to divide itself into several smaller companies.

Protecting Resources. Reformers were also concerned about the nation's resources. For example, lumber companies were cutting down many forests. People feared that soon the country would have no forests left. So in 1872, Congress set aside land for the first national park.

Reforming Voting Laws. Reformers also fought for laws that made the nation more democratic. Among them was the secret ballot. In the past, voters could not get a ballot until they announced which political party they wished to vote for. With the secret ballot, the names of all the candidates are listed on one ballot. Voters can choose among them without anyone knowing how they voted.

In 1913, reformers also helped to get the Seventeenth Amendment passed. It changed the way United States senators were elected. Before 1913, a state legislature chose senators. The people voted only for members of the House of Representatives. Since 1913, members of both houses of Congress are elected by the voters. Reformers, workers, inventors, and business people all helped the nation grow. Because of their hard work and talent, the United States was becoming a leading industrial nation.

Voters in Boston, Massachusetts, began using the secret ballot in 1889.

To Help You Remember

1. (a) Why did many workers join labor unions?   (b) What did unions do for their members?
2. List two ways the A.F. of L., under Samuel Gompers' leadership, helped its members.
3. List four ways Jane Addams helped to improve living conditions for poor people in Chicago.
4. (a) Why was Standard Oil considered a monopoly?   (b) What did Congress try to do about it and other monopolies?
5. List two laws that made the nation more democratic.

Chapter Review

Words to Know

1. How does the *Industrial Revolution* differ from other revolutions?
2. (a) What is a *corporation*? (b) What does it mean to own *stock*? (c) How does a *stockholder* earn *dividends*?
3. What is a *free enterprise* system?
4. What effect does a *monopoly* have on competition?
5. How is an *assembly line* organized?
6. Who belongs to a *labor union*?
7. Why were *settlement houses* important to *immigrants*?
8. How is a *suburb* linked to a city?
9. What does a *reformer* do?

Reviewing Main Ideas

1. List three reasons for the Industrial Revolution in the United States.
2. Why did many people move to cities in the early 1900's?
3. How did unions help workers?
4. List three ways reformers helped to improve American life.

In Your Own Words

Reformers saw many problems in the United States during the early years of the Industrial Revolution. They tried to alert other Americans to those problems. Choose a problem the country faced in the early years of the Industrial Revolution and write a paragraph *informing* others of that problem. Then write a paragraph in which you urge readers to solve that problem.

Keeping Skills Sharp

Make a line graph showing production of raw petroleum based on the following:

1860:   500,000 barrels
1880:   26,286,000 barrels
1900:   63,621,000 barrels
1920: 442,929,000 barrels

Under your graph, write two sentences. The first should explain why production increased after 1860. The second should explain the increase after 1900.

Challenge!

Study the political cartoon below. Then answer the following questions.

1. Why do you think the cartoonist drew Standard Oil as an octopus?
2. What are the tentacles on the octopus doing?
3. Write a sentence telling why the cartoonist feels that monopolies like Standard Oil are wrong.

19

Becoming a World Power

In the 1800's, inventions helped bring people closer to-
gether. Railroads and steamboats made it possible for
Americans to travel around the country faster than ever
before. Travelers carried with them news of other places.
By the 1860's, telegraph lines linked cities across the United
States, and news traveled even faster.

At the same time, huge ships steamed across the oceans.
Passengers on those ships brought back news from Europe.
Then, in 1866, an American businessman named Cyrus
Field laid a telegraph cable across the Atlantic Ocean. It
linked American cities to cities in Europe. Americans be-
came more interested in news from overseas.

As You Read

As you read this chapter, notice how a growing interest in
other lands caused the nation to expand. Notice too how
that interest involved Americans in two wars overseas. The
chapter is divided into three parts.

- A War with Spain
- Expanding the Nation
- World War I

◀ *The United States fleet on its way around the world*

A War with Spain

In the late 1800's, many newspapers in the United States made special efforts to attract readers. They found that people were more likely to buy a newspaper if it included stories that shocked them. In 1895, a revolution in Cuba provided hundreds of such stories.

Cuba is a small island just 90 miles (144 kilometers) off the coast of Florida. It had been ruled by Spain since the 1500's. In the early 1800's, the Cubans began to fight for their freedom. Time after time, the Spanish put down these revolts. Then, in 1895, the Cubans tried again. This time they were successful.

What part of the United States is closest to Cuba? Where in Cuba did the Maine *explode?*

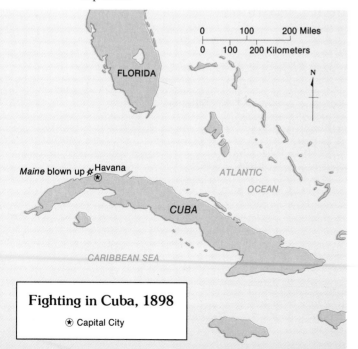

Fighting in Cuba, 1898

✪ Capital City

News of the Revolution

Dozens of American reporters poured into Havana, Cuba's capital. They had come to report on the fighting. The stories they wrote made many Americans want to help the Cubans. One story began this way: "Blood on the roadsides, blood in the fields, blood on the doorsteps, blood, blood, blood!"

Readers cheered news of the Cubans' gains. They worried about Spanish victories. As the fighting continued, many urged Congress and the president to help. Other Americans took matters into their own hands. They sent money and weapons to the Cubans.

These Americans believed that the United States had a duty to help Cuba. Cuba's fight for freedom reminded them of their country's war for independence from Great Britain.

The Fighting Spreads

At first, the United States government tried to stay out of the revolution. Instead, government leaders in the United States tried to persuade the Spanish to give Cuba its freedom. Then, on the night of February 15, 1898, an American battleship, the *Maine*, blew up in the harbor of Havana. The *Maine* was there to bring home United States citizens in danger from the fighting. Two hundred and sixty men were killed when the ship exploded.

To this day, no one knows why the ship exploded. American newspapers claimed the Spanish had blown up the ship. All over the United States, people called for war. Their slogan was "Remember the *Maine!*" On April 19, 1898, the United States declared war on Spain.

A Surprise in the Pacific. The Spanish thought the Americans would invade Cuba. To the amazement of the Spanish, the Americans struck first in the Pacific. On April 30, the American fleet in the Pacific steamed to the Philippines (fil'ə pēnz'), islands in the Pacific owned by Spain.

The next morning Commodore George Dewey gave the command to open fire on the Spanish fleet in the harbor at Manila, the Philippine capital. In seven hours, Dewey's men had captured or destroyed every Spanish ship there.

Dewey had the support of the people who lived in the Philippines. Like the Cubans, they too were trying to win their freedom. So they were eager to help the Americans fight Spain.

Victory in Cuba. While Dewey was fighting in the Philippines, 17,000

What facts does the Journal *tell? What opinions does it express?*

Americans sailed toward Cuba. Some were professional soldiers. Many were volunteers. Among them were black Americans, Indians, and immigrants who had had to struggle for their freedom.

One of the volunteers was a young New Yorker named Theodore Roosevelt. He gave up his job as assistant secretary of the navy to help lead a group of volunteers known as the Rough Riders. The group included

Teddy Roosevelt's Rough Riders (left) and the United States 10th Cavalry (right) fought bravely in the war against Spain.

cowboys, lumberjacks, Indians, and college football players.

Most of the soldiers, however, were not as well prepared for battle as Teddy Roosevelt's Rough Riders. The United States had rushed into war so fast that many soldiers did not even have rifles. In the end, it did not matter. The Americans had enough soldiers, guns, and supplies to defeat the Spanish. By the middle of August 1898, the fighting was over. Spain had surrendered.

At the peace talks, Spain freed Cuba. Spain also turned over the island of Guam (gwäm) in the Pacific and Puerto Rico (pwer'tō rē'kō) in the West Indies to the United States.

Spain also sold the Philippines to the United States for $20 million.

A Debate over the Peace Treaty

The United States Senate had to approve the treaty the president had worked out with Spain. Many senators disagreed with its terms. They thought the United States had no right to take over other lands.

Other senators pointed out that Great Britain, Germany, and other nations were taking over land in Africa and Asia as well as several islands in the Pacific. They wanted the United States to do the same.

After three months of debate, the Senate approved the treaty. Guam, Puerto Rico, and the Philippines became part of the United States.

The People of the Islands

The people of the Philippine Islands are called Filipinos (fil′ə pē′nōs). They were the first to respond to the news of the American takeover. Many were angry. The Filipinos had set up a republic when the war with Spain started. Now they would have to fight against the United States to win their independence.

It took the United States three years to put down the revolt in the Philippines. Yet most Filipinos still dreamed of independence. So, little by little, the United States gave Filipinos more say in their government. Finally in 1946, 48 years later, the Philippines became an independent nation.

Puerto Ricans were also upset by the peace treaty. Over the years, they had won some freedom from Spain. Now those gains were lost. American soldiers ruled the island. Congress appointed the governor for Puerto Rico. However, Puerto Ricans were allowed to make their own laws.

Slowly Puerto Ricans won more rights. In 1917, they became citizens of the United States. In 1947, the island became a **commonwealth.** A

Commodore George Dewey and the Pacific fleet take control of the Philippines.

commonwealth is like a state. Citizens have their own governor and their own lawmakers. The main difference between a commonwealth and a state is that citizens of a commonwealth do not have a say in Congress.

To Help You Remember

1. How did Americans find out about the revolution in Cuba?
2. Why did the Cubans rebel against Spain?
3. Why did the United States declare war on Spain?
4. (a) What did the Cubans gain as a result of their war with Spain? (b) What did the United States gain?

347

Expanding the Nation

The people of Puerto Rico and the Philippines were separated from the United States by miles of ocean. However, they were not the first American territories that were far away from the rest of the country.

Buying Alaska

The first such territory was Alaska. Until 1867, the Russians ruled Alaska. They had had a colony there since the 1700's. In 1867, they offered to sell it to the United States for $7,200,000. Secretary of State William H. Seward jumped at the chance to buy so much land for less than two cents an acre.

Many Americans rushed to Alaska when gold was discovered there in 1897.

Many Americans thought it was a foolish purchase. Who would want to live in a land of ice and snow? They called Alaska Seward's Ice Box.

Those who favored the purchase did not speak of ice and snow. Instead, they talked of a land rich in timber, fish, and furs. They spoke too of the importance of ports along the Pacific coast. Trade with Asia was growing, and these Americans wanted to take advantage of it.

In the end, the **expansionists,** those in favor of taking over land outside of the country, won the debate. Yet few Americans thought it was a good purchase until 1897. That year gold was discovered in Alaska. Suddenly many Americans rushed to Alaska.

By 1912, many Alaskans were eager to enter the Union. Yet it was not until 1959 that Alaska finally joined the Union. That year it became the 49th state.

Gaining Hawaii

In 1898, the same year the United States acquired the Philippines, Puerto Rico, and Guam, it also added the Hawaiian Islands to the United States. Americans had been trading with the Hawaiians since George Washington was president. The islands were also resting places for weary sailors headed for China. In the islands, they took on fresh water and food before continuing across the Pacific Ocean.

By 1830, many Americans had settled in the islands. Some were missionaries. They had come to teach the Hawaiians the Christian religion. Others sold goods to trading and whaling ships that stopped at the islands. Still others started sugar cane plantations. By 1890, Americans owned most of the farm land in Hawaii, and sugar had become the islands' most valuable crop.

As time passed, there were more foreigners in the islands than Hawaiians. Although Hawaiian kings and queens still ruled the islands, they found it harder and harder to govern without the help of foreigners.

Liliuokalani (lē lē′ü ō kä lä′nē) became queen of Hawaii in 1891. She wanted to return Hawaii to the Hawaiians. She tried to limit the influence of foreigners in Hawaii. American settlers were outraged. In 1893, they overthrew the queen and set up a republic. Then they asked President Cleveland to make Hawaii a part of the United States. He refused. He did not think the United States had the right to take over lands outside of the country.

In 1898, William McKinley became president of the United States. He favored expansion. So did many people

Bishop Museum

Queen Liliuokalani's rule of Hawaii lasted only two years.

in Congress. That same year Congress made Hawaii a territory of the United States. About 60 years later, in 1959, Hawaii became the nation's 50th state.

A Shortcut between Oceans

As trade grew with islands in the Pacific, American ships needed a faster way of getting from the Atlantic to the Pacific Ocean. The voyage around South America to the Pacific was long and dangerous.

The Spanish, French, British, and Americans had talked of building a

349

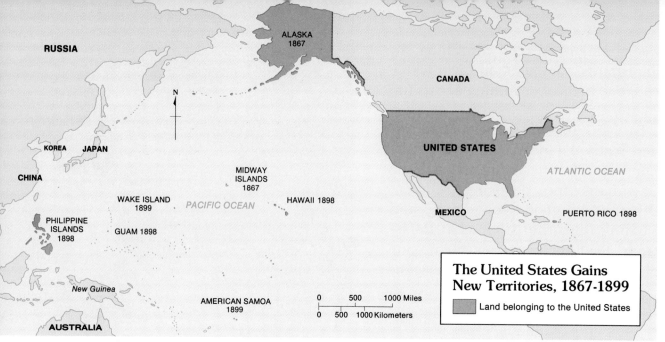

The United States Gains
New Territories, 1867-1899

Land belonging to the United States

By 1900, the United States had gained many territories. Name three territories the United States gained in the Pacific. What territory did the United States gain in North America?

canal across the Isthmus of Panama for a long time. The distance across the isthmus was only 50 miles (80 kilometers). However, the land was covered with thick rain forests, tall mountains, and muddy swamps. The swamps were a breeding place for disease-carrying mosquitoes.

Still many people dreamed of a canal that would connect the Atlantic to the Pacific. The French started one in the 1800's, but they did not get very far. Diseases like yellow fever and malaria killed off too many workers. Then, in 1903, the United States decided to try. Theodore Roosevelt was president of the United States then. He believed it was

important to the future of the United States to have that canal.

Panama was then a part of the Republic of Colombia. So Roosevelt tried to buy a 10-mile (16-kilometer) strip of land at the Isthmus of Panama from Colombia. However, the Colombian government refused to sell the land.

Panamanians were angry when they learned that Colombia would not sell the land. Many Panamanians wanted to break away from Colombia and form their own country. With help from the United States, leaders in Panama led a successful revolt. On November 3, 1903, Panama declared its independence from Colombia. The

350

leaders of the revolt quickly set up a new government.

Fifteen days later, Panama and the United States signed a treaty. The United States agreed to pay Panama $10 million then and a yearly rent of $250,000 for the land the canal would be built on.

Before work could begin on the canal, a way had to be found to stop yellow fever and malaria. A Cuban doctor named Carlos Finlay discovered that yellow fever is carried by a certain type of mosquito. An American doctor, Major William C. Gorgas, saw the way to end yellow fever by destroying the mosquito's breeding places.

Soon afterward another type of mosquito was found to cause malaria. It too was destroyed. The victory over yellow fever and malaria made it possible for people to work on the canal without getting sick.

In 1904, "the dirt began to fly" as Roosevelt put it. Each mile along the route presented its own special problems. Engineers had to find a way to slow down a fast-moving river. Workers had to cut a waterway through nine miles of solid rock. The canal took ten years to complete.

On August 15, 1914, the first ship passed through the canal. In just ten hours, it steamed from the Atlantic Ocean to the Pacific. The dream of centuries had come true at last.

Workers used steam shovels to dig the Panama Canal.

During the first year that the canal opened, 2,000 ships passed through it. They came from many different nations. Dozens of countries have benefited from the canal over the years, especially those in North and South America.

To Help You Remember

1. (a) How did the United States gain Alaska?   (b) Why did some Americans want Alaska?
2. (a) Why did many Americans want Hawaii?   (b) How did the United States gain Hawaii?
3. (a) Why did the United States want to build a canal across Panama?   (b) Why was it difficult to build?

The map below shows how the United States has grown. Use it to answer the following questions.

1. (a) Find the western border of the United States in 1783. What was the last state in this territory to enter the Union? (b) When did the last state in the Louisiana Purchase enter the Union? (c) When did the last states in the territory that once belonged to Mexico enter the Union?

2. Name four territories that are part of the United States today.

3. (a) How many states did the United States have in 1790? (b) In 1860? (c) In 1900? (d) In 1950?

4. (a) In what ten-year period did the United States add the most states? (b) How many states were added?

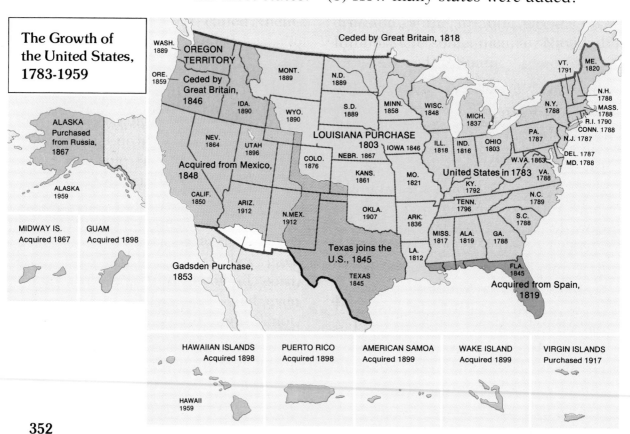

The Growth of the United States, 1783-1959

World War I

By the early 1900's, the United States was one of the richest nations in the world. Every year thousands of ships left ports like New York and New Orleans loaded with steel, machinery, and other goods. They sailed to countries in all parts of the world. Americans were also starting businesses in other countries.

As trade and industry grew overseas, the United States found itself more involved in events in distant lands. Americans liked taking a leading role in world affairs. However, they did not like the thought that they might be dragged into quarrels in other parts of the world. That concern grew in 1914.

On a Sunday afternoon in June, a young student from the small country of Serbia in eastern Europe shot and killed a nephew of the Emperor of Austria. When Americans read of the event on Monday morning, few dreamed it would lead to a world war. Yet within a few years, 30 countries were drawn into a world war, including the United States.

Taking Sides in the War

In the early 1900's, countries in Europe competed with one another for colonies, markets, and resources. None wanted war. Yet each feared its neighbors did. So they all built strong armies and navies. They also looked for **allies.** Allies are countries that promise to help one other in time of war.

A few weeks after the shooting, Austria declared war on Serbia. Germany was an ally of Austria. So Germany too went to war against Serbia. However, the Russians were allies of Serbia. So Russia declared war on Austria and Germany. One by one the rest of Europe took sides. Some joined the Central Powers as Germany and Austria were called. Others joined the Allied Powers. They included Russia, Great Britain, and France.

Countries on both sides had colonies in many parts of the world. These colonists were also drawn into the war. The British army, for example, included soldiers from India as well as soldiers from British colonies in Africa, Australia, and Canada.

Trying to Stay Out of War

Most Americans wanted their country to remain **neutral.** A neutral nation does not take sides in a war.

Staying neutral was very profitable for the United States. The Allies,

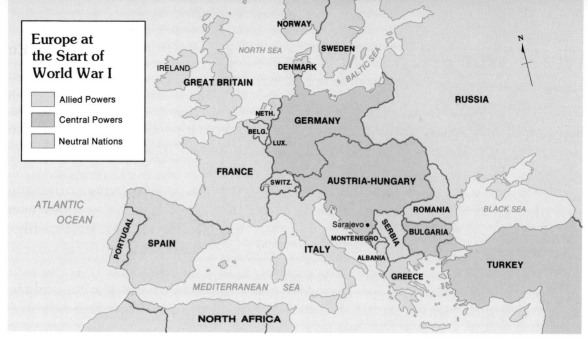

At the start of World War I, which countries in Europe joined the Allied Powers? Which countries joined the Central Powers? Which did not take sides?

Great Britain, France, and Russia, bought more and more goods from the United States as their factories were damaged in the war. Germany and the other Central Powers would have liked to have done the same. However, the British navy made it impossible for ships to enter or leave German ports.

The German effort to break Britain's naval blockade finally brought the United States into the war. The Germans had developed a new weapon, the submarine. It traveled underwater so it could not be seen. German submarines sank many ships headed for Great Britain. All of these ships carried war materials. Some also carried passengers. The Germans placed ads in many American newspapers warning of the dangers of crossing the Atlantic.

In May of 1915, the Germans proved that they meant what they said. A German submarine torpedoed the British ocean liner *Lusitania*. Nearly 1,200 passengers drowned. Among them were 128 Americans. People in the United States were outraged. President Woodrow Wilson demanded that the Germans stop using submarines. For almost two years they did.

Then, in 1917, the Germans decided to make an all-out effort to bring the war to an end. Once again they used their submarines to sink one ship after another. As a result, on April 2, 1917, Wilson asked Congress to declare war. Congress quickly did so. The United States joined the Allied Powers in their fight against the Central Powers.

Fighting a World War

By the time the United States entered the war, the fighting had been going on for over two years. When the war had first begun, most people thought it would be over in a few weeks. Instead, it had dragged on and on. Both sides had weapons that made a quick victory impossible.

One of the new weapons was a machine gun. It could be fired so rapidly that a soldier could shower the air with bullets. Soldiers on both sides had to dig deep trenches to protect themselves. Only in the trenches could soldiers escape the bullets.

For the soldiers, there seemed to be no end to the war. Those people who lived in lands torn up by the fighting shared that feeling. In the winter of 1918, the Russian people pulled out of the war. That year they overthrew their king. The new government immediately signed a peace treaty with Germany.

Germany no longer had to fight the Russians in eastern Europe. Thousands of German soldiers began to move from battlefields in eastern Europe to the trenches in western Europe. If the United States was going to make a difference in the war, it had to act quickly. It did. In June of 1918, more than 250,000 American soldiers arrived in France.

At the same time, American factories were working faster than ever. They were turning out guns, ships, and other war supplies. Everyone helped. As more and more men went off to war, women took their places in factories, fields, and mines.

Americans helped out in other ways too. People ate less so that more food could be shipped overseas. Many Americans had days when they ate no meat. Others planted gardens.

By the end of 1918, the Allied Powers were winning the war. Thanks to

The Allies battle the Central Powers near Mezy, France, in 1918.

Posters like the one above encouraged Americans to support the war effort.

the Americans, they had plenty of soldiers and supplies. The Germans were short of both. On November 11, 1918, the Germans agreed to an **armistice.** That is, they agreed to stop fighting. World War I was over.

The Peace Terms

In January 1919, representatives from each of the Allied Powers met at Versailles, near Paris, France.

They hoped to make a treaty that would bring lasting peace to the world. President Wilson played a major role at the peace talks.

Wilson wanted World War I to be the last world war. So he called for an end to empires. He suggested that the Allies join together in a League of Nations. The purpose of the League was to provide a place where countries could talk over their differences without going to war.

When Wilson returned from Paris, he presented the peace treaty to the Senate. Many senators did not like the treaty. They feared the League of Nations might somehow draw the United States into another war.

In the end, the United States worked out a separate treaty with the Central Powers. The United States never joined the League. Yet in the years ahead, the United States found that it could not stay out of world affairs.

To Help You Remember

1. What event set off World War I?
2. (a) List the Central Powers.
   (b) List the Allied Powers.
3. Why did the United States enter the war?
4. What was the armistice of 1918?
5. (a) Why was the League of Nations started? (b) Why did the United States refuse to join it?

Chapter Review

Words to Know

Complete the following sentences.

1. Puerto Rico is a United States *commonwealth*. A commonwealth is ____.
2. *Expansionists* won the debate over Alaska. Expansionists wanted ____.
3. As European nations prepared for war, they called on their *allies*. Allies are ____.
4. Most Americans wanted their country to stay *neutral*. A neutral nation is ____.
5. The *armistice* took effect on November 11, 1918. An armistice is ____.

Reviewing Main Ideas

1. How did each of the following get Americans involved in a war with Spain? (a) newspaper stories of the Cubans' fight against Spain (b) the explosion of the *Maine*.
2. (a) What lands did the United States gain from Spain at the end of the war? (b) How did senators in favor of expansion feel about new lands? (c) How did those against it feel?
3. (a) How did the United States get Alaska? (b) Hawaii?
4. (a) Why did the United States want to build a canal across the Isthmus of Panama? (b) How did President Roosevelt get the land for the canal? (c) What had to be done before work on the canal could begin?
5. How did the United States get Americans involved in World War I?
6. List two ways Americans helped the Allies in Europe during the war.

In Your Own Words

In the years between 1867 and 1898, the United States gained several territories. Write a paragraph telling when and how the United States gained two of those territories. Be sure to give each paragraph a title.

Keeping Skills Sharp

On an outline map of the world, show the territories the United States added between 1867 and 1914. Which territory lies the farthest west? Which is the farthest east? Use meridians of longitude to help you answer both questions.

Challenge!

Propaganda is the spreading of ideas or information for the purpose of helping or hurting a cause. When the New York *Journal* called the Spanish the enemy, it was slanting its stories in a way that would help the Cubans. Rewrite the sentences below so that each encourages people to support either the Cubans or the Spanish.

1. On the night of February 15, 1898, an American battleship, the *Maine*, blew up in the harbor of Havana.
2. Two hundred and sixty people were killed when the ship exploded.

20

From Good Times to Hard Times

When World War I ended in 1918, people danced in the streets. Bells rang. Whistles and horns blew. Americans were happy that the war was over. They also welcomed the changes that were taking place in American life. Some changes were due to the war. Others were the result of inventions such as the radio, moving pictures, and the automobile. These inventions made life more pleasant.

By 1929, Americans were buying about 100 million movie tickets a week. Americans were also buying millions of radios. People could buy movie tickets, radios, and even automobiles because they were earning more money than ever before. Life seemed to be getting better all the time. Few dreamed that the good times would suddenly end.

As You Read

In this chapter, you will learn about the the good times and the hard times that followed. You will also learn about the changes Americans welcomed and those they feared. The chapter has three parts.

- A Demand for Equal Rights
- The Good Years
- Hard Times

◀ *Allies Day celebration, New York City, 1917*

A Demand for Equal Rights

When the United States entered World War I, Americans rushed to help their country. Some fought on the battlefields. Others helped at home. Yet many of these people were denied the same rights and opportunities that other Americans enjoyed. After the war, these Americans began to demand equal rights.

Voting Rights for Women

Women's groups were among those who pushed for equal rights. They had been fighting for **suffrage,** the

In 1869, when Wyoming was still a territory, women were allowed to vote.

right to vote, long before the war began. As far back as 1848, more than 300 women had met at Seneca Falls, New York, to demand the same rights men had. Many Americans at the time were shocked at the idea of women voting or holding public office. They believed that voting and holding government office were things only men could do.

Although women's groups made some gains over the years, women could not vote in any state until 1890. That year Wyoming entered the Union. It became the first state to give women the right to vote. Slowly other states did the same. Still, by 1913, women could vote in only 12 out of 48 states.

Then came World War I. Women took over hundreds of jobs that people had always considered men's work. They made steel, built trucks and machine guns, and ran offices and shops across the nation. Some joined the army or the navy. They served as nurses, truck drivers, clerks, and cooks.

The war changed many people's ideas about women and what they could do. So in 1920, the Nineteenth Amendment was added to the Constitution. It gave women in every state the right to vote.

Citizenship for Indians

During World War I, thousands of Indians volunteered to fight even though they did not have to. They were not United States citizens.

After the war, many Indians wanted to be citizens. They wanted the same **civil rights** other Americans had. Civil rights are the rights guaranteed to citizens by the Constitution, including the right to vote. In 1924, Congress passed a law making Indians citizens of the United States.

Among those who fought for the new law was a senator from Kansas named Charles Curtis. His mother was part Kaw Indian. Because his father was an American citizen, Curtis was also a citizen. However, most Indians were not as fortunate.

Curtis tried to help those Indians. He supported many laws that made life better for the Indians, including the law that granted them citizenship. In 1929, Curtis was elected vice-president of the United States. Because of Curtis, the hopes of many Indians began to come true.

Disagreements over Civil Rights

Blacks too had high hopes after the war. Many had fought bravely. The French gave their highest medal for courage to four American army companies of black soldiers.

These Seminole Indians in Florida are voting for the first time.

Blacks had helped at home too. Over 500,000 moved north during the war to take jobs in factories, mills, and mines. Before the war, few companies in the North would hire black workers. During the war, they had no choice. There was a shortage of workers. Even though black workers did an outstanding job, most were fired as soon as the war was over.

In spite of their war record, blacks in the United States faced discrimination. Their civil rights were limited. They could not live wherever they wished. They could not attend the schools of their choice. They often could not get jobs that paid well no matter how qualified they were.

Members of the NAACP march in a parade in the early 1900's.

As early as 1909, a group of black and white Americans had formed the National Association for the Advancement of Colored People, or the (NAACP). The organization worked to get equal rights for black citizens. It brought cases of discrimination to both state and federal courts. It also fought for laws that would give equal rights to black citizens.

After the war, membership in the NAACP grew rapidly. Many blacks had risked their lives for their country. Now they wanted the government to grant them full rights as United States citizens.

Many people in the United States believed in equal rights for all citizens. Other Americans did not. These Americans did not believe that black citizens should have the same rights as white citizens. They did not trust the newcomers who had come to the United States in the early 1900's either.

These Americans wanted to keep control of the country in their own hands. They did not want blacks, Indians, Spanish-speaking Americans, and immigrants to have a say in the way the country was run.

In the 1920's, many of these Americans became concerned that too many immigrants were entering the country. They feared the immigrants would take away jobs from people already in the United States. So they persuaded Congress to pass laws to limit the number of people moving to the United States each year.

Some Americans who were against equal rights worked outside the law. They joined a secret group called the Ku Klux Klan. The Klan tried to frighten blacks, Jews, Catholics, Spanish-speaking Americans, and Indians. Klan members used threats, murder, and house burnings against people they did not like.

By the middle of the 1920's, the Klan had over 4 million members. Then membership began to drop off. More and more Americans became disgusted with its methods. Within a few years, the group disappeared from many parts of the country.

To Help You Remember

1. (a) How did women in all parts of the United States get the right to vote? (b) When did they get that right?

2. (a) How did Indians become United States citizens? (b) When did they become citizens?

3. (a) Why was the NAACP formed? (b) List two ways it helps people.

The Good Years

The ten years following World War I were called the good years. In the 1920's, the United States was the richest country in the world. It produced more iron and steel, more automobiles, more furniture, more clothes, and, in fact, more goods than all the other countries in the world combined.

Older industries expanded. At the same time, hundreds of new industries were started. Businesses were growing at an almost unbelievable rate. As they grew, profits and wages went up. **Consumers,** the people who buy and use goods and services, had more money to spend than ever before. The increased money supply brought many changes to American life. For most Americans, the 1920's were the good years.

The Age of the Automobile

In 1923, two scientists set out to study changes in American life. A friend asked them, "Why do you need to study what's changing this country? I can tell you what's happening in just four letters: *a-u-t-o!*"

Automobiles were not a new invention in the 1920's. They were first developed in the 1890's. However, at that time, only the rich could afford one. Then, in 1908, Henry Ford began producing the Model T. It was a car that almost everyone could afford. In 1912, it cost $600. By 1916, the price had dropped to $360. In 1925, a car cost only $260.

By 1925, over half of the families in the United States had a car or were about to buy one. As more and more people bought cars, other businesses grew and prospered. Before the 1920's, the United States had no gas stations, shopping centers, garages, parking lots, motels, or drive-ins. Within 30 years, they were common in most parts of the country. The automobile had become an important part of American life.

When people first began buying cars, there were no traffic lights or

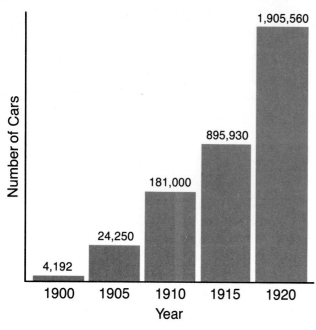

Cars Sold in the United States, 1900–1920

Number of Cars (y-axis)

Year (x-axis)

- 1900: 4,192
- 1905: 24,250
- 1910: 181,000
- 1915: 895,930
- 1920: 1,905,560

About how many automobiles were sold in 1910? In 1920?

road signs. In fact, there were very few good roads in the country. As the number of automobiles increased, so did the number of paved roads. By the middle of the 1920's, a driver could travel on good roads all the way from New York to Kansas. The Age of the Automobile had arrived.

The Age of Flight

During the 1920's, the Age of Flight began. Like the automobile, flying machines were invented long before the 1920's. However, they did not become popular until the 1920's.

During World War I, both the Allied Powers and the Central Powers used airplanes to scout, to spy, and to drop bombs. The men who flew those planes were the heroes of the war. Their adventures set many young men and women to dreaming. After the war, they too wanted to learn how to fly.

For several years, there were only a few jobs for pilots. Some found work with the United States Post Office. It had started air-mail service in 1918. A few were lucky enough to pilot airplanes for companies that offered passenger service. However, these companies did not have many customers. Most Americans were afraid to fly.

Then, on May 20, 1927, Charles Lindbergh of Minnesota became the first pilot to fly nonstop across the Atlantic Ocean. His flight took just 33 1/2 hours. Radio stations reported his progress hour by hour. Overnight he became a hero.

Interest in flying skyrocketed. Airlines began to carry four times as many passengers as they had the year before. Every year planes went a little faster and were a little safer. For many, air travel became part of the good life. By the end of the 1920's, the Age of Flight clearly had arrived.

Buy Today, Pay Later

Where were Americans getting the money for automobiles, radios, and airplane lessons? Many earned good wages. Some used their savings. Others went into debt. In the 1920's, more and more Americans were buying on **credit.** That is, they paid a small part of the total price of a car or a radio each month until it was finally paid for in full. The amount people paid each month included an extra charge called **interest.**

The **stock market** was another place people bought on credit. The stock market is where stocks, or shares in companies, are traded. In the past, people bought stock in a company hoping the company would make a profit. Then as stockholders, each would receive a dividend, or part of that profit. It was not a way of getting rich quickly. Now, however, many bought stock hoping it would rapidly rise in value. Then they could sell the stock for a higher price than they had paid for it.

For a few years, nearly everybody who bought stocks seemed to make money. Some became rich. The newspapers often told of taxi drivers or waiters who had made a fortune buying and selling stock.

Then, on October 24, 1929, stock prices suddenly started to fall. People who still owed money for their stock grew frightened. They tried to sell their stock to pay their debts. However, no one was willing to buy them. Day after day, stock prices continued

Worried stock owners wait for news outside the New York Stock Exchange.

to fall. Those people who could not sell their stocks lost everything they owned. The good years were over.

To Help You Remember

1. How did the automobile industry lead to the growth of many other businesses?
2. Why was the 1920's the beginning of the Age of Flight?
3. (a) What does buying on credit mean? (b) What did Americans buy on credit?
4. What happened to end the good years?

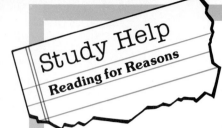

In the first two sections of the chapter, you read about some important changes that took place in the 1920's. A good way to keep track of those changes is to ask yourself two questions:

What happened?
Why did it happen?

What happened is called the *effect,* or result. Why it happened is the *cause,* or reason. Below is a list of several causes of change. Give at least two effects for each of the changes listed.

Causes

1. During World War I, women took over hundreds of jobs that many people considered men's work.
2. During World War I, thousands of Indians volunteered to fight even though they did not have to.
3. In the 1920's, some Americans were against civil rights for blacks, Jews, Catholics, and foreigners.
4. In the 1920's, workers earned more money than ever before.
5. Automobiles cost less in the 1920's than ever before.
6. Airplanes became very popular in the 1920's.
7. In the 1920's, many Americans bought more and more goods on credit.

As you read the rest of the chapter, look for the changes that took place in the 1930's. Remember to ask what happened and why it happened. Keep in mind that most changes have more than one cause and more than one effect.

Hard Times

In 1929, one event quickly led to another. When the prices of stocks fell, many banks closed. People who had put their life savings into these banks lost all their money. The banks had loaned too much money to people who could not repay it. Soon other businesses were forced to close too.

Fewer people could afford to buy radios, automobiles, refrigerators, and other goods. Many factories closed. Some factory owners laid off their workers. More people than ever before were out of a job. As more people lost their jobs, buying dropped even more sharply. As a result, still more businesses closed.

A Time of Broken Hopes and Dreams

By 1932, the United States was in the middle of a **depression.** A depression is a time when many businesses fail. Trade slows down and millions of people are put out of work.

A woman who lived in Chicago wrote that when the depression hit, it was "as if somebody had pulled a switch and everything had stopped running." She went on to say that Chicago had become "a place of broken hopes and dreams."

The same was true in other large cities. Thousands of people lost their jobs. Many people also lost their homes. They had borrowed money from a bank to buy them. Then, when the depression came, many could no longer afford the monthly payments to the bank. So the bank took their homes. Thousands drifted from town to town hoping to find work and a place to live.

Just as it seemed things could not get much worse, another disaster struck. In 1932, a drought hit the Great Plains. Little rain fell that year. Crops withered and died in the fields. Top soil turned to dust. The next

This painting was drawn by a Russian immigrant. It shows the hopelessness people felt during the depression.

Whitney Museum of American Art

The picture on the right shows what happened to a farm in Oklahoma as a result of dust storms in the 1930's. What other states were affected by those dust storms?

Dust Storms on the
Great Plains, 1935-1940

Land Destroyed by Dust Storms

spring, strong winds began to blow across the plains. Those winds picked up millions of tons of dirt and dust. Within hours, the dirt and dust formed huge black clouds that blocked out the sun and coated everything with dust.

Thousands of farms were ruined. Many farmers packed up their belongings and moved from place to place in search of work.

A Reason for Fresh Hope

In 1932, Americans voted for a new president. The Democratic candidate was Franklin D. Roosevelt of New York. He promised Americans a "new deal." Many were not sure what he meant, but it sounded good.

Roosevelt started in public office as a state senator. During World War I, he served as assistant secretary of the navy. Then in 1920, Franklin Roosevelt ran for the vice-presidency of the United States and lost. Shortly after the election, he got polio. It left him paralyzed from the waist down. However, he did not give up his career.

With the help of his wife Eleanor, Roosevelt returned to public office. He was governor of New York when the depression began. He worked hard to help the hungry and the jobless in the state. When he ran for president in 1932, he promised to do the same for all Americans. He won the election by nearly 7 million votes.

The day Roosevelt took office, Americans gathered around their radios to hear what their new president had to say. He told them, "The only thing we have to fear is fear itself." President Roosevelt called on Americans to fight the depression as hard as they would fight an enemy in war.

The New Deal.

The president did not have a fixed plan for ending the depression. To him, the **New Deal** meant he would try one new idea after another until he found one that worked. As he told one group of Americans, "It is common sense to take a method and try it. If it fails, admit it frankly and try another. But above all try something."

Roosevelt brought hundreds of new people into government to help fight the depression. He hired Republicans as well as Democrats, women as well as men, and blacks as well as whites. He also brought thousands of young people to Washington. He wanted fresh ideas. The old ways of doing things were clearly not working.

The president and his helpers did not waste any time. In his first 100 days in office, Roosevelt sent 15 ideas for laws to Congress. All 15 became law. Some of these laws provided help for the old, the homeless, and the hungry.

New Jobs.

The most serious problem the president faced was what to do about the 12 million people who were out of work. Roosevelt and his advisers decided to make jobs for them. The government hired workers to pave roads, lay water pipes, and build schools, theaters, playgrounds, and airports. It paid people to put on plays, paint murals, and write books.

By putting people to work, Roosevelt hoped businesses would open up again. If people had jobs, they would

Eleanor Roosevelt checks on working conditions in a coal mine for the president.

have money to buy things. As more people bought goods, businesses would grow, and they would hire more workers.

Protecting Resources.

Many of the projects started by the government were designed to protect the nation's resources. One of the most successful was the Tennessee Valley Authority (TVA). This project began in 1933. Government workers taught Tennessee farmers how to protect the soil by planting trees. The workers planted hundreds of trees. Most important of all, TVA workers built 16 large dams along the Tennessee River and its branches.

The dams stopped the flooding that had caused so much damage in the past. They also provided cheap electricity. Before they were built, only 1 out of 50 families in the Tennessee Valley had electricity. After they were built, almost everyone did.

Another project was aimed at ending the threat of dust storms on the plains. The government hired hundreds of young men to plant trees on the Great Plains. The roots of trees kept the rich top soil from blowing away.

The Norris Dam (left) was one of the many dams built by the TVA workers. How many dams were built along the Tennessee River? How did these dams help people in the Tennessee Valley?

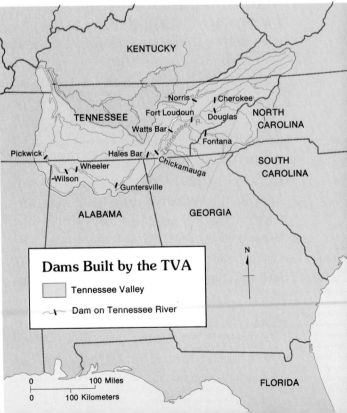

Dams Built by the TVA

▢ Tennessee Valley

⌁ Dam on Tennessee River

Help for the Old, Sick, Jobless. Government projects gave work to about 8 million Americans. Most of them were young men and women. What about those who were too old or sick to work?

To help those Americans, Congress passed the Social Security Act in 1935. It provides money for those who are over 65 and not working. It also helps states set up unemployment insurance plans. These plans provide money to people who are out of work for a short period of time. The Social Security Act also gives money to states to help support orphans and people with handicaps.

The money to pay for all of this help came from working people. Each month they paid money into a social security fund. Their employers put in the same amount of money, and the government added to it.

The Social Security Act still gives millions of families peace of mind. People no longer have to worry about having no money when they are too old or too sick to work.

Over the years, Roosevelt's projects cost the nation billions of dollars. Not all of them worked. Yet they gave Americans new hope for the future. The United States was beginning to recover from the depression. Still the depression did not really end until 1939. That year another world war began.

Americans saw Roosevelt as a strong leader. Few paid attention to his disability.

To Help You Remember

1. Why did many Americans lose their jobs in 1929?
2. What was the depression?
3. What happened in 1932 that made the depression worse?
4. What did Franklin Roosevelt ask Americans to do when he became president?
5. List three ways President Roosevelt put Americans to work.
6. (a) How does the Social Security Act help people? (b) Where does the money to pay for social security benefits come from?

Chapter Review

Words to Know

1. What is *suffrage?*
2. What does it mean to buy on *credit?*
3. What does it mean to pay *interest* on a loan?
4. Explain what happens during a *depression?*
5. What are *civil rights?*
6. Who are *consumers?*
7. What kind of activities takes place in a *stock market?*
8. What did President Roosevelt mean when he called for a *New Deal?*

Reviewing Main Ideas

1. (a) What groups of Americans fought for equal rights in the early 1900's? (b) What happened as a result of their fight?
2. (a) Why were the 1920's called the good years? (b) Why were the 1930's called the hard times?
3. How did President Roosevelt get Americans working again?
4. (a) Why was the TVA started? (b) Tell two ways it helped people along the Tennessee River.
5. What did the government do to help people on the Great Plains?
6. What did the projects started by Roosevelt give to many Americans?
7. How does the Social Security Act help many Americans?
8. When did the depression end in the United States?

In Your Own Words

In the 1930's, thousands of Americans lost their jobs. What happened as a result of so many Americans' being out of work? Write a paragraph that answers this question. Include as many results as you can think of.

Challenge!

In 1932, a city official told a group of Senators what happened in Philadelphia when private charities ran out of money.

One woman said she borrowed 50 cents from a friend and bought stale bread for 31½ cents per loaf, and that is all they had for eleven days except for one or two meals. Another family did not have food for two days. Then the husband went out and gathered dandelions. The family lived on them.

An Oklahoma newspaper editor told the House of Representatives:

The roads of the West and Southwest teem with hungry hitchhikers. The campfires of the homeless are seen along every railroad track. I saw men, women, and children walking over the hard roads. Most were tenant farmers who had lost their all in the late slump in wheat and cotton.

1. How does each speaker arouse sympathy for the hungry?
2. What do you think the speakers want Congress to do? Why?

Unit Review

Take Another Look

Below is a list of key events from the unit. Use the time line on this page to find out when each event took place. On a separate sheet of paper, list the events in the order in which they occurred. Next to each event, give one reason it was important.

a. The transcontinental railroad is completed.
b. Congress passes the Homestead Act.
c. The NAACP is formed.
d. The *Maine* explodes in the harbor of Havana.
e. Congress passes the Social Security Act.
f. Indians become United States citizens.
g. The United States enters World War I.
h. The Panama Canal opens.
i. The United States acquires Puerto Rico and some islands in the Pacific.
j. The United States has a depression.
k. Women get the right to vote.

You and the Past

1. Many of the changes that took place in the United States between 1865 and the 1930's affect the way you and others in your community live. Choose one of those changes and write a paper telling how that change made a difference to life in your community.
2. Many people who experienced the 1920's and 1930's are still living. Interview a person in your community who remembers the good times of the 1920's or the hard times of the 1930's. Find out what life was like in your community in those days. How have things changed?
3. The history of many individuals makes up our nation's history. Choose a person who was important in the years between 1865 and the 1930's. Write a report about how that person's accomplishment has affected your own life and that of various family members.

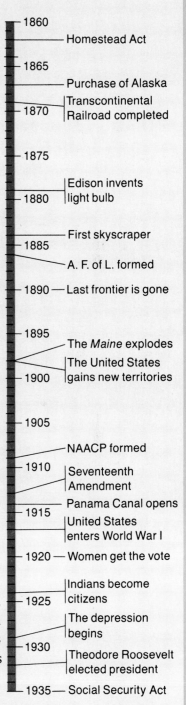

1860

Homestead Act

1865

Purchase of Alaska

Transcontinental Railroad completed

1870

1875

Edison invents light bulb

1880

First skyscraper

1885

A. F. of L. formed

1890 — Last frontier is gone

1895

The *Maine* explodes

The United States gains new territories

1900

1905

NAACP formed

1910

Seventeenth Amendment

Panama Canal opens

1915

United States enters World War I

1920 — Women get the vote

Indians become citizens

1925

The depression begins

1930

Theodore Roosevelt elected president

1935 — Social Security Act

Countdown in the Firing Room, Kennedy Space Center, Florida

Unit Eight

A Modern Nation

Just 20 years after World War I ended, a second world war began. World War II brought many changes not only to the United States but to countries throughout the world as well. After the war, the United States faced many new challenges. Americans worked hard to meet those challenges.

21

The United States in War and Peace

When World War I ended in 1918, many people prayed that it would be the war to end all wars. Yet, just 20 years later, armies were once again on the march. By September of 1939, a second world war had begun. Countries in every part of the world were drawn into the fighting.

At first, Americans tried to stay out of the war. They believed that the oceans around the United States would keep the nation safe from attack. On December 7, 1941, Americans discovered that there were no safe places in the world any more. That day, Japanese warplanes bombed Pearl Harbor in Hawaii. The United States declared war on Japan the next day.

As You Read

In this chapter, you will learn about World War II. You will see how the war changed life everywhere in the world. The chapter is divided into three parts.

- World War II
- The Search for Peace
- A Changing World

As you read, look for the changes that war brought both to the United States and to other countries.

◄ *War in the Pacific*

World War II

The depression that slowed business in the United States during the 1930's also brought hard times to other countries. In some, people turned to leaders who promised to bring power to their country. Instead, these leaders brought about the most terrible war in history.

Moving toward a World War

The Germans were among those who listened eagerly to talk of power and glory. Their country was especially

A businessman uses a wheelbarrow to cart the weekly pay for his workers. Money was almost worthless in Germany.

hard-hit by the depression. It was also hurt by the treaty that ended World War I. The treaty took land and resources away from Germany. Germany also had to pay the winning countries for the damage it had done during the war.

Germany's New Leader. Many Germans thought the treaty was unfair. A man named Adolf Hitler took advantage of that feeling. He told the Germans they were not to blame for the defeat in World War I. He placed the blame on the Jewish people.

Although the Jews had nothing to do with Germany's defeat, many Germans were eager to believe Hitler's lie. Some were prejudiced against Jews. These Germans did not trust anyone whose religion differed from their own. They found it all too easy to blame others for Germany's troubles.

By 1933, Hitler ruled Germany. He quickly made himself **dictator.** That is, he took complete charge of the country. He made the laws. His followers, who were known as Nazis (nä'tzēz), enforced those laws.

As dictator, Hitler ordered his police to round up all Jews and send them to prisons that were called **concentration camps.** Many Jews were killed immediately. Others were forced to work as slaves until they were too weak to work. Then they too were killed.

Concentration camps were part of a plan to wipe out the Jewish people. By 1945, over 6 million had been killed. So many died that people called it a **holocaust.** The word means great or terrible destruction.

Hitler did not just single out Jews for destruction. He also ordered the deaths of many other people. Thousands of Catholics, Poles, labor union members, Gypsies, and even handicapped people were killed.

Hitler's Allies. Hitler also wanted to build a new German empire. Several other countries had similar ideas. They too hoped to end the depression at home by conquering other lands. Japan was one of those countries. In 1931, Japan attacked a part of China known as Manchuria. Four years later Italy invaded Ethiopia in northeastern Africa.

In 1936, Germany, Italy, and Japan signed a treaty of friendship. They promised to help each other in time of war. The three countries were known as the Axis Powers.

As the leaders of the Soviet Union watched the Axis Powers take over more land, they decided to join in. The Soviet Union was a **communist** country. A communist country is one in which the government owns and

Thousands of Jews in Poland were rounded up and sent to prison camps.

runs all factories, mines, farms, and other businesses. There is very little freedom. The Soviet Union wanted to spread communism to other countries. So, in 1939, it signed an agreement with Germany. The two countries agreed to conquer and then to divide Poland. They also promised not to attack one another.

World War II Begins

On September 1, 1939, the German army roared into Poland. Two days later, Great Britain and France decided they could no longer stand by and watch one country after another

World War II

Major Axis Powers
Major Allied Powers
Neutral Countries
Areas Under Axis Control

List the Axis Powers. List two continents where the Axis Powers controlled large areas of land. Which side did Canada, Brazil, and Australia join during World War II?

fall under German rule. They declared war on the Axis countries. World War II had begun. On one side were the Allies led by Great Britain and France. On the other were the Axis countries led by Germany.

At first, there seemed to be no stopping the Germans. They fought a new kind of war. They called it a *Blitzkrieg* (blitz' krēg), the German word for lightning war. Rows of swiftly moving tanks and armored trucks would roar across the border of a country while airplanes bombed cities and towns. Within hours, hundreds of buildings lay in ruins. The roads were crowded with families fleeing for their lives.

Poland fell to Germany in just 11 days of brutal fighting. By the spring of 1940, the Germans also controlled much of northern and western Europe. In June, France fell. By August, Germany was bombing England.

In the meantime, the Japanese were taking over Southeast Asia. They were also threatening many islands in the Pacific. Italian soldiers were moving into eastern Europe and North Africa. The Soviet Union was busy as well. It now ruled part of Poland. It also controlled Latvia, Lithuania, and Estonia in northern Europe.

Then, on June 22, 1941, Hitler suddenly attacked the Soviet Union. This

380

proved to be a mistake. The Soviet Union was too large and too far from German bases and supplies to be conquered quickly. By winter, the Germans had settled in for a long, hard fight.

The United States at War

In 1941, many Americans still believed in **isolation**. That is, they believed that the United States should have as little to do with other countries as possible. These Americans wanted the United States to stay out of the war. Yet they, like other Americans, hoped that the Allies would win.

Pearl Harbor. Then, on Sunday, December 7, 1941, Japanese warplanes bombed a United States naval base at Pearl Harbor in Hawaii. Over 2,400 Americans were killed in the surprise attack, and more than 1,100 were wounded. The next day, President Franklin D. Roosevelt asked Congress to declare war on Japan. Three days later, Germany and Italy declared war on the United States. The two nations were allies of Japan.

A Time of Fear. Americans quickly discovered what people in other countries already knew. The battles of World War II were fought in the skies. Bombs did not just fall on the soldiers. They also hit houses, schools, and factories. No one was safe.

Many Americans were fearful of this new kind of war. They saw danger everywhere. People who lived along the Pacific coast were especially worried. Many feared the Japanese would bomb them next.

Some Americans directed their fears toward the Japanese Americans. As a result, the President ordered all Japanese Americans living on the West coast shipped to prison camps farther inland.

None of these Japanese Americans were ever found guilty of spying. Many proved their loyalty over and over again during the war. Japanese

Truckloads of Japanese Americans arrive at a camp in the Wyoming desert.

American soldiers won many honors and medals. Yet it was not until long after the war that many Americans realized how unfairly they had treated Japanese Americans.

Preparing to Fight. Japanese Americans were not the only United States citizens to show their loyalty during the war. Everyone pitched in. Even school children helped out. They collected old papers, tin cans, and scrap metal. Paper and metal were in short supply. Americans allowed nothing to go to waste.

Thousands of men and women took jobs in factories, mines, and farms. They built thousands of ships, tanks, and airplanes. They turned out enough food, weapons, clothing, and medicine to supply not only the American armed forces but also those of the Allies. No other country has ever produced so much so quickly.

Winning the War

By 1942, American troops were fighting in Europe, Africa, Asia, and on islands in the Pacific. Everyone knew it would be a long war. By 1944, the Allies were making headway both in Europe and in the Pacific.

Victory in Europe. In 1944, nearly 3 million soldiers from many different countries gathered in England. They were there to prepare for an invasion

Americans helped out in the war effort in many ways. Children collected scrap metal. Many women worked in defense plants.

that would free Europe. The invasion was led by an American general, Dwight D. Eisenhower.

The planning of the invasion took many months. Then, finally, on the morning of June 6, 1944, everything was ready. By dawn, 130,000 soldiers had landed on the beaches of Normandy in France. More soldiers arrived each day.

By August, France was free. By the spring of 1945, the Allies were moving east toward Berlin, Germany's capital. At the same time, Soviet soldiers were pushing west toward the same city. By May, the Germans had given up. Rather than face defeat, Hitler killed himself. The war in Europe was over.

Victory in the Pacific. The war in the Pacific continued. There the Allies captured one island after another. Each victory brought them closer to Japan. By 1945, the Allies had also destroyed most of Japan's navy and air force. Yet the Japanese refused to surrender.

An invasion of Japan seemed necessary. Yet many feared it would be a long fight. President Roosevelt was seeking another way of ending the war when he died suddenly. People all over the world mourned. Roosevelt, who had served longer than any other president, was beginning his fourth term of office.

Allied forces fought all day for this stretch of beach in Normandy, France.

Vice-President Harry S. Truman became president. He had to decide whether or not to invade Japan. Truman's advisors told him about a new weapon that had been secretly developed during the war. It was the atom bomb, the most powerful weapon developed at the time. It had more power than 20,000 tons (18,000 metric tons) of dynamite.

Many of the president's advisors urged him to use the bomb to force the Japanese to give up. Others were not sure it was a good idea. Unlike other weapons, this new bomb could have long-lasting effects. It gave off a deadly poison that could cause illness and even death long after the bomb had been dropped.

After much careful thought, President Truman made his decision. On

August 6, 1945, the United States dropped an atom bomb on the city of Hiroshima (hir′ō shē′mə). Three days later, another atom bomb was dropped on the city of Nagasaki (nä′gə sä′kē). The next day, August 10, 1945, the Japanese surrendered. The war was finally over.

To Help You Remember

1. What did the Axis Powers do to start World War II?
2. What did Americans do to help win the war?
3. (a) What events led to victory in Europe? (b) In the Pacific?

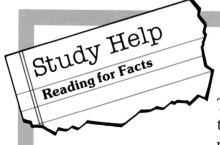

Study Help

Reading for Facts

The outline below contains the headings from the first section of the chapter. Copy the outline on a separate sheet of paper. Then, under each of the headings, list at least two events.

World War II

A. Moving toward a World War
  1. Germany's New Leader
    a. _____
    b. *Hitler becomes dictator of Germany.*
  2. Hitler's Allies
    a. _____
    b. _____
    c. _____
    d. _____
B. World War II Begins
  1. _____
  2. _____
  3. _____
  4. _____

C. The United States at War
  1. Pearl Harbor
    a. _____
    b. _____
  2. A Time of Fear
    a. _____
    b. _____
  3. Preparing to Fight
    a. _____
    b. _____
D. Winning the War
  1. Victory in Europe
    a. _____
    b. _____
  2. Victory in the Pacific
    a. _____
    b. _____

Continue the outline as you read the rest of the chapter.

The Search for Peace

Over 40 million people were killed during World War II. Millions of others were left homeless after bombs destroyed cities and towns throughout Europe, Asia, and Africa. Everywhere farms, factories, roads, bridges, and railways lay in ruins. In time, people would rebuild their homes and start new businesses. Their lives, however, would never be the same again.

Americans were luckier. Even though many Americans died on the battlefields, the United States was a richer and stronger nation when the war ended than before it began. Yet, even in the United States, the war changed people's ideas about the world and the role the United States should play in world affairs.

Changes in Outlook

In 1945, few Americans still believed in isolation. Even those who had wanted to avoid any involvement with foreign countries before the war now had a different point of view. With weapons like the atom bomb, there were no safe places in the world any more.

Organizing for Peace. In 1945, the United States was the only country to have an atom bomb. Yet Ameri-

cans realized that it was only a matter of time before other countries also had atomic weapons. The next world war was therefore likely to be fought with weapons even more terrible than those used in World War II.

To make sure there would never be another war, the United States joined the Allies in planning a new league of nations. It was to be called the United Nations (UN). The organization would include all the countries of the world. Members would work together to keep the peace. In 1945, representatives from 50 countries

President Harry S. Truman is shown here addressing a session of the United Nations.

gathered in San Francisco, California, to write a charter for the UN. The new group then set up headquarters in New York City.

An End to Empires. The war also changed people's ideas about empires. Many people now believed that no country has the right to rule another. In 1946, there were only four independent countries in Africa. Asia too was still divided into colonies. In the years after the war, however, one colony after another won its independence. Since 1945, over 50 new nations have been formed.

Americans saw many similarities between their own country's fight for freedom in 1776 and these modern struggles for independence. At the same time, many Americans feared that the Soviet Union would take advantage of the unrest in the world to spread communism. Increasingly, those fears seemed justified.

The Cold War

In February of 1945, the Allies agreed to hold elections in every country they had freed. From the start, the Soviet Union ignored the agreement. Instead, it set up communist governments in one Eastern European country after another.

President Truman was outraged. He and later American presidents set out to keep the Soviet Union from taking over any more land. The struggle that followed between the United States and the Soviet Union is called a **cold war**. A cold war is fought with words and money, not with guns or bombs. At the same time, each side prepares for a war it hopes will never come.

By 1949, the Soviets had their own atom bomb. Soon the two sides were competing in a deadly **arms race**. Each was determined to produce more weapons, and more destructive weapons, than the other side. The competition between the two countries took other forms too as each tried to win countries to its point of view.

American Gains. Just after the war, many countries did not have the money or the supplies they needed to rebuild. So, in 1947, President Truman offered to help the war-torn countries recover. Dozens of nations accepted the offer. American aid to these countries saved countless lives. It also strengthened the governments of Western Europe so that they could protect their countries from the Soviets. American aid kept Greece and Turkey free as well.

In 1953, Dwight Eisenhower became president of the United States. He expanded President Truman's aid program. It now included nations in

Africa and Asia. Some of the money the United States gave these countries was used for weapons. Much of the money, however, went for factories, roads, dams, railroads, schools, and hospitals.

In 1961, yet another president took office. John F. Kennedy continued to help other countries much as Truman and Eisenhower had. He also tried a new idea. In 1961, he persuaded Congress to set up the Peace Corps. The Peace Corps sent thousands of volunteers to countries in need of help. These volunteers taught African villagers how to read. They also dug wells in South America and improved harvests in India. They won friends for the United States.

Soviet gains. The Soviets had their own successes in the cold war. In 1949, China became a communist nation. Ten years later Fidel Castro (fi del′ ka′stro) set up a communist government in Cuba, an island just 90 miles (144 kilometers) from the southern coast of Florida.

Were most of the countries in the Western Hemisphere allied with the communist or the noncommunist in 1966? Find the two largest countries on the map. Name them.

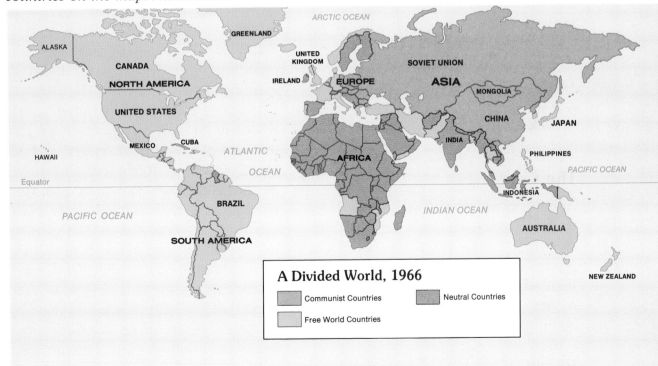

A Divided World, 1966

The Soviets' greatest success came in 1957. That year they launched the first **satellite** in space. A satellite is an instrument used to gather and send information as it circles Earth or other planets.

Americans were not pleased that the Soviets were the first in space. They were determined to catch up. In 1958, Congress set up the National Aeronautics and Space Agency (NASA). The competition between the two nations now included exploration of outer space.

The Cold War Warms Up

In the years since World War II, there have been many small wars. Some

Find Vietnam and Korea on the map. In what part of Asia is each located?

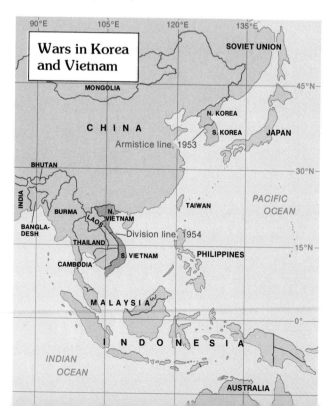

were wars of independence. Others were civil wars. Still others were fought to change borders established after World War II. From time to time, the Soviet Union and the United States have sent weapons, money, and even soldiers to help fight in these wars. Neither country, however, has allowed these wars to become another world war.

The first small war began in the East Asian country of Korea, not far from the Soviet Union. Before the war, Korea was under Japanese rule. It was freed by Soviet and American soldiers. After the war, the Soviets set up a communist government in the northern part of the country. South Korea had a government that was against communism.

In 1950, the North Koreans decided to unite the country by conquering South Korea. The United Nations sent troops to help the South Koreans. Among the troops were soldiers from the United States and 15 other countries. In the end, however, neither side won the war. The two Koreas are still separated by UN guards and barbed wire.

The war in Korea was a new kind of war. In the past, countries used their most deadly weapons whenever they had to fight a war. In Korea, countries chose not to use their most deadly weapons even if it meant that the war would have no winner.

A War in Vietnam

In the 1960's, the United States found itself involved in a war similar to the one in Korea. This time the war was in the Southeast Asian country of Vietnam. Before World War II, Vietnam was a French colony. During the war, it was conquered by the Japanese. When the war ended, Vietnam, like Korea, was divided.

Like the North Koreans, the North Vietnamese wanted to reunite the country under their own rule. They found some supporters in South Vietnam. Other South Vietnamese wanted to keep their own government. A civil war began in the 1950's.

A Widening War. The Soviets helped the North Vietnamese by giving them tanks and other weapons. At first, the United States tried to help the South Vietnamese in a similar way. In the 1950's, President Eisenhower sent aid and advisors to the country.

By the early 1960's, the South Vietnamese were losing the war. So President Kennedy stepped up aid to South Vietnam. He also sent the first United States troops to take part in the fighting. By 1964, Lyndon B. Johnson was president. He sent even more American troops to Vietnam. So did the next president, Richard M. Nixon. By the late 1960's, thousands of American soldiers were fighting in Vietnam, and the war was

Thousands of American soldiers fought in Vietnam between 1964 and 1973.

spreading to neighboring countries in Southeast Asia.

Disagreements in the United States. As American involvement in the war increased, Americans were becoming more and more divided. Some Americans thought that their country had no business in Vietnam. They did not think the United States should fight another country's war.

Other Americans had a different view. They thought the United States had a responsibility to stop the spread of communism. These Americans wanted to defeat the North Vietnamese and win the war.

389

The Vietnam Memorial in Washington, D.C., is a lasting tribute to those who gave their lives in the Vietnam War.

The End of the War. After nearly ten years of fighting, the war in Vietnam was no closer to ending than it had been in the 1960's. So the United States pulled out of Vietnam. By 1973, American soldiers were back home. Two years later the North Vietnamese took over the south and reunited the country.

The war left much bad feeling in the United States. It had become so unpopular that soldiers did not return to celebrations as other soldiers had. It was not until 1982 that many veterans felt that their sacrifices were recognized. That year the government dedicated a memorial in Washington, D.C., to honor those who had died in Vietnam.

To Help You Remember

1. How did World War II change people's ideas about isolation?
2. (a) How did people's ideas about empires change after the war? (b) Name one outcome of that change.
3. What events led to a cold war in the years after World War II?
4. How did the United States help other countries after the war?
5. Why did the United States send soldiers to Korea in 1950?
6. Why did the United States send soldiers to Vietnam in the 1960's and 1970's?
7. How did the war in Vietnam divide Americans?

A Changing World

There have been many small wars since the one in Vietnam. The United States has taken sides in a few of these wars. In most, however, it has tried to act as peacemaker.

Bad feelings between the United States and the communist countries can make a small war very dangerous. With atomic weapons on both sides, even the tiniest conflict can become a world war.

Relations with Communist Nations

In recent years, the United States has worked hard to improve its relations with communist countries. The two most powerful of these countries are China and the Soviet Union.

China. When China became a communist country in 1949, the United States refused to deal with the new government. Instead, it continued to regard the leaders of the old government, who now lived on the island of Taiwan, as China's true rulers.

In 1963, China exploded its first atom bomb. It was becoming a very powerful country in other ways too. It sent aid and advisors to many countries. By the 1970's, the United States could no longer ignore China.

In 1972, President Nixon flew to China for a meeting with the country's leaders. He visited famous places like the Great Wall of China and was guest of honor at a huge banquet. Nixon's visit marked the start of a new, more friendly relationship between China and the United States.

The flags of China and the United States fly side by side in this Chinese city.

The next two presidents, Gerald Ford and Jimmy Carter, continued Nixon's policies in China. In 1979, the United States formally recognized the communist government of China as the country's official government. The following year the two countries signed a trade agreement.

The Soviet Union. In 1972, President Nixon also visited the Soviet Union. He traveled there in an effort to improve relations between the two countries. He and the Soviet leaders promised to cooperate on scientific projects and improve trade. They also agreed to work together on a series of agreements that would slow down and perhaps some day end the arms race. In 1973, the first of these agreements went into effect. It was known as SALT I. SALT stands for Strategic Arms Limitation Treaty.

Soon after the treaty was signed, work began on SALT II. Little progress was made, however. Each side accused the other of not really wanting to end the arms race.

Then, in 1980, the Soviets invaded neighboring Afghanistan, a country in Central Asia. Americans were furious. The invasion convinced many Americans that it was time to take a tougher stand against the Soviet Union. When Ronald Reagan became president in 1981, he started a program to build up the United States military might. The Soviets responded by increasing their own supply of weapons.

The growing arms race has alarmed many people in the world. In case of a nuclear, or atomic, war, every nation would be affected. As a result of such concerns, the governments of the two countries have agreed to meet once again.

Rich Nations and Poor Nations

In 1950, many Americans saw the world as divided into two groups of countries: allies of the United States and allies of the Soviet Union. By the 1980's, there were over 160 countries in the world. Many of them were allies of neither nation.

These nations did not want close ties with the United States or the Soviet Union. They wanted to make their own choices and do whatever seemed best for their own countries.

To people in these countries, the divisions between rich and poor nations are more important than the divisions between the United States and the Soviet Union. Many new nations still have colonial economies. That is, they have few factories or industries. So they must import tools, machines, and other manufactured goods. To pay for these goods, they export raw materials like coffee,

This Peace Corps volunteer is helping the people of Costa Rica develop more modern farming methods.

cocao, and oil. The price of raw materials is always less than the price of goods manufactured from those materials. So most of these new nations are deeply in debt.

These countries would like more industry, but they do not have the money needed to build factories or even people trained to manage those factories. The United States is helping these countries in many ways. It sends money for factories, schools, and farm equipment. Peace Corps volunteers help to train workers for new jobs. So do many religious groups and private charities. American businesses help too. Many have built factories in countries throughout Asia, Africa, and Latin America. These factories provide needed jobs.

New Links and Old

Today the countries of the world are linked in many ways. An event in one country touches people everywhere. People today are linked not only by trade but also by newer and much faster systems of transportation and communication.

Jet airplanes were a weapon of war during World War II. Today they have a peaceful use. They transport people and goods to even the most distant countries within hours. As a result, more people than ever before are visiting other countries.

Telephones and televisions link people too. The president of the United States and the head of the Soviet Union are only a telephone call

In 1985, millions of people sent aid to Mexico City after two giant earthquakes tumbled buildings and killed thousands.

away. So are ordinary people in both nations.

Today, through the use of satellites, people throughout the world can watch the same event on television. For example, through television, people in countries around the world saw what happened when a drought hit Sudan and Ethiopia, two African nations, in 1984 and 1985. Millions of people responded in much the way they would to a call for help from a neighbor. They sent food, medicine, and other supplies.

The world is growing smaller. No place is isolated any more.

To Help You Remember

1. Name two ways the United States has tried to improve relations with China.
2. Name two ways the United States has tried to improve relations with the Soviet Union.
3. How did the Soviet invasion of Afghanistan affect Americans?
4. (a) What problems must the poorer nations in the world solve? (b) How is the United States helping them do so?
5. Name three links between countries today.

Chapter Review

Words To Know

1. In what way were German *concentration camps* a part of the *holocaust?*
2. How is the *arms race* a part of the *cold war?*
3. What do people favor who believe in the policy of *isolation?*
4. In what way was Adolf Hitler a *dictator?*
5. What is a *communist* country?
6. How does a *satellite* help scientists learn more about Earth?

Reviewing Main Ideas

1. (a) How did Germany help start World War II? (b) Japan? (c) Italy?
2. Tell three ways the United States prepared for war.
3. (a) How did the war end in Europe? (b) In the Pacific?
4. How did the United States work for peace after World War II?
5. How was the war in Korea different from other wars in history?
6. (a) How did the United States become involved in the war in Vietnam? (b) How did that war end?
7. (a) Why has the United States tried to improve relations with China and the Soviet Union in recent years? (b) How successful have these efforts been?

In Your Own Words

Write a paragraph about one of the following topics. Be sure that your paragraph has a topic sentence that tells what the paragraph is about.

1. Hitler Changes Germany
2. December 7, 1941, a Day Americans Will Never Forget
3. August 6, 1945, a Day the Japanese Will Never Forget
4. The United States Fights a Cold War
5. The United States Tries to Improve Relations with Communist Countries

Challenge!

On January 20, 1961, John F. Kennedy became the youngest elected President in American history. The speech he made on Inauguration Day inspired not only many Americans but also people around the world. He closed his speech with these words:

And so, my fellow Americans: Ask not what your country can do for you—ask what you can do for your country.

My fellow citizens of the world: Ask not what America will do for you, but what together we can do for the freedom of man.

What did President Kennedy think makes a person a good citizen of the United States? A good citizen of the world? Soon after he took office, Kennedy started the Peace Corps. How did the Peace Corps reflect his ideas about citizenship?

22

Changes at Home

World War II changed the way Americans viewed other countries. It also changed the way Americans saw themselves. New inventions changed American life too. Television is a good example. It seems hard to believe today, but in 1945, most Americans had never seen a television set. Yet by 1960, there was a set in almost every home.

Through television, Americans shared proud moments and sad ones. They saw the fighting in Vietnam in a way people had never seen a war before. In 1969, they also watched as two American **astronauts** planted the United States flag on the moon. Astronauts are people who explore outer space.

As You Read

Television has changed American life. So have many other inventions. In this chapter, you will see how they have opened new opportunities. You will see too how the struggle for equal rights has expanded those opportunities to include all Americans. As you read, notice the way one change often leads to many others. This chapter is divided into three parts.

- New Ways of Living
- The Struggle for Equal Rights
- Toward Equality for All

◄ *Edwin E. Aldrin, Jr., walking on the moon*

New Ways of Living

The years since World War II have been years of change in the United States. There have been changes in the places people live and in the kinds of jobs they hold. There have even been changes in the kinds of things people do for fun.

New Technology

Television is only one of the inventions that has changed American life in the last 40 years. Some, like TV, were developed in peacetime. Others grew out of the war effort.

Wartime Inventions. During the war, hundreds of raw materials were in short supply. So scientists looked for ways of using plastics as substitutes. From chemicals, they created solid plastics that could be used in place of glass, wood, and metal. They also created liquid plastics that could be used as paints or glues. They even developed yarns made of plastic that could be woven into cloth.

After the war ended, many factories continued to turn out plastic products. People liked the plastic products because they were cheaper and often lasted longer than the real thing. Today most goods are made at least in part of plastics.

Americans have also found new uses for other wartime inventions. Those inventions include everything from jet airplanes to frozen food. Scientists have even found peaceful uses for atomic energy. It is used to make electricity.

During the war, people had to get things done faster than ever before. So builders used assembly-line methods to put up army barracks and even factories. After the war, they used those same methods to build houses.

Machines That Think. During the war, the United States army asked scientists at Harvard University in Cambridge, Massachusetts, for help

The plastic molds made in this factory will be used for a variety of products.

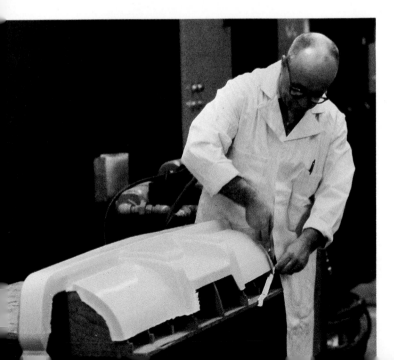

*Today, computers do everything from reading books for the blind
(left) to assembling parts of an automobile (right).*

in solving a complicated problem. To provide a solution, the scientists built a machine that could solve math problems quickly. It was the first **computer**. A computer not only solves problems. It also stores large amounts of information and then recalls it with great speed.

Its inventors nicknamed the first computer Mark I. It was built in 1944. Two years later it was out-of-date. In 1946, scientists at the University of Pennsylvania built a new computer. Its electric impulses carried messages 1,000 times faster than Mark I's mechanical system.

The new computer was quickly out-of-date as well. So was the one that took its place. Each new machine was smaller and more efficient than the old one it replaced. Each was also less expensive.

In 1961, there were only 4,000 computers anywhere in the world. By the middle of the 1970's, there were over 100,000 in the United States alone. Today there are millions. Computers are used in many different ways. They help people store information and solve problems. They also teach skills, draw maps and graphs, and even play games.

Computers are used in the space industry to help speed up work.

New Jobs

Computers have led to many new jobs. Until a few years ago, no one ever heard of a computer programmer, word processor, or data entry operator. Now these jobs regularly appear in the want ads of newspapers. Other jobs are disappearing. Computers can do the work faster and more efficiently than people.

With computers, workers in almost every industry can turn out more work in less time. As a result, fewer people are needed in mines, factories, and offices.

Before computers, almost every office had at least a few file clerks. They kept a company's records in order. Today those records are stored in large computers. Office workers can get them just by typing a few numbers on their computer terminal. When they are finished, the computer automatically stores them. Offices also use computers to pay bills, to transfer information from one office to another, and to solve complicated problems.

Other inventions have had similar effects. The widespread use of plastics has also opened many new jobs. It has closed some as well. There is less demand for steel, leather, and other goods now. So many of the factories that produced those goods have closed their doors.

Thanks to jets, the airline industry has also grown rapidly since the 1950's. It too has opened many new jobs. Thousands of Americans work in airports. Others service airplanes, write tickets, prepare in-flight meals, and do dozens of other jobs. On the other hand, there is less travel by train now. So fewer people work for the railroads.

Moving to the Suburbs

Many Americans have jobs that did not exist long ago. They also live in communities that did not exist long ago. Until the 1920's, no one had ever heard of a suburb. Today more than half of the people in the United States live in the suburbs.

Many families moved to the suburbs after the war. At the time, there was a housing shortage. Few houses were built during the depression. Even fewer went up during the war years. When the war ended, millions of Americans were eager to buy houses. Many builders bought up land outside large cities and put up houses as quickly and cheaply as Henry Ford once built his Model T's.

In just a few years, the nation had hundreds of new communities within easy reach of a city. Each was built near a highway. Before long, those who traveled on those highways were finding it harder and harder to tell where one suburb ended and another began. In some parts of the country, there was an almost unbroken line of cities and suburbs. Geographers called this type of development a **megalopolis.** The word means a very large city.

One megalopolis stretches from southern New Hampshire to Maryland. Another lies along the southern shores of the Great Lakes. Still another stretches along the coast of southern California from San Diego to San Francisco.

Every city and suburb in a megalopolis has its own schools, mayor, and city council. Yet they are linked in many ways. Every day thousands

Suburban housing developments like the one above were built in the 1950's.

of people travel from one part of a megalopolis to another to work, attend school, shop, or play. The people in a megalopolis are linked in other ways too. Fumes from factories and cars in one community affect all of the others. Many share water, electric power, and bus and train service.

Opening New Frontiers

In the last 30 years, life in the United States has been changing in still another way. Americans have begun to explore a new frontier, outer space. The Soviets were the first to open this new frontier. In 1957, they launched a successful satellite. Americans quickly expanded their own space program.

In 1961, President John Kennedy set a goal for the country. He said the United States would land a spacecraft on the moon by 1970. On July 20, 1969, the United States reached its goal.

Two American astronauts, Neil A. Armstrong and Edwin E. Aldrin, Jr., became the first humans to walk on the moon. They planted an American flag there. They also left a container carrying messages from 76 countries and a plaque describing their visit. A television camera the astronauts brought along allowed millions to watch as the two walked on the moon. They later rejoined Michael Collins, the third member of the crew, on the spaceship *Columbia* for the journey back to Earth.

Over the years, the space program has expanded knowledge in many ways. It has led to inventions like the communications satellite. It enables people to watch events as they happen. It is also used to send messages and photographs. Pictures taken from satellites help people forecast the weather, find minerals, and do hundreds of other tasks.

By the mid-1980's, the United States was making regular trips into space. A teacher was even asked to set up a classroom in space. Christa McAuliffe was to teach lessons from the spaceship *Challenger* to students around the nation.

However, on January 28, 1986, the *Challenger* exploded after takeoff, and all seven crew members were killed. President Ronald Reagan spoke to students about the tragedy. "I know it's hard to understand that sometimes painful things like this happen. It's all part of the process of exploration and discovery; it's all part of taking a chance and expanding horizons."

To Help You Remember

1. List three wartime inventions and tell how each is used today.
2. What are computers used for?
3. Where do most Americans live today?
4. What is a megalopolis?
5. What changes have taken place as a result of the space program?

This picture of New York City was taken from space.

This chapter looks at changes that have taken place in the United States since World War II. For each event listed below, write a change that took place as a result of it.

New Technology

1. Wartime Inventions
   (a) During the war, hundreds of raw materials were in short supply. As a result, _____.
   (b) After the war, many factories continued to turn out plastic products. As a result, _____.
   (c) During the war, people had to get things done faster than before. As a result, _____.
2. Machines That Think
   (a) During the war, the United States Army asked scientists at Harvard University for help in solving a complicated problem. As a result, _____.
   (b) Each new computer quickly became out-of-date. As a result, _____.

New Jobs

1. The invention of computers meant that people were needed to run them. As a result, _____.
2. Computers took over many jobs that used to be done by people. As a result, _____.
3. The widespread use of plastics reduced the demand for steel, leather, and other goods. As a result, _____.
4. Thanks to jets, the airline industry grew rapidly. As a result, _____.

Continue the list of changes for the remaining two sections of the lesson: *Moving to the Suburbs* and *Opening New Frontiers*. Add to the list as you complete the remaining sections of the chapter.

The Struggle for Equal Rights

New inventions were not the only way American life changed after World War II. The war also changed the way Americans saw themselves and others.

Those who fought in the war found their courage tested again and again. Thousands met the challenge. The list of those who won medals for bravery include black and white Americans, women and men. Indians, Spanish-speaking Americans, and immigrants all made the list.

Those who stayed home were challenged too. To get workers, factory owners hired more women and older people than ever before. For the first time, some factory owners were also willing to hire those who had a **disability**, or handicap. The achievements of these new workers showed what people could accomplish if they were only given a chance. In the years after the war, more and more Americans demanded that chance. Black Americans were among the first to work for equal rights.

An End to Segregation

The struggle of black Americans for equal rights was not a new one. When slavery ended in 1865, prejudice did not end. Many states had laws that **segregated** Americans. That is, the laws kept black and white Americans apart. In many places, blacks attended separate schools. They ate in separate restaurants. Many jobs, neighborhoods, and even parks were closed to black Americans. Some states even kept blacks from voting.

In the 1950's and 1960's, blacks worked harder than ever to change these laws. Many fought unfair laws in court. They argued that the laws ought to be thrown out because they went against the Constitution. Their first big victory came in 1954.

Three years earlier, a fourth grader named Linda Brown tried to attend the public school near her house in Topeka, Kansas. She was turned away. It was an all-white school, and she was black.

Linda's parents decided to fight for Linda's rights. The Browns took their case to court. In 1954, it reached the Supreme Court, the highest court in the nation. The justices agreed with Linda and her parents. They ordered that schools throughout the nation be **integrated**. An integrated school is one that is open to both black and white students.

The Struggle Continues

After the Supreme Court handed down its ruling, black Americans began to challenge other laws as well. Among them was a law in Alabama that said that blacks had to sit at the back of buses. If the buses became crowded, they had to stand so that white passengers could sit.

Rosa Parks. In December of 1955, Rosa Parks took the bus home from work as usual. She was a seamstress in a Montgomery, Alabama, department store. It had been a long, hard day, and she was tired. When the bus became crowded, the driver ordered her to give her seat to a white man. When she refused, she was arrested.

Rosa Parks took her case to court. While lawyers debated the law, the black people of Montgomery decided to take action. They refused to ride city buses until the law was changed. For 381 days, they walked to work or rode in car pools. Then, in 1956, the Supreme Court ordered that buses, trains, and airplanes be integrated.

Martin Luther King, Jr. The leader of the fight in Montgomery was a young minister from Atlanta, Georgia. His name was Martin Luther King, Jr. He believed that by protesting peacefully, black and white Americans could get the unfair laws changed.

King led many protests. The largest took place in August of 1963. More than 200,000 Americans gathered in Washington, D.C. They had come to

Rosa Parks is shown here as she enters the Montgomery County Courthouse.

urge Congress to pass laws that would protect the rights of all Americans. King spoke to the crowd. He said, "Now is the time to make real the promises of democracy." He told too of his dream of a nation in which all Americans could live in peace.

King spent much of his life speaking out against violence. Yet he could do little to stop it. In 1968, while in Memphis, Tennessee, he was shot and killed. The nation mourned the loss of a great leader.

New Laws. The work of Martin Luther King, Jr., and other Americans brought about many changes. In the 1960's, Congress passed several new

Martin Luther King, Jr., devoted his life to the struggle for equal rights. He was loved and admired by millions of people.

laws. They made it illegal to deny anyone a job or the right to vote because of his or her ancestors, color, or sex. Only integrated schools could receive government money. Companies that did not offer all workers an equal chance to get ahead could no longer do business with the federal government.

A Widening Struggle

Blacks were not the only Americans to work for the new laws. Many other groups also joined the struggle for equal rights. They too pushed for new laws and argued in the nation's courts for equal treatment.

Hispanic Americans. Hispanic, or Spanish-speaking, Americans come from many different countries. The largest number are Mexican Americans. Puerto Ricans make up the next largest group. (Puerto Rico has been part of the United States since 1898.) Still other Hispanic Americans are from Caribbean islands or countries in Central and South America. Although there are many differences among Hispanic Americans, they share a language.

Like black Americans, Hispanics have also suffered from prejudice. They too have found some jobs, schools, and neighborhoods closed to them. As a result, they too have worked for laws that would protect their rights, including their right to speak Spanish.

Some Hispanics fought for their rights in court. In 1974, they won an important victory. The Supreme Court ruled that schools must provide **bilingual education** for children who do not speak English. That is, schools must teach those children in their own language as well as in English. The word *bilingual* means "expressed in two languages."

Indian Groups. Indian groups also demanded fairer treatment. About half of the Indians in the United States live on or near a reservation. Others live in cities and towns throughout the country. Although some have managed to get ahead, Indians as a group are the poorest Americans.

By the late 1960's, many Indians were demanding more opportunities. To call attention to their problems, a few staged protests. Other Indians preferred to use the courts to force the United States to honor its treaties. Over the years, the government had taken away land from some groups without paying for it.

In the 1960's and 1970's, the courts ordered the government to honor the treaties it had signed by paying for the land. In other cases, the government was ordered to return land to the Indians.

These new citizens are registering to vote in Sacramento, California.

Immigrants. During the 1960's, a number of Americans were also concerned about unfair immigration laws. They wanted those laws changed because they favored some immigrants over others. Under these laws, for example, only 100 Chinese immigrants could settle in the United States each year. Yet thousands of people could come from many countries in Europe.

In 1965, Congress passed a new law. It limited the number of immigrants who could settle in the United States each year just as the old laws did. It did not, however, set limits by country. Instead, it set yearly limits by hemisphere. People with close relatives in the United States were allowed to come before those who did not have family in the country. **Refugees** were also given an advantage. Refugees are people who fled their country for political reasons. They cannot safely return home. The law also said that immigrants could not be turned away because of their skin color or their ancestors.

Women. The struggle for equal rights also made some women aware of the ways they too suffered from prejudice. Although women now had the vote, they still did not have the same opportunities as men. Men usually got the best jobs. They also received higher pay than women even when both did the same work.

In the 1960's and 1970's, many women wanted an amendment to the Constitution making unfair treatment based on sex illegal. In 1972, Congress passed the Equal Rights Amendment (ERA). It then went to the states for approval. Some women were against the amendment. They feared they would lose certain kinds of special protection they now had. They feared, for example, that women might be drafted into the armed forces. In the end, the ERA fell three states short of becoming part of the Constitution.

Even so, women were able to persuade Congress to pass a number of laws that protected their rights. Jobs could not no longer be closed to women because of their sex. Women were also entitled to equal pay.

Older Americans. Just as women fought against unfair treatment based on sex, so older Americans wanted an end to such treatment

Older Americans and handicapped Americans are among the groups of people who are working for equal rights.

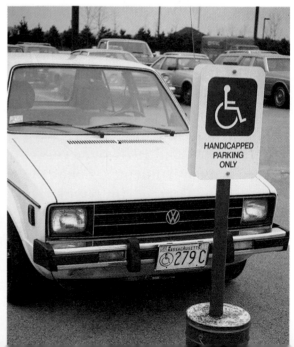

based on age. Many did not have much money. They had trouble finding housing and meeting the high cost of medical care. Some wanted to continue working. They formed groups like the American Association of Retired People to push for their goals. As a result of the efforts of these groups, Congress raised the age when people must retire from 65 to 70 years old.

Americans with Disabilities. Encouraged by the success of other groups, Americans with disabilities also demanded their rights as citizens. In the 1970's, Congress stated that disabled Americans cannot be denied a job just because of their disability. They have a right to use public buildings, too. For example, these buildings must have elevators and ramps for wheelchairs. Children with disabilities have the same right to an education as other children.

To Help You Remember

1. (a) What laws did blacks try to change in the 1950's and 1960's? (b) What part did Martin Luther King, Jr., play in those efforts?
2. How did court decisions and laws passed by Congress affect (a) black Americans, (b) Hispanic Americans, (c) Indians?
3. Why did many Americans favor the immigration law of 1965?
4. (a) What goals did women work for? (b) Older Americans? (c) Americans with disabilities?

Toward Equality for All

Court decisions and new laws have brought many changes to the United States. The country has always been home to people of many different cultures. Today there is more variety than ever. Today more Americans than ever are able to make the most of the opportunities the nation offers.

The New Immigrants

One reason for the greater variety of cultures in the United States today is a change in immigration. In 1965, Congress passed a new immigration law. The law went into effect in 1968. Before 1968, four out of every five

In the 1970's and 1980's, many Vietnamese sought refuge in the United States.

immigrants were from Europe. Today four out of every five newcomers are from Latin America and Asia. Between 1970 and 1980, the number of Asian immigrants alone more than doubled.

The Asians come from countries like South Korea, China, and the Philippines. Many are also from countries in Southeast Asia. When the Communists took over all of Vietnam in 1975, thousands of people fled the country. The number of refugees grew as neighboring Cambodia (now Kampuchea) and Laos also became communist countries. Between May 1975, and March 1982, over 600,000 men, women, and children left Southeast Asia. Many of them settled in the United States.

Other new immigrants are Hispanics. The population of many Latin American countries is growing faster than the number of jobs. So thousands have come to the United States in search of work. Others come for political freedom. When the Communists took over Cuba, many Cubans became refugees. Other Hispanics are from countries in Central America that are torn by revolution or civil war.

Like earlier immigrants, all of these newcomers face many problems. They have to learn a new language as well as new customs and traditions. They often have to learn new skills too. Yet they too have taken advantage of the opportunities opened by the new laws. The number of immigrants who work in science, business, the arts, and education is growing every year.

A number of communities have benefited too. Miami, Florida, is a good example. It has become a business center for many people who live in countries throughout Central and South America. They come to Miami because many people there speak their language and understand their customs.

Modern Pioneers

In some ways, the new immigrants are pioneers. So too are many Americans whose families have lived in the United States for generations. In the early 1800's, pioneers like Daniel Boone led the way west. Today's pioneers lead in a different way. They are the first to make the most of opportunities opened by the new laws. In doing so, they have encouraged others to follow. In the 1960's and 1970's, Barbara Jordan was one of those modern pioneers.

Barbara Jordan. In 1962, the young black woman from Houston, Texas, decided to run for a seat in the Texas House of Representatives. She lost the election. Two years later she ran again and lost again. In 1966, she decided to try for a seat in the Texas state senate. Many people thought her chances of winning were poor. There had not been a black state senator since 1883. No black woman had ever been elected to the state senate.

Barbara Jordan did not change her mind. She ran and this time she won. Winning the election, however, was only a beginning. Now she had to prove she could handle the job. She had to work for laws that would help the people she represented. To do so, she had to get along with other senators—even those with different points of view. By the end of her first year, Barbara Jordan had come a long way toward proving herself. The other senators voted her the outstanding new member.

In 1972, Barbara Jordan decided to run for a seat in the House of Representatives in Washington, D.C. This time she received over 80 percent of the vote. She had proved to voters that a black could represent both black and white Americans. She had proved too that a woman could represent both men and women.

Barbara Jordan is a modern pioneer who made the most of new opportunities.

411

A Growing List. Since the 1960's, one pioneer after another has opened new fields and new opportunities. Some, like Barbara Jordan, are famous. Others are known only in their hometowns. Over the years local newspapers have written countless stories about the community's first black police officer, first woman firefighter, and first Hispanic principal. Photographs have shown the first girl to play on a boys' Little League team and the first immigrant to win a local spelling bee or science fair.

Sally Ride was this country's first woman astronaut. Thurgood Marshall was the first black to serve on the Supreme Court, and Sandra Day O'Connor the first woman.

Other pioneers were honored only at family gatherings. Thousands of families took pride in their first high school graduate, the first in the family to get a college education, or the first to become a doctor or a lawyer.

By the middle of the 1980's, more blacks, Hispanics, and Indians were finishing high school than ever before. Their number of college graduates increased too. So did those who entered professions like medicine, law, and education. The number of businesses owned and operated by blacks, Hispanics, and various Indian groups was increasing rapidly as well.

Changing Attitudes. The new laws have not ended prejudice. Nor have they promised instant success. They simply give people a chance to get ahead. In making the most of that chance, modern pioneers have helped change the way Americans see themselves and others. They have also inspired everyone to try a little harder, even those who choose not to explore new fields. A young man who lost a leg to cancer expressed it best.

In 1985, Jeff Keith ran across the United States to raise money for cancer research. He told reporters he had another goal too. He said, "My message is that if I can run across America on one leg, then anything can be accomplished."

Today's college graduates include many young people with minority backgrounds.

To Help You Remember

1. What changes resulted from the immigration law passed in 1965?
2. (a) Who are the modern pioneers? (b) How do they change people's ideas about themselves and others?
3. (a) Why have there been so many firsts since the 1960's? (b) How have they expanded opportunities for all Americans?

413

Chapter Review

Words to Know

1. What does an *astronaut* explore?
2. Name three things a *computer* can do.
3. What is a *megalopolis?*
4. How is a *segregated* school different from an *integrated* one?
5. What is *bilingual education?*
6. What is a *disability?*
7. How is a *refugee* different from other immigrants?

Reviewing Main Ideas

1. Give two examples of the ways each of the following has changed American life: (a) television, (b) plastic products, (c) jet airplanes, (d) computers, (e) satellites.
2. Give three examples of the ways Americans fought for equal rights after World War II.
3. How did the new immigration law Congress passed in 1965 change American life?
4. How did the civil rights laws Congress passed in the 1960's open opportunities for many Americans?

In Your Own Words

Write a paragraph telling how one of the following changes has made a difference to the way people in your community live and work.

The Growing Use of Computers
The Growth of Suburbs
The Civil Rights Laws of the 1960's

Challenge!

Barbara Jordan of Houston, Texas, was the first black woman to represent a southern state in Congress. In 1973, she said this of the preamble, or introduction, to the Constitution.

"We, the people"—it is a very eloquent beginning. But when the Constitution of the United States was completed on the 17th of September in 1787, I was not included in that "We, the people." I felt for many years that somehow George Washington and Alexander Hamilton just left me out by mistake. But through the process of amendment, interpretation, and court decision, I have finally been included in "We, the People."

1. Which amendments helped include Barbara Jordan in "We the people?" (If you cannot remember, use your index to find the right amendments.)
2. Which court decisions helped include Barbara Jordan?
3. Today do the words "We, the people" include all Americans? Give reasons for your answer.
4. Barbara Jordan ended her speech by saying, "My faith in the Constitution is whole, it is complete, it is total." Why do you think she places such a high value on the Constitution even though it did not include her when it was written?

Keeping Skills Sharp

There are nearly 240 million people in the United States. Over one half of those Americans live in ten states. Those states are shown below on the map. So are the ten states that have the fewest people.

Beside the map there is a graph. It tells the kinds of communities most Americans live in today. Use the graph and the map to answer the following questions.

1. In what states do most Americans live?

2. (a) What states have the fewest people? (b) How do you explain why they do not have more people?

3. (a) What states are growing rapidly? (b) How do you think that growth will affect a map that shows where Americans live in the year 2000? (c) Why?

4. (a) What does the graph and the map tell about where most people in California live? (b) Most Georgians live? (c) Most people in Washington State live?

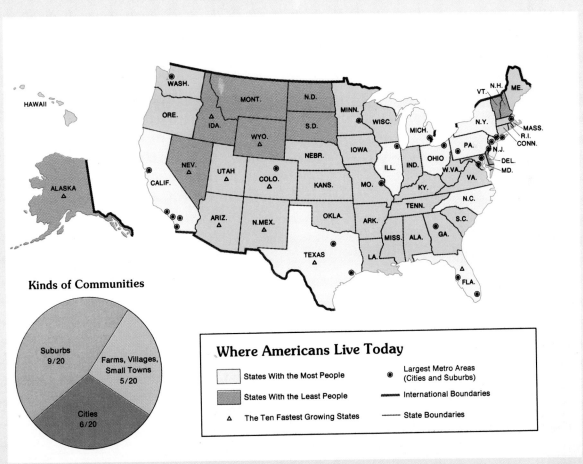

Kinds of Communities

Suburbs 9/20

Farms, Villages, Small Towns 5/20

Cities 6/20

Where Americans Live Today

☐ States With the Most People

▨ States With the Least People

△ The Ten Fastest Growing States

⬤ Largest Metro Areas (Cities and Suburbs)

▬ International Boundaries

— State Boundaries

23

The United States Today

Nearly 240 million people live in the United States today. They come from many different backgrounds and have a great variety of skills and interests. The land they live on is as varied as they are. The United States is the fourth-largest country in the world. It covers over 3½ million square miles. Over the years, the American people have used that land and its resources in many different ways. They have cleared forests, drained marshes, brought water to the desert, and turned grasslands into wheat fields. There have been other changes too. The country looks very different today from the way it looked long ago. It has even changed since World War II. Those changes can be seen in every part of the nation.

As You Read

In this chapter, you will learn what each part of the country is like today. As you read, look for signs of change. Notice too the things that have stayed the same. The chapter is divided into four parts.

- The Northeast
- The South
- The Middle West
- The West

◄ *Connecticut Avenue, Washington, D.C.*

The Northeast

Throughout the history of the United States, the Northeast has been the most crowded part of the country. Today it is hard to tell where one state in the region ends and the next begins. An almost unbroken line of cities and suburbs stretches from southern New Hampshire to northern Maryland.

Although other parts of the nation are growing faster, nearly one out of every four Americans still lives in the Northeast. Yet the Northeast takes up only ¹/₂₀ of the country's land.

The Northeast is a very crowded region. What states make up the Northeast?

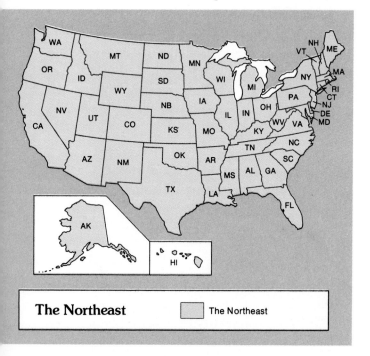

The Northeast | The Northeast

Trade and Manufacturing

Most of the people in the Northeast live near the North Atlantic coast. In the Northeast, the coastline is broken by many inlets and bays where ships can safely harbor. The colonists built cities along these harbors. Among those cities were New York, Boston, Philadelphia, and Baltimore.

Buying and Selling. From the start, each of those ports was a center of trade. Farmers sold their corn and wheat in the markets of these cities. Loggers came too with timber from the many forests in the region. Fishing crews also gathered in the markets to sell their catches. Before long, these port cities had many businesses that served buyers and sellers. Banks were started. So were companies that hauled and stored goods.

Other cities in the Northeast grew up along rivers like the Connecticut, the Hudson, the Susquehanna, and the Delaware. From these cities, goods were shipped to the coast.

Today both the seaports and the river cities of the Northeast are still flourishing. Farmers, lumbering companies, and fishing crews still sell their goods there. So do factory owners. The cities of the Northeast are now centers of manufacturing as well as trade.

Making Goods. The Northeast is the place where the Industrial Revolution began. Today, nearly 200 years later, the region's factories are still humming. Although some factories have left the region, many new ones have taken their place.

In parts of Massachusetts, workers build computers in the same buildings where cotton cloth was once made. Other factories in the region use steel from nearby mills to make scientific equipment and parts for spacecraft. Some turn out plastic and products made from plastic. There are also many chemical plants and oil refineries.

Why have these industries remained in the Northeast? Good transportation is one reason. A large supply of workers is another. A third reason is that cities in the Northeast offer factory owners a wide variety of services.

Service Industries

Today the fastest-growing industries in the Northeast are the **service industries**. These are industries that help people in some way. Banks provide a service. So do hospitals, radio and television stations, schools, and government agencies.

Long ago, service industries in the Northeast helped only people who lived nearby. Today more and more of these industries serve people throughout the United States and the world.

New York City is a world center for entertainment and banking. The city is also home to the New York Stock Exchange. There people buy and sell shares of stock in companies throughout the nation. Many companies that publish books, magazines, and newspapers are located in the city. So are the country's main radio and television networks. All these serve not only New Yorkers but also people in every other state and in countries around the world.

The skyscrapers of New York City tower over crowded city streets.

Other cities in the region also provide services for the nation. Boston with its many colleges and universities is a center for research in science, medicine, and other fields. The first computer, for example, was built at Harvard, the nation's oldest university, in nearby Cambridge.

Washington, D.C., is the capital of the nation. Nearly half of the workers there are employed by the federal government. They too serve people throughout the United States.

Not every service industry in the region serves factories and other large businesses. **Tourism**, the business of serving visitors, is an important industry in the Northeast too. Millions of people visit the Northeast each year. They enjoy the forests, the mountains, and the seashore. They see places important to all Americans. They visit the battlefields of the American Revolution. They tour Independence Hall in Philadelphia. They go to Washington to watch their government at work. Thousands of people in the northeast part of the country have jobs that depend on these tourists.

To Help You Remember

1. Where were the first cities in the Northeast located?
2. What kinds of goods do factories in the region produce?
3. (a) What are the fastest-growing industries in the Northeast? (b) Why?

The South

The South looks very different today from the way it did at the end of World War II. Before the war, most Southerners farmed for a living. Many were very poor. Today most Southerners live in cities. They work in factories or have jobs in a great variety of service industries. Signs of change are everywhere. Those changes have brought much prosperity to the region.

Changes in Farming

Today fields of cotton, rice, and tobacco are still a common sight in many parts of the South. Those fields, however, are not worked the way they used to be. There are fewer farmers today. With machines, one farmer, however, can plant and harvest more crops than 10 or even 20 workers could in the past.

The land that a farmer works produces bigger harvests today. Why?

Farmers have learned to **conserve** the land. That means they use the resource wisely. They rotate, or change, the crops they grow from year to year so that the soil does not wear out. They have learned better ways of plowing and planting their fields. Farming has become a science.

Farmers have taken advantage of improvements in technology too. They are specializing in such crops as celery, oranges, peaches, and tomatoes. In the past, these crops often spoiled before they could get to market. Now thanks to refrigeration and faster transportation, they can be safely shipped almost anywhere in the world.

There has been another change too. Long ago, Southerners shipped their cotton and other farm products to cities in the Northeast for processing. There were few factories in the South. Today most of the nation's cotton mills are located in cities from Virginia to Georgia. In fact, North Carolina turns out more cloth than any other state. Other factories process rice, peanuts, and sugar. Still others turn Florida oranges into juice and lemons into lemonade.

Putting Resources to Work

The South is changing in other ways too. People there are making better use of their other resources.

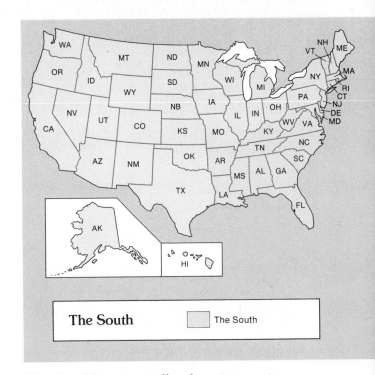

The South is a rapidly changing region. What states are shown on this map of the South?

Southerners are now using their forests to provide lumber for furniture and pulp for paper. In fact, wood has become so valuable that some farmers grow it as a crop. Mississippi has many tree farms. So do a number of other states in the region. Mills that process lumber or make paper dot the region. So do furniture factories.

The rivers of the South have always been a valuable resource. Today they too are more valuable than ever. Since the 1930's, dams like those built by the Tennessee Valley

421

Oil rigs in Louisiana and horse farms in Kentucky are two of the ways Southerners are putting resources to work.

Authority have allowed people to use these rivers not only to transport goods but also as a needed source of **hydroelectric power.** Hydroelectric power is the use of water power to make electricity.

Fishing too has always been an important way of earning a living. Today it is more important than ever. Fish can now be shipped almost anywhere without fear of spoiling. To serve those new markets, fishing crews bring in huge catches from the Atlantic Ocean and the Gulf of Mexico. Some people fish the rivers. Others have created fish farms. They raise catfish and other fish in small ponds.

The South is also rich in mineral resources. Resources like iron ore and coal turned Birmingham, Alabama, into a steel-making center in the late 1800's. Today workers in Alabama also mine bauxite, which is used in making aluminum. In Louisiana and Mississippi, workers drill for oil and natural gas. Nearby refineries turn these resources into gasoline, heating oil, plastic, and many other products.

Transportation Systems

As factories have grown, so has transportation. Dozens of new highways link Southern cities with each other and with other parts of the nation. Those cities are also connected to distant places by rail and air routes.

Highways, railroads, and airplanes carry people as well as goods. Many older Americans move to the South when they retire. In this way, they can escape the ice and snow of Northern winters.

Other Americans spend their vacations in the South. Some come to see the old South. They visit Charleston, South Carolina, and St. Augustine, Florida. Others come to see the new South. They watch the space launches from Cape Canaveral in Florida, visit amusement parks, or just relax at hotels that dot the Atlantic coast and the Gulf of Mexico.

The Growth of Southern Cities

By the 1980's, five **metropolitan areas** in the South had a million people or more. A metropolitan area is made up of one or more large cities and surrounding suburbs. Some metropolitan areas have been important in the South since the early 1800's. Others are new.

New Orleans has been an important seaport for over 150 years. Long ago, farmers from as far north as Illinois shipped their goods down the Mississippi to New Orleans. Today barges still come down the river. They carry not only farm products but also industrial goods.

Three of the other large metropolitan areas are in the state of Florida. They are Miami, the Fort Lauderdale-Hollywood metropolitan area, and Tampa-St. Petersburg. All three are major centers for tourism. Many retired people live in these cities as well. Miami is also an important business center for many Latin American companies.

The fifth city is Atlanta, Georgia. It is a business center for Southerners. It has many banks and insurance companies. It has the largest airport in the region as well. Many foreign countries have **consulates** in the city. In a consulate, representatives of a foreign country help their business people work out trade agreements with local companies. Today Southerners trade with people in every country in the world.

To Help You Remember

1. How has farming changed in the South?
2. Name three ways Southerners are now making better use of their resources.
3. How have new highways and airports helped the South grow?
4. Name three metropolitan areas with over one million people.
5. Tell why each of the cities you named above has grown.

A land use map tells how people use land and key resources. It can also help you see similarities and differences between the various parts of the country.

The land use map on page 425 has color and a number of small picture symbols. The colors show economic activities. That is, the colors show how most of the land in the region is used. The picture symbols show key resources. Use both colors and symbols to answer the following questions.

1. (a) Which part of the country has the most manufacturing? (b) Which part has the least?
2. How do manufacturing centers in the Northeast seem to differ from those in the South?
3. Name the main manufacturing cities in the South and tell what energy resources each is near.
4. Minneapolis, St. Louis, Memphis, and New Orleans have at least two things in common. What are they?
5. Where in the United States is fishing an important economic activity?
6. Which parts of the country have many farms and ranches?
7. In which part of the country will you find more ranches than farms?
8. Name five cities that can use hydroelectric power in their factories.
9. Where in the United States will you find places with little or no economic activity?
10. Name the three main land uses along the Great Lakes.
11. Name at least three parts of the country where forestry is an important industry.
12. What important economic activity cannot be shown on a land use map?

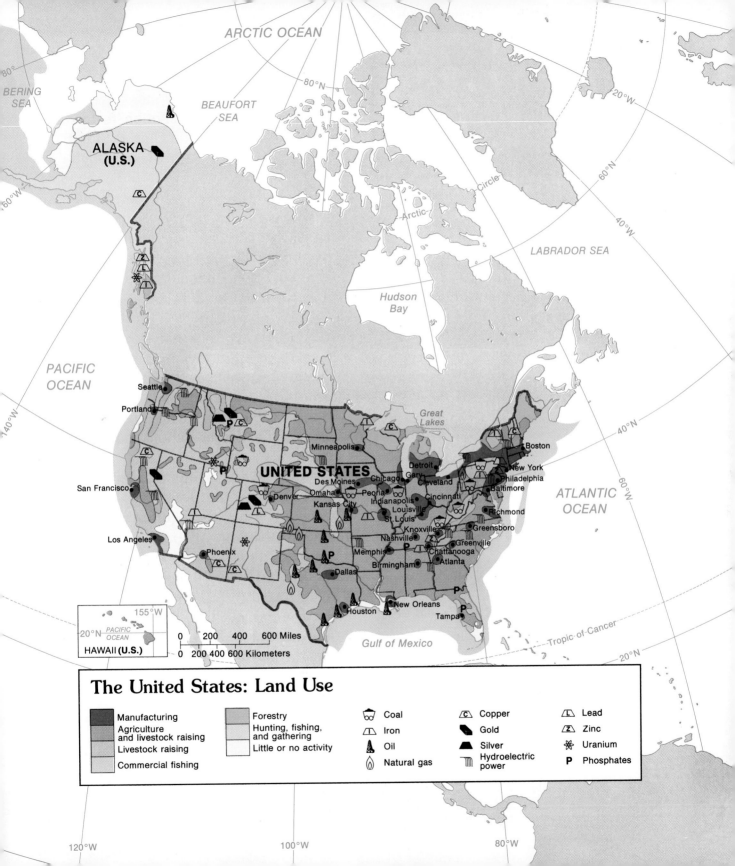

The United States: Land Use

Manufacturing
Agriculture and livestock raising
Livestock raising
Commercial fishing
Forestry
Hunting, fishing, and gathering
Little or no activity

Coal
Iron
Oil
Natural gas
Copper
Gold
Silver
Hydroelectric power
Lead
Zinc
Uranium
Phosphates

ARCTIC OCEAN

BEAUFORT SEA

BERING SEA

ALASKA (U.S.)

PACIFIC OCEAN

Seattle
Portland

San Francisco

Los Angeles

Phoenix

155°W
20°N PACIFIC OCEAN
HAWAII (U.S.)

0 200 400 600 Miles
0 200 400 600 Kilometers

UNITED STATES

Minneapolis

Denver

Des Moines
Omaha
Kansas City

Peoria
Indianapolis
St. Louis
Louisville

Chicago

Memphis

Dallas

Houston

New Orleans

Birmingham

Nashville
Knoxville
Chattanooga
Atlanta

Tampa

Gulf of Mexico

Detroit
Gary
Cleveland
Cincinnati

Richmond
Greensboro
Greenville

New York
Philadelphia
Baltimore

Boston

ATLANTIC OCEAN

Great Lakes

Hudson Bay

LABRADOR SEA

Arctic Circle

Tropic of Cancer

120°W   100°W   80°W

The Middle West

The Middle West covers about ⅕ of the United States. Like the South, the Middle West is also changing. The changes there, however, have been less dramatic.

A Farming Center

Long ago the Middle West was a farming center. Settlers there turned even the dry plains into the bread-basket of the world. Today the Middle West is still a farming center.

Several states in the Middle West border the Great Lakes. What are those states?

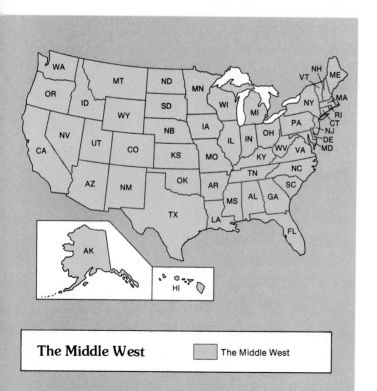

The Middle West — The Middle West

Farmers there grow enough to feed not only people in the United States but also people in countries throughout the world.

Yet there are fewer farmers today than ever before. They can produce more because they have the latest machines and the help of scientists who can show them how to get the most from their land.

Many farmers in the Middle West still remember the dust storms that howled across the plains in the 1930's. Therefore, farmers today are careful to conserve both land and water. Today, for example, many farmers plant trees to hold the soil in place.

Middle West farmers have found ways to water the land even in dry years. They use the **aquifer** that lies beneath the Great Plains. An aquifer is a huge underground lake. The one under the Great Plains is almost as big as the state of California. Farmers discovered it in the 1930's. However, they could not use it until after World War II. Only then did engineers build the kind of pumps farmers needed to use the underground water.

Most of the country's corn is grown in an area called the Corn Belt. It stretches from central Ohio to eastern Nebraska. Twice as much corn is grown there than before World War II. Since the war, scientists have developed new kinds of corn that resists disease and ripens early. Most of that corn does not find its way to the supermarket. Instead, it is used to fatten livestock.

Omaha, Nebraska, has become the country's meat-processing center. From there, beef and pork are shipped in refrigerated trucks and railroad cars to other parts of the country.

Wheat is another major crop. In states like North Dakota, where winters are very cold, farmers plant spring wheat. Its name comes from the fact that it is planted in the spring. In Kansas and other places where winters are not as hard, farmers grow winter wheat. It is planted in the fall so that its roots can grow strong before winter comes. In the spring, the wheat grows rapidly and is ready for harvest by early summer.

Dairy farming is also important in the Middle West. The country's largest dairy farms are located west of the Great Lakes in Wisconsin and Minnesota.

A Manufacturing Center

The Middle West has been a center of industry since the late 1800's. It still is, but the factories there are also changing.

Circular fields are easier to irrigate. Trees provide windbreaks to protect crops.

The first factories in the region processed farm products. Many still turn wheat into flour and milk into cheese. Today, however, some factories use farm products in ways people never dreamed of. For example, factories in the Middle West make such products as cooking oil, baby powder, and chewing gum from corn. They also make gasahol, a fuel that runs cars.

The Middle West has other resources for industry as well. It has rich deposits of coal and iron. About 70 percent of all the iron ore in the United States comes from the Mesabi Range in Minnesota. The Middle West also has limestone.

427

This factory in Illinois makes sweeteners and alcohol fuel from corn.

By the early 1900's, there were many steel mills along the Great Lakes. Thousands of factories that depended on steel grew up nearby. Detroit, Michigan, became the center of the nation's automobile industry. In other cities of the Middle West, workers made machines for factories around the country.

Some factories in the Middle West are in trouble. Since the 1970's, the steel and automobile industries have lost business to companies in Japan and West Germany. Today too the factories of the Middle West are using more plastic and less iron and steel.

Yet the Middle West remains an important manufacturing center partly because, like the Northeast, it is also a transportation center.

A Transportation Center

Long ago, cities like Cincinnati, Ohio, and St. Louis, Missouri, grew up along the rivers of the Middle West. Others like Chicago were located on the Great Lakes. In those days, water was the cheapest way of shipping goods. It still is. Today barges on the rivers and lakes carry goods to and from the Middle West.

Until 1959, people in the Middle West had no way of shipping their goods directly to countries other than Canada. They were **landlocked**. That is, they had no ocean ports. Today they do. In 1959, the United States and Canada opened the St. Lawrence Seaway. It allows oceangoing ships to travel up the St. Lawrence River to the Great Lakes. As a result, Chicago and other cities along the Great Lakes have become ocean ports.

The Middle West is the place where the country's railroads come together. So do the nation's highways. Many railroads and trucking companies have their headquarters in the Middle West. Many airlines are also based in the Middle West. Chicago's O'Hare Airport is one of the busiest in the world.

Chicago itself is the third largest city in the nation. It is the busiest port on the Great Lakes. It is also a major railroad center. Chicago is also the center for business in the Middle West. Many of its companies have dealings with businesses throughout the nation and the world.

To Help You Remember

1. How has farming in the Middle West changed?
2. How has manufacturing changed?
3. Give three reasons why the Middle West is an important transportation center.

The West

No part of the country has changed more than the West. Until World War II, few people lived in any Western state. Today California has more people than any other state, and the region as a whole is the fastest-growing part of the country.

The Southwest

Long ago much of the Southwest was too dry for farming. People thought most land there was useful only for grazing sheep and cattle. Then, in the early 1900's, the federal government built huge dams like the Hoover Dam on the Colorado River and the Coolidge Dam on the Gila River. These dams provided water for people, animals, and crops. As a result, farming has become very important.

Name the three regions that make up the West. Which of these regions includes the state of Texas? Which includes California?

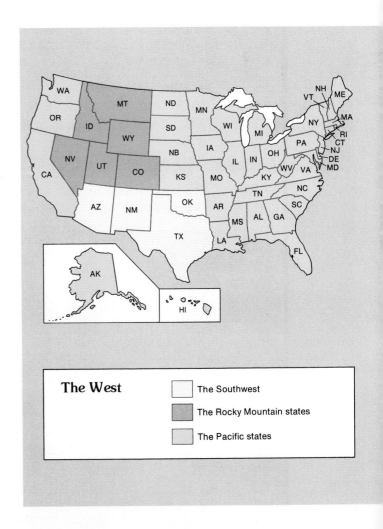

The West
☐ The Southwest
■ The Rocky Mountain states
▨ The Pacific states

Today Texas, New Mexico, and Arizona are all major cotton-growing states. Many farmers in the region also grow such crops as grapefruit, oranges, melons, and lettuce. Many get more than one harvest a year because of the long growing season.

Mining too is a big industry. Much of the region's wealth comes from energy resources. These are resources people use to power machines. Oklahoma and Texas have oil and natural gas. New Mexico and Texas are rich in uranium, a mineral used to make atomic energy.

The Southwest has other mineral resources too. Among those resources are sulfur, salt, helium, copper, and silver. Long ago most of these resources were shipped to other parts of the country for processing. Today much of that work takes place in the Southwest. Many refineries and mills were built during World War II. The need for these resources did not end after the war. So the refineries and mills are as busy as ever.

In recent years, many other factories have been started in the region. Some turn oil into **petrochemicals**. Petrochemicals are chemicals made from petroleum. They are used to make medicine, fertilizer, plastic, soap, and even paint. In other new factories, workers build computers, airplanes, and other equipment.

Hoover Dam (left) supplies water and electricity to people in the Southwest. Houston, Texas (right), is one of the fastest-growing cities in the United States.

As industry has grown so have the cities of the Southwest. Today Texas has three of the ten largest cities in the United States—Houston, Dallas, and San Antonio. The largest of these cities is Houston. It has grown because of its nearness to oil and natural gas. Today Houston has many refineries. It is also the center of the petrochemical industry. It is an important seaport too, even though it is 50 miles from the Gulf of Mexico. In the early 1900's, the people of Houston built the Houston Ship Canal, linking the city to the Gulf. The port helped the city grow.

The Rocky Mountain States

Like the Southwest, the Rocky Mountain States have also been experiencing rapid growth. Long ago, prospectors eager for gold and silver opened the region for settlement. Today miners search for uranium, petroleum, coal, and other energy resources. The Rockies are also rich in copper, lead, phosphate rock, silver, and zinc.

Yet there are few factories in the region. The tall mountains that make up the Rockies are difficult to cross. Building highways and railroad lines is very expensive. The Rocky Mountain States also lack a large, dependable supply of water. There is, however, some manufacturing. It takes

People from all over the world come to the Rocky Mountain region. Here, a family enjoys a picnic near Lake Jackson in the state of Wyoming.

431

Every year the Denver Mint makes millions of pennies and other coins.

place in such cities as Denver, Colorado. It is one of the nation's main meat-packing centers. It also has a **mint**. A mint is a place where the United States government manufactures coins. Denver is a service center for businesses in the Rockies too. So it has many banks, trading companies, and other service industries.

The same is true of Salt Lake City in Utah.

Tourism is a growing industry in the region too. Every year thousands of people come to the Rockies to ski. Others visit the many national parks in the region. The Rockies are no longer as cut off from the rest of the country as they once were.

The Pacific States

Since World War II, the states that border the Pacific are also not as isolated as they once were. New highways and improvements in air travel have helped the region grow. As a result, people there can make better use of their resources.

For example, some states along the Pacific are rich in energy resources. Swiftly flowing rivers in Oregon and Washington can be used to make electricity. California and Alaska have large supplies of oil and natural gas. Now that they can get their goods to market, people in the Pacific States are using those resources to process fish, timber, and farm products. They have built other factories too. There workers build automobiles, airplanes, and ships. Still others turn out computers. The center of the computer industry is the area around San Jose, California.

With better transportation, tourism has become a very important in-

The mild climate and beautiful scenery of the Los Angeles area is well suited to making movies.

dustry in every state in the region. Tourists now come by car, on ships, and in airplanes. They relax on the beaches of Hawaii and southern California. They camp in the forests of Oregon and Washington. A few trek to Alaska to see the tall mountains and sparkling lakes.

As in other parts of the country, the growth of new industries has affected cities in the region. Los Angeles, California, is a good example. Most people think of it as a center for film-making and tourism. Few realize it is also a manufacturing center. Workers in Los Angeles build airplanes, refine oil, and make clothing. These industries have helped make Los Angeles the second largest city in the nation.

Like other parts of the country, the Pacific States are changing rapidly. Change has been a part of the United States from its very beginning. Americans are still trying out new inventions and other new ideas. No one yet knows how these inventions will change the nation in years to come.

To Help You Remember

1. Name three ways the Southwest has changed since World War II.
2. (a) In what ways have the Rocky Mountain States changed?
(b) How have they stayed the same?
3. How have improvements in transportation helped the Pacific States grow?

433

Chapter Review

Words to Know

1. What is an *aquifer?*
2. Name three *service industries.*
3. What do farmers do when they *conserve* land?
4. What is a *consulate?*
5. What is *tourism?*
6. What goods are made from *petroleum chemicals?*
7. What is manufactured at a *mint?*
8. What is a *landlocked* state?
9. What is *hydroelectric* power?
10. What is a *metropolitan area?*

Reviewing Main Ideas

1. Give two examples of the ways each of the following regions has changed in recent years: (a) the Northeast, (b) the South, (c) the Middle West, (d) the West.
2. (a) Which regions have grown most rapidly in recent years? (b) Why?
3. Give two reasons why each of the following cities is important: (a) New York, (b) Atlanta, (c) Miami, (d) Chicago, (e) Houston, (f) Denver, (g) Los Angeles.
4. (a) How is farming in the Middle West like farming in the South? (b) How is it different?

In Your Own Words

Write a short essay describing a trip across every section of the United States. Begin your trip in the Northeast. End it in Hawaii or Alaska.

Keeping Skills Sharp

In 1790, nine out of every ten Americans worked on farms. By 1890, most Americans were working in manufacturing. Use the graphs below to answer the questions about the kinds of jobs Americans had in the 1970's and early 1980's.

1. (a) What kinds of jobs did most Americans have in 1970? (b) In 1980?
2. (a) Which kinds of jobs grew between 1970 and 1980? (b) Which kinds offered fewer jobs in 1980 than in 1970?

Challenge!

1. Use the information on the graphs to predict what kinds of jobs most Americans will have in the year 2000. Give reasons for your answer.
2. Fewer people work at some jobs. Yet Americans are producing more goods than ever. How do you explain this?

How Jobs Have Changed 1970–1980

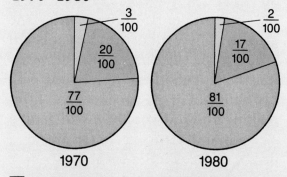

1970

1980

☐ Agriculture, Forestry, Fisheries
▨ Mining, Construction, Manufacturing
☐ Service Jobs

Unit Review

Take Another Look

1. What events important to understanding World War II took place in each of the following years: (a) 1939, (b) 1941, (c) 1944, (d) 1945?
2. Describe how World War II changes the way people viewed (a) war (b) empires.
3. (a) What kind of war is a cold war? (b) When did the cold war with the Soviet Union begin? (c) How has it affected efforts for world peace?
4. World War II brought many changes to the United States. Explain how it changed (a) the role the United States played in world affairs, (b) ideas about equal rights, (c) the kinds of jobs Americans have.
5. Tell two ways improvements in technology have affected life in each of the following parts of the country: (a) the Northeast, (b) the South, (c) the Middle West, (d) the West.
6. How have improvements in transportation changed life in the United States?
7. For each section of the country, choose an important city. Tell how that city has changed or grown in recent years.
8. Describe three new things you have learned about your region in this unit.

You and the Future

1. Changes in technology have opened many new jobs in the United States. To find out what those jobs are, study your local newspaper. The list of jobs available can give you clues to work in your community. What can you learn from other advertisements? From news stories on the business pages? From the food section of the paper? Share what you learn from the newspaper with your classmates. Then use your findings to predict what your community will be like when you are grown up.
2. Computers are already changing the way Americans live and work. How do you think they will affect life 15 years from now? Life 30 years from today? Why? What other inventions do you think will make a difference in the ways people live and work in the future?

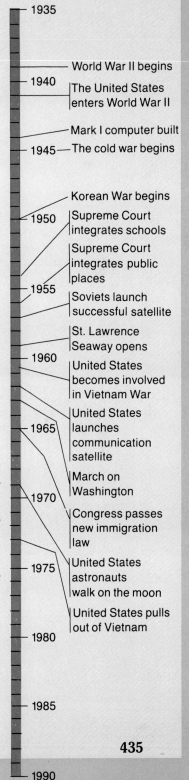

1935

World War II begins

1940

The United States enters World War II

Mark I computer built

1945 — The cold war begins

Korean War begins

1950 Supreme Court integrates schools

Supreme Court integrates public places

1955 Soviets launch successful satellite

St. Lawrence Seaway opens

1960 United States becomes involved in Vietnam War

United States launches communication satellite

1965

March on Washington

1970

Congress passes new immigration law

1975 United States astronauts walk on the moon

United States pulls out of Vietnam

1980

1985

1990

435

Waterton-Glacier International Peace Park

Unit Nine

Canada and Latin America

Canada and the countries of Latin America have much in common with the United States. All are countries in the Western Hemisphere. All were once European colonies. Over the years, the United States has come to take a great interest in its neighbors to the north and the south.

24

Exploring Canada

Canada lies directly north of the United States. The two countries share a border nearly 4,000 miles (6,400 kilometers) long. Canada and the United States have many other things in common too. The Great Lakes and the St. Lawrence River are a part of both countries. So are the Rockies and the Appalachian Mountains and the Great Plains. The two countries share a part of their history as well. Both were once British colonies.

In spite of these similarities, the United States and Canada are different in many ways. As one Canadian said, "Americans tend to take us for granted. They think we are very much like them. This just is not true."

As You Read

In this chapter, you will study Canada's past. You will also explore life in Canada. As you read, look for ways Canada differs from the United States. Notice too similarities between the two nations. The chapter is divided into two parts.

- Canada's Past
- Living in Canada Today

◄ *Thousand Island Bridge on the St. Lawrence Seaway, Canada*

Canada's Past

Canada is one of the largest countries in the world. It covers more than one third of North America. Canada is a land of thick forests, tall mountains, green river valleys, and huge grasslands. Canada's rich resources have attracted many people. The first to settle there were the Indians.

The First Canadians

Long before Europeans first came to the Americas, many groups of Indians lived in what is now Canada. They were the first Canadians. They lived in every part of Canada but only

What type of forest covers most of Canada?

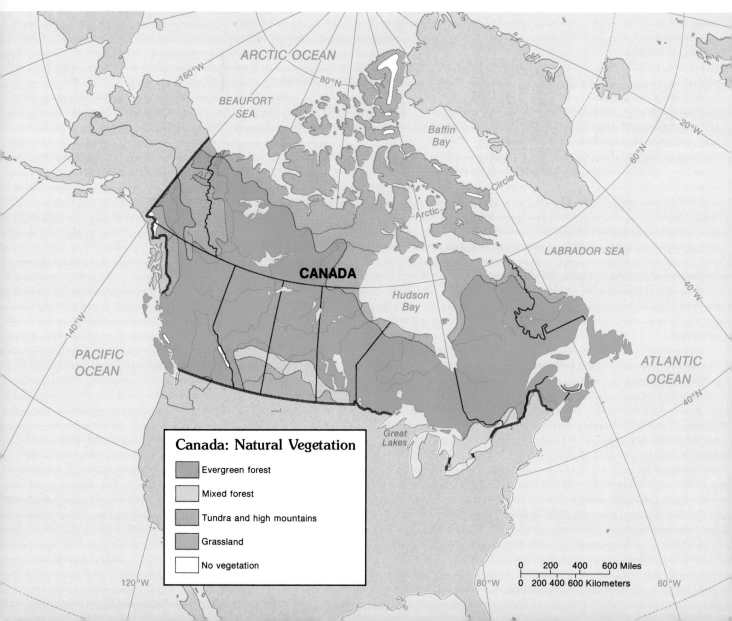

ARCTIC OCEAN

BEAUFORT SEA

Baffin Bay

LABRADOR SEA

CANADA

Hudson Bay

PACIFIC OCEAN

ATLANTIC OCEAN

Great Lakes

Canada: Natural Vegetation

- Evergreen forest
- Mixed forest
- Tundra and high mountains
- Grassland
- No vegetation

0   200   400   600 Miles

0 200 400 600 Kilometers

a few made their homes in the frozen north or in the rugged mountains in the west. Most lived near the St. Lawrence River or along the Great Lakes.

Along River and Lakes. The Indians of the lowlands had much in common with the Indians who lived in what is now the eastern part of the United States. They spoke the same language and shared many customs. They also used the land in similar ways.

Both groups depended on the forests for many things. They hunted deer, beaver, and other forest animals for food and clothing. They gathered berries and nuts in the forests. The forests also provided wood for houses, canoes, and tools.

Many groups fished in the rivers and streams that flowed through the forests. Some also farmed. They grew corn, squash, and beans.

On the Grasslands. Other groups of Canadian Indians lived on the grasslands west of the lowlands. They planted crops along rivers and streams. Like the Indians who lived on the Great Plains in the United States, they too hunted buffalo.

In the Far West. Few Indians lived in the far western part of Canada. Those who did made their homes

The Indians on the grasslands followed the buffalo during hunting season.

along the Pacific coast. They lived in a part of the country that has mild winters and warm summers. Yet they did not farm. They did not need to. Thick forests grew in the mountains that lined the coast. There the Indians gathered berries and nuts. They also hunted forest animals.

The ocean and the many rivers that flowed through the Indians' lands were filled with fish. The most important of these fish was salmon. Each year millions of salmon swam up the rivers and streams. In just a few days, the Indians could catch enough fish to last the year.

In the Far North. Only a few people lived in the far north of Canada. Most of them were not Indians. Their language and their way of life were very different from those of the Indians. The people who lived along the Arctic Ocean called themselves the *Inuit* (i'nü it). In their language, the word means "the people."

The Indians called the Inuit Eskimos. The name *Eskimo* means "eater of raw meat." Unlike the Indians, the Inuit did not gather food or farm. Instead, they depended on animals for all of their food. During the long, cold winters, they hunted seal through holes in the icy Arctic Ocean. In summer, hunting was a little easier. Then the caribou and other animals moved north for a few months. So the Inuit did not have to cut through thick ice to get their food.

Europeans Arrive

The first Europeans began arriving in Canada in 1497. They did not come to settle. They were searching for an all-water route to the riches of Asia.

Explorers and Fishermen. The first to come was the Italian explorer John Cabot. Like later explorers, he never found a route to Asia. He did, however, claim Newfoundland and eastern Canada for England.

By 1534, French explorers were also claiming land in Canada. That year Jacques Cartier sailed up the St. Lawrence River to where Montreal is located today. He too was looking for an all-water route to Asia.

When Cartier returned to Europe with tales of great forests and rich fishing grounds, French fishermen listened with great interest. Before long, many of them came to see for themselves. Cartier's stories proved to be true.

Every spring dozens of French fishermen sailed to North America. They fished in the waters off the coast of Newfoundland. Before returning home, they dried their catch along the coast. Many also traded with the Indians who lived there. They exchanged knives and other metal tools

Indians and fur traders meet in Montreal to exchange goods.

for furs. They were able to sell the furs for such high prices that in time many people in France were eager to come to North America. They hoped to become rich from the fur trade.

In 1608, Samuel de Champlain built the first permanent French settlement in Canada. He named it Quebec. Quebec was to be a center of the fur trade. From there, French trappers pushed farther west and south.

Competition. By 1670, the French had competition in the fur trade. The British had landed in Hudson Bay. They too were eager to trade for furs. Before long, the two countries were fighting for control of Canada and the fur trade.

Great Britain and France fought many wars. The last of these wars is the one people in the United States call the French and Indian War. It began in 1754. It continued until 1763. Great Britain won that war. As a result, France lost most of its land in North America.

Under British Rule. Canada belonged to the British in 1763. They ruled their new colony much as they did their 13 colonies farther south.

In 1776, those 13 southern colonies declared their independence from Great Britain. Early in the war that followed, Americans invaded Canada. They expected support from people there. It never came. Most Canadians were French. Although they were not happy about British rule, they were pleased that the British allowed them to keep their language, customs, and other parts of their culture. So they had little reason to rebel.

Yet the war brought many changes to Canada. The most noticeable change was in its population. Many colonists who remained loyal to Great Britain left the United States. They settled in British North America. A few moved to British colonies such as Nova Scotia, New Brunswick, and Prince Edward Island. However, most settled in the part of Canada the French once ruled. So many people came that the British divided French Canada into two parts, Upper and Lower Canada. Most of the English-speaking settlers lived in Upper Canada. Lower Canada remained mostly French.

The Road to Independence

After the American Revolution, the British watched their remaining colonies carefully. They did not want to lose them too. So when the people of British North America demanded more and more freedom to govern themselves, they got it.

By the 1840's, colonial assemblies in British North America had more

Loyalists from the United States build a settlement at Johnston, on the banks of the St. Lawrence River in Canada.

power than they did before the American Revolution. The people of British North America were also freer to trade with other countries. They no longer had to buy only from Great Britain.

As British North America won more freedom, many more people settled there. Still the colonies did not grow as quickly as the United States. They had fewer railroads and highways than the United States. The colonies did not have as many factories either. Many believed that as long as British North America was divided into many colonies, it would never grow as quickly as the United States.

By the 1860's, some leaders were calling for a united Canada. They wanted to create a confederation, or union of colonies. Each colony was called a province. The provinces would handle local matters. A central government would handle matters that affected the whole country.

Great Britain's Parliament agreed to the idea. Upper and Lower Canada, New Brunswick, and Nova Scotia united on July 1, 1867. Later other colonies joined the confederation. The new country was known as Canada. Although it was united, it was not an independent country.

Little by little, Canada won its freedom from Great Britain. By 1949, Canada was fully independent. Canadians control their own country. They also choose their own leaders.

Governing Canada

Today Canada is an independent nation. Like the United States, it is a democracy. Yet Canada's national government is very different from that of the United States. Power is divided between Congress and the president in the United States. In Canada, **Parliament** makes the laws and then sees to it that those laws are carried out.

Parliament is divided into two parts, the Senate and the House of Commons. Voters in each province elect members of the House of Commons. As in the United States, they choose candidates from different political parties. The party that wins the most seats in the House of Commons chooses the **prime minister.** The prime minister heads Canada's government. He or she is responsible to the House of Commons.

Senators, on the other hand, are not elected. They are appointed by the prime minister. Although senators can serve until they retire at the age of 75, they have little power. They cannot write new laws. They can only approve or reject those passed by the House of Commons. However, they cannot reject any laws that deal with taxes or expenses.

Canada also has many courts. In the courts, judges deal with people accused of breaking the laws. The judges are appointed by the prime minister. They serve until they retire. As in the United States, people who are unhappy with a judge's decision can take their case to a higher court. The highest court in Canada is the Supreme Court. It decides the most important cases in the country.

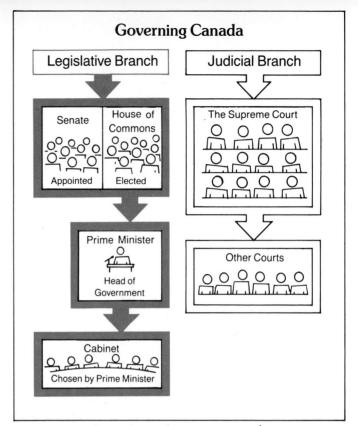

How many branches of government does Canada have? Name them.

To Help You Remember

1. (a) Who were the first Canadians? (b) Where did they settle?
2. Give three reasons other Europeans came to Canada.
3. How did Great Britain gain most of France's colonies in North America?
4. Why did Great Britain give people in British North America a larger voice in government?
5. (a) When did the provinces of Canada unite? (b) When did Canada become independent?

445

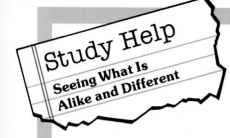

In the first part of the chapter, you read about ways Canada is similar to the United States. You also read about ways the two nations are different. A chart is a good way to keep track of similarities and differences.

Fill in the chart below. It should help you see how Canada and the United States are alike and how they differ.

	First Settlers and How They Lived	First European Settlers and How They Lived	The Road to Independence	Government Today
Canada				
United States	The Indians Farmed, fished, hunted, gathered	The English Farmed, fished, traded fur		

As you read the next part of the chapter, make another chart. This one should compare the provinces and territories in Canada today.

Living in Canada Today

Today many Indians and Inuit still live in Canada. However, most Canadians are from families that once lived in Europe. The rest have ancestors who came to Canada from other parts of the world. They have all helped Canada grow into one of the strongest countries in the world.

Quebec

Quebec is Canada's oldest province and its largest. It is where the first French settlements were built.

Quebec is still home to most of the French-speaking people in Canada. Over 80 percent of the people in Quebec have French ancestors. Many still

How is much of the land in Canada used today?

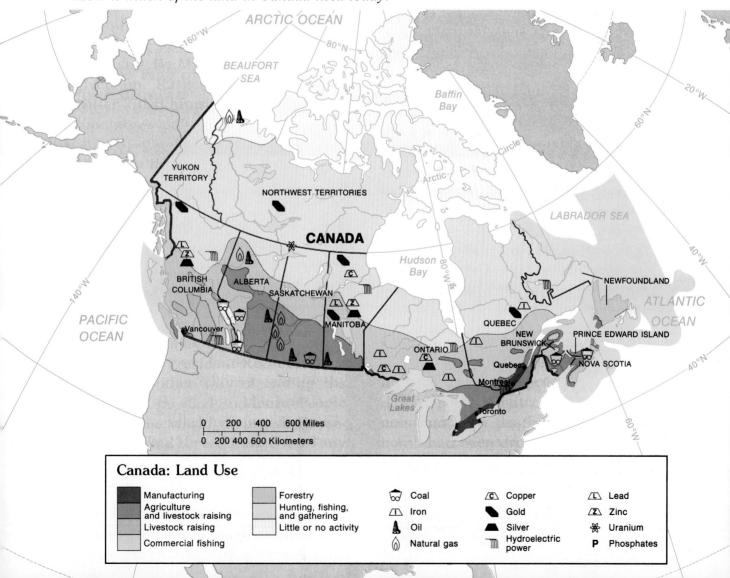

Canada: Land Use

Manufacturing
Agriculture and livestock raising
Livestock raising
Commercial fishing

Forestry
Hunting, fishing, and gathering
Little or no activity

Coal
Iron
Oil
Natural gas

Copper
Gold
Silver
Hydroelectric power

Lead
Zinc
Uranium
P Phosphates

In Quebec City, Quebec, street signs are written in both English and French.

They make clothing, smelt aluminum, process food, refine oil, and turn out electrical equipment. They are also the leading producers of paper products in North America.

Quebec's many natural resources have helped industry grow. The province is rich in asbestos, copper, gold, zinc, and iron ore. Its forests are thick with fir, spruce, and other trees. Its many rivers provide much of the electric power needed to keep machines working.

The largest city in Quebec and all of Canada is Montreal. Half of the province's factories are located there. Like most of the other cities and towns in Quebec, Montreal is located in the south. The same is true of Ontario, Quebec's neighbor to the west.

Ontario

Ottawa, the capital of Canada, lies on the border between Quebec and Ontario. It is a fitting place for the nation's capital. Quebec is the largest province in size. Ontario is the largest in population. It is also Canada's leading province in many ways. Some call it the nation's heartland.

Ontario produces more goods than the other nine provinces combined. Many people in Ontario make cars. Almost all of Canada's automobiles are made in cities that lie along the western shores of Lake Ontario.

speak only French. Today it is one of Canada's two official languages.

The heart of French Quebec is its capital, Quebec City. There road signs, newspapers, and restaurant menus are printed in French as well as in English. In many schools, classes are taught only in French. The people of Quebec take great pride in their French heritage.

Although the past is important to the people of Quebec, they are also concerned about the present and the future. They have turned their province into a center for manufacturing, mining, and trade. The people of Quebec make about one fourth of all the goods manufactured in Canada.

Lumber mills are only one of the many different kinds of factories located in Ontario.

Hamilton, one of those cities, is also Canada's main iron and steel center. Toronto is another city that lies along Lake Ontario. Toronto is the country's leading port.

Ontario is a center for mining too. It alone produces one fourth of all the minerals mined in Canada. The province is rich in gold, copper, zinc, and uranium. It also has the world's largest supply of nickel.

Ontario is a farming center as well. Farmers there produce about a third of Canada's food. Beef and dairy cattle graze near Lake Huron and Lake Ontario. Peaches, cherries, and other fruit grow along the Niagara River.

Atlantic Provinces

East of Quebec lie Canada's four smallest provinces, New Brunswick, Nova Scotia, Prince Edward Island, and Newfoundland. They are known as the Atlantic Provinces because they face the Atlantic Ocean.

The four provinces have been fishing centers for hundreds of years. The Grand Banks lie just southeast of Newfoundland. It is a shallow part of the ocean where thousands of fish live. In the 1500's, those rich fishing grounds drew French fishermen to North America. Today many fishing boats from the Atlantic Provinces still head for the Grand Banks.

Fishers unload snow crabs at Shippegan Harbor in New Brunswick.

The fishing crews return home with cod, herring, flounder, and salmon. Other fishing crews search the coast of Nova Scotia and Prince Edward Island for lobsters, scallops, and other shellfish.

Even though fishing is still an important industry, most people in the Atlantic Provinces earn their living in other ways today. Some work on farms, in factories, or in mines. Others have jobs in the tourist industry.

Prairie Provinces

In the center of Canada lie Manitoba, Alberta, and Saskatchewan. These three provinces are often called the

Prairie Provinces. A **prairie** is a land covered by tall grasses. Like the grasslands in the United States, the prairies of Canada have plenty of rich soil. The climate, however, is much colder in Canada than it is in the United States. In winter, cold Arctic winds blow across Canada's plains. Summers are very short.

Over the years, many people from Eastern and Northern Europe have settled in the Prairie Provinces. They came from lands where winters are long and summers short. So they knew how to farm in a cold climate. Many even came with seeds that do well in such a climate. As a result, the Prairie Provinces today grow

Grain elevators like this one in Arcola, Saskatchewan, store wheat grown in the Prairie Provinces.

almost all of Canada's wheat, rye, and oats. Farmers there also raise most of the nation's beef cattle.

Wheat and cattle were the main products of the Prairie Provinces for many years. Today, however, one third of the region's workers have mining jobs. Many drill for oil. Others mine coal. The three provinces supply nearly all of Canada's oil and natural gas. They also have half of Canada's coal deposits. The discovery of these resources has brought many people to the Prairie Provinces. It has also encouraged many factories to locate there.

British Columbia

To the west of the Prairie Provinces lies British Columbia. Steep, forested mountains and rugged highlands cover much of the province. At first, only a few people dared to cross those mountains. Then, in 1857, gold was discovered in the southern part of British Columbia. Thousands of people headed there.

Today British Columbia is sometimes called Canada's treasure house. In addition to gold, it has silver, copper, zinc, nickel, and oil. British Columbia also has another important resource, its forests. The lower mountains are covered with trees. They provide 70 percent of Canada's lumber.

British Columbia's breathtaking scenery attracts many visitors.

Long ago the Indians of British Columbia lived mainly in the southwestern part of the province. That is where most people live today. It has the mildest climate in all of Canada. It also has fertile land that is good for farming. Farmers there raise dairy cattle and grow vegetables.

British Columbia is a fishing center too. Today, as in the past, people fish along the coast or in the province's many rivers and streams. However, today people also use the rushing rivers for electric power.

Canada's Territories

Few people live in northern Canada. It is a cold, frozen land that the Canadians have divided into two territories. One is the Yukon Territory. It

451

lies just north of British Columbia. The other is known as the Northwest Territories. It covers about one third of the country. Parts of it are just 500 miles (800 kilometers) from the North Pole.

In both territories, mining is the most important activity. It was gold that first brought people to the Yukon in the late 1800's. Today people also come to mine the territory's large deposits of coal, copper, lead, zinc, and silver.

Mining is also important in the Northwest Territories. Scientists think that almost every known mineral can be found somewhere in the territory. Yet only a few minerals are being mined there today. It is very hard to bring ores across the frozen wilderness.

Today, as long ago, most of the people who live in the two territories are Inuit and Indians. Some live as their ancestors did. Yet, even in the frozen north, things are changing. Today many Inuit and Indians work on government defense projects. Some serve as guides for tourists. Still others have found jobs as miners, truck drivers, teachers, carpenters, doctors, and nurses.

Today the two territories are no longer as isolated as they once were. Roads and railroads now connect much of the territories to the rest of Canada. As they do, Canada's last frontier is closing.

A group of Inuit unload a supply barge in Umingmaktok, Northwest Territories.

To Help You Remember

1. (a) Why is Quebec called the French Canadian homeland?
   (b) How do people earn a living there?
2. Give three reasons Ontario is called Canada's heartland.
3. How do most people in the Atlantic Provinces earn a living?
4. How do most people in the Prairie Provinces earn a living?
5. (a) Why is British Columbia called Canada's treasure house? (b) How do people there make a living?
6. How do people in the territories make a living?

Chapter Review

Words to Know

1. The *prime minister* has a very important job. What does that person do?
2. *Parliament* has two important jobs. What are they?
3. A large part of Canada is covered by *prairies*. What is a prairie?

Reviewing Main Ideas

1. List at least three types of land that are found in both Canada and the United States.
2. (a) Who were the first people to settle in Canada?   (b) How did they make a living?
3. (a) Who were the first Europeans to settle in Canada?   (b) How did they make a living.
4. (a) How did Great Britain gain control of France's land in North America?   (b) When?
5. When and how did Canada become independent?
6. (a) How is Canada's government similar to the government in the United States?   (b) How is the government of Canada different?
7. Match each part of Canada with the sentence that best describes it.

Atlantic Provinces   Ontario
British Columbia   Quebec
Prairie Provinces   The Territories

   (a) Canada's largest province
   (b) Canada's smallest provinces
   (c) Canada's breadbasket
   (d) Canada's manufacturing center
   (e) Canada's last frontier
   (f) Canada's mining center

In Your Own Words

Write a paragraph comparing the United States and Canada. Choose from the list of topics below. Be sure to give at least one way the two countries are alike. Also tell how the two differ.

   land   government   history

Challenge!

The walls of the Canadian House of Commons are made of stone. An artist carved symbols into that stone. The symbols show something of importance to each of Canada's ten provinces. Look carefully at the list of symbols and then give a reason the artist chose it. What part of Canadian life do all ten carvings show? Explain your answer.

Alberta	cowboy on horseback
British Columbia	airplane
Manitoba	farmer with hayfork
New Brunswick	sailing ship
Newfoundland	lumberman with ax
Nova Scotia	sailor with anchors
Ontario	miner
Prince Edward Island	fisherman with nets
Quebec	turbine engine
Saskatchewan	farmer with tractor

25

Latin America: Past and Present

Latin America lies to the south and east of the United States. It is a large region that includes 8 countries in North America, many island nations in the Caribbean, and 12 countries in South America.

The region is called *Latin* America because it once belonged to Spain and Portugal. Even today most people there speak Spanish or Portuguese. Both languages developed from Latin, a language spoken in Southern Europe over 2,000 years ago. Beside their languages, Spain and Portugal brought their religion and customs to the region.

The Spanish and Portuguese also brought Africans to Latin America. Yet neither the Europeans nor the Africans were the first to live in Latin America. The Indians were the first settlers. Over the years, all three groups have helped to shape life throughout Latin America.

As You Read

As you read this chapter, keep track of the people who settled in Latin America and the ways they have helped to shape life there. The chapter is divided into three parts.

- The First Settlers
- Colonial Rule in Latin America
- The Struggle for Independence

◀ *Signs written in both Latin and Spanish, Hidalgo, Mexico*

ATLANTIC OCEAN

Tropic of Cancer

20°N

MEXICO

Gulf of Mexico

CARIBBEAN SEA

CENTRAL AMERICA

PACIFIC OCEAN

Equator 0°

SOUTH AMERICA

Tropic of Capricorn

20°S

Latin America: Natural Vegetation

Evergreen forest

Mixed forest

Tropical rain forest

Tundra and high mountains

Grassland

Grassland with scattered trees

Desert and other dry land

40°S

| 0 | 500 | 1000 Miles |
| 0 | 500 | 1000 Kilometers |

456

120°W   100°W   80°W   60°W   40°W   20°W

The First Settlers

The first people to settle in Latin America were the Indians. They made their homes in almost every part of the region. Like their neighbors to the north, the Indians of Latin America lived in a variety of ways.

In Mexico and Central America

Many groups of Indians made their homes in Mexico and Central America. This is the part of Latin America that lies on the continent of North America. Rugged mountains cover much of the land there.

The first farmers in the Americas lived in the highlands of Mexico. Most of them made their homes in small farming villages in the mountain valleys. Others farmed along the edge of the thick rain forests that lie along the Gulf of Mexico.

At first, people farmed in similar ways. Every few years they would clear a new patch of land by burning the brush and trees. The ashes helped to fertilize the soil. In time, however, the soil would wear out. Then villagers cleared a new field.

Over the years, farmers found ways to improve their land and the size of their harvests. They learned to irrigate their fields and to use fertilizers

◀ *Describe the vegetation of Mexico.*

that worked better than ashes. Farmers no longer had to clear new fields every few years. Before long, some were raising so much food that not everyone had to farm. With the improvements in farming, a few people were free to work at other jobs.

About 2,000 years ago, some Indian groups in Mexico and Central America started building large cities. One of those cities was Teotihuacán (tā ō tē wə' kän). It was located about

Find the Mayan empire. Where was it located? Which Indian empire was the farthest south? The farthest north?

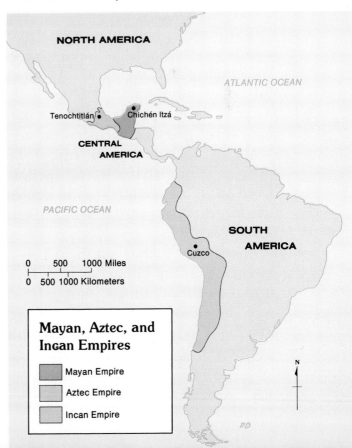

Mayan, Aztec, and Incan Empires

■ Mayan Empire
■ Aztec Empire
■ Incan Empire

From this observatory in Chichen Itza, Mayan priests studied the stars.

30 miles (48 kilometers) from what is today Mexico City.

Teotihuacán had many stone pyramids where people gathered to worship their gods. One pyramid was as tall as a building 20 stories high. Around the pyramids stood the palaces of the priests and rulers. Beyond them lay the homes of the rest of the people. More than 50,000 people lived in Teotihuacán. It was one of the largest cities in the world about 2,000 years ago.

In the rain forests south of Teotihuacán, a group known as the Maya (mī'ə) built pyramids and palaces too. They lived about 1,700 years ago in what is today southern Mexico and northern Guatemala. The Maya were not only great builders but also great inventors. They invented a calendar and a system of writing.

Then, about a thousand years ago, the Maya abandoned their cities. No one knows why. Perhaps their crops failed. They may have been invaded by another group. They never again built great cities.

After the Maya, other groups in Mexico and Central America began building large cities. Among them were the Aztecs. In 1325, they built the city of Tenochtitlán in the middle of a lake in the Valley of Mexico. It was their capital. By the 1500's, it had grown into the largest city in the world. More than 300,000 people lived there.

From their capital, the Aztecs sent fierce warriors to conquer neighboring towns. By 1500, they had defeated most of their enemies. They controlled a huge empire in Mexico.

In the Highlands of South America

Far to the east of Mexico lay another great Indian empire. It belonged to the Incas of Peru.

The Incas lived high in the Andes Mountains, along the west coast of South America. The Andes Mountains are the longest mountain range in the world. They also have the tallest mountains in the Americas. Over

458

50 mountains in the Andes soar 20,000 feet (6,100 kilometers) or more above sea level.

Between the tall mountains are many green valleys. Thousands of people settled in those valleys. By 1500, all were a part of the Incan empire. The capital of the empire was Cuzco, a city in the Andes Mountains in what is today Peru.

The Incan empire stretched over 2,500 miles (4,020 kilometers) from present-day Colombia in the north to Chile in the south. More than 3½ million people lived there.

Like the Aztecs, the Indians of the Andes were also farmers. They too grew corn. They also grew potatoes, a crop their ancestors had developed. They raised alpacas and llamas as well. The animals were used to carry goods from one city to another. They were also a source of wool and meat.

The Indians of the Andes did not have much flat land. So they cut giant step-like fields called **terraces** into the sides of steep mountains. They also dug canals to bring water to these fields.

Today many people in the Andes still farm on terraced fields. They use the old canals too. Many travel on roads paved with stones the Incas built hundreds of years ago. Over 6 million people still speak the language of the Incas. The old ways live on high in the mountains.

This terraced field is located in the highlands of Bolivia.

In the Rain Forests and Grasslands of South America

Fewer people lived east of the Andes. There the land was too wet or too dry for farming. The climate was also not as cool as it was in the mountains.

The Amazon River Valley. Just east of the Andes lies the Amazon River Valley. It is covered by the largest rain forest in the world. The climate there is warm and steamy all year. It rains almost every day. As a result, trees grow so tall and close together that it is hard to see the sky.

Life was not easy for those who lived in the steamy Amazon River

459

Valley. A rain forest is hard to clear, and its soil is not very good for growing crops. The rains wash away the minerals that keep the soil fertile. Still the Indians of the rain forest did farm. Their main crop was a root called cassava. They ground it into flour to make bread.

The Indians also hunted and gathered food. They knew which plants in the rain forest were safe to eat and which were poisonous. They learned to use the poison from the plants as weapons.

On the Grasslands. Only a small number of Indians lived on the grassy plains to the south of the Amazon River Valley. Most were hunters and gatherers. Unlike the Indians who lived on the grasslands of North America, the Indians of South America did not have buffalo to hunt. Instead, they hunted the guanaco, a greyish brown animal that looks like a camel without a hump.

On the Caribbean Islands

Many Indians lived on the 7,000 islands that dot the Caribbean Sea. Here temperatures are mild all year long. Only heavy rains mark the start of one season and the end of another.

The Indians of the Caribbean were farmers. They also fished. Most lived on narrow plains along the coasts or in mountain valleys. Many of the islands are the tops of an underwater mountain range. So these islands are very mountainous.

Some of the Indians who lived in the Caribbean were fierce warriors. They used spears, slings, clubs, and blow guns. Those weapons, however, were no match for the guns and cannons of the Europeans. They began arriving in the Caribbean in 1492.

Indians in the rain forest clear land by cutting and burning brush and trees.

To Help You Remember

1. Where did the first farmers in the Americas live?
2. What did the people who built Teotihuacán have in common with the Maya and the Aztecs?

3. (a) How did people living in the Andes Mountains farm? (b) What crops did they grow? (c) What animals did they raise?

4. (a) How did the Indians in the Amazon River Valley get food? (b) The Indians on the grasslands? (c) The Indians of the Caribbean?

Colonial Rule in Latin America

In 1492, Christopher Columbus made his famous journey across the Atlantic. He never found the great cities of Asia he was searching for. Yet he did explore many islands in the Caribbean Sea. He claimed each of them for Spain.

Before long, the Spanish were building colonies in the Caribbean. Then, in 1521, Hernando Cortés conquered the Aztecs of Mexico. Twelve years later, Francisco Pizzaro defeated the Incas of Peru. Spain then had a huge empire in the Americas. Soon other European countries were challenging Spain's rights to the region. In time, many of them would also build colonies in Latin America.

Spain's Colonies

At first, Spain divided its new lands among the leaders of the armies that conquered it. The soldiers were given huge pieces of land and the right to rule the people who lived on that land. The soldiers, however, were mainly interested in finding gold and silver. So they ordered the Indians to search for the precious minerals.

Wherever there was no gold or silver, the Spanish turned to farming. Some landowners rented small plots of land to Indian farmers. Others raised cattle and sheep on their land. Still others set up plantations. They grew sugar cane, cotton, and other cash crops.

The plantation owners did not work the land themselves. They forced the Indians to do the planting, plowing, and harvesting.

In the years just after the Spanish arrived, thousands of Indians died. Some were killed fighting for their freedom. Others died from overwork. Many more died of diseases the Spanish unknowingly brought to the Americas.

More Caribbean Indians died than any other Indian group. By the 1600's, there were only a few left. So the Spanish brought slaves from Africa to work on the plantations.

461

In time, a new way of life developed in Spanish America. The Spanish ruler divided the people in the colonies into four groups. The most important people were government officials from Spain. They ruled the colonies.

Next in importance were the Spaniards born in Latin America. They were known as creoles (krē'ols). Although many were very rich, they could not take part in government. The Spanish did not trust anyone born outside of their country to look out for their interests.

The third group were the mestizos (me stē'zōs). These were people who had both Spanish and Indian ancestors. Most worked on large estates. A few owned their own land, but their farms were very small. These people had very little money or influence.

The Indians and the Africans made up the last group. They were the poorest and least powerful. Even though they were in the majority in many parts of Latin America, they were slaves. From time to time, some would rebel. However, their handmade weapons were useless against the armor, guns, and cannons of the Spanish army.

Portugal's Colonies

Spain was only one of the European countries to claim land in Latin America. In 1500, Pedro Cabral (kə'bräl), a Portuguese explorer, claimed the eastern part of South America for Portugal. The Portuguese called their colony Brazil. They named it for a tree that grew in the forests there. It was called brazilwood. The Portuguese settlers used it long ago to make a red dye.

The early settlers shipped brazilwood back to Portugal. They had few other ways of making money in their new land. Later, they found diamonds and gold. They also discovered that they could make money farming the country's fertile land. They grew valuable cash crops like sugar cane, coffee, and cotton.

Like the Spanish, the Portuguese tried to get the Indians to work in their fields. They had very little success. Brazil did not have as many Indians as other parts of Latin America. Also, the Indians could easily escape into the rain forest. So the Portuguese turned to Africa for workers. They brought many thousands of slaves to Brazil. Today many Brazilians have both Portuguese and African ancestors.

More Colonies in the Caribbean

As other countries watched Spain and Portugal grow rich, they were eager to get a share of the wealth.

El Morro Fortress in Puerto Rico was built by the Spanish in the 1500's to guard the Bay of San Juan in Puerto Rico.

Some encouraged pirates to attack Spanish treasure ships. By the 1500's, the islands in the Caribbean Sea had become hideouts for pirates from England and France.

When the pirates were finally brought under control in the 1600's, several countries took over the pirates' old hideouts. The English took over Jamaica, the Bahamas, and the Virgin Islands. The French sent settlers to Haiti, Martinique, St. Martin, and St. Lucia. The Netherlands also took over a few islands in the Caribbean.

Like the Spanish, all three countries built large plantations on their islands. They too grew cash crops like sugar cane. They also used African slaves to do the work. There was very little freedom anywhere in Latin America in the 1700's.

To Help You Remember

1. How did Spain get its huge empire in the Americas?
2. When the Spanish found no gold or silver on their land, what did they do to earn a living?
3. (a) How did the Spanish divide people in their colonies? (b) Who had the most power? (c) Which group had the least?
4. (a) How did the Portuguese gain Brazil? (b) How did the people there make money? (c) Why did they bring Africans to Brazil?
5. Besides Spain, what countries claimed land in the Caribbean?

A good way to see some of the changes that have taken place in Latin America is to look at maps of the region from different time periods.

Look at the maps on this page. One shows the way Spain divided Latin America in 1790. The other map shows the countries of Latin America today. Use the maps to answer the questions that follow.

1. Find the Viceroyalty of New Spain.   (a) What continent is it on?   (b) List the names of the present-day countries that were part of New Spain.
2. Find the Viceroyalty of Peru.   (a) What continent is it on?   (b) What present-day countries were part of that colony?
3. What countries were once part of   (a) the Viceroyalty of New Granada?   (b) The Viceroyalty of La Plata?

European Colonies in Latin America, 1790

Latin America Today
—— International Boundaries

The Struggle for Independence

In 1783, the United States became the first of Europe's colonies in the Americas to win its freedom. During the next 50 years, many of the colonists in Latin America fought for and won their independence too.

The Road to Independence

The first people to win independence were African slaves in Haiti. In 1791, they drove their French rulers off the island. They then set up the first independent black republic in the world. In the years that followed, the push for independence spread to other parts of Latin America.

In Mexico and Central America. The Mexicans were next to rebel. On September 16, 1810, a Catholic priest, Father Miguel Hidalgo (mē gel′ ē däl′gō), led an army of Indians and mestizos against the Spanish. A year later, Hidalgo was killed. Yet his dreams of independence lived on. Other leaders took up the fight.

Over the next ten years, the rebels had little success. Then, in 1821, the creoles joined the revolution. They were no longer willing to take orders from Spain. With the help of the Creoles, Mexico won its independence that same year.

Unlike the Mexicans, the people of Central America did not have to fight for their freedom. The region became independent when Mexico did. In those days, all of Central America was part of Mexico. A few years later, however, people in Central America broke away from the new nation. They wanted their own countries.

In South America. The fight against Spain in South America was led by two brilliant generals, Simon Bolivar (sē mōn′ bō lē′vär) and Jose de San Martín (hō zā′ dā sän mär tēn′). Bolivar freed Ecuador, Colombia,

Mexicans call Father Hidalgo the father of their country.

When Mexico won its independence from Spain in 1821, people throughout Mexico celebrated their newly won freedom.

and Venezuela from Spanish rule. San Martín won independence for Argentina and Chile. In 1824, the armies of the two generals met in Peru and fought together to free that country. Two years later, the last Spanish soldiers left Peru.

By 1826, most of Spain's colonies in Latin America were independent. Only a few islands in the Caribbean Sea remained under Spanish rule.

In Brazil. Independence came more quickly and with less fighting in Brazil. In the early 1800's, Europe was torn by wars. So in 1808, the king of Portugal decided to move to Brazil. He believed he would be safer

there. When the wars ended in 1821, he returned home. His son Pedro, however, refused to go. In 1822, he declared Brazil an independent nation and himself emperor.

Only the Portuguese soldiers in Brazil put up a fight. Everyone else in the colony favored independence. The Portuguese soldiers were finally defeated in 1826. That year Portugal finally recognized Brazil as an independent nation.

Governing the New Nations

When the Spanish and Portuguese colonies became independent countries, they each had to form their own

On December 1, 1822, Dom Pedro I was crowned emperor of Brazil.

governments. Three hundred years of control by other countries did little to prepare them for freedom.

Latin Americans had many different ideas about how their countries ought to be governed. These disagreements often led to violence. Some countries had dozens of different governments within just a few years. As a result, few governments were able to do much to improve life for their people.

As violence grew, armies took control of many countries. People were willing to accept the rule of a general for the sake of peace. These generals were **dictators**. A dictator is a ruler who has complete control over a country. Dictators in Latin America made the laws. They then used the army to make sure those laws were obeyed by everyone.

Some dictators did help their countries. One in Argentina helped to unite the nation. Another in Mexico encouraged new businesses and helped build trade.

For the most part, Latin America's dictators caused more problems than they solved. Some used their power to get rich at the expense of others. For example, many dictators sold the rights to mine valuable resources like copper and tin to foreign companies. Others took away land from anyone who disagreed with them. These actions angered many people.

By the 1900's, Latin Americans were eager for a change. Revolutions began in several countries.

The first revolution started in Mexico in 1910. It lasted for 14 years. When the rebels finally won the war, they set up a new government. It gave people more freedom. It also tried to improve the lives of ordinary people by building roads, schools, and hospitals.

In the 1950's, a revolution also began in Cuba. A young lawyer named Fidel Castro led the fight against Cuba's dictator. In 1959, Castro and his supporters took control of the country. They too started many programs to help the poor.

The central library of the University of Mexico is used by more than 110,000 students every year.

Many Cubans welcomed the changes. However, some lost their enthusiasm when Castro announced that he was going to make Cuba a communist country. Thousands fled their homes. Many of them settled in the United States. Those who stayed behind found that they were not as free as they had hoped to be.

In the late 1970's and early 1980's, revolutions spread to many nations in Central America. In 1979, the people of Nicaragua overthrew their dictator. Other revolutions broke out in El Salvador and Guatemala.

Today many countries in Latin America are still ruled by dictators. However, several countries now have democratic governments. In Costa Rica, Mexico, Venezuela, Colombia, and Peru the people elect their leaders. Yet even in many of these nations, the voters have little choice. People who disagree with the government cannot run for office.

To Help You Remember

1. Who were the first colonists in Latin America to win independence from European control?
2. (a) Who led the fight for Mexican independence? (b) When did Mexico finally become an independent nation?
3. How did Central America become independent?
4. (a) Who led the fight for independence in Spanish South America? (b) When did the last Spanish colony there win its freedom?
5. How did Brazil finally become independent?
6. Why were many newly independent nations in Latin America ruled by dictators?
7. Why did revolutions break out in several Latin American countries in the 1900's?

Chapter Review

Words to Know

1. What Latin Americans were known as *creoles?*
2. What Latin Americans were known as *mestizos?*
3. What is a *dictator?*

Reviewing Main Ideas

1. How did the Indians of Latin America use the land and its resources (a) in Mexico and Central America? (b) In the Andes Mountains? (c) In the Amazon River Valley? (d) In the grasslands of South America? (e) In the Caribbean?
2. How did the first Spanish settlers use their land and its resources?
3. How did Spain group the people in their colonies?
4. (a) How did the Portuguese use the land and its resources? (b) Who did most of the work in Brazil?
5. (a) How did most of the Spanish colonies become independent? (b) How did the Portuguese colony gain its independence?
6. (a) Why did dictators take control of many Latin American countries? (b) What problems did they solve? (c) What problems did they create?

In Your Own Words

Write a paragraph explaining how one of the groups listed in the next column used its land and other resources. Be sure your paragraph has a topic sentence that tells the main idea.

  The Indians of Mexico and
    Central America
  The Indians of the Andes
  The First Spanish Settlers

Challenge!

The Aztecs used a form of picture writing to record stories of their past. Each symbol, or glyph, stood for a word. Sometimes two or more glyphs were combined to make up a longer word. For example, look carefully at the glyph for Tenochtitlan. What two glyphs were combined to make the word? Use the glyphs below to write a story about the Aztecs. Then share your story with your classmates.

motion   deer   house   dog

stone   water   rain   traveling

Montezuma II   tree   Tenochtitlan   crocodile

Things to Do

Most Latin Americans think of Father Miguel Hidalgo, Simon Bolivar, and Jose de San Martín as great heroes. Choose one of these men and use the library to find out why.

26

Living in Latin America Today

Latin America is a land of sharp contrasts. In parts of the region, tiny farming villages dot the land. In other parts, crowded, busy cities stretch out over the land. Everywhere there are contrasts between rich and poor. In the cities, the homes of wealthy business people are just a few blocks from the homes of the poor.

There are also contrasts between the old and the new in Latin America. Some people still work in much the same way as their ancestors did. They farm on mountain terraces. They use hand looms to weave wool and cloth. Others work in modern factories. They refine oil and build trucks. They weave cloth too. However, they have up-to-date machines in factories to do the work.

As You Read

This chapter looks at life in Latin America today. As you read, look for contrasts between life in the country and life in the city. Also look for contrasts between old and new, rich and poor. The chapter is divided into three parts.

- Life in the Country
- Life in the Cities
- Old Industries and New

◀ *Blending of the old and the new, La Paz, Bolivia*

Life in the Country

Long before Europeans came to Latin America, many people there lived as farmers. Many still do. About 40 percent of the people in Latin America farm for a living.

Farming for Food

Most families in Latin America work small plots of land. They grow barely enough food to feed their families.

On Small Farms. Some farmers live in tiny villages high in the Andes Mountains. Their farms are tiny. Few farms are much larger than a football field. This land is not all in one place. Each farmer's land is divided among several tiny fields scattered over a terraced moutainside.

Although it takes a lot of climbing to get from one field to another, most families prefer this arrangement. It is a guard against hunger. If a disease or some other disaster hits one field, the others may be safe.

Villagers guard against hunger in other ways too. They plant many different kinds of potatoes. If one kind fails, the others may not. These ideas about farming began long before the days of the Incas. They have been passed down from one generation to the next since then.

The tools the farmers use are also like those used long ago. Many farm with a hoe and a foot plow. Water is carried to their fields through stone canals. They too were built long ago.

Most families do not own the land they farm. They are **sharecroppers.** They rent land from a large landowner. Each year they give a large part of their crops to the landowner who sells it in a nearby market town. The villagers live on the rest of their harvest.

The landowner must be paid even if the crops fail or if there is an illness in the family. If times are hard, most families have no savings to fall back on. The fear of hunger is as much a

Stone canals built by the Incas 2,000 years ago are still being used today.

part of their lives as the tall mountains and the cool mountain air.

Farmers in the lowlands also work small plots of land. They too work their land much as their ancestors did. For example, many still clear a new part of the forest every few years much as people did centuries ago.

Helping Small Farmers. In recent years, many governments in Latin America have been trying to help small farmers. As cities grow larger, farmers will have to grow more food to feed the people in the cities.

Some countries like Brazil are opening new lands for farming. Others rent modern tools to small farmers. All are building roads to make it easier to get crops to market. They are teaching farmers the latest farming methods too.

Private groups are also helping. For example, the International Potato Center is located in Peru. There is a similar center for corn in Mexico. In both centers, scientists are trying to develop seeds that will produce more food. They are also searching for seeds that can grow almost anywhere.

Still changes come slowly in a land where many people value the old ways. Changes also come slowly because many people cannot afford to experiment. They must constantly guard against hunger.

Scientists from many countries study at the International Potato Center.

Farming for Trade

Those who own large farms, plantations, and ranches are more willing to experiment. They can afford to buy the latest tools and try out the newest farming methods. These people are called **commercial farmers**. They grow crops or raise animals to sell to people in their own country and to people in other countries too.

The families who own the large plantations and ranches produce almost all of the food products Latin America sells abroad. These families live very differently from people who work tiny plots of land.

The large landowners do not have to worry about having enough to eat. They can buy as much as they need. They can also afford to put money

473

This busy marketplace in Bolivia shows how programs aimed at helping farmers improve their harvest are succeeding.

aside to protect themselves against hard times. After all, owning a large farm does not protect a farmer from drought, flooding, crop diseases, or other disasters.

Commercial farmers can be hurt in another way too. They are dependent on the people they sell to. In the last 20 years, for example, the demand for coffee dropped sharply because fewer people were buying coffee.

Coffee is not the only crop for which the market has boomed and then dropped. The markets for bananas, cocoa, cotton, and rubber have also skyrocketed from time to time and then dropped sharply.

As long as there is a demand for their crops, the large landowners will live in comfort. However, their farm workers face an uncertain future. Today many farm workers are leaving the country in hopes of finding better jobs in the city.

To Help You Remember

1. (a) Why do many farmers in Latin America work several small fields?   (b) How are their farming methods similar to those used long ago?
2. How are governments in Latin America helping farmers?
3. (a) Why is life easier for the large landowners than it is for the farm workers?   (b) What problems do the large landowners face?
4. Why are many farm workers leaving the country?

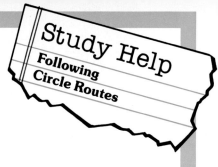

On paper, the shortest distance between the United States and Latin America is a straight line. Earth, however, is not flat the way a sheet of paper is. Earth is round. So the shortest distance between two places is always a curved line. That curved line is part of a **great circle route.** A great circle route is any route that divides Earth in half. The equator is a great circle route. So are all lines of longitude and their opposites. For example, the prime meridian and longitude 180 degrees form a great circle route. So do longitude 100 degrees east and longitude 80 degrees west.

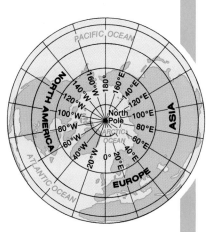

1. Name four cities in North and South America that lie along longitude 80 degrees west.
2. Dodge City, Kansas, and Mexico City, Mexico, are on the same great circle route. What is it?

Following Great Circle Routes

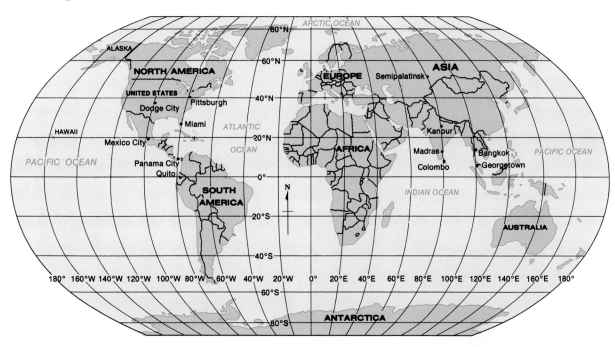

Life in the Cities

Cities have been a part of Latin America for many hundreds of years. The Incas of Peru and the Aztecs of Mexico built many large cities. So did Spanish and Portuguese settlers. Since Latin American countries have become independent, cities have grown faster than ever.

In Search of Opportunity

Latin American cities have grown most rapidly within the last 30 years. Millions of people have flocked to the cities and towns. They come for the same reasons people have always moved to cities. They come in hopes of finding work in factories, shops, and other businesses. They also come in search of opportunity.

Many are disappointed. Factories do not need as many workers as they once did. Machines now do more of the work. So there are not enough jobs for everyone who wants one. The best jobs also require special training. Yet many of the newcomers have not had any schooling at all.

In spite of these disappointments, only a few of the newcomers leave the cities. Most have nothing to go back to. Jobs are even harder to find in the country. So they try to make the best of whatever opportunities the city offers.

The Role of Families

Old traditions have helped many people in Latin America adjust to city life. For example, families there have always worked together as a team. In the cities, many families find that they can get ahead more easily if they help each other. The Molinas are a good example of such a family. They live in Mexico.

The Molinas live in a small but comfortable house just outside the

This factory in Colombia is only one of many new factories that have opened.

city of Guadalajara (gwä′dl ə ha′rə). The father works in an automobile factory. The mother runs the family business, a small grocery store.

There are six children in the family, four girls and two boys. The two oldest girls have finished school. They work in a local clothing factory. They give all their earnings to their parents to help pay for their house.

The children's grandmother also lives with the family. She helps too. She watches the younger children while their mother works. She also mends the family's clothes.

Like most families in Latin America, the Molinas know they can depend on each other. The oldest daughter will soon marry. She and her husband-to-be have very little money. Yet they know they can live with either her parents or his until they can afford their own home.

The Role of the Church

The Molinas are Roman Catholics. So are more than 90 percent of the people in Latin America. Religion unites people throughout the region. It also helps make city life a little easier.

Many people turn to the Church when they are in trouble. Priests and nuns offer prayers and guidance. They help in other ways too. The Church runs hospitals, orphanages, and schools throughout Latin America.

People in Ecuador wear traditional clothes during a religious celebration.

Religious ceremonies also brighten and give meaning to people's lives. For example, most cities have a special saint. They hold a festival to honor that saint every year. During these festivals, there are special church services, parades, fireworks, and a variety of games and contests.

To Help You Remember

1. Why are some Latin Americans disappointed after moving from the country to the city?
2. How do members of many Latin American families work together?
3. How does the Roman Catholic Church help Latin Americans?

Old Industries and New

People come to the cities to find work. Some take jobs in industries that have been important to Latin Americans for hundreds of years. Others are working in industries that are still very new.

Mining

Long ago the Aztecs, the Incas, and other Indian groups mined gold and silver. When Europeans arrived, mining became more important than ever. It is still very important.

Since independence, however, gold and silver have become less important. In Mexico, earnings from lead, zinc, and copper are now greater than earnings from gold or silver. Chile gets much of its income from its huge deposits of copper. Tin is far more important to people in Bolivia than silver. Brazilians now sell more iron ore than gold or diamonds.

The most valuable mineral resource today, however, is oil. People are as eager to find it as they once were to find gold. Nine countries in the region have oil, but only two are major producers. They are Venezuela and Mexico.

Yet, like the price of cash crops, the demand for mineral resources often depends on events that take place in other countries. The demand for sodium nitrate in the early 1900's is a good example. Sodium nitrate is a salt used to make explosives and fertilizers. The Atacama (ä'tä kä'mä) Desert, which lies along the west coast of South America, has the world's largest supply of this salt.

In the early 1900's, there was a huge demand for sodium nitrate. During World War I nearly 300,000 people flocked to the desert to mine the salt.

Then a scientist in Germany found a way to make nitrates from gases in the air. Suddenly there was no interest in sodium nitrate. Dozens of salt mines closed. Workers had to move on to other jobs.

Sometimes a resource becomes less important for other reasons. Venezuela, for example, is running out of oil. Its supplies are not expected to last many more years. On the other hand, Mexico still has large amounts of oil. However, because of falling oil prices it is no longer as profitable as it once was to drill for oil.

Some governments in Latin America are using the money they make from oil, copper, iron, and other minerals to start new businesses. They do not want to be dependent on only one resource.

How is much of the land used in Argentina? ▶

Latin America: Land Use

Manufacturing

Agriculture and livestock raising

Livestock raising

Forestry

Hunting, fishing, and gathering

Commercial fishing

Little or no activity

Coal

Iron

Oil

Natural gas

Copper

Bauxite

Gold

Silver

Diamonds

Hydroelectric power

Tin

Lead

Zinc

Uranium

Nickel

Tungsten

ATLANTIC OCEAN

Tropic of Cancer

20°N

Gulf of Mexico

THE BAHAMAS

Monterrey

MEXICO

Mexico City

CUBA

DOMINICAN REPUBLIC

HAITI

PUERTO RICO (U.S. COMM.)

VIRGIN ISLANDS (U.S./U.K.)

ANTIGUA-BARBUDA

JAMAICA

BELIZE

HONDURAS

GUATEMALA

EL SALVADOR

NICARAGUA

COSTA RICA

PANAMA

CARIBBEAN SEA

ST. CHRISTOPHER AND NEVIS

DOMINICA

SAINT LUCIA

ST. VINCENT AND THE GRENADINES

BARBADOS

GRENADA

TRINIDAD AND TOBAGO

Barranquilla

Cartagena

Caracas

VENEZUELA

GUYANA

SURINAME

FRENCH GUIANA (FR.)

Medellín

Bogotá

COLOMBIA

GALÁPAGOS ISLANDS (ECUADOR)

ECUADOR

Equator

0°

PACIFIC OCEAN

BRAZIL

PERU

Lima

BOLIVIA

Tropic of Capricorn

20°S

PARAGUAY

São Paulo

Rio de Janeiro

CHILE

URUGUAY

Valparaíso

Santiago

Rosario

Buenos Aires

Montevideo

Concepción

ARGENTINA

40°S

500

1000 Miles

500

1000 Kilometers

FALKLAND ISLANDS (U.K.)

SOUTH GEORGIA ISLANDS (U.K.)

120°W

100°W

80°W

60°W

40°W

20°W

Cattle ranching is an important industry in Argentina.

Manufacturing

Until recently, Latin America had very few factories. People in most countries there earned money by selling raw materials like food and minerals to other countries. During World War II, these goods were in great demand. When the war ended, the demand fell sharply.

As a result, the governments of several Latin American countries decided to make use of those resources themselves. They encouraged local business people to start factories. They also invited European and American companies to open businesses in Latin America.

As a result of these efforts, hundreds of new factories opened. Many of them use nearby resources. For example, Argentina has many cattle ranches and wheat farms. So food processing has become an important industry there.

Other countries are using their resources too. There are steel mills in Brazil. It also has factories that use the steel to make cars and trucks. Many people in Central America refine sugar, roast coffee beans, or turn cocoa into chocolate. Factories in Latin America also turn out chemicals, furniture, clothing, and many other goods. The leading manufacturing nations are Argentina, Brazil, Chile, Mexico, and Venezuela.

The Tourist Industry

Many Latin Americans are also finding jobs in another new industry. It is the tourist industry.

Since World War II, the cost of air travel has dropped sharply. More people can now afford to travel. Many of them visit Latin America. They come to enjoy the white sandy beaches and to swim in the warm waters of the Caribbean. Many also come to see the pyramids in Mexico and the ruins of ancient Incan cities in the mountains of Peru.

These visitors have created thousands of new jobs. Workers are needed to run hotels and restaurants, guide tours, sell souvenirs, and handle dozens of other jobs.

The tourists have also created a demand for goods like those made in Latin America hundreds of years ago. As a result, many Latin Americans are working at the same jobs their ancestors once held. They are potters, weavers, and goldsmiths.

There is, however, an important difference. Potters and weavers sold their goods long ago in local markets. People bought them for everyday use. Today things made by potters, weavers, and other artisans are considered works of art. They are sold in stores and shops in all parts of the world.

Looking Ahead

The future of countries in Latin America, like the future of countries everywhere, depends on its children. They will one day start new industries and expand older ones.

To prepare for the future, children need a good education. Yet providing schooling for everyone in Latin America is not easy. Many families live far from the nearest school. Others need the help of every family member to survive. So even young children have to work.

Governments in Latin America are spending more on education every year. They know that their countries

These children play outide the Museum of Anthropology in Mexico City.

cannot advance unless their people are educated. They also know that the children are their best hope for a brighter future.

To Help You Remember

1. (a) What minerals were mined in Latin America long ago?   (b) What minerals are mined there today?
2. (a) When were many factories built in Latin America?   (b) Why were they built?
3. How are Latin Americans benefiting from the growth of the tourist industry?
4. Why do many Latin Americans believe education is the key to a brighter future?

Chapter Review

Words to Know

1. What is a *sharecropper*?
2. What is a *commercial farmer*?

Reviewing Main Ideas

1. (a) How is farming in Latin America today similar to the way it was long ago? (b) Tell two ways it differs.
2. Why have Latin American cities grown so rapidly over the last 30 years?
3. How do family and religion help Latin Americans adjust to life in the city?
4. How are governments in Latin America using the money earned from their mineral resources?
5. Why is the tourist industry important to Latin Americans?
6. Why are Latin Americans trying to improve education?

In Your Own Words

1. (a) Why is life hard for many families living in farming villages? (b) Why is it hard for many families living in cities?
2. Use your answers to write a paragraph that explains why life today is difficult for many Latin Americans.

Keeping Skills Sharp

The coldest parts of Earth lie near both the North Pole and the South Pole. The warmest parts lie along the equator.

Keep these facts in mind as you study the map below.

1. (a) Which part of North America is coldest? (b) Warmest?
2. (a) Which part of South America is coldest? (b) Warmest?
3. Explain why the south is not always warmer than the north.

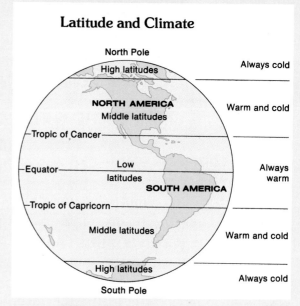

Latitude and Climate

Challenge!

Latitude affects climate. So do other things. Try to solve as many of these climate mysteries as you can.

1. Why are there snow-covered mountains along the equator?
2. Olympia in the state of Washington and Bismarck in North Dakota are about equally far north. Why then are Bismarck's winters so much colder?

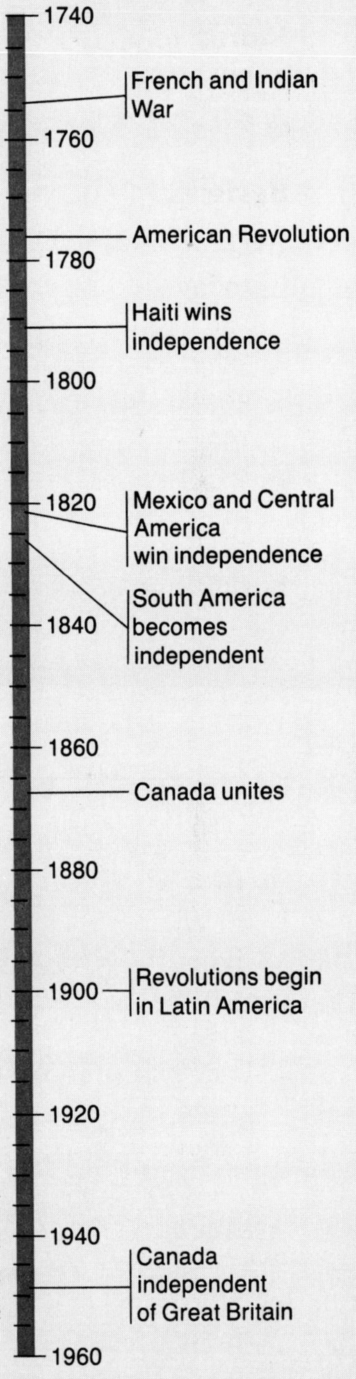

Take Another Look

Use the time line on this page and the information in the text to answer the questions.

1. When did Europeans first come (a) to Canada? (b) to Latin America?
2. (a) Why is 1776 an important date to Canadians? (b) to Latin Americans?
3. Why is the year 1867 important to Canadians?
4. (a) Why is the year 1791 important to people in Haiti?
   (b) Why is 1821 important to people in Mexico and Central America? (c) Why is 1826 important to South Americans?
5. How did people in Latin America use their resources (a) before 1492? (b) between 1492 and the 1820's? (c) after the 1820's? (d) How do they use them today?
6. How did people in Canada use their resources (a) before 1498? (b) when they were under French rule? (c) when they were under British rule? (d) today?

You and Current Events

1. The United States has many ties to other countries in the Americas. Newspapers and magazines can help you see some of those links. Study your local newspaper carefully to see how many of those ties you can find. Be sure to study not only the news articles but also the food pages, advertisements, business section, travel pages, and entertainment news.
2. In the 1940's, people in the Americas began to build a highway linking countries throughout the Americas. That highway is called the Pan-American Highway. On a map of the Americas, show the highway. Then write a report telling what products might travel along this highway.
3. Countries in the Americas have many common interests. They discuss many of these at organizations like the Pan American Union. Make a list of concerns that affect countries in the Americas. Why might it be hard for one country to solve these problems without involving its neighbors?

Time line (right side):

- 1740
- French and Indian War
- 1760
- American Revolution
- 1780
- Haiti wins independence
- 1800
- 1820 — Mexico and Central America win independence
- South America becomes independent
- 1840
- 1860
- Canada unites
- 1880
- 1900 — Revolutions begin in Latin America
- 1920
- 1940
- Canada independent of Great Britain
- 1960

Atlas

Countries of the World

----- Disputed boundaries

| 0 | 1000 | 2000 | 3000 Miles |
| 0 | 1000 | 2000 | 3000 Kilometers |

GREENLAND (DEN.)

ALASKA (U.S.)

CANADA

UNITED STATES

ATLANTIC OCEAN

PACIFIC OCEAN

HAWAII (U.S.)

Tropic of Cancer

THE BAHAMAS
DOMINICAN REPUBLIC
PUERTO RICO (U.S. COMM.)
CUBA
VIRGIN ISLANDS (U.S.)
MEXICO
JAMAICA HAITI
ANTIGUA AND BARBUDA
BELIZE
ST. CHRISTOPHER
AND NEVIS
DOMINICA
GUATEMALA
SAINT LUCIA
BARBADOS
EL SALVADOR
NICARAGUA
GRENADA
ST. VINCENT AND
THE GRENADINES
HONDURAS
TRINIDAD AND TOBAGO
COSTA RICA
PANAMA
VENEZUELA
GUYANA
SURINAME
COLOMBIA
FRENCH GUIANA (FR.)

Equator

KIRIBATI

ECUADOR

PERU

BRAZIL

WESTERN SAMOA

TONGA

Tropic of Capricorn

BOLIVIA

PARAGUAY

CHILE

URUGUAY

ARGENTINA

EUROPE

80°N

0°

20°E

ATLANTIC

Arctic Circle

OCEAN

ICELAND

SWEDEN

FINLAND

NORWAY

60°N

UNITED KINGDOM

DENMARK

IRELAND

NETHERLANDS
EAST
POLAND
GERMANY
BELGIUM
WEST
CZECHOSLOVAKIA
LUXEMBOURG
GERMANY

SOVIET UNION

SWITZERLAND
AUSTRIA HUNGARY
FRANCE
LIECHTENSTEIN
ROMANIA

MONACO
SAN
YUGOSLAVIA
MARINO
BULGARIA
ANDORRA
ITALY
ALBANIA

40°N

SPAIN

PORTUGAL

GREECE

TURKEY

GIBRALTAR (U.K.)

MALTA

CYPRUS

| 0 | 500 | 1000 | 1500 Miles |
| 0 | 500 | 1000 | 1500 Kilometers |

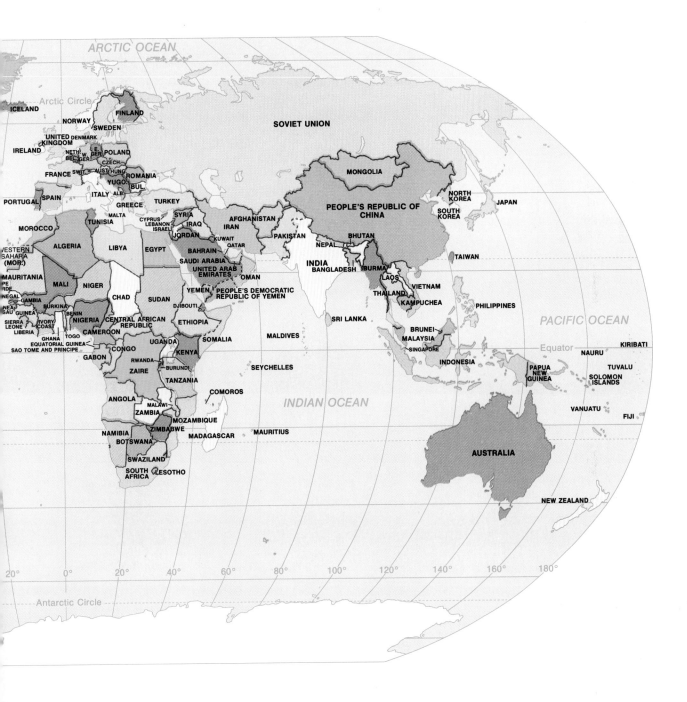

ARCTIC OCEAN

Arctic Circle

ICELAND

NORWAY
SWEDEN
FINLAND

UNITED DENMARK
KINGDOM
IRELAND
NETH. POLAND
BEL. GER.
FRANCE SWIT. AUST. HUNG.
ITALY YUGO. ROMANIA
CZECH.
ALB. BUL.

PORTUGAL SPAIN

SOVIET UNION

MONGOLIA

PEOPLE'S REPUBLIC OF
CHINA

NORTH
KOREA

SOUTH
KOREA

JAPAN

GREECE TURKEY

MALTA
TUNISIA CYPRUS SYRIA
LEBANON IRAQ
ISRAEL
JORDAN

MOROCCO

WESTERN
SAHARA
(MOR.)

ALGERIA LIBYA EGYPT

AFGHANISTAN
IRAN

KUWAIT
QATAR

PAKISTAN

NEPAL BHUTAN

TAIWAN

BAHRAIN
SAUDI ARABIA
UNITED ARAB
EMIRATES OMAN

INDIA
BANGLADESH BURMA

LAOS

VIETNAM

MAURITANIA
PE
RDE
NEGAL
GAMBIA
NEA
SAU GUINEA
SIERRA
LEONE
LIBERIA

MALI NIGER

CHAD SUDAN

YEMEN
PEOPLE'S DEMOCRATIC
REPUBLIC OF YEMEN
DJIBOUTI

THAILAND

KAMPUCHEA

PHILIPPINES

PACIFIC OCEAN

BURKINA
BENIN
IVORY
COAST
GHANA TOGO
EQUATORIAL GUINEA
SAO TOME AND PRINCIPE

NIGERIA
CENTRAL AFRICAN
REPUBLIC

CAMEROON

ETHIOPIA

SRI LANKA

MALDIVES

BRUNEI
MALAYSIA
SINGAPORE

Equator
NAURU

KIRIBATI

GABON CONGO

UGANDA
KENYA

SOMALIA

INDONESIA

PAPUA
NEW
GUINEA

TUVALU
SOLOMON
ISLANDS

RWANDA
ZAIRE BURUNDI

TANZANIA

SEYCHELLES

VANUATU

FIJI

ANGOLA

MALAWI
ZAMBIA

COMOROS

INDIAN OCEAN

MOZAMBIQUE

AUSTRALIA

NAMIBIA ZIMBABWE
BOTSWANA

MADAGASCAR MAURITIUS

SWAZILAND
SOUTH LESOTHO
AFRICA

NEW ZEALAND

20°   0°   20°   40°   60°   80°   100°   120°   140°   160°   180°

Antarctic Circle

485

World Population Density

Persons per square mile	Persons per square kilometer
Uninhabited	Uninhabited
Less than 2	Less than 1
2–25	1–10
25–125	10–50
125–250	50–100
250–500	100–200
Over 500	Over 200

• Major cities

NORTH

AMERICA

Chi

New York

ATLANTIC OCEAN

Los Angeles

Tropic of Cancer

Mexico

PACIFIC OCEAN

Equator

SOUTH

AMERICA

Rio de J

São P

Tropic of Capricorn

Buenos Aires

ARCTIC OCEAN

Arctic Circle

Leningrad
Moscow

EUROPE

London

Paris

ASIA

Beijing

Seoul

Tokyo

Tehran

Cairo

Delhi
Karachi

Shanghai

Calcutta

Bombay

Bangkok

Manila

PACIFIC OCEAN

AFRICA

Equator

Jakarta

INDIAN OCEAN

AUSTRALIA

20° 0° 20° 40° 60° 80° 100° 120° 140° 160° 180°

Antarctic Circle

ANTARCTICA

ARCTIC OCEAN

BERING
SEA

BEAUFORT
SEA

GREENLAND
(DENMARK)

Baffin
Bay

Nome •
Prudhoe Bay •
• Thule

ALASKA
(U.S.)

• Anchorage

Yukon

LABRADOR SEA

Denmark Strait

Davis Strait

Circle Strait

• Godthåb

Gulf of
Alaska

Juneau •

Mackenzie R.

Great Bear
Lake

Arctic

Great Slave
Lake

Hudson
Bay

PACIFIC
OCEAN

Edmonton •

CANADA

Peace R.

Saskatchewan R.

Nelson R.

Lake
Winnipeg

ST. PIERRE AND
MIQUELON (FR.)

Vancouver •
Calgary •

Fraser R.

Columbia R.

Seattle •

Portland •

Winnipeg •

Lake Superior

Lawrence R.

Quebec •
Montreal •
Ottawa ★

ATLANTIC
OCEAN

Snake R.

Missouri R.

Minneapolis •

Lake Michigan

Lake Huron

Lake Ontario
Lake Erie

Toronto •
Hamilton •

Boston •
Hartford •

Milwaukee •

Buffalo •

Omaha •

Chicago •

Detroit •

Pittsburg •

New York •

Great
Salt Lake

San Francisco •
San Jose •

Salt Lake City •

Platte R.

Denver •

UNITED STATES

Cleveland •

Philadelphia •

Indianapolis •

Baltimore •

Kansas City •

St. Louis •

Cincinnati •

Washington, D.C. •

Colorado R.

Arkansas

Ohio R.

Los Angeles •

San Diego •

Phoenix •

Oklahoma
City •

Memphis •

Atlanta •

BERMUDA
(U.K.)

El Paso •

Dallas •

Red R.

Birmingham •

Rio Grande

Brazos R.

New
Orleans •

Jacksonville •

Tropic of Cancer

San
Antonio •

Houston •

Mississippi R.

Gulf of Mexico

Miami •

THE BAHAMAS
★ Nassau

TURKS AND CAICOS
ISLANDS (U.K.)

ST. CHRISTOPHER
AND NEVIS
Basseterre ★

Monterrey •

VIRGIN ISLANDS
(U.S.)

ANTIGUA-BARBUDA
St. Johns ★

MEXICO

Havana ★

CUBA

DOMINICAN
REPUBLIC

PUERTO RICO
(U.S. COMM.)

DOMINICA
Roseau ★

San Juan •

SAINT LUCIA
Castries ★

Guadalajara •

CAYMAN ISLANDS
(U.K.)

Mexico City ★

HAITI
Port-au-
Prince ★

MONTSERRAT (U.K.)
GUADELOUPE (FR.)

BARBADOS

Kingston ★

Santo
Domingo ★

MARTINIQUE (FR.)

Bridgetown ★

JAMAICA

SAINT VINCENT AND
THE GRENADINES
Kingstown ★

BELIZE
★ Belmopan

NETHERLANDS
ANTILLES
(NETH.)

GRENADA
St. Georges ★

TRINIDAD
AND
TOBAGO

CARRIBBEAN
SEA

Port-of-Spain ★

Guatemala ★

HONDURAS
★ Tegucigalpa

Panama
Canal

GUATEMALA

San Salvador ★

NICARAGUA
★ Managua

EL SALVADOR

San José ★

Panama City •

COSTA RICA

PANAMA

N

160°W

HAWAII
(U.S.)

PACIFIC
OCEAN

Kauai

Oahu

Honolulu •

Molokai
Maui

20°N

Lanai

0   150 Miles

Hawaii

0   150 Kilometers   155°W

North America: Political

★ Capital city   • Other city

0   500   1000 Miles

0   500   1000 Kilometers

Equator

ATLANTIC OCEAN

Gulf of Mexico

Tropic of Cancer

30°N

20°N

CARIBBEAN SEA

10°N

PACIFIC OCEAN

Barranquilla
Cartagena

Maracaibo
Caracas ★

VENEZUELA

Georgetown
Paramaribo
Cayenne

GUYANA
SURINAME

FRENCH GUIANA (FR.)

Medellín
Cali

★ Bogotá

COLOMBIA

Orinoco R.

GALÁPAGOS ISLANDS
(ECUADOR)

Quito ★
ECUADOR

Guayaquil

Negro R.

Equator

0°

Amazon R.

Fortaleza

N

PERU

Recife

BRAZIL

São Francisco R.

Lima ★

10°S

Salvador

Lake
Titicaca

BOLIVIA

★ La Paz

Brasília ★

Arequipa

★ Sucre

Belo Horizonte

Paraná R.

20°S

Tropic of Capricorn

PARAGUAY

São Paulo

Rio de Janeiro

★ Asunción

Curitiba

Tucumán

CHILE

South America: Political

★ Capital city   • Other city

Córdoba

Valparaíso
Santiago ★

Rosario

URUGUAY

Pôrto Alegre

30°S

0   500   1000 Miles

Buenos Aires ★
★ Montevideo
Río de la
Plata

0   500   1000 Kilometers

Concepción

ARGENTINA

Bahía Blanca

40°S

FALKLAND ISLANDS (U.K.)
Stanley

50°S

Tierra del
Fuego

Cape Horn

SOUTH GEORGIA ISLANDS
(U.K.)

120°W   110°W   100°W   90°W   80°W   70°W   60°W   50°W   40°W   30°W   20°W

Countries of the Americas

North America

Country and Capital	Largest City	Total Area, sq. mi.	Population	Languages
Antigua and Barbuda St. Johns	St. John's	171	80,000	English
The Bahamas Nassau	Nassau	5,380	232,000	English
Belize Belmopan	Belize City	166	161,000	English, Spanish Maya, Carib
Canada Ottawa	Montreal	3,852,000	24,900,000	English, French
Costa Rica San Jose	San Jose	19,653	2,655,000	Spanish
Cuba Havana	Havana	44,216	9,995,000	Spanish
Dominica Roseau	Roseau	291	74,000	English, French patois
Dominican Republic Santo Domingo	Santo Domingo	18,816	6,588,000	Spanish
El Salvador San Salvador	San Salvador	8,083	5,072,000	Spanish, Nahuati
Grenada St. George's	St. George's	133	88,000	English, French patois
Guatemala Guatemala	Guatemala	42,042	8,070,000	Spanish, Indian languages
Haiti Port-au-Prince	Port-au-Prince	10,683	5,762,000	French, Creole
Honduras Tegucigalpa	Tegucigalpa	43,277	4,394,000	Spanish, Indian languages
Jamaica Kingston	Kingston	4,244	2,428,000	English
Mexico Mexico City	Mexico City	761,600	79,662,000	Spanish
Nicaragua Managua	Managua	50,193	3,038,000	Spanish, Indian languages
Panama Panama	Panama	29,762	2,038,000	Spanish, English
Saint Lucia Castries	Castries	238	122,000	English, French patois

Country and Capital	Largest City	Total Area, sq. mi.	Population	Languages
Saint Vincent and the Grenadines Kingstown	Kingstown	150	102,000	English, French patois
Trinidad and Tobago Port of Spain	Port of Spain	1,980	1,185,000	English, others
United States Washington, D.C.	New York City	3,615,105	236,690,000	English

South America

Country and Capital	Largest City	Total Area, sq. mi.	Population	Languages
Argentina Buenos Aires	Buenos Aires	1,077,000	30,708,000	Spanish
Bolivia La Paz	La Paz	424,162	6,037,000	Spanish Quechua, Aymara
Brazil Brasilia	Rio de Janeiro	3,286,000	134,380,000	Portuguese
Chile Santiago	Santiago	292,257	11,706,000	Spanish
Colombia Bogota	Bogota	439,735	28,901,000	Spanish
Ecuador Quito	Guayaquil	104,505	8,648,000	Spanish, Quechua
Guyana Georgetown	Georgetown	83,000	794,000	English
Paraguay Asuncion	Asuncion	157,047	3,623,000	Spanish, Guaroni
Peru Lima	Lima	496,222	19,006,000	Spanish, Quechua, Aymara
Suriname Paramaribo	Paramaribo	60,239	363,000	Dutch, English, others
Uruguay Montevideo	Montevideo	68,536	2,926,000	Spanish
Venezuela Caracas	Caracas	352,143	17,279,000	Spanish, Indian languages

ESABI
RANGE

Lake Superior

St. Paul
Minneapolis

WISCONSIN

Milwaukee
Madison

Green
Bay

Straits
of Mackinac

Lake Huron

MICHIGAN

Lansing

Lake Michigan

Detroit

Chicago

ILLINOIS

INDIANA

CENTRAL PLAINS

Springfield

Indianapolis

MISSOURI

Jefferson
City

St. Louis

Cincinnati

OHIO

Columbus

Cleveland

Lake Erie

Buffalo

Lake Ontario

Pittsburgh

ALLEGHENY
PLATEAU

PENNSYLVANIA

Harrisburg

MAINE

Augusta

Penobscot Bay

Montpelier

VT.

N.H.

Concord

NEW YORK

Albany

ADIRONDACK
MOUNTAINS

Boston

Cape Cod

MASS.

Providence

Hartford

CONN.

R.I.

Nantucket
Martha's Vineyard

Long Island Sound

Long Island

New York

NEW JERSEY

Trenton

Philadelphia

Baltimore

Cape May

Dover

Delaware Bay

DELAWARE

MD.

D.C.

Annapolis

Washington

**ARK
PLATEAU**

KENTUCKY

Frankfort

Charleston

**WEST
VIRGINIA**

CUMBERLAND PLATEAU

Richmond

VIRGINIA

Chesapeake Bay

RKANSAS

Little Rock

Nashville

TENNESSEE

Kentucky Lake

ALABAMA

Atlanta

**NORTH
CAROLINA**

Raleigh

Hatteras
Cape Hatteras

**SOUTH
CAROLINA**

Columbia

MISSISSIPPI

Jackson

Montgomery

GEORGIA

PLAIN

COASTAL

PLAIN

BLUE RIDGE

APPALACHIAN

MOUNTAINS

BLUE RIDGE

ATLANTIC OCEAN

COASTAL

LOUISIANA

Baton
Rouge

New Orleans

Pontchartrain

Mississippi
Delta

Gulf of Mexico

Mobile Bay

Pensacola
Bay

Tallahassee

FLORIDA

Cape Canaveral

Tampa Bay

Lake
Okeechobee

The
Everglades

Cape Sable

Miami

FLORIDA
KEYS

Straits of Florida

The United States Today

Elevation key

Feet		Meters
14,000		4,000
7,000		2,000
1,500		500
700		200
0		0
Below sea level		Below sea level

★ Capital city

◉ State capital city

• Other city

| 0 | 100 | 200 | 300 | 400 | 500 Miles |

| 0 | 100 | 200 | 300 | 400 | 500 Kilometers |

0   100 Miles

0   100 Kilometers

20°N

ATLANTIC

OCEAN

**PUERTO RICO
(U.S. COMM.)**

San Juan

CARIBBEAN SEA

90°W

85°W

80°W

75°W

70°W

65°W

60°W

45°N

40°N

35°N

30°N

25°N

Tropic of Cancer

70°W

60°W

The States by Region

State and Its Capital	Date Became State	Rank in Order of Statehood	Area in Square Miles	Rank in Size	Population	Rank in Population
The Northeast						
Connecticut Hartford	1788	5	5,018	48	3,153,000	26
Delaware Dover	1787	1	2,044	49	602,000	47
Maine Augusta	1820	23	33,265	39	1,133,000	38
Maryland Annapolis	1788	7	10,460	42	4,265,000	19
Massachusetts Boston	1788	6	8,284	45	5,781,000	11
New Hampshire Concord	1788	9	9,279	44	951,000	42
New Jersey Trenton	1787	3	7,787	46	7,438,000	9

494

State and Its Capital	Date Became State	Rank in Order of Statehood	Area in Square Miles	Rank in Size	Population	Rank in Population
New York Albany	1788	11	49,108	30	17,659,000	2
Pennsylvania Harrisburg	1787	2	45,308	33	11,865,000	4
Rhode Island Providence	1790	13	1,212	50	958,000	41
Vermont Montpelier	1791	14	9,614	43	516,000	48
Washington D.C.			69		638,000	

The South

State and Its Capital	Date Became State	Rank in Order of Statehood	Area in Square Miles	Rank in Size	Population	Rank in Population
Alabama Montgomery	1819	22	51,705	29	3,943,000	22
Arkansas Little Rock	1836	25	53,187	27	2,291,000	33
Florida Tallahassee	1845	27	58,664	22	10,416,000	27
Georgia Atlanta	1788	4	58,910	21	5,639,000	12
Kentucky Frankfort	1792	15	40,409	37	3,667,000	23
Louisiana Baton Rouge	1812	18	47,752	31	4,362,000	18
Mississippi Jackson	1817	20	47,689	32	2,551,000	31
North Carolina Raleigh	1789	12	52,669	28	6,019,000	10
South Carolina Columbia	1788	8	31,113	40	3,203,000	24
Tennessee Nashville	1796	16	42,144	34	4,651,000	17
Virginia Richmond	1788	10	40,767	36	5,491,000	13
West Virginia Charleston	1863	35	24,231	41	1,948,000	34

State and Its Capital	Date Became State	Rank in Order of Statehood	Area in Square Miles	Rank in Size	Population	Rank in Population
The Middle West						
Illinois Springfield	1818	21	56,345	24	11,448,000	5
Indiana Indianapolis	1816	19	36,185	38	5,471,000	14
Iowa Des Moines	1846	29	56,275	25	2,905,000	28
Kansas Topeka	1861	34	82,277	14	2,408,000	32
Michigan Lansing	1837	26	58,527	23	9,109,000	8
Minnesota St. Paul	1858	32	84,402	12	4,133,000	21
Missouri Jefferson City	1821	24	69,697	19	2,905,000	28
Nebraska Lincoln	1867	37	77,355	15	1,586,000	35
North Dakota Bismarck	1889	39	70,702	17	670,000	46
Ohio Columbus	1803	17	41,330	35	10,791,000	6
South Dakota Pierre	1889	40	77,116	16	691,000	45
Wisconsin Madison	1848	30	56,153	26	4,765,000	16
The West						
The Southwest						
Arizona Phoenix	1912	48	114,000	6	2,860,000	29
New Mexico Santa Fe	1912	47	121,593	5	1,359,000	37
Oklahoma Oklahoma City	1907	46	69,956	18	3,177,000	25
Texas Austin	1845	28	266,807	2	15,280,000	3
The Rocky Mountain States						
Colorado Denver	1876	38	104,091	8	3,045,000	27

State and Its Capital	Date Became State	Rank in Order of Statehood	Area in Square Miles	Rank in Size	Population	Rank in Population
Idaho Boise	1890	43	83,564	13	965,000	40
Montana Helena	1889	41	147,046	4	801,000	44
Nevada Carson City	1864	36	110,561	7	881,000	43
Utah Salt Lake City	1896	45	84,899	11	1,554,000	36
Wyoming Cheyenne	1890	44	97,809	9	502,000	49
Pacific States						
Alaska Juneau	1959	49	591,004	1	438,000	50
California Sacramento	1850	31	158,706	3	24,724,000	1
Hawaii Honolulu	1959	50	6,471	47	994,000	39
Oregon Salem	1859	33	97,073	10	2,649,000	30
Washington Olympia	1889	42	68,139	20	4,245,000	20

How the United States Has Grown

Year	Population	Number of People per Square Mile	Area (Land Only) in Square Miles
1790	3,929,214	4.5	864,746
1810	7,239,881	4.3	1,681,828
1830	12,866,020	7.4	1,749,462
1850	23,191,876	7.9	2,940,042
1870	39,818,449	13.4	2,969,640
1890	62,947,714	21.2	2,969,640
1910	91,972,266	31.0	2,969,640
1930	122,775,048	41.2	2,977,128
1950	151,325,798	42.6	3,618,770
1970	203,302,031	57.4	3,618,770
1990 (est.)	245,500,000	67.8	3,618,770

From the Source:
Documents and Songs from American History

A Step toward Self-Government

When the 41 Pilgrims aboard the *Mayflower* signed the Mayflower Compact, they were taking an important step toward self-government. The compact, or agreement, provided for a "civil body politic" to make laws. In other words, the compact said that the people of the colony could make their own laws. It also allowed the people of the colony to change laws when it was necessary. The Mayflower Compact remained the basis of the Plymouth Colony's government until 1691, when that colony became part of Massachusetts.

The original Mayflower Compact has disappeared. This version is close to the original. It follows the spelling and punctuation printed in a book written by the second governor of Plymouth Colony, William Bradford.

The Mayflower Compact

In ye name of God Amen. We whose names are underwritten, the loyall subjects of our dread soveraigne Lord King James, by ye grace of God, of Great Britaine, Franc, &c. Ireland king, defender of ye faith, &c. Haveing undertaken, for ye glorie of God, and advancemente of ye Christian faith and honour of our king & countrie, a voyage to plant ye first colonie in ye Northerne parts of Virginia, doe by these presents solemnly & mutualy in ye presence of God, and one of another, covenant, & combine ourselves togeather into a Civil body politick; for our better ordering, & preservation & furtherance of ye ends aforesaid; and by vertue hereof to enacte, constitute, and frame such just & equall Lawes, ordinances, Acts, constitutions, & offices, from time to time, as shall be thought most meete & convenient for ye generall good of ye colonie: unto which we promise all due submission and obedience. In witnes whereof we have hereunder subscribed our names at Cap-Codd ye -11- of November, in ye year of ye raigne of our soveraigne Lord King James of England, France, & Ireland ye eighteenth, and of Scotland ye fiftie fourth.

Ano Dom. 1620.

Toward Independence

By the summer of 1776, many American colonists felt that for their good and the good of their children, they had to break away from the British government and rule themselves. Delegates from the 13 colonies met in Philadelphia to decide what to do. There, Thomas Jefferson wrote the Declaration of Independence to explain to the world why Americans should separate from Britain. On July 4, 1776, the delegates voted to approve the Declaration of Independence.

The Declaration stated that all people are entitled to certain human rights—the right to life, liberty, and the pursuit of happiness. People, it said, also have the right to choose their government. That government must protect the rights of the people it governs. The Declaration then listed the abuses of the king. Finally, the men who signed the Declaration pledged themselves and everything they had to the cause of independence.

The Declaration of Independence
IN CONGRESS, JULY 4, 1776

The Unanimous Declaration of the Thirteen United States of America

When in the course of human events, it becomes necessary for one people to dissolve the political bands which have connected them with another, and to assume among the powers of the earth, the separate and equal station to which the laws of Nature and of Nature's God entitle them, a decent respect to the opinions of mankind requires that they should declare the causes which impel them to the separation.

We hold these truths to be self-evident, that all men are created equal, that they are endowed by their Creator with certain unalienable rights, that among these are life, liberty and the pursuit of happiness. That to secure these rights, governments are instituted among men, deriving their just powers from the consent of the governed,—That whenever any form of government becomes destructive of these ends, it is the right of the people to alter or to abolish it, and to institute new government, laying its foundation on such principles and organizing its powers in such form, as to them shall seem most likely to effect their safety and happiness. Prudence, indeed, will dictate that governments long established should not be changed for light and transient causes; and accordingly all experience hath shown, that mankind are more disposed to suffer, while evils are sufferable, than to right themselves by abolishing the forms to which they are accustomed. But when a long train of abuses and usurpations, pursuing invariably the same object evinces a design to reduce them under absolute despotism, it is their right, it is their duty, to throw off such government, and to provide new guards for their future security.—Such has been the patient sufferance of these Colonies; and such is now the necessity which constrains them to alter their former systems of government. The history of the present King of Great Britain is a history of repeated injuries and usurpations, all having in direct object the establishment of an absolute tyranny over these States: To prove this, let facts be submitted to a candid world.

He has refused his assent to laws, the most wholesome and necessary for the public good.

He has forbidden his Governors to pass laws of immediate and pressing importance, unless suspended in their operation till his assent should be obtained; and when so suspended, he has utterly neglected to attend to them.

He has refused to pass other laws for the accomodation of large districts of people, unless those people would relinquish the right of representation in the legislature, a right inestimable to them and formidable to tyrants only.

He has called together legislative bodies at places unusual, uncomfortable, and distant from the depository of their public records, for the sole purpose of fatiguing them into compliance with his measures.

He has dissolved Representative Houses repeatedly, for opposing with manly firmness his invasions on the rights of the people.

He has refused for a long time, after such dissolutions, to cause others to be elected; whereby the legislative powers, incapable of annihilation, have returned to the people at large for their exercise; the State remaining in the mean time exposed to all the dangers of invasion from without, and convulsions within.

He has endeavoured to prevent the population of these States; for that purpose obstructing the laws for naturalization of foreigners; refusing to pass others to encourage their migrations hither, and raising the conditions of new appropriations of lands.

He has obstructed the administration of justice, by refusing his assent to laws for establishing judiciary powers.

He has made judges dependent on his will alone, for the tenure of their offices, and the amount and payment of their salaries.

He has erected a multitude of new offices, and sent hither swarms of officers to harass our people, and eat out their substance.

He has kept among us, in times of peace, standing armies without the consent of our legislatures.

He has affected to render the military independent of and superior to the civil power.

He has combined with others to subject us to a jurisdiction foreign to our constitution, and unacknowledged by our laws; giving his assent to their acts of pretended legislation:

For quartering large bodies of armed troops among us:

For protecting them, by a mock trial, from punishment for any murders which they should commit on the inhabitants of these States:

For cutting off our trade with all parts of the world:

For imposing taxes on us without our consent:

For depriving us in many cases, of the benefits of trial by jury:

For transporting us beyond seas to be tried for pretended offenses:

For abolishing the free system of English laws in a neighbouring province, establishing therein an arbitrary government, and enlarging its boundaries so as to render it at once an example and fit instrument for introducing the same absolute rule into these colonies:

For taking away our charters, abolishing our most valuable laws, and altering fundamentally the forms of our governments:

For suspending our own legislatures, and declaring themselves invested with power to legislate for us in all cases whatsoever.

He has abdicated government here, by declaring us out of his protection and waging war against us.

He has plundered our seas, ravaged our coasts, burnt our towns, and destroyed the lives of our people.

He is at this time transporting large armies of foreign mercenaries to complete the works of death, desolation and tyranny, already begun with circumstances of cruelty and perfidy scarcely paralleled in the most barbarous ages, and totally unworthy the head of a civilized nation.

He has constrained our fellow citizens taken captive on the high seas to bear arms against their country, to become the executioners of their friends and brethren, or to fall themselves by their hands.

He has excited domestic insurrections amongst us, and has endeavoured to bring on the inhabitants of our frontiers, the merciless Indian savages, whose known rule of warfare is an undistinguished destruction of all ages, sexes and conditions.

In every stage of these oppressions we have petitioned for redress in the most humble terms: Our repeated petitions have been answered only by repeated injury. A prince, whose character is thus marked by every act which may define a tyrant, is unfit to be the ruler of a free people.

Nor have we been wanting in attentions to our British brethren. We have warned them from time to time of attempts by their legislature to extend an unwarrantable jurisdiction over us. We have reminded them of the circumstances of our emigration and settlement here. We have appealed to their native justice and magnanimity, and we have conjured them by the ties of our common kindred to disavow these usurpations which, would inevitably interrupt our connections and correspondence. They too have been deaf to the voice of justice and of consanguinity. We must, therefore, acquiesce in the necessity which denounces our separation, and hold them, as we hold the rest of mankind, enemies in war, in peace friends.

WE, THEREFORE, the Representatives of the United States of America, in General Congress, Assembled, appealing to the Supreme Judge of the world for the rectitude of our intentions, do, in the name, and by authority of the good people of these Colonies, solemnly publish and declare, That these United Colonies are, and of right ought to be FREE AND INDEPENDENT STATES; that they are absolved from all allegiance to the British Crown, and that all political connection between them and the State of Great Britain, is and ought to be totally dissolved; and that as free and independent States, they have full power to levy war, conclude peace, contract alliances, establish commerce, and to do all other acts and things which independent States may of right do. And for the support of this Declaration, with a firm reliance on the protection of Divine Providence, we mutually pledge to each other our lives, our fortunes and our sacred honor.

John Hancock.

Button Gwinnett	Thos. Nelson jr.	Tho M:Kean
Lyman Hall	Francis Lightfoot Lee	Wm. Floyd
Geo Walton.	Carter Braxton	Phil. Livingston
Wm. Hooper	Robt. Morris	Frans. Lewis
Joseph Hewes,	John Adams	Lewis Morris
John Penn	Robt. Treat Paine	Richd. Stockton
Edward Rutledge.	Elbridge Gerry	Jno Witherspoon
Thos. Heyward Junr.	Step. Hopkins	Fras. Hopkinson
Thomas Lynch Junr.	William Ellery	John Hart
Arthur Middleton	Benjamin Rush	Abra Clark
Samuel Chase	Benja. Franklin	Josiah Bartlett
Wm. Paca	John Morton	Wm: Whipple
Thos. Stone	Geo Clymer	Saml. Adams
Charles Carroll of Carrollton	Jas. Smith.	Roger Sherman
George Wythe	Geo. Taylor	Saml. Huntington
Richard Henry Lee	James Wilson	Wm. Williams
Th: Jefferson	Geo. Ross	Oliver Wolcott
Benja. Harrison	Caesar Rodney	Matthew Thornton
	Geo Read	

Setting Up a Government

Starting here, you can read the Constitution of the United States just as it was written in 1787. Some parts of the Constitution, however, are no longer in effect. They have been changed by later amendments. These parts of the Constitution appear in *italic* type. Beside the Constitution, inside the tan block, are explanations that will help you with your reading.

Constitution of the United States of America

PREAMBLE

WE THE PEOPLE of the United States, in order to form a more perfect Union, establish justice, insure domestic tranquility, provide for the common defense, promote the general welfare, and secure the blessings of liberty to ourselves and our posterity, do ordain and establish this Constitution for the United States of America.

ARTICLE I

SECTION 1. All legislative powers herein granted shall be vested in a Congress of the United States, which shall consist of a Senate and House of Representatives.

SECTION 2. The House of Representatives shall be composed of members chosen every second year by the people of the several States, and the electors in each State shall have the qualifications requisite for electors of the most numerous branch of the State Legislature.

PREAMBLE
The Preamble says that the people have the power to set up the government. It also tells why they set up a new government: (1) to bind the states together, (2) to see that everyone is treated fairly by the laws, (3) to keep peace in the country, (4) to defend the country against foreign enemies, (5) to work for the good of all the people, and (6) to give the people freedom for generations to come.

ARTICLE I   MAKING LAWS
Section 1.   Congress
Lawmaking power   The power to make laws belongs to Congress. But Congress can make only those laws permitted by the Constitution. Congress has two parts—the Senate and the House of Representatives.

Section 2.   The House of Representatives
Choosing members   Members of the House of Representatives are elected from each state every two years. Anyone a state allows to vote for members of the state legislature must also be allowed to vote for members of the House of Representatives.

No person shall be a representative who shall not have attained to the age of twenty-five years, and been seven years a citizen of the United States, and who shall not, when elected, be an inhabitant of that State in which he shall be chosen.

Representatives *and direct taxes* shall be apportioned among the several States which may be included within this Union, according to their respective numbers, *which shall be determined by adding to the whole number of free persons, including those bound to service for a term of years, and excluding Indians not taxed, three-fifths of all other persons.* The actual enumeration shall be made within three years after the first meeting of the Congress of the United States, and within every subsequent term of ten years, in such manner as they shall by law direct. The number of representatives shall not exceed one for every thirty thousand, but each State shall have at least one representative; and until such enumeration shall be made, the State of New Hampshire shall be entitled to choose three, Massachusetts eight, Rhode Island and Providence Plantations one, Connecticut five, New York six, New Jersey four, Pennsylvania eight, Delaware one, Maryland six, Virginia ten, North Carolina five, South Carolina five, and Georgia three.

Who may be a representative   A representative must be at least 25 years of age, must have been a United States citizen for at least 7 years, and must live in the state he or she represents.

Representation based on population   The number of representatives each state has in the House of Representatives is based on the number of people living in the state. At the time the Constitution was written, taxes were collected by each state government to be paid to the United States government. These taxes were also based on the number of people living in the state. This rule was changed later as far as income taxes were concerned. The rules for counting the number of people living in a state also changed. Today all the people living in each state are counted. Slavery is against the law today. Indians are citizens, so they are now counted. Congress must count the number of people in the states every ten years. No matter how few people a state has, it gets at least one representative. Since 1929, the total size of the House of Representatives has been set at 435.

When vacancies happen in the representation from any State, the Executive authority thereof shall issue writs of election to fill such vacancies.

The House of Representatives shall choose their Speaker and other officers; and shall have the sole power of impeachment.

SECTION 3. The Senate of the United States shall be composed of two senators from each State, *chosen by the legislature thereof,* for six years and each senator shall have one vote.

Immediately after they shall be assembled in consequence of the first election, they shall be divided as equally as may be into three classes. The seats of the senators of the first class shall be vacated at the expiration of the second year, of the second class at the expiration of the fourth year, and of the third class at the expiration of the sixth year, so that one-third may be chosen every second year; and if vacancies happen by resignation, or otherwise, during the recess of the legislature of any State, the executive thereof may make temporary appointments until the next meeting of the legislature, which shall then fill such vacancies.

Filling vacancies   A vacancy exists when a representative dies or resigns before his or her term has ended. Then the state's governor must call for a special election to replace the representative.

Choosing officers; impeachment   Members of the House of Representatives choose their own leaders. Their leaders include a Speaker, or chairperson. Only the House of Representatives has the power of impeachment. That is, the House of Representatives may bring charges of serious misbehavior against any official of the United States government.

Section 3.   The Senate
Choosing members   Each state has two senators. Each senator serves a six-year term and has one vote. Before 1913, senators were chosen by state legislatures. Since then, senators have been chosen by the voters of each state.

Three groups of senators   During the first years under the Constitution, senators were divided into three groups. One group served for six years; one group served for four years; one group served for two years. In this way, their terms did not end at the same time. All senators are now elected for six-year terms. However, only one third are chosen at a time.

No person shall be a senator who shall not have attained to the age of thirty years, and been nine years a citizen of the United States, and who shall not, when elected, be an inhabitant of that State for which he shall be chosen.

The Vice President of the United States shall be President of the Senate, but shall have no vote, unless they be equally divided.

The Senate shall choose their other officers, and also a President pro tempore, in the absence of the Vice President, or when he shall exercise the office of President of the United States.

The Senate shall have the sole power to try all impeachments. When sitting for that purpose, they shall be on oath or affirmation. When the President of the United States is tried, the Chief Justice shall preside: And no person shall be convicted without the concurrence of two thirds of the members present.

Judgment in cases of impeachment shall not extend further than to removal from office, and disqualification to hold and enjoy any office or honor, trust or profit under the United States: but the party convicted shall nevertheless be liable and subject to indictment, trial, judgment and punishment, according to law.

Who may be a senator A senator must be at least 30 years of age, must have been a United States citizen for at least nine years, and must live in the state that he or she represents.

President of the Senate The Vice President of the United States is the president, or chairperson, of the Senate. However, the Vice President can vote only when there is a tie vote.

Other officers Members of the Senate choose all their other leaders. One of these, the President pro tempore, is the chairperson when the Vice President is absent. *Pro tempore* means "for a time."

Impeachment trials The Senate holds a trial for any official impeached by the House of Representatives. The official is found guilty if two thirds of the senators present vote him or her guilty. If the President of the United States is on trial, the Chief Justice of the United States acts as chairperson of the Senate. The Chief Justice is the highest official on the Supreme Court.

Punishment If an official is found guilty in an impeachment trial, the Senate can order the official out of office. The Senate can also order that the person never serve in the government again. After being put out of office, the person can be tried in a regular court for the crimes that the Senate has already judged.

SECTION 4. The times, places and manner of holding elections for senators and representatives, shall be prescribed in each State by the legislature thereof; but the Congress may at any time by law make or alter such regulations, *except as to the places of choosing senators*.

The Congress shall assemble at least once in every year, *and such meeting shall be on the first Monday in December, unless they shall by law appoint a different day*.

SECTION 5. Each house shall be the judge of the elections, returns and qualifications of its own members, and a majority of each shall constitute a quorum to do business; but a smaller number may adjourn from day to day, and may be authorized to compel the attendance of absent members, in such manner, and under such penalties as each house may provide.

Each house may determine the rules of its proceedings, punish its members for disorderly behaviour, and, with the concurrence of two-thirds, expel a member.

Section 4. Elections and Meetings of Congress

How elections are held The states may make rules about elections to Congress. But Congress may change state election laws. As a result of later changes, both senators and representatives are chosen by the people.

Meetings of Congress Congress must meet at least once a year. A later amendment changed the beginning of each session from the first Monday in December to January 3.

Section 5. Rules of Congress

How Congress is organized Both the House of Representatives and the Senate can set rules for membership. Each can keep out any newly elected member who does not meet those rules. Neither the House nor the Senate can carry out official business unless there is a quorum—that is, unless more than half the members are present. If there is no quorum, members adjourn, or end their meeting for the day. Both houses may use penalties to force absent members to attend.

Rules of Congress Each house of Congress may make its own rules. Each may punish members who do not obey those rules. In both houses, a member can be expelled, or required to leave, by two thirds of those present.

Each house shall keep a journal of its proceedings, and from time to time publish the same, excepting such parts as may in their judgment require secrecy; and the yeas and the nays of the members of either house on any question shall, at the desire of one-fifth of those present, be entered on the journal.

Neither house, during the session of Congress, shall, without the consent of the other, adjourn for more than three days, nor to any other place than that in which the two houses shall be sitting.

SECTION 6. The senators and representatives shall receive a compensation for their services, to be ascertained by law, and paid out of the Treasury of the United States. They shall in all cases, except treason, felony and breach of the peace, be privileged from arrest during their attendance at the session of their respective houses, and in going to and returning from the same; and for any speech or debate in either house, they shall not be questioned in any other place.

No senator or representative shall, during the time for which he was elected, be appointed to any civil office under the authority of the United States, which shall have been created, or the emoluments whereof shall have been increased during such time; and no person holding any office under the United States, shall be a member of either house during his continuance in office.

Journal of meetings of Congress Each house must keep a record of what goes on at its meetings, and from time to time those records must be published. But members may decide to keep some things secret. How members vote on a question is published only if one fifth of the members there agree to do so.

Ending a meeting of Congress Neither house may adjourn, or end a meeting, for more than three days or move to another city unless the other house agrees.

Section 6. What Members of Congress Can and Cannot Do

Pay and privileges of members Members of both houses are paid out of the United States Treasury. The amount they are paid is decided by law. Members cannot be arrested at meetings of Congress or on their way to and from meetings unless they are suspected of treason, serious crimes, or disturbing the peace. They cannot be punished for anything they say in their meetings except by other members of their house.

Holding other official positions No one can become a member of Congress without giving up other national positions. No member can take a position in the national government if that position was created, or the pay for that position was increased, while the member served in Congress.

SECTION 7. All bills for raising revenue shall originate in the House of Representatives; but the Senate may propose or concur with amendments as on other bills.

Every bill which shall have passed the House of Representatives and the Senate, shall, before it become a law, be presented to the President of the United States; if he approves he shall sign it, but if not he shall return it, with his objections to that house in which it shall have originated, who shall enter the objections at large on their journal, and proceed to reconsider it. If after such reconsideration two thirds of that House shall agree to pass the bill, it shall be sent, together with the objections, to the other House, by which it shall likewise be reconsidered, and if approved by two thirds of that House, it shall become a law. But in all such cases the votes of both Houses shall be determined by yeas and nays, and the names of the persons voting for and against the bill shall be entered on the journal of each House respectively. If any bill shall not be returned by the President within ten days (Sundays excepted) after it shall have been presented to him, the same shall be a law, in like manner as if he had signed it, unless the Congress by their adjournment prevent its return, in which case it shall not be a law.

Section 7. Ways of Passing Laws

Taxes Only the House of Representatives may propose a law for raising money. But the Senate has the right to make changes in such proposals.

How a bill becomes a law After a bill, or proposed law, has passed both houses of Congress, it must be sent to the President. If the President signs the bill, it becomes law. If the President does not approve of the bill, he or she may veto it—that is, refuse to sign it. The President then sends the bill, with a list of reasons stating why he or she does not approve of it, to the house that passed it first. The members of that house vote on the bill again. If two thirds pass it a second time, it is sent to the other house, along with the President's reasons for not wanting it to be law. If two thirds of that house also favor the bill, it becomes law. The President's reasons for not wanting the law must be published. The records of Congress must also show how each member voted. The President has ten days (not counting Sundays) to consider a bill. If the President takes longer, the bill becomes law without his or her signature as long as Congress has not adjourned in the meantime. If Congress has adjourned, the unsigned bill does not become law. This is known as a pocket veto.

Every order, resolution, or vote to which the concurrence of the Senate and House of Representatives may be necessary (except on a question of adjournment) shall be presented to the President of the United States; and before the same shall take effect, shall be approved by him, or being disapproved by him, shall be repassed by two thirds of the Senate and House of Representatives, according to the rules and limitations prescribed in the case of a bill.

SECTION 8. The Congress shall have power to lay and collect taxes, duties, imposts and excises, to pay the debts and provide for the common defense and general welfare of the United States; but all duties, imposts and excises shall be uniform throughout the United States.

To borrow money on the credit of the United States;

To regulate commerce with foreign nations, and among the several States, and with the Indian tribes;

To establish a uniform rule of naturalization, and uniform laws on the subject of bankruptcies throughout the United States;

Actions that need the President's approval Any action that needs the approval of both the House and the Senate must also be sent to the President for approval the same way that bills are. The only exceptions are votes to adjourn Congress.

Section 8.   Powers of Congress
Taxing the people Congress may raise taxes in order to pay the nation's debts, defend the nation, and provide for the good of all the people. Those taxes must be the same throughout the United States.

Borrowing money Congress may borrow money to run the national government.

Trade relations Congress may control trade, transportation, communication, and related matters with other countries, among the states, and with Indian groups.

Becoming a citizen and paying debts Congress decides how citizens of foreign countries can become citizens of the United States. Congress may make laws for the whole country concerning the treatment of those who cannot pay their debts.

To coin money, regulate the value thereof, and of foreign coin, and fix the standard of weights and measures;

Coining money Congress may coin, or make, money and say how much it is worth. It may also put a value on foreign money. Congress also has the power to set weights and measures so they will be the same everywhere.

To provide for the punishment of counterfeiting the securities and current coin of the United States;

Punishment for making fake money Congress may pass laws to punish those who make false bonds, stamps, or money.

To establish post offices and post roads;

Rules concerning mail Congress may set up post offices and build the roads over which the mail travels.

To promote the progress of science and useful arts, by securing for limited times to authors and inventors the exclusive right to their respective writings and discoveries;

Protecting people's work Congress may help science, industry, and the arts by making laws that protect the works of authors, composers, artists, and inventors. These laws would punish other people who try to copy the original work without permission.

To constitute tribunals inferior to the Supreme Court;

Setting up lower courts Congress may set up national courts that have less authority than the Supreme Court of the United States.

To define and punish piracies and felonies committed on the high seas, and offenses against the law of nations;

Laws in places outside the United States Congress may decide what acts committed at sea are a crime and how they are to be punished. It may also make laws about crimes in which foreign countries and foreign citizens are involved.

To declare war, grant letters of marque and reprisal, and make rules concerning captures on land and water;

Declaring war Congress, and only Congress, may declare war. Until 1856, it could also set rules about warfare carried on by private citizens. Such warfare is no longer allowed.

To raise and support armies, but no appropriation of money to that use shall be for a longer term than two years;

To provide and maintain a Navy;

To make rules for the government and regulation of the land and naval forces;

To provide for calling forth the militia to execute the laws of the Union, suppress insurrections and repel invasions;

To provide for organizing, arming, and disciplining the militia, and for governing such part of them as may be employed in the service of the United States, reserving to the States respectively, the appointment of the officers, and the authority of training the militia according to the discipline prescribed by Congress;

To exercise exclusive legislation in all cases whatsoever, over such district (not exceeding ten miles square) as may, by cession of particular States, and the acceptance of Congress, become the seat of the Government of the United States, and to exercise like authority over all places purchased by the consent of the legislature of the State in which the same shall be, for the erection of forts, magazines, arsenals, dock-yards, and other needful buildings;—And

Supporting armed forces Congress may raise and support armed forces. It cannot, however, provide money for the army for more than two years at a time. Congress may also make rules for the organization and control of the armed forces.

Rules about militia Congress may call out militias to enforce national laws, put down rebellions, and drive out invaders. Militias are groups of citizen-soldiers in the various states. Congress may organize the militias, furnish weapons to them, and make rules for them while they are in the service of the United States. Each state may appoint officers of its militia, but it must train the militia as Congress directs.

Control of the capital Congress may make all the laws for governing the District of Columbia, which includes the national capital. Congress shall govern all places bought from the states for use as forts, arsenals, navy yards, and public buildings.

To make all laws which shall be necessary and proper for carrying into execution the foregoing powers, and all other powers vested by this Constitution in the Government of the United States, or in any department or officer thereof.

SECTION 9. The migration or importation of such persons as any of the States now existing shall think proper to admit, shall not be prohibited by the Congress prior to the year one thousand eight hundred and eight, but a tax or duty may be imposed on such importation, not exceeding ten dollars for each person.

The privilege of the writ of habeas corpus shall not be suspended, unless when in cases of rebellion or invasion the public safety may require it.

No bill of attainder or ex post facto law shall be passed.

No capitation, or other direct, tax shall be laid, unless in proportion to the census or enumeration herein before directed to be taken.

Changing laws of the Constitution
Congress may make any laws needed to carry out the powers given to the government of the United States by the Constitution. This part of the Constitution is known as the elastic clause, because it can be stretched to fit the changing needs of the nation.

Section 9.   Powers Denied Congress
Tax on slaves   Before 1808, Congress could not outlaw the slave trade. But it could tax the people who brought slaves into the country. The tax could not be more than ten dollars for each slave.

Writ of habeas corpus   Only when the country is in danger from a rebellion or invasion can Congress keep courts from issuing writs of habeas corpus. A writ of habeas corpus forces a jailor to bring a prisoner to court so that a judge can decide whether that person is being held lawfully.

Punishing individuals   Congress can never pass a law punishing a particular person. Congress cannot pass a law punishing people for doing something that was lawful at the time they did it.

Direct taxes   Congress cannot set a capitation, or direct tax on individuals, except in proportion to population figures. The only exception is the income tax. Congress may not tax goods sent from one state to another.

No tax or duty shall be laid on articles exported from any State.

No preference shall be given by any regulation of commerce or revenue to the ports of one State over those of another: nor shall vessels bound to, or from, one State, be obliged to enter, clear, or pay duties in another.

Trade taxes Congress may not favor one state or city over the others in matters of trade. Ships from any state may enter the ports of any other state without paying charges.

No money shall be drawn from the Treasury; but in consequence of appropriations made by law; and a regular statement and account of the receipts and expenditures of all public money shall be published from time to time.

Spending government money Congress cannot spend government money without passing a bill for that purpose. An account of all money taken in and spent must be made public.

No title of nobility shall be granted by the United States: And no person holding any office of profit or trust under them, shall, without the consent of the Congress, accept of any present, emolument, office, or title, of any kind whatever, from any King, Prince, or foreign State.

Official titles Congress may not create titles such as that of lord, duchess, or count. No national official can accept a title, gift, or position from another country without the permission of Congress.

SECTION 10. No State shall enter into any treaty, alliance, or confederation; grant letters of marque and reprisal; coin money; emit bills of credit; make any thing but gold and silver coin a tender in payment of debts; pass any bill of attainder, ex post facto law, or law impairing the obligation of contracts, or grant any title of nobility.

Section 10.   Powers Denied to the States
What states cannot do No state can make treaties with foreign countries. No state can give private citizens permission to wage a war. No state can coin money. These powers belong to the national government. Like the national government, a state government may not punish people for things that were lawful when they did them, and it may not grant titles of nobility.

No State shall, without the consent of the Congress, lay any imposts or duties on imports or exports, except what may be absolutely necessary for executing its inspection laws: and the net produce of all duties and imposts, laid by any State on imports or exports, shall be for the use of the Treasury of the United States; and all such laws shall be subject to the revision and control of the Congress.

No State shall, without the consent of Congress, lay any duty of tonnage, keep troops, or ships of war in time of peace, enter into any agreement or compact with another State, or with a foreign power, or engage in war, unless actually invaded, or in such imminent danger as will not admit of delay.

ARTICLE II

SECTION 1. The executive power shall be vested in a President of the United States of America. He shall hold his office during the term of four years, and, together with the Vice President, chosen for the same term, be elected, as follows:

Each State, shall appoint, in such manner as the legislature thereof may direct, a number of electors, equal to the whole number of senators and representatives to which the State may be entitled in the Congress; but no senator or representative, or person holding an office of trust or profit under the United States, shall be appointed an elector.

States' power to charge inspection fees A state cannot tax goods entering or leaving the state without the permission of Congress. But states may charge an inspection fee. Any profit from that fee must go to the United States Treasury. Congress has the power to change state inspection laws.

More things states cannot do Unless Congress gives permission, no state may tax ships, keep troops other than a militia, or keep warships in peacetime. States cannot ally with other states or with foreign countries unless Congress agrees. States cannot go to war without the permission of Congress unless invaded or in such danger that delay is impossible.

ARTICLE II THE EXECUTIVE BRANCH
Section 1. President and Vice President
Terms of the President and Vice President The President of the United States enforces the nation's laws. The President serves a four-year term. The Vice President also serves for four years.

The selection of electors The President and Vice President are to be chosen by electors in each state. These electors are selected according to rules set by state legislatures. The electors from all the states form the electoral college. The number of electors in each state is equal to the number of representatives and senators the state has in Congress. No person who has a position in the national government may be an elector.

The electors shall meet in their respective States, and vote by ballot for two persons, of whom one at least shall not be an inhabitant of the same State with themselves. And they shall make a list of all the persons voted for, and of the number of votes for each; which list they shall sign and certify, and transmit sealed to the seat of the Government of the United States, directed to the President of the Senate. The President of the Senate shall, in the presence of the Senate and House of Representatives, open all the certificates, and the votes shall then be counted. The person having the greatest number of votes shall be the President, if such number be a majority of the whole number of electors appointed; and if there be more than one who have such majority, and have an equal number of votes, then the House of Representatives shall immediately choose by ballot one of them for President; and if no person have a majority, then from the five highest on the list the said House shall in like manner choose the President. But in choosing the President, the votes shall be taken by States, the representation from each State having one vote; a quorum for this purpose shall consist of a member or members from two thirds of the States, and a majority of all the States shall be necessary to a choice. In every case, after the choice of the President, the person having the greatest number of votes of the electors shall be the Vice President. But if there should remain two or more who have equal votes, the Senate shall choose from them by ballot the Vice President.

Duties of the electors   The electors, meeting in their respective states, vote for President and Vice President on one ballot. Their votes are recorded and then sent to the President of the Senate, who counts them in front of both houses of Congress. The candidate with the highest number of electoral votes becomes President, and the one with the second highest total becomes Vice President. If there is a tie, or no candidate has a majority, the House of Representatives shall choose the President from the five candidates with the highest totals. In the balloting, each state has one vote. At least two thirds of the states must be present. The candidate who wins a majority of all states becomes President. The person who comes in second will be the Vice President. This section of the Constitution was changed by a later amendment.

The Congress may determine the time of choosing the electors, and the day on which they shall give their votes; which day shall be the same throughout the United States.

No person except a natural born citizen, or a citizen of the United States, at the time of the adoption of this Constitution, shall be eligible to the office of President; neither shall any person be eligible to that office who shall not have attained to the age of thirty-five years, and been fourteen years a resident within the United States.

In case of the removal of the President from office, or of his death, resignation, or inability to discharge the powers and duties of the said office, the same shall devolve on the Vice President, *and the Congress may by law provide for the case of removal, death, resignation, or inability, both of the President and Vice President, declaring what officer shall then act as President, and such officer shall act accordingly, until the disability be removed, or a President shall be elected.*

The President shall, at stated times, receive for his services, a compensation, which shall neither be increased nor diminished during the period for which he shall have been elected, and he shall not receive within that period any other emolument from the United States, or any of them.

Election day   Congress can decide on what day electors are to be chosen and on what day they are to cast their ballots. Each day is to be the same throughout the United States. (The day set for choosing electors is the first Tuesday after the first Monday in November. The electors cast their ballots on the first Monday after the second Wednesday in December.)

Qualifications for President   The President must be a citizen of the United States by birth or must have become a citizen by the time the Constitution was adopted. He or she must be at least 35 years old and must have lived in the United States for 14 or more years.

Who can take the place of the President   If the President dies, resigns, or is unable to carry out the duties of the office, the Vice President becomes President. Congress can decide by law who becomes President when neither the President nor the Vice President can serve. This part of the Constitution was changed by a later amendment.

The President's salary   The salary of a President cannot be raised or lowered during his or her term of office. The President cannot receive any other salary from national or state governments.

Before he enter on the execution of his office, he shall take the following oath or affirmation:—"I do solemnly swear (or affirm) that I will faithfully execute the office of President of the United States, and will to the best of my ability, preserve, protect and defend the Constitution of the United States."

SECTION 2. The President shall be Commander in Chief of the Army and Navy of the United States, and of the militia of the several States, when called into the actual service of the United States; he may require the opinion, in writing, of the principal officer in each of the Executive Departments, upon any subject relating to the duties of their respective offices, and he shall have power to grant reprieves and pardons for offenses against the United States, except in cases of impeachment.

He shall have power, by and with the advice and consent of the Senate, to make treaties, provided two thirds of the Senators present concur; and he shall nominate, and by and with the advice and consent of the Senate, shall appoint ambassadors, other public ministers and consuls, Judges of the Supreme Court, and all other officers of the United States, whose appointments are not herein otherwise provided for, and which shall be established by law: but the Congress may by law vest the appointment of such inferior officers, as they think proper, in the President alone, in the courts of law, or in the heads of departments.

The President's oath of office   Before starting a term of office, the President is to make a solemn promise to carry out faithfully the duties of President and to protect the government that was set up by the Constitution.

Section 2.   Powers of the President

Military and civil powers   The President is Commander in Chief of the armed forces of the United States. He or she is also the Commander in Chief of the state militias when they are called to national service. The President may order written reports from Cabinet officers about the work of their departments. The President may pardon people accused of crimes against the national government or delay their punishment. The President cannot, however, pardon or delay the punishment of an impeached government official.

Making treaties and appointing officers The President can make treaties with foreign countries. At least two thirds of the Senators present must vote for each treaty before it becomes binding.

The President can appoint people to represent the United States in other countries, judges of the Supreme Court, and other government officials unless the Constitution says differently. In each case, a majority of the Senate must vote for the President's choice. Congress may pass laws giving the President, the courts, or heads of government departments the right to select people for less important government positions. The President may appoint individuals to fill open positions that occur

The President shall have power to fill up all vacancies that may happen during the recess of the Senate, by granting commissions which shall expire at the end of their next session.

SECTION 3. He shall from time to time give to the Congress information of the state of the Union, and recommend to their consideration such measures as he shall judge necessary and expedient; he may, on extraordinary occasions, convene both houses, or either of them, and in case of disagreement between them, with respect to the time of adjournment, he may adjourn them to such time as he shall think proper; he shall receive ambassadors and other public ministers; he shall take care that the laws be faithfully executed, and shall commission all the officers of the United States.

SECTION 4. The President, Vice President and all civil officers of the United States, shall be removed from office on impeachment for, and conviction of, treason, bribery, or other high crimes and misdemeanors.

when the Senate is not meeting. These temporary appointments come to an end at the close of the next session of the Senate.

Section 3.   Duties of the President
Other presidential powers   The President is to inform Congress from time to time about the condition of the country. Traditionally the President does so at the beginning of each session of Congress. The speech is called the State of the Union message. In it, the President recommends changes or improvements in government. In emergencies, the President may call meetings of the House of Representatives or the Senate or both. If the two houses of Congress disagree about the ending of a session, the President may end it. The President deals with representatives of other countries. It is the President's duty to see that the laws of the country are obeyed. The President signs official papers appointing individuals to jobs in the national government.

Section 4.   Impeachments
Who can be impeached   The President, Vice President, and other officials of the national government (except members of Congress and military officers) can be removed from office if they are accused of wrongdoing by the House of Representatives and then found guilty by the Senate.

519

ARTICLE III

SECTION 1. The judicial power of the United States, shall be vested in one Supreme Court, and in such inferior courts as the Congress may from time to time ordain and establish. The judges, both of the supreme and inferior courts, shall hold their offices during good behaviour, and shall, at stated times, receive for their services, a compensation, which shall not be diminished during their continuance in office.

SECTION 2. The judicial power shall extend to all cases, in law and equity, arising under this Constitution, the laws of the United States, and treaties made, or which shall be made, under their authority;—to all cases affecting ambassadors, other public ministers and consuls;—to all cases of admiralty and maritime jurisdiction;—to controversies to which the United States shall be a party;—to controversies between two or more States;—*between a State and citizens of another State;*—between citizens of different States,—between citizens of the same State claiming lands under grants of different States, and between a State, or the citizens thereof, and foreign States, citizens or subjects.

In all cases affecting ambassadors, other public ministers and consuls, and those in which a State shall be a party, the Supreme Court shall have original jurisdiction. In all the other cases before mentioned, the Supreme Court shall have appellate jurisdiction, both as to law and fact, with such exceptions, and

ARTICLE III THE JUDICIAL BRANCH
Section 1. Judicial Power

Judges and what they can do The Supreme Court of the United States makes the final decisions in matters of law. Congress may set up other national courts with less power than the Supreme Court. Judges of all national courts hold office for life or until they are proved guilty of wrongful acts. Their salaries cannot be lowered while they are in office.

Section 2. Cases Heard in the United States Courts

Powers of the federal courts The national courts settle disputes that have to do with the Constitution, laws of the United States, treaties, and laws about ships and shipping. These courts also settle legal disputes between people of different states, disputes in which people of the same state claim land in other states, and disputes between a state or citizen of a state and a foreign country. Until a later amendment was passed, the national courts also settled disputes between a state and a citizen of another state.

Jurisdiction of the Courts If a representative of a foreign country or a state is involved in a dispute, the trial may go directly to the Supreme Court. All other cases described above are tried in a lower national court first. These cases are brought to the Supreme Court only if one of the parties objects to the decision of the lower court and appeals to the Supreme Court. After the case has been tried in the Supreme Court, there is no higher court to which either side may appeal.

under such regulations as the Congress shall make.

The trial of all crimes, except in cases of impeachment, shall be by jury; and such trial shall be held in the State where the said crimes shall have been committed; but when not committed within any State, the trial shall be at such place or places as the Congress may by law have directed.

SECTION 3. Treason against the United States, shall consist only in levying war against them, or in adhering to their enemies, giving them aid and comfort. No person shall be convicted of treason unless on the testimony of two witnesses to the same overt act, or on confession in open court.

The Congress shall have power to declare the punishment of treason, but no attainder of treason shall work corruption of blood, or forfeiture except during the life of the person attainted.

ARTICLE IV

SECTION 1. Full faith and credit shall be given in each State to the public acts, records, and judicial proceedings of every other State. And the Congress may by general laws prescribe the manner in which such acts, records and proceedings shall be proved, and the effect thereof.

SECTION 2. The citizens of each State shall be entitled to all privileges and immunities of citizens in the several States.

Trial by jury for criminal cases Except for an impeached official, anyone accused of a crime by the national government has the right to a trial by jury. The trial must be held in the state where the crime was committed. If the crime took place outside of any state—at sea, for example—the trial is to be held in a place Congress has chosen by law.

Section 3. Treason
Definition of treason Treason is carrying on war against the United States or helping the enemies of the United States. No one can be punished for treason unless two or more witnesses swear they saw the same act of treason or unless the accused person confesses to the crime in court.

Punishment for treason Congress can pass laws fixing the punishment for treason. However, the family of a person found guilty of treason cannot be punished in any way.

ARTICLE IV   THE STATES AND THE NATION
Section 1.   Official Acts of the States
Laws of other states Each state must respect the laws, records, and court decisions of all other states.

Section 2.   Rights of Citizens of Other States
Rights of a person legally in another state Citizens of one state who move to or do business in another state have the same rights as citizens who live in that state.

A person charged in any State with treason, felony, or other crime, who shall flee from justice, and be found in another State, shall on demand of the executive authority of the State from which he fled, be delivered up, to be removed to the State having jurisdiction of the crime.

No person held to service or labour in one State, under the laws thereof, escaping into another, shall, in consequence of any law or regulation therein, be discharged from such service or labour, but shall be delivered up on claim of the party to whom such service or labour may be due.

Section 3. New States may be admitted by the Congress into this Union; but no new State shall be formed or erected within the jurisdiction of any other State; nor any State be formed by the junction of two or more States, or parts of States, without the consent of the legislatures of the States concerned as well as of the Congress.

The Congress shall have power to dispose of and make all needful rules and regulations respecting the Territory or other property belonging to the United States; and nothing in this Constitution shall be so construed as to prejudice any claims of the United States, or of any particular State.

Rights of a person illegally in another state A person accused of a crime in one state and found in another is to be returned for trial to the state in which the crime was committed. The request for the accused person's return must come from the governor of that state.

Rights of a slave illegally in another state Slaves did not become free by escaping to a state that did not allow slavery. Instead, they had to be returned to their owners. Because slavery is no longer legal, this part of the Constitution is no longer in effect.

Section 3. New States and Territories
Adding new states Congress has the right to add new states to the United States. No state can be divided to make a new state without the consent of Congress and the original state. No new state can be formed from parts of two or more states without the agreement of the legislatures of all the states involved and without the agreement of Congress.

National territory Congress has the power to make rules about all government lands and property. Congress also may set up a government for any territory before it becomes a state.

SECTION 4. The United States shall guarantee to every State in this Union a republican form of Government, and shall protect each of them against invasion; and on application of the legislature, or of the executive (when the legislature cannot be convened) against domestic violence.

Protecting the States It is the duty of the national government to see that every state has a government in which the people rule and that each state is protected against invasion. If a state asks the national government for help in putting down a riot or other disturbance, the United States must provide that help.

ARTICLE V

The Congress, whenever two thirds of both Houses shall deem it necessary, shall propose amendments to this Constitution, or on the application of the legislatures of two thirds of the several States, shall call a convention for proposing amendments, which, in either case, shall be valid to all intents and purposes, as part of this Constitution, when ratified by the legislatures of three fourths of the several States, or by conventions in three fourths thereof, as the one or the other mode of ratification may be proposed by the Congress; provided that no amendment which may be made prior to the year one thousand eight hundred and eight shall in any manner affect the first and fourth clauses in the Ninth Section of the First Article; and that no State, without its consent, shall be deprived of its equal suffrage in the Senate.

ARTICLE V AMENDING THE CONSTITUTION

Changing the Constitution The Constitution can be changed by amendment. There are two ways to propose an amendment. An amendment can be proposed (1) by the vote of two thirds of the Senate and two thirds of the House of Representatives or (2) by Congress, called together in a special convention. This happens when two thirds of all state legislatures have asked for the special convention. There are two ways in which the amendment may become part of the Constitution. The amendment becomes part of the Constitution when it is approved (1) by the legislatures of at least three fourths of the states or (2) by special conventions in at least three fourths of the states. Before 1808, no amendment could change the first and fourth clauses in Article I, Section 9. No amendment may take away a state's right to have the same number of senators as other states unless the state affected agrees.

ARTICLE VI

All debts contracted and engagements entered into, before the adoption of this Constitution, shall be as valid against the United States under this Constitution, as under the Confederation.

This Constitution, and the laws of the United States which shall be made in pursuance thereof; and all treaties made, or which shall be made, under the authority of the United States, shall be the supreme law of the land; and the judges in every State shall be bound thereby, any thing in the Constitution or laws of any State to the contrary notwithstanding.

The senators and representatives before mentioned, and the members of the several State legislatures, and all executive and judicial officers, both of the United States and of the several States, shall be bound by oath or affirmation, to support this Constitution; but no religious test shall ever be required as a qualification to any office or public trust under the United States.

ARTICLE VII

The ratification of the conventions of nine States shall be sufficient for the establishment of this Constitution between the States so ratifying the same.

Done in convention by the unanimous consent of the States present the seventeenth day of September in the year of

ARTICLE VI THE SUPREME LAW OF THE LAND

Public debt Loans made by Congress before the Constitution was adopted were to be paid.

Laws of the Constitution The Constitution, the laws made by Congress as permitted by the Constitution, and treaties made by the United States are the highest laws of the United States. Judges must follow these laws even if state laws contradict them. All national government and state government officials must promise to uphold the Constitution and abide by it.

No religious requirements Anyone who meets the requirements to hold a position in the United States government cannot be kept out of the position because of religion.

ARTICLE VII RATIFICATION

Accepting the Constitution When nine states have held conventions and agreed to the Constitution, the government set up by this Constitution shall begin in those states. The states represented in the Constitutional Convention on September 17, 1787, agreed to the Constitution as a plan of government to be proposed to the states. (Only Rhode

our Lord one thousand seven hundred and eighty seven and of the Independence of the United States of America the twelfth. In witness whereof we have here unto subscribed our names.

Go. Washington—*Presid't.*
and deputy from Virginia

Island refused to take part in the Constitutional Convention. The other 12 states chose 65 delegates to the convention; 55 attended most of the meetings. The day the Constitution was signed, 43 delegates were present, but only 39 actually put their signatures on the document.)

Attest William Jackson *Secretary*

New Hampshire
John Langdon
Nicholas Gilman

Massachusetts
Nathaniel Gorham
Rufus King

Connecticut
Wm. Saml. Johnson
Roger Sherman

New York
Alexander Hamilton

New Jersey
Wil: Livingston
David Brearley.
Wm. Paterson.
Jona: Dayton

Pennsylvania
B Franklin
Thomas Mifflin
Robt Morris
Geo. Clymer
Thos. FitzSimons
Jared Ingersoll
James Wilson
Gouv Morris

Delaware
Geo: Read
Gunning Bedford jun
John Dickinson
Richard Bassett
Jaco: Broom

Maryland
James McHenry
Dan of St Thos. Jenifer
Danl. Carroll

Virginia
John Blair—
James Madison Jr.

North Carolina
Wm. Blount
Richd. Dobbs Spaight
Hu Williamson

South Carolina
J. Rutledge
Charles Cotesworth Pinckney
Charles Pinckney
Pierce Butler

Georgia
William Few
Abr Baldwin

Amendments

The First Ten Amendments:
The Bill of Rights

1st Amendment: Religious and Political Freedom

Congress shall make no law respecting an establishment of religion, or prohibiting the free exercise thereof; or abridging the freedom of speech, or of the press; or the right of the people peaceably to assemble, and to petition the Government for a redress of grievances.

2nd Amendment: Right to Bear Arms

A well regulated militia, being necessary to the security of a free State, the right of the people to keep and bear arms, shall not be infringed.

3rd Amendment: Quartering of Soldiers

No soldier shall, in time of peace be quartered in any house, without the consent of the owner, nor in time of war, but in a manner to be prescribed by law.

4th Amendment: Searches and Seizures

The right of the people to be secure in their persons, houses, papers, and effects, against unreasonable searches and seizures, shall not be violated, and no warrants shall issue, but upon probable cause, supported by oath or affirmation, and particularly describing the place to

---

THE FIRST TEN AMENDMENTS: THE BILL OF RIGHTS

1st Amendment   Congress cannot pass the following kinds of laws: laws that would establish an official religion; laws that would keep people from following any religion; laws that would prevent people from speaking freely or publishing their ideas and beliefs; laws that would stop people from meeting peacefully or from asking the government to right a wrong.

2nd Amendment   Because the people have a right to have militias, Congress cannot stop people from keeping and carrying firearms.

3rd Amendment   In peacetime, citizens cannot be forced to give either room or board to soldiers. In wartime, however, Congress may pass a law instructing citizens to give soldiers room and board.

4th Amendment   A person's house or belongings cannot be searched or seized unless a warrant—an official order from a judge—gives permission to do so. A judge cannot issue a warrant unless there is sufficient evidence to indicate that doing so will aid in capturing a criminal. The warrant must describe the place that is to be searched and identify the persons or things that will be seized.

be searched, and the persons or things to be seized.

5th Amendment: Rights of Those Accused of Crimes

No person shall be held to answer for a capital, or otherwise infamous crime, unless on a presentment or indictment of a Grand Jury, except in cases arising in the land of naval forces, or in the militia, when in actual service in time of war or public danger; nor shall any person be subject for the same offense to be twice put in jeopardy of life or limb; nor shall be compelled in any criminal case to be a witness against himself, nor be deprived of life, liberty, or property, without due process of law; nor shall private property be taken for public use, without just compensation.

6th Amendment: Protection in Criminal Courts

In all criminal prosecutions, the accused shall enjoy the right to a speedy and public trial, by an impartial jury of the State and district wherein the crime shall have been committed, which district shall have been previously ascertained by law, and to be informed of the nature and cause of the accusation; to be confronted with the witnesses against him; to have compulsory process for obtaining witnesses in his favor, and to have the assistance of counsel for his defense.

5th Amendment No person may be tried in a national court for a serious crime unless a grand jury has decided there is enough evidence against that individual to warrant a trial. The only individuals not covered by this rule are those serving in the armed forces in time of war or public danger. If a person has been tried in a national court and found innocent of a crime, he or she cannot be tried a second time for the same offense. However, if the offense is a crime under state law, the person can be tried for that offense in a state court. Also, if the offense injures another party, the person accused can be made to pay damages, even though innocent of a crime.

No person can be forced to say anything in national court that would help to prove his or her guilt.

No person can be executed, imprisoned, or fined except as a punishment after a fair trial.

The government cannot take a person's property for public use without paying a fair price for it.

6th Amendment A person accused of a crime must be tried promptly and in public. The trial is held in the district or state where the crime took place. The accused must be told what he or she is being tried for. The accused must be present when witnesses speak against him or her in court. The accused is entitled to call witnesses and to have the help of a lawyer.

7th Amendment: Civil Suits

In suits at common law, where the value in controversy shall exceed twenty dollars, the right of trial by jury shall be preserved, and no fact tried by a jury, shall be otherwise reexamined in any court of the United States, than according to the rules of the common law.

7th Amendment In disputes over property that is worth more than $20, either party can insist on a jury trial or both can agree not to have a jury.

8th Amendment: Bails, Fines, Punishments

Excessive bail shall not be required, nor excessive fines imposed, nor cruel and unusual punishments inflicted.

8th Amendment A person accused of a crime can get out of jail until the trial if he or she hands over a sum of money to the court. This money, called bail, is returned when the accused person appears at the trial. If the accused person fails to appear, the bail is lost. Courts cannot force the accused to pay unreasonably large amounts of bail. A person tried in a national court and found guilty cannot be punished with an unreasonably large fine or unreasonably long prison sentence. That person also cannot be punished in cruel or unusual ways—such as torture or branding.

9th Amendment: Other Rights of the People

The enumeration in the Constitution, of certain rights, shall not be construed to deny or disparage others retained by the people.

9th Amendment The mention of certain rights in the Constitution does not mean that these are the only rights that people have. They still have rights that are not listed in the Constitution.

10th Amendment: Powers Kept by the States or the People

The powers not delegated to the United States by the Constitution, nor prohibited by it to the States, are reserved to the States respectively, or to the people.

10th Amendment All of the powers that are not given by the Constitution to the national government and not denied to the states belong to the states or to the people.

The First Bill of Rights

In 1776, Virginia voted to become independent of Great Britain. Virginians wrote a constitution, and to it they added a bill of rights, the Virginia Declaration of Rights. Thomas Jefferson borrowed many of its ideas and used them in the opening paragraphs of the Declaration of Independence. The Bill of Rights in the United States Constitution was also based on it.

George Mason wrote the Declaration of Rights. The Virginia Constitutional Convention adopted it on June 12, 1776. Here are some selections from that document.

Virginia Declaration of Rights

SECTION 1.   That all men are by nature equally free and independent and have certain inherent rights, of which, when they enter into a state of society, they cannot, by any compact, deprive or divest their posterity; namely, the enjoyment of life and liberty, with the means of acquiring and possessing property, and pursuing and obtaining happiness and safety.

SECTION 8.   That in all capital or criminal prosecutions a man has a right to demand the cause and nature of his accusation, to be confronted with the accusers and witnesses, to call for evidence in his favor, and to a speedy trial by an impartial jury of twelve men of his vicinage, without whose unanimous consent he cannot be found guilty; nor can he be compelled to give evidence against himself; that no man be deprived of his liberty except by the law of the land or the judgment of his peers.

SECTION 9.   That excessive bail ought not to be required, nor excessive fines imposed, nor cruel and unusual punishments inflicted.

SECTION 10.   That general warrants, whereby an officer or messenger may be commanded to search suspected places without evidence of a fact committed, or to seize any person or persons not named, or whose offense is not particularly described and supported by evidence, are grievous and oppressive and ought not to be granted.

SECTION 13.   . . . in all cases the military should be under strict subordination to, and governed by, the civil power.

SECTION 16.   That religion, or the duty which we owe to our Creator, can be directed only by reason and conviction, not by force or violence; and therefore all men are equally entitled to the free exercise of religion . . .

A Message from the Alamo

William B. Travis was commander of the Texas volunteers defending the Alamo as Texas fought for its independence from Mexico. In February of 1836, a unit of Santa Anna's army was rapidly surrounding the Alamo. Santa Anna demanded that Travis and his troops surrender. Travis answered the note by firing a cannon. He then wrote a letter asking for support. Part of that letter appears below.

Travis's Message from the Alamo

Commandancy of the Alamo—
Bejar, Feby, 24th, 1836

To the People of Texas and all Americans in the world. Fellow citizens & Compatriots

I am besieged, by a thousand or more of the Mexicans under Santa Anna— I have sustained a continued Bombardment & cannonade for 24 hours & have not lost a man—The enemy has demanded a surrender at discretion, otherwise, the garrison are to be put to the sword, if the fort is taken—I have answered the demand with a cannon shot, & our flag still waves proudly from the walls—*I shall never surrender or retreat.* Then, I call on you in the name of Liberty, of patriotism & everything dear to the American character, to come to our aid, with all dispatch—The enemy is receiving reinforcements daily & will no doubt increase to three or four thousand in four or five days. If this call is neglected, I am determined to sustain myself as long as possible & die like a soldier who never forgets what is due to his own honor & that of his country—*Victory or Death.*

(signed) William Barret Travis
Lt. Col. comdt

P.S. The Lord is on our side. When the enemy appeared in sight we had not three bushels of corn. We have since found in deserted houses 80 or 90 bushels & got into the walls 20 or 30 head of Beeves—

Travis

Texas Becomes an Independent Nation

On March 2, 1836, Texas delegates met at Washington-on-the-Brazos to talk about becoming independent of Mexico. After much discussion, they decided to adopt the Texas Declaration of Independence. Although several committee members had been assigned to write the document, George C. Childress was the actual author of the declaration. In the declaration, the people of Texas proclaimed themselves the independent Republic of Texas.

The Texas Declaration of Independence

When a government has ceased to protect the lives, liberty, and property of the people from whom its legitimate powers are derived, and . . . becomes an instrument in the hands of evil rulers for their oppression . . . the first law of nature, the right of self-preservation—the inherent and inalienable right of the people to appeal to first principles and take their political affairs into their own hands in extreme cases—enjoins it as a right towards themselves and a sacred obligation to their posterity to abolish such government and create another in its stead, calculated to rescue them from impending dangers, and to secure their future welfare and happiness.

Nations, as well as individuals, are amenable for their acts to the public opinion of mankind. A statement of a part of our grievances is, therefore, submitted to an impartial world . . .

The Mexican government, by its colonization laws, invited and induced the Anglo-American population of Texas to colonize its wilderness under the pledged faith of a written constitution, that they should continue to enjoy that constitutional liberty and republican government to which they had been habituated in the land of their birth, the United States of America. In this expectation they have been cruelly disappointed . . .

It has failed and refused to secure on a firm basis, the right of trial by jury . . .

It has failed to establish any public system of education . . .

It denies us the right of worshiping the Almighty according to the dictates of our own consciences . . .

We, therefore, the delegates . . . do hereby resolve and declare that our political connection with the Mexican nation has forever ended; and that the people of Texas do now constitute a free, sovereign, and independent republic . . .

A Peace Treaty with Mexico

In 1848, the United States and Mexico signed a treaty that ended the Mexican War. It was negotiated at Villa de Guadalupe Hidalgo, a small town that is now a part of Mexico City. Several important parts of that treaty appear below.

Treaty of Guadalupe Hidalgo

ARTICLE I

There shall be firm and universal peace between the United States of America and the Mexican Republic . . .

ARTICLE V

The boundary line between the two Republics shall commence in the Gulf of Mexico, three leagues from land, opposite the mouth of the Rio Grande, otherwise called Rio Bravo del Norte, or opposite the mouth of its deepest branch, if it should have more than one branch emptying directly into the sea; from thence up the middle of that river, following the deepest channel, where it has more than one, to the point where it strikes the southern boundary of New Mexico; thence, westwardly, along the whole southern boundary of New Mexico (which runs north of the town called Paso) to its western termination; thence, northward, along the western line of New Mexico, until it intersects the first branch of the river Gila; (or if it should not intersect any branch of that river, then to the point on the said line nearest to such branch, and thence in a direct line to the same;) thence down the middle of the said branch and of the said river, until it empties into the Rio Colorado; thence across the Rio Colorado, following the division line between Upper and Lower California, to the Pacific Ocean . . .

ARTICLE VIII

Mexicans now established in territories previously belonging to Mexico . . . who prefer to remain in said territories may either retain the title and rights of Mexican citizens, or acquire those of citizens of the United States. . .

ARTICLE IX

The Mexicans who . . . shall not preserve the character of citizens of the Mexican Republic . . . shall be maintained and protected in the free enjoyment of their liberty . . .

ARTICLE XII

. . . the Government of the United States engages to pay to that of the Mexican Republic the sum of fifteen millions of dollars. . .

A Call for Equal Rights

On August 28, 1963, more than 200,000 people gathered in front of the Washington Monument in Washington, D.C. They had come to urge Congress to pass laws that would protect the rights of all Americans. The featured speaker on that day was Martin Luther King, Jr.

King spoke of the promise of America. He reminded his listeners of the Emancipation Proclamation, the Declaration of Independence, and the Constitution. Then he spoke about his dream: a dream to rid the world of prejudice and segregation, a dream to bring freedom and justice to every American. Part of that speech appears below.

I Have a Dream

I have a dream that one day on the red hills of Georgia, sons of former slaves and sons of former slave-owners will be able to sit down together at the table of brotherhood. . .

I have a dream my four little children will one day live in a nation where they will not be judged by the color of their skin but by the content of their character. I have a dream today!

I have a dream that one day every valley shall be exalted, every hill and mountain shall be made low, the rough places shall be made plain, and the crooked places shall be made straight and the glory of the Lord will be revealed and all flesh shall see it together.

With this faith we will be able to work together, to pray together, to struggle together . . . to stand up for freedom together, knowing that we will be free one day. This will be the day when all of God's children will be able to sing with new meaning—"my country 'tis of thee; sweet land of liberty; of thee I sing; land where my fathers died, land of the pilgrim's pride; from every mountain side, let freedom ring"—and if America is to be a great nation, this must become true.

And when we allow freedom to ring, when we let it ring from every village and hamlet, from every state and city, we will be able to speed up that day when all of God's children—black men and white men, Jews and Gentiles, Catholics and Protestants—will be able to join hands and to sing in the words of the old Negro spiritual, "Free at last, free at last; thank God Almighty, we are free at last."

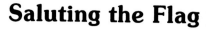

Saluting the Flag

Francis Bellamy wrote the Pledge of Allegiance in 1892. It was printed in a magazine called *The Youth's Companion*. Americans who read the magazine liked the pledge. It captured the feeling of devotion that they felt toward the United States. Today students recite the Pledge of Allegiance in classrooms across the country.

The Pledge of Allegiance

I pledge allegiance to the flag of the United States of America and to the republic for which it stands, one nation under God, indivisible, with liberty and justice for all.

American Political Faith

In 1917, William Tyler Page won a nationwide contest for the "best summary of American political faith." His entry was called the American's Creed. Page used several sources to write the creed. You may recognize phrases in it from the Constitutiion and the Declaration of Independence.

The American's Creed

I believe in the United States of America as a government of the people, by the people, for the people; whose just powers are derived from the consent of the governed; a democracy in a Republic; a sovereign Nation of many sovereign States; a perfect Union, one and inseparable; established upon those principles of freedom, equality, justice, and humanity for which American patriots sacrificed their lives and fortunes.

I therefore believe it is my duty to my country to love it; to support its Constitution; to obey its laws; to respect its flag, and to defend it against all enemies.

534

The National Anthem

Francis Scott Key wrote "The Star-Spangled Banner" in 1814, during the War of 1812. You can read about the battle that inspired the song on page 232 of this book.

The Star-Spangled Banner

Words by Francis Scott Key
Composer Unknown

Oh, say, can you see by the dawn's ear-ly light,

What so proud-ly we hailed at the twi-light's last gleam-ing?

Whose broad stripes and bright stars, through the per-il-ous fight,

O'er the ram-parts we watched were so gal-lant-ly stream-ing?

And the rock-ets' red glare, the bombs burst-ing in air,

Gave proof through the night that our flag was still there.

Oh, say, does that star-span-gled ban-ner yet wave

O'er the land of the free and the home of the brave?

The Flag and Seal of Texas

The single star on the flag and seal of Texas gives the state its nickname, the Lone Star State. The front of the seal shows an oak branch on the left. Oak stands for strength. The olive branch on the right stands for peace. On the back of the seal are the flags of the six nations that have governed Texas.

The Texas State Pledge

One hundred and fifty years ago, the people of Texas went to war to become independent of Mexico. Their flag flew in every battle. Today the flag still stands for freedom for Texas. Texans salute it to show loyalty to their state.

Salute to the Texas Flag

Honor the Texas Flag!
We pledge our loyalty to thee,
Texas, one and indivisible.

The Texas State Song

The state song of Texas is "Texas, Our Texas." The people who sing the song are proud of their state. They are happy to live in Texas.

Texas Our Texas

Words by
Gladys Yoakum Wright
and William J. Marsh

Music by
William J. Marsh

Facts About the Presidents and Their First Ladies

The table that follows gives the years each president served and the state from which each president was elected. It also tells a little about the presidents and the women who served as their official hostesses, or first ladies.

The nation's presidents have had much in common. Over two thirds served in the armed forces. All but eight graduated from college. Although some have been teachers, storekeepers, and farmers, most have been lawyers. A surprising number were related. Franklin D. Roosevelt, for example, was related by blood or marriage to eleven presidents (Washington, the two Adamses, Madison, Van Buren, the two Harrisons, Taylor, Grant, Theodore Roosevelt, and Taft).

 **1789-1797**

Virginia

George Washington   **Martha Washington**

George Washington was the only president elected unanimously. He was "first in war, first in peace, and first in the hearts of his countrymen."

 **1801-1809**

Virginia

Thomas Jefferson   **Martha Randolph**

Jefferson, a widower, had his married daughter act as his first lady. His collection of books (6,000 in all) helped start the Library of Congress.

 **1797-1801**

Massachusetts

John Adams   **Abigail Adams**

The Adamses were the first to live in the White House. It was not finished when they moved in, so they used the East Room to dry laundry.

 **1809-1817**

Virginia

James Madison   **Dolley Madison**

The White House burned during the War of 1812. Dolley Madison became a hero by saving important papers and a portrait of Washington.

1817-1825

Virginia

James Monroe   **Elizabeth Monroe**

By late 1817, the White House had been repaired. The Monroes had their daughter's wedding there, the first in the White House.

1825-1829

Massachusetts

John Quincy Adams   **Louisa Adams**

John Quincy Adams was the only son of a president to be president. Louisa Adams was the only first lady born in England.

1829-1837

Tennessee

Andrew Jackson   **Rachel Jackson**

Andrew Jackson was the first president born in a log cabin. He was the first to be elected from a state west of the Appalachian Mountains.

1837-1841

New York

Martin Van Buren   **Angelica Van Buren**

Van Buren was the first president born in the United States rather than a colony. A widower, his daughter-in-law served as first lady.

1841

Ohio

William Henry Harrison   **Anna Harrison**

Harrison gave the longest inaugural speech ever, two hours long. He spoke outdoors on a cold day, caught pneumonia, and died one month later.

1841-1845

Virginia

John Tyler   **Julia Tyler**

Tyler was the first vice-president to replace an elected president. Later he would also be the only former president to take part in the Confederacy.

1845-1849

Tennessee

James K. Polk   **Sarah Polk**

Sarah Polk was the only first lady to be a president's official secretary. Polk's government issued the nation's first postage stamp.

1849-1850

Lousiana

Zachary Taylor   **Mary Taylor Bliss**

Taylor was the first professional soldier to become president. His wife had no interest in politics, so their daughter acted as first lady.

1850-1853

New York

Millard Fillmore   **Abigail Fillmore**

Abigail Fillmore was the first president's wife to work after marriage (as a teacher). In the 1800's, wives usually worked only if the family was poor.

1853-1857

New Hampshire

Franklin Pierce   **Jane Pierce**

The years of Pierce's presidency were sad ones. Two months before the inauguration, their eleven-year-old son was killed in a train accident.

1857-1861

Pennsylvania

James Buchanan   **Harriet Lane**

Buchanan was the only president not to marry. His niece acted as his first lady. She later willed her art collection to the nation.

1861-1865

Illinois

Abraham Lincoln   **Mary Lincoln**

Lincoln was the first president born west of the Appalachians and, at six foot four inches, the tallest. He was the first killed in office.

1865-1869

Tennessee

Andrew Johnson   **Eliza Johnson**

Johnson was the only president never to attend school. He did not learn to read or write until he was an adult. His wife, Eliza, taught him.

1869-1877

Illinois

Ulysses S. Grant   **Julia Grant**

Grant was the first president to graduate from the U.S. Military Academy. While he was president, the nation celebrated its 100th birthday.

1877-1881

Ohio

Rutherford B. Hayes   **Lucy Hayes**

Lucy Hayes was the first president's wife to take a stand on the issues of the day. She worked to end slavery, stop liquor sales, and help the poor.

1881

Ohio

James A. Garfield   **Lucretia Garfield**

Garfield was the last president born in a log cabin and the first college president to be president. He was the second president to be killed in office.

1881-1885

New York

Chester A. Arthur   **Mary Arthur McElroy**

Arthur traveled more than earlier presidents. He visited Florida and Yellowstone National Park. A widower, he had his sister act as his hostess.

1885-1889

New York

Grover Cleveland   **Frances Cleveland**

The Clevelands married in the White House. At 21, Frances Cleveland was the youngest president's wife. She had a baby in the White House.

1889-1893

Indiana

Benjamin Harrison   **Carolina Harrison**

Harrison was the only grandson of a president to be president. While he was president, electric lights were installed in the White House.

1893-1897

New York

Grover Cleveland   **Frances Cleveland**

Cleveland was the only president to serve two separated terms. His wife held Saturday receptions so working women could attend.

1897-1901

Ohio

William McKinley   **Ida McKinley**

McKinley was the third president killed in office. He was also the last Civil War veteran to be president and the first twentieth-century President.

1901-1909

New York

Theodore Roosevelt   **Edith Roosevelt**

At 42, Roosevelt was the youngest president. After a cartoon showed him with a bear cub, the teddy bear became a popular toy.

1909-1913

Ohio

William H. Taft   **Helen Taft**

Taft was the only president to later head the Supreme Court. He was the first to name a woman to a high government post, the Children's Bureau.

1913-1921

New Jersey

Woodrow Wilson   **Edith Wilson**

Wilson's first wife, Ellen, died in the White House. He remarried and his second wife, Edith, ran the government after her husband suffered a stroke.

1921-1923

Ohio

Warren G. Harding   **Florence Harding**

Harding was the only newspaper publisher to be elected president. He and his wife turned the *Marion Star* in Ohio into a prosperous newspaper.

1923-1929

Massachusetts

Calvin Coolidge   **Grace Coolidge**

Grace Coolidge was the first president's wife to graduate from college. She taught at the Clarke School for the Deaf in Massachusetts.

1929-1933

California

Herbert Hoover   **Lou Hoover**

Hoover was the first president to have his own telephone. A wealthy man, he was also the only president to refuse to accept a salary.

1933-1945

New York

Franklin D. Roosevelt   Anna Eleanor Roosevelt

Roosevelt was the only president elected four times. His wife was the most politically active first lady. She later was a United Nations delegate.

1945-1953

Missouri

Harry S Truman   **Elizabeth Truman**

Truman was the only modern president who did not attend college. He was also the first president since Grant to have farmed as an adult.

1953-1961

Pennysylvania

Dwight D. Eisenhower   Mamie Eisenhower

Eisenhower visited more countries than any earlier president, 27 in all. He was also the first president since Grant to graduate from West Point.

1961-1963

Massachusetts

John F. Kennedy   **Jacqueline Kennedy**

Kennedy was the first president born in the 1900's and the first Catholic to be president. He was the fourth president to be killed in office.

1963-1969

Texas

Lyndon B. Johnson   **Claudia (Lady Bird) Johnson**

Johnson was the first to take office on an airplane and to be sworn in by a woman. He named the first black American to the Supreme Court.

1969-1974

California

Richard M. Nixon   **Thelma (Pat) Nixon**

Nixon was the first president born west of the Rocky Mountains. He was also the first president to resign his position.

1974-1977

Michigan

Gerald R. Ford   **Betty Ford**

Ford was the only unelected president. When Nixon's vice president resigned, Ford took his place. When Nixon resigned, Ford became president.

1977-1981

Georgia

James E. (Jimmy) Carter   **Roslyn Carter**

Carter was the only president to graduate from the U.S. Naval Academy. He was also the first president born in a hospital.

1981-

California

Ronald Reagan   **Nancy Reagan**

Ronald Reagan was the oldest person to be elected president. He was also the first president to appoint a woman to the Supreme Court.

Glossary

A

abolitionist (ab'ə lish'ə nist) A person who wants to end slavery. (p. 282)

ally (al'ī) A country that helps another country in time of war. (p. 353)

almanac (ôl'mə nak) A book with interesting information arranged by days for a given year. (p. 143)

amend (ə mend') To change. (p. 210)

amendment (ə mend'mənt) A change in a bill, law, or constitution. (p. 210)

apprentice (ə pren'tis) A person who learns a trade. (p. 143)

aquifer (ak'wə fər) A huge underground lake. (p. 426)

armistice (är'mə stis) A truce. (p. 356)

artisan (är'tə zən) A craftsworker. (p. 142)

assembly line A system in which a moving belt brings parts of a product to workers who then add other parts to them. (p. 331)

astronaut (as'trə nôt) A member of the crew of a spacecraft. (p. 397)

axis (ak'sis) An imaginary line that runs through Earth from the North Pole to the South Pole. (p. 16)

B

barter (bär'tər) To trade by exchanging goods. (p. 82)

basin (bā'sn) The land drained by a river and its tributaries. (p. 20)

bay (bā) Part of a larger body of water that extends into land. (p. 20)

bilingual education Education in two languages. (p. 407)

bill of rights A list of freedoms and liberties. (p. 205) The first ten amendments to the Constitution. (p. 211)

blockade (blo kād') A military action that closes a port. (p. 297)

boom (büm) A sudden increase in business or some other activity. (p. 268)

boycott (boi'kot) To protest by refusing to buy a product or service. (p. 173)

C

cabinet (kab'ə nit) The people who advise the head of a government. (p. 214)

canal (kə nal') A narrow waterway made by people. (p. 242)

canyon (kan'yən) A narrow valley with high, steep sides. (p. 20)

cape (kāp) A piece of land that extends into water. (p. 20)

capital (kap'ə təl) The city where the government of a state or country meets. (p. 10)

cash crop A crop grown for sale. (p. 222)

century (sen'chər ē)   A period of 100 years. (p. 88)

charter (chär'tər)   A legal paper that gives permission to explore or settle land. (p. 62)

checks and balances   A system in which the power of each branch of the government is limited by the powers of the other branches. (p. 212)

civil rights   Rights guaranteed to citizens by the Constitution. (p. 361)

civil war   A war between the citizens of a country. (p. 291)

claim (klām)   To take control. (p. 31)

climate (klī'mit)   The usual weather of a place. (p. 18)

clipper (klip'ər)   A large sailing ship built for speed. (p. 267)

coast (kōst)   Land along an ocean. (p. 20)

cold war   A war fought with words, ideas, and money. (p. 386)

colonist (kol'ə nist)   A person who lives in a colony. (p. 45)

colony (kol'ə nē)   A settlement far from the home country. (p. 45)

commercial farmer   A farmer who grows crops or raises animals to sell. (p. 473)

common (kom'ən)   Land set aside for grazing. (p. 100)

commonwealth (kom'ən welth')   A governing unit similar to a state. (p. 347)

communist (kom'yə nist)   Favoring an economic and social system in which most or all property is owned by the government. (p. 379)

compact (kom'pakt)   A contract. (p. 70)

compass (kum'pəs)   An instrument that shows direction. (p. 8)

compass rose   A device on a map that shows direction. (p. 8)

compromise (kom'prə mīz)   An agreement in which both sides give up some things in order to get something they value more. (p. 210)

computer (kəm pyü'tər)   A machine that solves problems and also stores information quickly. (p. 399)

concentration camp   A prison where political prisoners are kept. (p. 378)

Congress (kong'gris)   The lawmaking branch of the United States government. (p. 209)

conserve (kən serv')   To use wisely. (p. 421)

constitution (kon'stə tü'shən)   A plan for a government. (p. 204)

consulate (kon'sə lit)   The offices of an official appointed by a foreign government to look out for its interests and those of its citizens. (p. 423)

consumer (kən sü'mər)   One who buys and uses goods or services. (p. 363)

continent (kon'tə nənt)   One of seven large landmasses on Earth. (p. 8)

continental divide   In the Rocky Mountains, the highest ridge of land that separates rivers flowing east from those flowing west. (pp. 251–252)

corporation (kôr'pə rā'shən)   A business owned by stockholders. (p. 330)

county (koun'tē)   A political division within a colony or state. (p. 124)

cow town   A railroad town that serves ranchers. (p. 320)

credit (kred'it)   Payment for something in small amounts until it is paid for in full. (p. 365)

creole (krē'ol)   A Spaniard born in Latin America. (p. 462)

culture (kul'chər)   A way of life. (p. 39)

D

dame school   A classroom set up in a colonial home. (p. 155)

decade (dek'ād)   A period of 10 years. (p. 68)

delta (del′tə) Land built by deposits of soil at the mouth of a river. (p. 20)

democracy (di mok′rə sē) A government in which citizens hold political power. (p. 248)

depression (di presh′ən) A time when many businesses fail and many people are out of work. (p. 367)

dictator (dik′tā tər) A person who has complete control of a country. (p. 378)

disability (dis′ə bil′ə tē) The lack of an ability or power. (p. 409)

discriminate (dis krim′ə nāt) To treat one group of people differently from another. (p. 305)

dividend (div′ə dend) A share of the profits made by a corporation. (p. 330)

dock (dok) A platform built over water. (p. 141)

draft (draft) A law that requires people to sign up for military service. (p. 294)

E

economy (i kon′ə mē) The ways a group of people produce goods and services. An economy also includes ways of getting those goods and services to people. (p. 109)

elder (el′dər) A colonial leader. (p. 100)

electors (i lek′tərs) People chosen by voters to elect the President and Vice-President of the United States. (p. 213)

elevation (el′ə vā′shən) The height of land above sea level. (p. 4)

emancipate (i man′sə pāt) To set free. (p. 297)

environment (en vī′rən mənt) All of the living and nonliving things in a place. (p. 36)

equator (i kwā′tər) The 0° line of latitude, the starting point for measuring distances north and south. (p. 12)

executive branch The part of government that enforces laws. (p. 204)

expansionist (ek span′shə nist) A person who favors taking over land outside of a country. (p. 348)

explore (ek splôr′) To search for new things or new places. (p. 32)

export (ek′ spôrt) To sell goods to another country. (p. 54)

F

fall line The place where rivers from a highland form rapids as they tumble down to a lowland. (p. 117)

federal system A government in which power is divided between national and state governments. (p. 207)

free enterprise An economy in which people are free to own and run their own businesses with little or no control by the government. (p. 328)

frontier (frun tir′) The land just beyond a settled area. (p. 126)

fugitive (fyü′jə tiv) A person who has run away. (p. 280)

G

geography (jē og′rə fē) The study of places on Earth and life in those places. (p. 2)

globe (glōb) A model of Earth. (p. 14)

gold rush A great or sudden effort of people to find gold. (p. 267)

great circle route Any route that follows Earth's curve. (p. 447)

grid (grid) A series of lines that cross one another at right angles. The lines are labeled to help locate places on a map. (p. 10)

gulf (gulf) A body of water that extends into land; a large bay. (p. 20)

H

harbor (här′bər) An area of deep water protected from winds and ocean currents. (p. 20)

hemisphere (hem′ə sfir) One half of a sphere or globe. (p. 13)

heritage (her'ə tij)   Values, beliefs, and other parts of a culture that are handed down from one generation to the next. (p. 151)

hill (hil)   A raised part of Earth's surface, smaller than a mountain. (p. 20)

history (his'tər ē)   An account of important events in the past. (p. 25)

holocaust (hol'ə kôst)   A great or terrible destruction. (p. 379)

homesteader (hōm'sted'ər)   A person granted public land. (p. 322)

House of Representatives The house of Congress whose membership is based on a state's population. (p. 210)

hydroelectric (hī'drō i lek'trik)   Developing electricity from water power. (p. 422)

I

immigrant (im'ə grənt)   A person who leaves his or her homeland to settle in another country. (p. 239)

impeach (im pēch')   To put a public official on trial for not carrying out his or her duties. (p. 303)

import (im'pôrt)   To buy goods from a foreign country. (p. 56)

inauguration (in ô' gyə rā'shən)   The act of installing a person in office. (p. 213)

indentured servant   A person who promises to work for a colonist for seven years. (p. 122)

independent (in'di pen'dənt)   Free to rule oneself. (p. 179)

indigo (in'də gō)   A plant from which a blue dye is made. (p. 119)

industrial (in dus'trē əl)   Of or having to do with manufacturing, trade, or business. (p. 141)

Industrial Revolution   The great changes that resulted from the use of powerful machines that made many jobs easier and faster. (p. 327)

inlet (in'let)   A small bay. (p. 20)

integrate (in'tə grāt)   To open to people of all races. (p. 404)

interchangeable (in'tər chan'jə bəl)   Capable of being used or put in place of something else. (p. 224)

interest (in'tər ist)   Money paid for the use of money. (p. 365)

invest (in vest')   To put money or other resources in something that is expected to produce income or a profit or both. (p.119)

irrigate (ir'ə gāt)   To bring water from streams to farm fields. (p. 323)

island (ī'lənd)   A body of land, smaller than a continent. (p. 8)

isolation (ī'sə lā'shən)   A policy of avoiding relations with other nations. (p. 381)

isthmus (is'məs)   A narrow body of land that connects two larger bodies of land. (p. 59)

J

joint-stock company   A business owned by many people. (p. 63)

judicial branch (jü dish'əl)   A branch of government that explains the meaning of laws in court. (p. 204)

justice (just'tis)   Fairness. (p. 204)   A judge. (p. 209)

L

labor union   An organization of workers who have united to win better working conditions and higher wages. (p. 337)

lake (lāk)   A body of water surrounded by land. (p. 21)

landlocked (land'lokt')   Shut in by land. (p. 428)

legend (lej'ənd) The key to a map. (p. 2)

legislative branch   A branch of government that makes laws. (p. 204)

legislature (lej'ə slā'chər)   A group of people who make laws. (p. 161)

liberty (lib′ər tē)   Freedom. (p. 171)

Loyalist (loi′ə list)   A colonist who sided with England during the American Revolution. (p. 184)

M

map (map)   A drawing of all or part of Earth. (p. 2)

market (mär′kit)   A place where goods are bought and sold. (p. 220)

massacre (mas′ə kər)   The killing of people who are not able to defend themselves. (p. 174)

megalopolis (meg′ə lop′ə lis)   A region made of up several metropolitan areas. (p. 401)

merchant (mėr′chənt)   A person who buys and sells goods. (p. 26)

meridian of longitude (mə rid′ē ən ov lon′jə tüd)   A line that stretches from the North Pole to the South Pole. (p. 12)

mestizo (me stē′zō)   A person of both Indian and Spanish ancestry. (p. 462)

metropolitan area   An area that includes one or more large cities and surrounding suburbs. (p. 423)

militia (mə lish′ə)   A group of citizens trained as soldiers. (p. 145)

mint (mint)   A place where the government coins money. (p. 432)

minuteman (min′it man′)   A colonist trained to fight at a moment's notice during the American Revolution. (p. 176)

mission (mish′ən)   A settlement where people of one religion teach their faith to others. (p. 56)

missionary (mish′ə ner′ē)   A person who teaches his or her religion to people of other faiths. (p. 55)

monopoly (mə nop′ə lē)   Complete or almost complete control of the sales of a product or service. (p. 339)

mountain (moun′tən)   The highest landform on Earth. (p. 21)

mountain range   A row of connected mountains. (p. 21)

mouth (mouth)   The place where a river empties into a larger body of water. (p. 21)

N

natural vegetation   The kind of plant life that grows wild in a place. (p. 2)

naval stores   Products such as turpentine, pitch, and tar. (p. 127)

navigable (nav′ə gə bəl)   Deep enough for oceangoing ships. (p. 118)

neutral (nü′trəl)   Not taking sides. (p. 353)

New Deal   The policies used to fight the Depression of the 1930's. (p. 369)

O

ocean (ō′shən)   The largest body of water on Earth; one of four large bodies of water. (p. 8)

open range   Unused land owned by the government. (p. 321)

P

parallel of latitude (par′ə lel ov lat′ə tüd)   A line drawn on a map or globe used to measure distances north or south of the equator. (p. 12)

parliament (pär′lə mənt)   A branch of government that makes laws and also sees that they are carried out. (p. 445)

Patriot (pā′trē ət)   A colonist who fought for the independence of the American colonies. (p. 184)

patroon (pə trün′)   A wealthy Dutch person who received land in return for paying the passage of other colonists. (p. 92)

peninsula (pə nin′sə lə)   Land almost totally surrounded by water. (p. 21)

petition (pə tish′ən)   A formal request to a government. (p. 172)

petrochemicals (pe′trō kem′ə kəls) Chemicals made from petroleum or natural gas. (p. 430)

Piedmont (pēd′mont) The hilly land at the foot of the Appalachian Mountains. (p. 21)

pilgrim (pil′grəm) A person who makes a journey for religious reasons. (p. 69)

pioneer (pī′ə nir′) The first to explore or settle an area. (p. 245)

plain (plān) A stretch of level or gently rolling land. (p. 21)

plantation (plan tā′shən) A large commercial farm. (p. 116)

plateau (pla tō′) Flat or gently rolling land high above sea level. (p. 21)

political party (pə lit′ə kəl) A group that works to get its members elected to office. (p. 214)

prairie (prer′ē) Land covered by tall grasses. (p. 450)

president (prez′ə dənt) The head of a country; the head of the executive branch of the United States. (p. 209)

prime meridian (prīm mə rid′ē ən) The 0° line of longitude. (p. 12)

prime minister The head of a government that has a parliament. (p. 445)

privateer (pri′və tir′) A trading ship armed for war. (p. 186)

proclamation (prok′lə mā′shən) An order issued by a government. (p. 168)

profit (prof′it) Money left over after paying costs. (p. 62)

proprietor (prə prī′ə tər) An owner. (p. 118)

R

ratify (rat′ə fī) To approve. (p. 211)

reconstruction (rē′kən struk′shən) The process of rebuilding. (p. 302)

reformer (ri fôr′mər) A person who wants to make improvements. (p. 338)

refugee (ref′yə jē′) One who flees his or her country for political reasons. (pp. 405–406)

relief (ri lēf′) Differences in height between highlands and lowlands. (p. 4)

repeal (ri pēl′) To do away. (p. 172)

represent (rep′ri zent′) To speak or act in another's name. (p. 67)

representative (rep′ri zen′tə tiv) A delegate. (p. 172) A member of the House of Representatives. (p. 210)

republic (ri pub′lik) A government in which the right to rule comes from the people. (p. 203)

reservation (rez′ər vā′shən) Land set aside by the government for a particular group. (p. 314)

resource (rē′sôrs) A part of the environment that is used to meet needs. (p. 36)

revolution (rev′ə lü′shən) A great change. (p. 176)

river (riv′ər) Water that flows from highland to lowland. (p. 21)

S

satellite (sat′l īt) An instrument that gathers and sends information from space. (p. 388)

scale (skāl) A way of showing size on a map or model. (p. 6)

scurvy (skėr′vē) A sickness caused by lack of fresh fruits and vegetables. (p. 81)

sea (sē) A large body of salt water, partly closed in by land. (p. 21)

sea level The height of the surface of the ocean. (p. 4)

secede (si sēd′) To leave. (p. 287)

segregate (seg′rə gāt) To separate or keep apart one group from the other(s). (p. 404)

Senate (sen′it) The house of Congress with two representatives from each state. (p. 210)

senator (sen′ə tər) A member of the Senate. (p. 210)

service industries Industries that help people in some way. (p. 419)

settlement house A community center where people gather for help, information, or recreation. (p. 338)

sharecropper (sher′krop′ər) A farmer who rents land by paying the owner with part of the harvest. (p. 472)

slave (slāv) A person who is owned by another person. (p. 54)

sod (sod) A thick, tough layer of tangled grass roots. (p. 323)

sound (sound) A long, narrow body of water that connects two larger bodies of water. (p. 21)

source (sôrs) The place where a river begins. (pp. 21, 250)

stock (stok) A share in a company. (p. 330)

stockholder (stok′hōl′dər) A person who buys shares in a business. (p. 330)

stock market The place where stocks are bought and sold. (p. 365)

strait (strāt) A small sound. (p. 21)

suburb (sub′ėrb′) A small community near a large city. (p. 335)

suffrage (suf′rij) The right to vote. (p. 360)

Supreme Court The highest court in the United States. (p. 209)

T

tanner (tan′ər) A person who turns animal skins into leather. (p. 140)

tax (taks) The money people must pay for government services. (p. 155)

technology (tek nol′ə jē) All the tools and ideas a group of people develop to meet their needs. (p. 39)

tenant farmer A person who rents land. (p. 85)

terrace (ter′is) A step-like field cut into the side of a hill or mountain. (p. 459)

territory (ter′ətôr′ē) An organized part of the United States whose land is not included within any state. (p. 227)

tidewater (tīd′wo′tər) The plain that borders the Atlantic coast. (p. 116)

tourism (tùr′iz′əm) Businesses that provide services to travelers. (p. 420)

transcontinental (tran′skon tə nen′tl) Reaching across a continent. (p. 316)

treaty (trē′tē) A formal agreement between nations. (p. 167)

trial by jury The deciding of a case in court by a group of citizens who have examined the charges by listening to the testimony. (p. 159)

triangular trade (trī ang′gyə lər) The name given to trade among the 13 English colonies, Africa, the West Indies, and Europe. (p. 110)

tributary (trib′yə ter′ē) A river that flows into a larger river. (p. 21)

tyranny (tir′ə nē) Cruel or unjust use of power. (p. 175)

V

valley (val′ē) Lowland that lies between hills or mountains. (p. 21)

vice-president The official who takes the president's place when necessary. (p. 209)

viceroyalty (vīs′roi′əl tē) One of Spain's large colonies in the Americas. (p. 54)

Index

The letter *m* stands for map.
The letter *g* stands for graph, chart, table, or diagram.

176: Culver Pictures. **177:** "Battle of Lexington" by Doolittle and Barber. Lexington Historical Society. **179:** "The Battle of Bunker Hill" by Winthrop Chandler. Acc.# 1982. 281. Gift of Mr. and Mrs. Gardner Richardson. Museum of Fine Arts, Boston. **180:** NYPL. **182:** "The Declaration of Independence" by John Trumbull. Yale University Art Gallery. **184:** *l&m* Culver Pictures; *r* Historical Pictures Service. **189:** "Washington Crossing the Delaware" by Emanuel Leutze. Metropolitan Museum of Art; gift of John Steward Kennedy. **191:** "The March to Valley Forge" by W. Trego. Valley Forge Historical Society. **193:** George Rogers Clark National Historical Park. **194:** Courtesy, United States Naval Academy Museum. **197:** "The Surrender of Lord Cornwallis at Yorktown" by John Trumbull. Yale University Art Gallery.

Unit Four: 200-201: "Salute to General Washington in New York Harbor" by L.M. Cooke (detail from #1203). National Gallery of Art, Washington. Gift of Edgar William and Bernice Chrysler Garbisch. **202:** Library of Congress. **205:** Portrait of Abigail Adams, attributed to Ralph Earl, c. 1785. New York State Historical Association, Cooperstown. **206:** Historical Society of Pennsylvania. **207:** John Carter Brown Library, Brown University. **209:** "Signing the Constitution" by Thomas Richard Rossiter (detail from #7570). Independence National Historical Park Collection. **210:** Culver Pictures. **213:** "The Republican Court" by Daniel Huntington. The Brooklyn Museum; gift of the Crescent-Hamilton Athletic Club. **215:** "President Washington and His First Cabinet" by E. Pollah Ottendorf. Continental Paintings Collection, Continental Insurance. **216:** U.S. State Department. **218:** 42.138 Draw & W.C. Am. Burton: View of the Capitol, Washington, D.C. in 1824. 3c. Courtesy Metropolitan Museum of Art, New York. **221:** "View of the Island of Woahoo", unsigned watercolor; gift of Charles H. Taylor. Peabody Museum of Salem/Mark Sexton. **223:** Smithsonian Institution, Division of Textiles. **224:** *Harper's New Monthly,* Vol. V. No. 26, July 1852, p. 148. **226:** Kentucky Historical Society. **229:** Field Museum of Natural History, Chicago. **232:** Anne S.K. Brown Military Collection, Brown University Library. **233:** I.N. Phelps Stokes Collection, New York Public Library. Astor, Lenox and Tilden Foundations. **234:** Ship's prow: eagle with motto "Don't Give up the Ship", #ME-CA7, *Index of American Design.* National Gallery of Art Washington.

Unit Five: 236-237: "The Oregon Trail" by Albert Bierstadt (detail). The Butler Institute of American Art, Youngstown, OH. **238:** "Daniel Boone Escorting Settlers through the Cumberland Gap" by George Caleb Bingham (detail). Washington University Art Gallery, St. Louis. **240, 241:** Culver Pictures. **243:** Detail from painting by H.D. Stitt. B&O Railroad Museum, Baltimore. **247:** Culver Pictures. **248:** "The Verdict of the People" by George Caleb Bingham (detail). Used by permission of the Boatmen's National Bank of St. Louis. **249:** 06.197 Ptgs. Am. Waldo: General Andrew Jackson, 2E. Courtesy Metropolitan Museum of Art, New York. **251:** "Bird's-eye view of Mandan Village" by George Catlin. National Museum of American Art, Smithsonian Institute, Washington, D.C. Gift of Mrs. Joseph Harrison, Jr. **253:** #7647, Independence National Historical Park Collection. **254:** "Trail of Tears" by Robert Lindneaux. Woolaroc Museum, Bartlesville, OK. **256:** "Barlow Cutoff" by William Henry Jackson, Scotts Bluff National Monument, National Park Service. **261:** "Handcart Pioneers" by C.C.A. Christensen. Reproduced by permission of the Church of Jesus Christ of the Latter-Day Saints. **264:** Museo Nacional de Historia, Mexico City. **265:** "General Scott's Entry into Mexico", lithograph after painting by Carl Nebel (detail). Chicago Historical Society. **267:** New York Historical Society. **268:** I.N. Phelps Stokes Collection, New York Public Library. Astor, Lenox and Tilden Foundations. **269:** California State Library.

Unit Six: 272-273: "The Army of the Potomac" by James Hope (detail). American, 1818/19-1892. Oil on canvas, 1865. 45.1 x 106 cm. #45.890, M. and M. Karolik Collection. Museum of Fine Arts, Boston. **274:** "The Old Print Shop" by Kenneth M. Newman. Photo courtesy Time-Life Books. **277:** *l* "The Book Bindery", anonymous, American (detail). Pencil and watercolor. 6 x 8⅞ in. #58.835, M. and M. Karolik Collection. Museum of Fine Arts, Boston; *r* The Granger Collection. **278:** *t* Portrait of Henry Clay attributed to Chester Harding; transfer from National Collection of Fine Arts. National Portrait Gallery, Smithsonian Institution, Washington; *b* Portrait of John C. Calhoun by Rembrandt Peale. Carolina Art Association, Gibbes Art Gallery. **280:** The Granger Collection. **282:** Ambrotype portrait of Frederick Douglass; gift of anonymous donor. National Portrait Gallery, Smithsonian Institution, Washington. **283:** Library of Congress. **284:** "The Underground Railroad" by Weber (detail). Cincinnati Art Museum. **286, 287:** University of Hartford, J. Doyle DeWitt Collection. **290:** Library of Congress. **292:** Anne S.K. Brown Military Collection, Brown University Library. **294:** Schomburg Center for Research in Black Culture, New York Public Library. Astor, Lenox and Tilden Foundations. **295:** Library of Congress. **296:** The Anne S.K. Brown Military Collection, Brown University Library. **299:** "Let Us Have Peace" © J.L.G. Ferris. Archives of '76, Bay Village, OH. **301:** Library of Congress. **302:** From *Harper's Weekly*, June 23, 1866. New York Public Library. Astor, Lenox and Tilden Foundations. **303:** Culver Pictures. **304:** Library of Congress. **305:** Valentine Museum, Richmond, VA.

Unit Seven: 308-309: "The Bowery at Night" by W. Louis Sonntag, Jr. (detail). Museum of the City of New York. **310:** "Conquest of the Prairie" by Irving R. Bacon, 1908 (detail). Oil on canvas. 48" x 120". Buffalo Bill Historical Center, Cody, WY. **312:** The Architect of the U.S. Capitol. **314:** *r* Denver Public Library, Western History Department. **316:** "Discovery of the Comstock Lode" by James Harrington (detail). Permission of the Fine Arts Museums of San Francisco; gift of Mrs. E.C. Lacey. **319:** "The Chisholm Trail" by Clara McDonald Williamson (detail). Wichita Art Museum, Roland P. Murdock Collection. **320:** Kansas State Historical Society. **322:** Solomon D. Butcher Collection, Nebraska State Historical Society. **323:** "The Homesteader's Wife" by Harvey Dunn. South Dakota Memorial Art Collection, Brookings. **326:** "The Gun Foundry" by John Ferguson Weir (detail). Putnam County Historical Society, Foundry School Museum, Cold Spring, N.Y. **329:** *tl, bl* Culver Pictures; *tr* The Granger Collection, New York; *ml* The Bettmann Archive; *m, br* Historical Pictures Service, Chicago. **330:** Portrait of Andrew Carnegie by unidentified artist. National Portrait Gallery, Smithsonian Institution, Washington; gift of Mrs. Margaret Carnegie Miller. **331:** Henry Ford Museum, The Edison Institute. **333:** *l* The Granger Collection; *r* The Granger Collection, New York. **335:** Avery Architectural and Fine Arts Library, Columbia University. **337:** The Granger Collection. **338:** Library of Congress. **339:** Wallace Kirkland, *Life* Magazine, © 1961 Time, Inc. **340:** The Granger Collection. **341:** Library of Congress. **342:** "U.S. Fleet in the Straits of Magellan the Morning of Feb. 8, 1908" by Henry Reuterdahl (detail). Courtesy U.S. Naval Academy Museum. **345:** Newspaper Collection, New York Public Library. Astor, Lenox and Tilden Foundations. **346:** *l* Library of Congress; *r* The Granger Collection. **347:** "Battle of Manila Bay, May 1898" by James G. Taylor (detail). Franklin D. Roosevelt Library, NARS-GSA. **348:** Historical Photography Collection, University of Washington Libraries/Eric A. Hegg. **349:** Original in Liliuokalani Trust. Photo: Bishop Museum, Honolulu, HI. **351, 355:** The Granger Collection. **356:** Library of Congress. **358:** "Allies Day, May 1917" by Childe Hassam (detail). National Gallery of Art, Washington. Gift of Ethelyn McKinney in memory of her brother, Glen Ford McKinney, 1943. **360:** Historical Pictures Service. **361:** UPI. **362:** Library of Congress. **365:** American Stock Exchange. **367:** "Employment Agency" by Isaac Soyer, 1937. Oil on canvas. 34¼ x 45 inches. Collection of Whitney Museum of American Art. Acq. #37.44. **368:** Library of Congress. **369:** UPI. **370:** Tennessee Valley Authority. **371:** Franklin D. Roosevelt Library.

Unit Eight: 374-375: NASA. **376:** "War" by Frederick Hortez. Photo by Henry Groskinsky. **378:** Wide World Photos. **379:** Yivo Institute for Jewish Research. **381:** Myron H. Davis, *Life* Magazine, © 1977 Time, Inc. **382:** *l* Wide World Photos; *r* National Archives. **383:** "Beachhead in Normandy" by Dwight Shepler (detail). Combat Art Center, Department of the Navy. **385:** Wide World Photos. **389:** Marilyn Silverstone (Magnum). **390:** Ellis Herwig (Stock Boston). **391:** Wally McNamee (Woodfin Camp & Associates). **393:** Suzanne L. Murphy (FPG). **394:** Thierry Campion (Sygma). **396:** NASA. **398:** © 1983 Joel Gordon. **399:** *tl* Tom Pantages; *tr* Ken Kaminsky (Uniphoto). **401:** Joe Scherschel, *Life* Magazine, © 1970 Time, Inc. **405:** Wide World Photos. **406:** Frances Miller, *Life* Magazine, © 1963 Time, Inc. **407:** Tom Myers. **408:** *l* Elaine Powell (Uniphoto); *r* Joseph A. DiChello. **410:** Alex Webb (Magnum). **411:** Carol Bernson (Black Star). **412** *t* NASA; *b* Black Star. **413:** Christopher S. Johnson (Stock Boston). **416:** Stacy Pick (Uniphoto). **419:** Carl Purcell. **422:** *l* Chuck O'Rear (Woodfin Camp & Associates); *r* Ruth Dixon. **427:** Grant Heilman Photography. **428:** Robert Frerck (Woodfin Camp & Associates). **430:** *l* Terrance Moore (Woodfin Camp & Associates); *r* Richard L. Miller (The Picture Cube). **431:** Paul Conklin. **432:** Jim Amos (Photo Researchers, Inc.). **433:** George Hall (Woodfin Camp & Associates).

Unit Nine: 436-437: Diane Ensign-Caughey. **438:** E. Sparks (The Stock Market). **441:** "Half Breed Encampment" by Paul Kane. Royal Ontario Museum. **442:** "The Fur Traders at Montreal" by George Agnew Reid. Picture Division, Public Archives of Canada, Ottawa. **444:** "Encampment of the Loyalists at Johnston" by James Peachey. Picture Division, Public Archives of Canada, Ottawa. **448:** Owen Franken (Stock, Boston). **449:** Templeman (Valan Photos). **450:** *tl* Val Wheelan (Valan Photos); *br* Craig Aurness (Woodfin Camp & Associates). **451:** John Fowler (Valan Photos). **452:** Momatiuk/Eastcott (Woodfin Camp & Associates). **454:** Richard Steedman (The Stock Market). **458:** Adrian Bodek. **459:** © 1983 Victor Englebert. **460:** © 1981 Loren McIntyre (Woodfin Camp & Associates). **463:** Richard Weiss (Peter Arnold, Inc.). **465:** Portrait of Father Miguel Hidalgo y Costilla, anonymous, c. 1810. Photo by Bradley Smith from *Mexico: A History in Art*. **466:** "Entrance of the Army of the Three Guarantees, September 27, 1821", anonymous painting. Museo Nacional de Historia, Mexico. Photo by Bradley Smith from *Mexico: A History in Art*. **467:** The Granger Collection. **468:** © 1983 Jesus Carlos, Mexico, D.F. **470:** Yoram Lehmann (Peter Arnold, Inc.). **472:** © 1983 Victor Englebert. **473:** International Potato Center (CIP). **474:** Courtesy CIMMYT. **476:** © 1983 Victor Englebert. **477:** Chip and Rosa Maria Peterson. **480:** Rene Burri (Magnum). **481:** Chip and Rosa Maria Peterson. **498-503:** all Library of Congress except Martha Jefferson Randolph: Dept. of State.